A Voice but No Power

A VOICE BUT NO POWER

Organizing for Social Justice in Minneapolis

DAVID FORREST

University of Minnesota Press
Minneapolis
London

The University of Minnesota Press gratefully acknowledges the financial assistance provided for the publication of this book by Oberlin College.

Portions of chapter 2 were published as "Consensus and Crisis: Representing the Poor in the Post–Civil Rights Era," *New Political Science* 35, no. 1 (March 2013): 19–43; reprinted by permission of the publisher, Taylor & Francis Ltd, http://www.tandfonline.com. Portions of chapter 6 were published as "Legitimacy without Mobilization? How Social Justice Organizations Defend Their Democratic Credentials," *Qualitative Sociology* 42 (2019): 71–92.

Published by the University of Minnesota Press
111 Third Avenue South, Suite 290
Minneapolis, MN 55401-2520
http://www.upress.umn.edu

ISBN 978-1-5179-1351-9 (hc)
ISBN 978-1-5179-1352-6 (pb)

A Cataloging-in-Publication record for this book is available from the Library of Congress.

Printed on acid-free paper

To Jenny

CONTENTS

INTRODUCTION 1

ONE Social Justice Organizations and the Struggle to Abolish Oppression 13

TWO Neoliberalism in a Progressive City 39

THREE The Political Hazards of Contentious Identity-Building 67

FOUR Organizing for Moderation 93

FIVE Misleading the Public 141

SIX Seeking Legitimacy without Mobilization 185

CONCLUSION After George Floyd 215

ACKNOWLEDGMENTS 223

APPENDIX Research Methods 227

NOTES 235

BIBLIOGRAPHY 261

INDEX 293

INTRODUCTION

On October 12, 2010, Bernadeia Johnson, then superintendent of Minneapolis Public Schools (MPS), issued a proposal to "phase out" and close North Community High School. Since taking her first job in the MPS administration in 2006, Johnson—an African American woman who previously worked as a financial analyst and a teacher—had pursued multiple initiatives aimed at undermining teachers' unions and marketizing public education. For example, in addition to proposing the closure of North High, she led the effort to hire teachers trained by Teach for America—a national nonprofit organization known for supporting high-stakes standardized testing and non-union charter schools.[1] Johnson herself was also a strong proponent of such schools.

North High, as it is more commonly called, was and still is one of the poorest and most disproportionately Black schools in Minneapolis. The 120-year-old school is located in Near North, a heavily policed north Minneapolis neighborhood with the highest poverty rate and largest percentage of Black residents in the city. At the time that Superintendent Johnson made her proposal, North High was also the most publicly maligned high school in Minneapolis. Local civic and political leaders harped on the fact that it had experienced several years of below-average standardized test scores and dwindling enrollment (from 2003 to 2010 its enrollment declined from 1,300 to only 265 students). Don Samuels, the African American city council member who represented the Near North neighborhood, once exclaimed that he wanted to "burn North High School down!"[2]

In explaining her proposal, the superintendent built on the stigma surrounding North High, painting it as the epitome of a "failing" school. She blamed the school itself for its low standardized test scores and enrollment numbers and claimed that it was incorrigibly challenged and in decline.[3] Her plan was to address North High's apparent failure by opening a new charter school, Minneapolis College Prep, in its place.[4] This plan comported with the rules established by No Child Left Behind (NCLB)—the federal education reform passed in 2001 that required school districts to swiftly discipline and "restructure" public schools with low standardized test scores.[5] It also extended established trends

North High School. Photograph by Tom Weber. Copyright 2010 Minnesota Public Radio®. Reprinted with permission. All rights reserved.

in MPS, a district that had already closed several public schools and, following its five-year "strategic plan," authorized multiple new non-union charter schools.

A recently formed group calling itself the Save North High Coalition immediately mobilized against the superintendent's proposal.[6] The coalition was racially, economically, and ideologically diverse and led mostly by civically active, African American, and middle-class residents of north Minneapolis. Its key member groups included North High's Alumni Association, the Friends of North High Foundation (a very small nonprofit foundation that provided fund-raising and volunteer support for the school), the Public Education Justice Alliance of Minnesota (a citywide group of socialist and student activists, current and former teachers, parents, and progressive city residents), Neighborhoods Organizing for Change (a nonprofit community organization focused on issues of racial and economic justice), a few North High parents and students, several north Minneapolis residents, and a handful of additional supporters from around the city.

Initially, many coalition organizers seemed poised to rally North High supporters around an emerging national movement against the marketization of education and for well-funded, inclusive, and demo-

North High supporters march outside an October 2010 school board meeting. Photograph by Tom Weber. Copyright 2010 Minnesota Public Radio®. Reprinted with permission. All rights reserved.

cratic public schools.[7] They turned out dozens—in some cases, upwards of one hundred—of supporters to rallies and other events and gained much attention from local media.[8] At these events they argued that North High's predominantly low-income and African American student body suffered not from a failing school but from a district and state government that had abandoned them—a trend perpetuated by the superintendent's proposal. As proof of this abandonment, coalition members pointed to several recent MPS decisions, each of which perpetuated an inegalitarian system of school choice and privatization and ignored the social and economic challenges facing north Minneapolis students and their families. These decisions included, for example, the closing of North High's public feeder schools, the elimination of its guaranteed attendance zone,[9] the implementation of poorly designed open-enrollment programs, and the aforementioned authorization of charter schools in north Minneapolis. Some members of the coalition also suggested that individual district employees actively discouraged families from enrolling their children at or supporting North High.

Rather, however, than attack problematic district initiatives and foster more egalitarian aspirations—such as smaller class sizes and more and better-staffed support services—the Save North High Coalition ultimately settled for backing an alternative plan devised by the superintendent to "redesign" the school. As part of this plan, MPS hired the Institute for Student Achievement, a national consulting firm. This firm's assigned mission was to lead district officials and school and community "stakeholders"—including coalition members—in creating a "new North High" that would raise the school's performance on standardized tests and make it a more attractive option for students.[10] While saving the school from closure, the redesign effort also affirmed the system of school choice and privatization that imperiled North High in the first place. It normalized more than challenged the market-like competition between schools that this system created; it also ignored the ways in which such competition conjoins with persistent discrimination, gentrification, growing economic insecurity, and expanded policing to further destabilize and racialize low-income students' access to quality education.[11] In the end, under the redesign plan, North High School remained open and began to attract a larger student body with very slightly raised academic performance.[12] But the Save North High Coalition and the oppositional fervor it had begun to generate quickly dissipated along with any threat it posed to racialized educational and economic inequality in the city, which remains abysmal.[13]

For over a century, social justice organizations like the Save North High Coalition have been a key source of political representation for low- and moderate-income people, people of color, women, and other disadvantaged constituencies in the United States.[14] Since the "advocacy explosion" and "backyard revolution" of the 1960s and 1970s, their political reach and importance has only grown.[15] These organizations include national groups like the Human Rights Campaign and the National Organization for Women as well as community-based groups like the Save North High Coalition. They include informal collectives as well as formally incorporated nonprofits. And they include groups that see themselves primarily as civic participants or service providers as well as those that explicitly understand themselves as social movement actors. But what they all have in common is that they grant an institutionalized voice to the disadvantaged, a voice that America's two major political parties often fail to provide.[16] In addition, and most importantly, they have the potential to help create a freer and more equal society.[17]

Yet, overall, social justice organizations in the United States have fallen well short of reaching this potential. Indeed, as numerous scholars and activists have noted, these organizations sometimes shield as much as challenge exploitation, racial discrimination, and other forms of systemic oppression.[18] Even since the Great Recession, as protest and rebellion have occurred with growing frequency, many social justice activists have continued to displace as much as empower popular struggles for egalitarian and emancipatory change.[19]

This book explains why contemporary social justice organizations often—and despite the best intentions—fail to realize their potential as representatives of disadvantaged groups. More specifically, it explains why so many of these organizations suppress rather than advance *abolitionist* demands—that is, demands that outline far-reaching but realistic paths toward eliminating systemic oppression in the United States and other capitalist societies.[20] It also explores how these organizations can set themselves up to better promote such demands, such as those calling for stronger welfare entitlements, restorative (rather than punitive) criminal justice, or, in the case of the Save North High Coalition, well-funded and inclusive public schools.

To answer these questions, I draw on immersive fieldwork that I conducted in Minneapolis from the fall of 2009 until the fall of 2012, during the aftermath of the Great Recession. Using evidence gathered from planning and strategy meetings, public events, informal interviews, and various documentary sources, I lead readers through an in-depth examination of the Save North High Coalition—which in December 2010 renamed itself the North High Community Coalition and was commonly known as the North High Coalition—and two other organizations, the Minnesota Coalition for a People's Bailout (commonly known as the Bailout Coalition) and the Minnesota Welfare Rights Committee (commonly known as the Welfare Rights Committee).[21] The Bailout Coalition was a socialist coalition led mostly by white and working-class female organizers. It formed near the end of 2008 and primarily worked to advance a fairer response to the rise of foreclosure-related evictions and unemployment among Minneapolis's lower-income residents. The Welfare Rights Committee was a multiracial social welfare organization led entirely by current or former welfare recipients. It formed in 1991 to oppose budget cuts and disciplinary reforms to Minnesota's social welfare programs and push for more generous and accessible benefits.[22]

Despite representing overlapping groups of lower-income people and facing what I show were similar political-economic conditions, these three organizations followed remarkably divergent trajectories. On the one hand, like most contemporary social justice organizations, the Bailout Coalition and the North High Coalition partially suppressed abolitionist demands for freedom and equality. More precisely, each of them came to either oppose (rather than embrace) these demands, rely on conventional rhetoric that obscures (rather than condemns) the interlocking oppressions targeted by these demands, or pursue limited approaches to mobilization that diminish (rather than foster) constituent engagement around these demands. On the other hand, the Welfare Rights Committee mostly avoided such problematic choices and, as a result, more effectively promoted abolitionism and bolstered struggles to eliminate oppression.

By contextualizing and analyzing the divergent trajectories of the Bailout Coalition, the North High Coalition, and the Welfare Rights Committee, *A Voice but No Power* develops a novel argument for why social justice organizations in general tend not to advance abolitionist demands, and how more of them could. A growing body of important work has argued that, and shown how, external forces—especially long-standing disparities in political participation and the strictures of the nonprofit sector—hinder social justice organizations and lead them to make counterproductive decisions.[23] In contrast, my analysis shows how processes directed, in part, by organizers themselves influence these decisions. Building on leading scholarship about power, civic and political organization, and social movements, I argue that the process through which social justice organizers fashion their constituents' public identities plays a crucial role in reinforcing (or mitigating) important contextual pressures and in motivating decisions that suppress (or advance) abolitionist demands. In particular, I assert that to explain and address the unfulfilled potential of these organizations, we must understand how they assemble, publicize, and legitimate what I call *contentious identities.*

Contentious identities are public identities that social justice organizers fashion to counter the stigmatizing identities—such as "welfare queen," "irresponsible borrower," and "the underclass"—ascribed to disadvantaged groups in policy debates.[24] They are contentious not only because they counter such stigmatizing identities but also because they construe the interests of the disadvantaged in ways that question some aspect of dominant social and political relations. For example, in 2011, organizers working with Occupy Wall Street constructed and popularized a contentious identity, "the 99%," that countered the stigmatizing identities surrounding students, low-wage workers, and other economically disadvantaged groups and questioned the link between extreme affluence and political influence in U.S. society.[25]

In addition to being contentious, identities like "the 99%" are also a *necessary* part of social justice organizations' representational efforts. Without fashioning these identities, they can neither explain why sociopolitical change is needed to meet their constituents' interests nor foster movement activity in support of this change. Each contentious identity suggests a set of barriers standing between their constituents and a better social, economic, and political position. And each one also provides a sense of how to overcome these barriers, around which movement activists can orient their collective actions.[26]

Yet, as essential as contentious identities are, I argue that the process through which social justice organizers fashion them can also create problems. As with many crucial tasks performed by organizers, constructing these identities may undermine as well as enhance their ability to realize their emancipatory and egalitarian potential.[27] For example, organizers may assemble contentious identities in ways that foster more moderate political aspirations among their followers and thus reduce their ability to even support (much less defend) abolitionist demands.[28] Or they may legitimate contentious identities in ways that normalize low constituent engagement and, as a result, limit the potential base of support for abolition.[29] In general, while enabling social justice organizations to accomplish one major representational goal—countering stigmatizing identities and giving voice to disadvantaged groups—efforts to construct contentious identities can also reproduce obstacles to achieving another—the advancement of powerful calls for equality and freedom.

Through my analysis of Minneapolis, the Bailout Coalition, the North High Coalition, and the Welfare Rights Committee, I demonstrate that, in the process of fashioning contentious identities, social justice organizations in the United States encounter three types of political hazards—each of which can easily lead them to suppress abolitionist demands. The first and most basic hazard is that they must usually operate in settings where dominant ideologies foreclose abolitionist aspirations.[30] These ideologies encourage them to assemble contentious identities that endorse more moderate aspirations and rationalize opposition to demands geared toward dismantling oppression. The second hazard is that they must often engage with audiences whose comprehension of oppression is extremely limited and for whom attacks on the systems underlying this oppression can sound unintelligible.[31] The presence of such audiences tempts organizers to publicize contentious identities using misleading rhetoric that obscures widely accepted systems of oppression and undermines the moral justification for abolitionist demands. The third hazard is that social justice organizations represent disadvantaged groups whose capacity for sustained and independent political engagement is often constrained.[32] This limited capacity motivates organizers to legitimate contentious identities using tactics that rely only on the engagement of professional staff or a handful of already committed activists, curbing the potential collective strength behind abolitionist demands.

As I explain in chapter 1, the foregoing hazards are endemic to capitalist societies, even those governed by left-wing regimes. At the same time, I show, each one has been dramatically heightened over the last forty years by the turn to what many academics and activists call neoliberalism—that is, a form of governance that rolls back social-democratic checks on the accumulation of private wealth and "treats market rationality as a normative ideal to be pursued through applications of public authority."[33] In particular, I clarify how, under neoliberalism, America's national, state, and local political institutions have promoted a widespread ideological belief in the primacy of capitalist markets—what social theorist Mark Fisher called "capitalist realism"[34]—and discouraged the extra-market aspirations that inform many abolitionist demands; engendered particularly rampant ignorance about the market-based roots of exploitation, discrimination, and other injustices; and reduced the political capacity of the poor and working class, which includes the majority of all disadvantaged individuals represented by social justice organizations.

In early 2000s Minneapolis, organizations such as the Bailout Coalition, the North High Coalition, and the Welfare Rights Committee encountered a left-leaning but neoliberalized political terrain that was increasingly defined by the foregoing hazards. In the process of assembling contentious identities, they had to unite activists who had become skeptical of abolitionist demands centered on circumscribing market rule (which is to say, most abolitionist demands). In the process of publicizing these identities, they had to engage with progressive as well as conservative audiences who regularly ignored the market-based systems of oppression—such as gentrification or deunionization—targeted by abolitionist demands. And in the process of legitimating these identities, they had to work with many poor and working-class constituents who, as a starting point, lacked the capacity for independent and assertive political action. The result was that each organization faced intense baseline pressures to either disregard abolitionist demands altogether or adopt misleading rhetoric and selective approaches to mobilization that weaken these demands.

Nevertheless, I demonstrate that, even in such a challenging context, the hazards of contentious identity-building do not inevitably propel social justice organizations to suppress abolitionist demands for equality and freedom. These organizations can still lead the charge in support of such demands. Whether or not they do so, I show, depends on how they craft what sociologists call their political "etiquette" or "footing"—that is, their collectively assumed guide for action.[35] Faced with limited time and energy, most organizations settle for adopting etiquettes that treat the hazards they encounter as fixed constraints on what they can do, effectively resigning themselves to the suppression of abolitionist struggle. However, through purposeful and strategic action some organizations have been able to follow an alternative trajectory. These organizations adopt etiquettes that treat the hazards of contentious identity-building for what they actually are—namely, enduring but mutable problems to be solved through long-term struggles.[36] They push themselves to operate as what Sanford Schram calls "radical incrementalists"—slowly but surely redressing each hazard, thus creating more opportunities to fashion contentious identities in ways that advance abolitionist demands.[37]

This difference in etiquette was, I show, ultimately why the Welfare Rights Committee more effectively pursued abolitionist demand-making than either the Bailout Coalition or the North High Coalition. Whereas the latter two organizations adopted etiquettes that, in different ways, accommodated and reproduced their hazardous political terrain, the Welfare Rights Committee did the inverse. They adopted an etiquette that drove them to steadily check capitalist realism's influence on their supporters, educate the public about oppression's market-based roots, and rebuild the political capacity of their poor and working-class constituents. Because of this difference, the Welfare Rights Committee's organizers were able to assemble and unite around a contentious identity that linked their constituents' interests to the goal of stronger welfare entitlements, particularly guaranteed cash assistance. Likewise, they were able to consistently publicize this identity using rhetoric that illuminated and condemned the oppressive processes facing their constituents—including those based in markets—and clarified the rationale for stronger entitlements. Finally, they were able to legitimate this identity without neglecting the long-term need to build up their poor and working-class constituents' political capacity and mobilize a larger base of support. Through its representational efforts, the Welfare Rights Committee made itself a steadfast conduit for the promotion of hard-to-win abolitionist demands. Moreover, it did so in settings such as the Minnesota State Capitol where those demands are often absent.

My goal in developing the foregoing claims is not only to contribute to theories about political representation, political organization, and social justice. I also hope to chart possibilities for further empowering egalitarian and emancipatory movements of ordinary people—such as those that have already emerged out of the 2020 coronavirus pandemic and economic catastrophe. Of course, social justice organizations are not the only possible source of empowerment for these movements. But if effective, they can be a vital one, expanding opportunities to unsettle politics as usual and to demand the elimination of systemic oppression.

The rest of this book further explicates my argument about why social justice organizations often fall short of their egalitarian and emancipatory potential and how, moving forward, they could more consistently reach for this potential. Chapter 1 offers a more detailed exposition of the book's theoretical framework, empirical focus, and contributions to scholarly debates about social justice organizing. (Readers primarily interested in the book's cases studies and analysis of Minneapolis may skim this chapter.) It unpacks the concept of abolitionist demands and specifies how the hazards of contentious identity-building typically, but not necessarily, lead social justice organizations to suppress these demands. It also clarifies how neoliberalism has worsened the hazardous terrain confronting organizers and summarizes the immersive research experiences that informed my analysis.

Chapter 2 outlines the post–Great Recession political economy that enveloped Minneapolis and the social justice organizations I studied. It examines the simultaneously progressive and neoliberal mode of governance that structured this political economy, specifies its oppressive and heavily racialized socioeconomic consequences, and explains why building a fairer political economy will require social justice organizers to more steadfastly promote abolitionist struggles.

Chapter 3 looks into how neoliberal governance has exacerbated the political hazards of contentious identity-building and representing disadvantaged individuals—even in cities like Minneapolis, which are ruled by progressive coalitions. It explains how, by the time of the Great Recession, Minneapolis's turn to neoliberalism had fostered the ideological dominance of capitalist realism, widespread public ignorance about oppressive market processes, and the political incapacitation of poor and working-class people. It also identifies the agency that social justice organizers have in how they respond to their hazardous landscape, a central feature of the book's remaining chapters.

Chapter 4 analyzes the meetings and internal deliberations of the North High Coalition and the Welfare Rights Committee, comparing how the organizers in these two groups differently *assembled* contentious identities on behalf of their constituents. Drawing on this comparison, it explains and shows how the spread of ideologies like capitalist realism leads social justice organizations to assemble contentious identities around moderate—rather than abolitionist—demands. It also demonstrates that, by developing alternative political etiquettes, more organizations could avoid this outcome.

Chapter 5 analyzes the public actions of the Bailout Coalition and the Welfare Rights Committee, both of which supported important abolitionist demands. In particular, it compares how they differently *publicized* contentious identities on behalf of their constituents. Drawing on this comparison, it explains and shows how societal ignorance about systemic oppression leads social justice organizations—even some that support abolitionist demands—to publicize contentious identities using conventional and misleading rhetoric. It also demonstrates that organizers can, with the right political etiquette, push and embolden themselves to instead use oppositional rhetoric, which truly clarifies the failure of the status quo and articulates the need for abolitionism.

Chapter 6 analyzes the overall representational efforts of all three organizations, comparing how they *legitimated* the contentious identities at the heart of their efforts. Through this comparison, it explains and shows how the low political capacity of many poor and working-class individuals leads social justice organizations to legitimate contentious identities using disempowering tactics—that is, tactics that rely only on the engagement of professional staff or a handful of already committed activists. It also demonstrates, once again, that organizers can develop political etiquettes that instead enable and motivate grassroots mobilization efforts, which expand the base of support for abolitionist demands.

Finally, the book's Conclusion summarizes my overall argument and brings the analysis to the end of 2020. It reflects on the uprising that began in Minneapolis after the police killing of George Floyd, assessing what that uprising reveals about the future prospects for social justice organizing, contentious identity-building, and abolitionist politics in the United States.

SOCIAL JUSTICE ORGANIZATIONS AND THE STRUGGLE TO ABOLISH OPPRESSION

The recession that struck the United States in 2007 and 2008 both resulted from and fed into several interrelated forms of socioeconomic hardship, such as underemployment, school closures, and, of course, foreclosures and evictions. Just as they did in ostensibly better economic times, these hardships disproportionately fell on lower-income people, people of color, women, and other disadvantaged groups—groups that they continued to burden throughout the ensuing economic recovery.[1]

Their negative effects included measurable changes such as increased housing instability, wage loss, and student mobility as well as the traumatic and stressful experiences that sometimes stem from losing one's home, job, or school.[2] Such disparate outcomes suggest that the recession was shaped, at least in large part, by federal, state, and local officials' persistent failure to adequately represent the interests of disadvantaged groups.[3]

At the heart of this failure has been these same officials' support since the 1970s for an increasingly neoliberal and market-centered approach to governance. This approach has valued, above all, active and often state-led promotion of the capitalist market as a model for organizing society. For disadvantaged groups, its emergence has been devastating. It has reinforced stigmatizing images of poverty that attribute the marginalization of disadvantaged individuals to welfare dependency and other seeming behavioral deficiencies.[4] Furthermore, to induce more "productive" behavior, its proponents have not only deregulated and expanded the sphere of market competition but also advanced policy initiatives—such as welfare reform, public housing demolition, and school choice—that intensify disadvantaged individuals' participation in this sphere. According to neoliberal theory, such market-centered initiatives mitigate widespread social marginalization by promoting greater self-sufficiency. In reality, however, they have exacerbated this marginalization by compounding labor exploitation, racial discrimination, financial predation, and other injustices.[5] As a result, when the Great Recession hit, many members of disadvantaged groups—especially lower-income members—were already struggling and especially vulnerable to hardships associated with periods of economic instability.

In the fall of 2009, spurred by the glaring representational failures of local and national politicians and the advice of a friend, I began following the Minnesota Coalition for a People's Bailout. The Bailout Coalition was a multiracial and ardently socialist organization, led mostly by politically experienced white and working-class women. It formed in October 2008 to mitigate the rising socioeconomic hardships facing, in their words, "poor and working people." The coalition's most dedicated members came from a wide range of local and small-budget activist groups, such as the Minnesota Welfare Rights Committee, the Minnesota Immigrant Rights Action Committee, Communities United against Police Brutality, and multiple antiwar groups. It also included Local 3800 of the American Federation of State County and Municipal Employees, which represents the University of Minnesota's clerical workers.

The Bailout Coalition organized primarily in the gentrifying but still diverse and working-class neighborhoods of south Minneapolis, where many of the city's Latino and Black residents lived. While Minneapolis experienced fewer foreclosures and other related hardships than most cities, those that did occur were highly concentrated among this group.[6] And although north Minneapolis—the highest poverty, most disproportionately African American, and most policed section of the city—saw the highest foreclosure and unemployment rates, a significant cluster of foreclosures and unemployment also hit families in the south Minneapolis neighborhoods where the Bailout Coalition organized.[7]

To promote an egalitarian response to the issues surrounding the recession, Coalition organizers called on public officials to "Bail out the people!" and "Make the rich pay for their crisis!" They lobbied state legislators to enact a more progressive tax system, extend and expand eligibility for unemployment insurance and other welfare benefits, protect and create public jobs, and institute a two-year moratorium on home foreclosures and evictions from foreclosed properties. This last demand became the centerpiece of their efforts.[8] They also pursued direct action, using protest, home occupations, and civil disobedience to

South Minneapolis home occupied by the Bailout Coalition. Photograph by Jeffrey Thompson. Copyright 2009 Minnesota Public Radio®. Reprinted with permission. All rights reserved.

delay and disrupt foreclosure-related evictions. In making their demand for a moratorium, organizers sought to problematize neoliberalism and challenge the systems of financial predation, exploitation, and discrimination that destabilize ordinary people's access to decent housing. Moreover, they implored people to imagine a world beyond these systems, where, as their supporters chanted, "Housing is a human right!" (rather than a commodity) and "Eviction is a crime!" (rather than a routinized fact of life).

A long-standing tradition of scholarship treats social justice organizations such as the Bailout Coalition as political participants or "pressure groups" seeking to influence policy makers. More hopeful versions of this tradition have suggested that these organizations—whether national or community-based—can create an open and pluralistic political environment where policy influence is evenly dispersed across social groups.[9] More realistic versions have shown how the affluent and other advantaged groups enhance their own influence at the expense of others, and how people fighting for social justice sometimes redistribute this influence.[10]

Helpful as this tradition is for explaining how social justice organizations struggle to influence the policy-making process, it misses the extent to which these organizations also play an important representational role. In addition to acting as political participants, they provide an institutionalized source of what political scientist Dara Strolovitch calls "compensatory representation" for disadvantaged groups who are ignored or stigmatized by elected officials, the two major political parties, and other dominant political actors.[11] They step into the representational gap left by these dominant actors and work to alter prevailing political practices and power relations surrounding their constituents. The Bailout Coalition, for example, not only sought to gain representation *from* elected officials in and around Minneapolis; they also positioned themselves as a source of compensatory political representation *for* "poor and working people," making demands on this constituency's behalf and contesting elected officials' harmful accounts of its interests. As Mick Kelly—a cook at the University of Minnesota and one of the coalition's founders and most active members—stated in a media interview, "our [that is, poor and working people's] interests aren't going to be represented unless we do it ourselves."[12]

Just like all representatives, the Bailout Coalition and other social justice organizations have shaped the boundaries of the U.S. political system and affected when and how different groups can gain political voice.[13] The express promise of these organizations is that their efforts will bolster movements for a freer and more equal world.[14] Yet, as many scholars have shown, they often fall short of their potential to meet this promise.[15]

The rest of this chapter outlines the theoretical framework and research methods I use to explain why social justice organizations so regularly fail to realize their potential, and to better understand how they could reverse this trend. First, I locate their potential in their ability to advance demands geared toward the abolition of systemic oppression, and I outline how they often wind up suppressing these demands. Second, I explicate my main argument. This argument is that social justice organizations' struggles to fashion what I call *contentious identities*—identities that depict and give voice to their constituents—often, but not inexorably, lead them to either displace or weaken abolitionist demand-making. I also clarify this argument's complementary relationship to two others, which attribute social justice organizations' missteps to the persistence of unequal political participation and the growth of the nonprofit sector. Third, I explain how neoliberal capitalism has deepened the hazards and challenges involved in fashioning contentious identities and, in doing so, reinforced the tendency of social justice organizations to fall short of their potential. Finally, I briefly review the immersive research methods I used to complete my study (a more detailed discussion of my research methods can be found in the appendix).

FROM RESPONSIVENESS TO ABOLITION

What is the source of social justice organizations' egalitarian and emancipatory potential? If they want to empower movements for greater equality and freedom, what kinds of demands should they make on behalf of disadvantaged groups, and how should they promote these demands?

Many activists and scholars locate the potential of social justice organizations and other representational actors in their capacity to advance responsive demands—that is, policy demands that reflect the expressed and unmanipulated preferences of their constituents. These activists and scholars assume (or at least hope) that, in the absence of political manipulation, disadvantaged groups will tend to support thoroughgoing egalitarian and emancipatory reforms.[16] Research has demonstrated, however, that large segments of these groups sometimes oppose such reforms; moreover, they often do so under circumstances where strategic manipulation is absent or hard to discern.[17] Other research shows that even if disadvantaged individuals are not manipulated per se, their preferences for (or against) egalitarian and emancipatory reforms are partly the *product* of social justice organizations' and other political actors' representational efforts. As these actors mobilize around different demands, they shape the scope of political competition in ways that can either cultivate or discourage individuals' desires for greater freedom and equality.[18] Thus, although many political observers appeal to responsiveness, it is an inadequate standard for evaluating whether social justice organizations live up to their potential as representatives.

I focus instead on whether these organizations effectively promote *abolitionist* demands—that is, demands for single-payer health care, workplace democracy, restorative criminal justice, and other far-reaching but realistic reforms that bolster long-term efforts to eliminate systemic oppression. From an abolitionist perspective, social justice organizations must not merely respond to and reflect but *incite* and *deepen* their constituents' actionable desires for egalitarian and emancipatory social change.[19] In the words of scholar–organizer Jane McAlevey, they must "raise expectations."[20]

Abolitionist demands, if effectively advanced, meet this standard in two ways. First, they problematize the systems of oppression that cut across the United States and other capitalist societies. Second, they intimate future possibilities for dismantling these systems. For example, as Kathi Weeks has explained, the demand for a guaranteed minimum income put forth by welfare rights activists in the 1960s and 1970s problematized the exploitative wage relations and patriarchal family arrangements that regulate many ordinary people's access to income. It also intimated the possibility of eventually delinking access to income from participation in these systems and, thus, from the performance of excessive or abusive waged and familial work obligations.[21] By demanding a guaranteed minimum income, welfare rights activists not only tendered a progressive policy idea that welfare recipients and poor women may support. They also incited and deepened many poor women's actionable desires to abolish extreme wage dependency and patriarchy and build a freer and more equal world.[22]

Much research shows that contemporary social justice organizations tend to (at least partly) suppress rather than effectively advance such abolitionist demands. Many of these organizations simply forgo the idea of abolition in favor of pursuing more moderate demands, such as those calling for higher-performing public schools, increased work supports, or health insurance subsidies.[23] In contrast to abolitionist demands, such moderate demands usually temper rather than cultivate disadvantaged constituents' desires for greater emancipation and equality. Instead of inciting people to oppose accepted and interlocking systems of oppression, they partly normalize these systems; in addition, instead of articulating previously underappreciated possibilities for creating a better world, they needlessly circumscribe what seems politically possible. For example, the demand for increased work supports—such as job training and employment-based tax credits—helps to normalize the systems of labor exploitation facing low-income people of color, single mothers, and other disadvantaged groups. It also limits consideration of possibilities for further and more equally freeing people from these systems.[24] In general, despite sometimes leading to helpful reforms, moderate demands prevent social justice organizations from realizing their broader emancipatory and egalitarian potential.

There are also many social justice organizations that nominally support abolitionist demands but make tactical choices that substantially weaken these demands. Some of them do so by relying on what I would call conventional and misleading (rather than oppositional) rhetoric—which obscures the oppressive systems or processes targeted by demands for abolition and, thus, weakens the moral justification for these demands.[25] For example, as political scientist Rose Ernst has shown, many contemporary welfare rights organizations undermine their own demands for generous income entitlements by leaning on a misleading and "color-blind"—that is, race-neutral—rhetoric.[26] This rhetoric makes their cause more accessible to mainstream audiences because it diverts attention from poorly understood racial differences surrounding welfare recipients, especially the fact that African American women participate in means-tested welfare programs at higher rates than white women. However, it also obscures the market-based systems of exploitation, discrimination, and abuse that create these differences and that demands for income entitlements are meant to address.[27] As a result, color-blind rhetoric ultimately enervates rather than strengthens the rationale for such demands.

Other organizations weaken abolitionist demands by focusing too much on selectively mobilizing staff and already committed activists and not enough on building and mobilizing a grassroots base of disadvantaged constituents.[28] This narrow approach to mobilization promotes low constituent engagement and thus inhibits the emergence of a base that is strong enough to force abolitionist demands to the center of political and policy debates.[29] For example, as McAlevey has shown, most trade unions in the United States have weakened their demands for workplace democracy by merely advocating for and selectively mobilizing rather than, in her words, "organizing" workers.[30] Whereas the former approach relies on professional staff and committed activists to protest and negotiate with employers, the former emphasizes building and mobilizing a majority base that can assert abolitionist goals through strikes and other disruptive actions. Unions and labor advocacy organizations that overrely on selective mobilization efforts have tended to lose rather than gain ground in battles for workplace democracy.[31] Despite providing an important modicum of influence, this approach weakens long-term efforts to abolish oppression.

Ultimately, because of their decisions about demands, rhetoric, and mobilization, social justice organizations regularly fall short of their potential as representatives. Many of them disregard rather than support abolitionist demands, and even when they support such demands, they often weaken them by turning toward misleading rhetoric and away from grassroots mobilization. These decisions yield representational efforts that temper more than cultivate ordinary people's desires for greater equality and freedom. They also circumscribe rather than expand opportunities for egalitarian and emancipatory movements to grow and push against the limits of the status quo. The future of these movements partly depends on whether a larger number of community-based and national social justice organizations can begin to embrace not only abolitionist demands but also the rhetoric and mobilizing tactics appropriate for advancing them.

UNEQUAL PARTICIPATION AND THE NONPROFIT SECTOR

Social justice organizations' strategic missteps are well documented and widely noted among left-leaning observers of American politics. However, much uncertainty still exists about why these missteps are so persistent and pervasive, and, consequently, how to correct them. Building on prior studies of interest groups, social movements, and political economy, I argue that this persistence and pervasiveness is largely a by-product of the difficult and hazardous process through which organizers fashion *contentious identities.* These are the public identities that they use to counter stigmatizing identities—such as "illegal immigrant," "irresponsible borrower," and "the underclass"—often ascribed to their constituents in policy debates.[32] This argument, which I outlined in the book's introduction and unpack in the next section, complements two other important theories. Rather than focus, as my argument does, on the internal processes of social justice organizations, these other theories emphasize how external forces lead organizations to suppress abolitionist demands.

The first theory attributes social justice organizations' strategic missteps to disparities in political participation, especially the fact that socioeconomically advantaged individuals participate in politics at higher rates than their disadvantaged counterparts. Its proponents build on E. E. Schattschneider's famous dictum that the "chorus" of voices in the U.S. political system "sings with a strong upper-class accent."[33] This "unheavenly chorus"—to borrow the title of one prominent study—pervades not only the overall political system but social justice organizations as well.[34] Indeed, even activists who come from disadvantaged groups tend to be among the more socioeconomically well-off members of those groups.[35] Although social justice organizations have become more inclusive over time, they continue to be led disproportionately by relatively advantaged and educated professionals.

Several studies have shown that such unequal participation pushes social justice organizations to favor perspectives that undercut abolitionist demand-making. While socioeconomically advantaged organizers often contribute important skills and resources to social justice efforts, they also frequently introduce perspectives that ignore or misread how different oppressions affect their constituents.[36] For example, as Ernst showed, white women professionals in welfare rights organizations tend to adopt perspectives that minimize or superficially address how racialized systems of oppression shape poor people's experiences.[37] As relatively advantaged leaders promote these types of perspectives, social justice organizations become less likely to support and effectively advance abolitionist struggles.

The second theory attributes social justice organizations' representational shortcomings to the expansion of the nonprofit sector. This sector includes many types of voluntary and philanthropic groups that register with the federal government as tax-exempt—501(c)(3) or 501(c)(4)—organizations. While it has existed for over a century, the nonprofit sector has ballooned since the 1960s. Between 1967 and 2008 the number of nonprofit organizations grew from 309,000 to over 1.5 million.[38] In 2013 these organizations employed more than 14 million people, a sum that rose even as the overall U.S. workforce shrunk in the wake of the Great Recession.[39] Although not every social justice organization is a government-registered nonprofit, the expanded presence of these organizations in national and local politics is closely tied to the growth of the nonprofit sector. Many of them register as public charities or social welfare groups in order to receive tax-exempt status and become eligible for grants awarded by private foundations and government agencies.[40] Even social justice organizations that are not registered as public charities or social welfare groups are indirectly affected by the nonprofit sector, as their members and potential allies often work within it.

Several studies have shown that the expanded nonprofit sector subjects social justice organizations to rules and expectations that reinforce the status quo and dent abolitionist demand-making. As Frances Fox Piven highlighted in 1970, this sector brings social justice organizations "into a narrowly circumscribed form of political action . . . for which they are least equipped" and that requires "powerful group support, stable organization, professional staff, and money—precisely those resources which the poor do not have."[41] In exchange for their tax-exempt status and access to these resources, social justice organizations must submit to terms set by the state institutions and private foundations that govern the nonprofit sector. Most noted among these terms are the formal limits the federal government places on nonprofit organizations' level of political activity.[42] In addition, government agencies and private foundations craft grant requirements that draw organizers' agendas toward moderate rather than abolitionist goals, encourage these organizers to frame oppressions as technical and episodic rather than political and systemic problems, and push them to invest resources in hiring professional staff and mobilizing committed activists rather than building and mobilizing their constituent base.[43] Just like the political perspectives of advantaged individuals, the rules and expectations of the nonprofit sector can easily lead social justice organizations to suppress abolitionist demands.

Theoretical accounts of social justice organizations' strategic missteps that look toward unequal participation and the nonprofit sector reveal much of importance. First and foremost, they clarify broader social forces that predispose many of these organizations to suppress abolitionist demands. If left unchecked, educated professionals' limited perspectives and elite funders' rules and expectations can significantly hinder social justice organizations' capacity to rebel against systemic oppression. Second, theories focused on unequal participation and the nonprofit sector also point toward important strategies for enabling social justice organizations to better reach their emancipatory and egalitarian potential. In particular, they show that fostering more equal political participation and building organizational support outside of the nonprofit sector are both important steps toward enabling better representation of disadvantaged groups.[44]

Nonetheless, there is also much about the politics of social justice organizing that these two theories cannot explain. For example, they cannot explain how—despite the influence of unequal participation and the nonprofit sector—some groups have nevertheless advanced (rather than abandoned) abolitionist politics. One such group, which I introduced in the introduction and discuss throughout this book, is the Welfare Rights Committee. Some might point out that these groups are precisely those that tend to have *more* participation from disadvantaged individuals and *weaker* ties to the nonprofit sector.[45] But this observation only raises further questions about how, in practice, they encourage that participation from below and maintain such weak ties.[46]

In addition, theories centered on unequal participation and the nonprofit sector cannot explain why many groups who *do* have more equal participation and weaker nonprofit ties nevertheless undercut abolitionism. As I will discuss more in the coming pages and chapters, two of the organizations I studied—the Welfare Rights Committee and the Bailout Coalition—were almost wholly led by poor and working-class people and had weak and combative relationships to the nonprofit sector, and even the third—the North High Coalition—had more equal participation and weaker nonprofit ties than many social justice organizations. Yet only one of these three groups, the Welfare Rights Committee, effectively developed and advanced an abolitionist politics. Perhaps this is because advantaged political actors and the nonprofit sector exert a broader ideological influence on social justice organizing, guiding what even nonprofessional and disadvantaged activists see as reasonable. But, again, this observation only raises further questions about why some groups are more susceptible to that influence than others.

CONTENTIOUS IDENTITIES

My argument aims to fill the aforementioned explanatory gaps by devoting greater attention to how social justice organizers fashion contentious identities, such as "the community," "the poor," "Black lives," and, most generally, "the people." I focus specifically on how they *assemble* these identities among themselves and, in turn, *publicize* and *legitimate* them for public officials, reporters, potential supporters, and other audiences. Through this process, organizers not only counter stigmatizing depictions of their constituents; they also implicitly clarify their constituents' interests in social and political change and suggest the appropriate role for their constituents in achieving this change. Contentious identity-building is, in short, their way of answering a fundamental question that weighs on every political organization—namely, Whom are we representing? A relatively homogeneous and discrete constituency, or one rife with crosscutting hierarchies? One with an adversarial relationship to the status quo social order, or one merely waiting to be incorporated into this order? One that is generally passive and quiescent, or one with meaningful potential for mass engagement?

Each stage of the contentious identity-building process directly informs whether social justice organizations reproduce different strategic missteps and reach their egalitarian and emancipatory potential as representatives. In assembling contentious identities among themselves, they can cultivate more or less organizational support for abolitionist demands. In publicizing these identities, they can rely more or less on oppositional rhetoric that strengthens the justification for abolitionist demands. And in legitimating these identities, they can invest more or less energy in expansive, grassroots mobilizing strategies that grow the base of support for abolitionist demands.

Across these stages, social justice organizations encounter three political hazards that, I will show, encourage them to abandon abolition. The first hazard is that they that they typically work in settings where dominant ideologies favor more limited aspirations for egalitarian and emancipatory change.[47] These ideologies encourage organizers to assemble contentious identities that endorse moderate goals and make abolitionist demands seem reckless and unrealistic. For example, since the postwar era, labor, women's, and civil rights organizations have contended with a consumerist ideology that prioritizes the ability to purchase important goods through commercial markets. This ideology has encouraged organizers to assemble contentious identities that endorse moderate demands for greater access to the marketplace—through, for example, financial aid or more diverse choices—and silence abolitionist demands for greater entitlements to housing, health care, education, and other goods.[48] The result is that many organizations have found themselves normalizing rather than problematizing reliance on predatory, exploitative, and discriminatory companies for the provision of basic human needs.

The second hazard is that social justice organizations often engage with audiences whose comprehension of systemic oppression is lacking and for whom condemnations of this oppression can sound unintelligible.[49] The presence of these audiences encourages organizers to publicize contentious identities using broadly accessible but misleading rhetoric, which sidesteps discussion of important oppressive processes and weakens the moral justification for abolitionist demands. For example, in the post-civil-rights era, antipoverty organizations have encountered many audiences who attribute poverty among working-class Black people to behavioral deficiencies, such as bad "people skills," low education, and welfare dependency. For these audiences, critiques of Black poverty that instead primarily target deunionization, racialized divisions of labor, gentrification, and other systems of oppression can easily sound outlandish. Their tendency to associate Black poverty with behavioral deficiency has encouraged organizers to publicize contentious identities using color-blind rhetoric, which sidesteps consideration of racialized differences and, in doing so, makes poor families seem more "normal" and relatable.[50] However, by ignoring racialized differences and the intersecting systems of oppression that create them, color-blind rhetoric also makes abolitionist measures seem less necessary.

The third hazard is that social justice organizations' constituents and most likely supporters often lack the capacity for sustained and independent political engagement.[51] This diminished political capacity encourages organizers to legitimate contentious identities using tactics that only require the engagement of professional staff and already committed activists and, thus, narrow the base of support for abolitionist demands. For example, social justice organizations' low-income constituents often lack important political resources, including time, transportation, and reliable modes of communication. This resource scarcity has encouraged organizers to legitimate contentious identities by acting as what one study calls "rational prospectors," selectively mobilizing individuals who already possess some political resources and can claim to stand in for broader disadvantaged constituencies.[52] Although this behavior seems rational in the short term, it routinizes the low engagement of their constituents and undermines the collective strength needed to push abolitionist demands over the long term.

Both unequal participation and the nonprofit sector exacerbate the hazards of contentious identity-building. Unequal participation, for instance, increases the relative presence of audiences who remain blind to various patterns of systemic oppression and thus have trouble deciphering rhetorical attacks on this oppression. Similarly, the nonprofit sector disseminates ideologies that foreclose radical aspirations for freedom and equality. It also diminishes the political capacity of disadvantaged individuals by encouraging the professionalization of social justice organizing. However, as I explain next and show in chapter 3, the political hazards faced by social justice organizers ultimately stem from broader institutional arrangements, of which unequal participation and the nonprofit sector are only a part.

In sum, my argument is that the fashioning of contentious identities is a double-edged sword that can easily lead social justice organizations to suppress abolitionist demands and undermine their own egalitarian and emancipatory potential. On the one hand, this process allows organizers to counter stigmatizing perceptions of their disadvantaged constituents and clarify these constituents' interests in social and political change. It enables them to give a greater voice to disadvantaged groups and is, in this sense, a basic and vital part of their representational efforts. On the other hand, it comes with hazards that encourage organizers to oppose abolitionist demands and to embrace misleading rhetoric and narrow approaches to mobilization that weaken these demands. The result has been that, even while granting disadvantaged groups a greater voice in political and policy debates, social justice organizers often (unintentionally) direct this voice against movements for a freer and more equal world.

And yet, social justice organizations can and sometimes do fashion contentious identities without actively suppressing abolitionist demands.[53] They can strike this balance, I argue, by developing a political "etiquette"—or guide for action—that requires them to treat the hazards of contentious identity-building as enduring problems in need of resolution (rather than as hardwired constraints on what they can do).[54] For example, by learning to approach the diminished political capacity of their disadvantaged constituents as a hurdle rather than a barrier, they can motivate themselves to help build this capacity and support grassroots mobilization through disciplined outreach and organizing. Following this type of political etiquette cannot, of course, simply erase the hazards I described. However, as I demonstrate at length in later chapters, it can help them to minimize each one, enabling organizers to commit to abolitionist demand-making without sacrificing their more immediate need to fashion contentious identities. It can also underscore the political fallout of simply accommodating each hazard, pressing organizers to endure substantial costs and risks to embrace and keep their abolitionist commitments.[55]

NEOLIBERAL CAPITALISM

Where do the hazards of fashioning contentious identities come from? Broadly speaking, they are endemic to the United States and other capitalist societies—that is, societies dependent upon the maintenance of corporate profits and the accumulation of private wealth through competitive markets. Political institutions in these societies tend to solidify the central role that markets play in ordering economic exchange and producing the affluence needed to maintain society. In doing so, they bolster ideologies, such as consumerism, that take this centrality for granted; they also delegitimate calls for universal and generous entitlements, workplace democracy, and other abolitionist goals that would subordinate market principles.[56] In addition, these same institutions tend to treat market competition as a nonpartisan good, which is at least compatible with the maximization of freedom and equality. They thus promote ignorance about the market-based roots of labor exploitation, housing discrimination, financial predation, and other oppressive practices, in the process rendering critiques of market rule less intelligible for many people.[57] Finally, political institutions in capitalist societies tend to restrict poor and working-class people's ability to access goods like housing and income outside of markets. They make this class—which constitutes the vast majority of disadvantaged individuals—reliant on employers and other privileged market actors for its well-being. Consequently, they grant these actors an extraordinary ability to impede independent political engagement from below.[58]

Although the hazards of fashioning contentious identities are deeply tied to capitalism, the strength of this tie has fluctuated over time. The Keynesian and social-democratic regimes that ruled North America and Western Europe between World War II and the 1970s partially tempered the hazardous terrain facing social justice organizations. America's New Deal regime instituted national welfare programs, consumer rights, collective bargaining rights, and other socioeconomic protections that encouraged more expansive aspirations for egalitarian change, the politicization of previously ignored systems of oppression, and the political engagement of ordinary people.[59] This regime did not erase the political hazards of contentious identity-building, and in some ways it even further discouraged making demands geared toward abolishing exploitative wage relations and imperial expansion. Nevertheless, it created more room for social justice organizations to formulate abolitionist demands against Jim Crow segregation and other systems that violated basic liberal ideals.[60]

By the late 1970s, the left-wing political coalitions and Fordist economic configurations that made Keynesian capitalism possible in America had collapsed and began ceding ground to today's neoliberal regime.[61] Rather than check capitalism's lifeline to the hazards of contentious identity-building, neoliberal governance has nurtured it in at least three ways.

First, under neoliberalism, America's political institutions have not only solidified but universalized the role of markets in society. These institutions do not settle for merely structuring private economic exchange around market principles. Rather, they apply the capitalist market as a model for organizing the public sphere as well. For example, many state and local governments have decentralized the provision of public services and contracted these services out to nonprofit and for-profit corporations.[62] Likewise, following incentives created by federal education policy, many school districts have used school choice initiatives and charter schools to place public schools in a market-like competition over students and resources.[63] By universalizing the market, neoliberal governance has affirmed Margaret Thatcher's ideological dictum that "there is no alternative" to a pro-market world. It has also, thus, discouraged even formulating, much less embracing, abolitionist demands that challenge market supremacy.[64]

Second, and relatedly, neoliberal-era institutions have construed marketization as not only compatible but concomitant with maximizing freedom and equality. Instead of attempting to square market relations with the realization of important outcomes like free speech or upward mobility, these institutions have increasingly designated market expansion and participation itself as the best measure of those outcomes. For example, means-tested welfare programs such as Temporary Assistance to Needy Families have used reductions in caseloads and increases in labor market participation to evaluate whether their recipients are becoming full and independent members of society.[65] In U.S. cities, civil society organizations, public agencies, private foundations, and developers have used growth in real estate values as the benchmark for evaluating their contributions to the betterment of struggling communities.[66] By idealizing markets in these and other ways, neoliberal governance has further distracted attention from how they perpetuate oppression. It has also framed social-democratic redistribution—a central check on markets and important tool in the fight against oppression—as threatening to the public good.[67]

Finally, under neoliberalism, political institutions in the United States have not just restricted poor and working-class people's ability to exit the marketplace; they have also commanded these people to embrace ever more active and compliant market participation. For instance, federal and state governments have made labor market participation a requirement for receiving different forms of social welfare assistance. They have also encouraged prisons to make greater use of inmates as a cheap and relatively unprotected workforce.[68] Following a similar logic, urban housing authorities have moved toward using rental certificates and vouchers—which require participation in rental markets—to provide low-income housing assistance (and for many low-income people, even this assistance is unavailable).[69] By actively intensifying working-class market participation, neoliberal governance has exacerbated the already significant influence that wealthy interests have over their lives. It has also instilled greater cynicism about the government's ability to provide a democratic counterweight to this power. The result has been fewer resources and motivation for grassroots engagement among disadvantaged individuals and an increase in economic elites' ability to channel and co-opt the engagement that does exist.[70]

In recent history, especially since the emergence of the coronavirus pandemic, neoliberalism has begun to lose its legitimacy in the United States. More and more movements have challenged its parameters, including—to name a few—Occupy Wall Street, Black Lives Matter, the Fight for 15, and the campaign against the Dakota Access Pipeline. Furthermore, many voters are expressing support for policy reforms that would restore and extend social-democratic checks on capitalist society.[71] The moment portends good things for social justice organizations, a number of which—particularly the Democratic Socialists of America—have reported growth in membership and taken a greater role in the politics of the street, the ballot box, and the policy-making process.

However, despite neoliberalism's declining legitimacy, the political hazards surrounding social justice organizations' efforts to fashion contentious identities will likely remain strong for the indefinite future. For one, an alternative, more liberating and egalitarian approach to governance has yet to garner enough electoral or institutional support to replace neoliberalism. Politicians like Bernie Sanders and Alexandria Ocasio-Cortez and a range of movement activists have certainly articulated the elements of potential alternatives; they can be found in various left-wing manifestos and policy platforms.[72] Nevertheless, until a nationwide electoral and governing coalition brings these elements together, neoliberalism—or perhaps something worse—and the political hazards associated with it will remain a significant part of U.S. society.

Furthermore, as I previously explained, the political hazards of contentious identity-building are endemic not just to neoliberalism but also to capitalism. Even a significant rollback of neoliberal governance cannot erase the problems associated with ordering society around the accumulation of profits and private wealth. Only a social order geared more purposefully toward the fulfillment of human needs can make struggles to abolish oppression a normal part of politics. Until such an order emerges—a moment that, realistically speaking, may never arrive—social justice organizations will have to negotiate a contentious identity-building process rife with political hazards that encourage them to suppress abolitionist demands.

STUDYING SOCIAL JUSTICE ORGANIZATIONS

The representational efforts of social justice organizations and the contentious identity-building processes underlying these efforts do not occur in general. They emerge unevenly across different organizations operating in specific locales. Thus, to study them properly it is often best to immerse oneself among particular organizations in a particular place. Between the fall of 2009 and the fall of 2012—in the wake of the Great Recession—I conducted immersive fieldwork among community-based social justice organizations in Minneapolis, Minnesota. During that time I focused primarily on three of these organizations, each of which was—with the exception of one individual—entirely volunteer-run:[73] the Bailout Coalition, the North High Coalition, and the Welfare Rights Committee. I participated in these three groups as both an academic observer of their representational efforts and a highly engaged but less influential volunteer. In the latter role, I performed many low-profile tasks, such as holding banners at rallies, phone-banking petition signees, engaging in community outreach, and making occasional contributions to strategy discussions.

My choice to focus on the Bailout Coalition, the North High Coalition, and the Welfare Rights Committee was intentional inasmuch as it stemmed from a conscious desire to examine variation in how social justice organizations fashion contentious identities and represent disadvantaged groups. However, as I explain in the coming paragraphs, it was also serendipitous.

I started in the fall of 2009 by studying the Bailout Coalition. As I indicated at the outset of this chapter, the coalition had formed several months prior and engaged in different activities aimed at pushing the city and state government to enact a fairer response to the Great Recession. Their efforts addressed a wide array of issues, such as extending unemployment benefits and taxing the rich. But their main focus, by far, was stopping foreclosures and evictions. Working with another group—the Minnesota Poor People's Economic Human Rights Campaign—they used rallies, occupations, and other protest actions to halt foreclosure-related evictions, mostly in south Minneapolis; they also pushed the state government to pass a two-year moratorium on foreclosures and evictions from foreclosed properties.

Their calls to end foreclosure-related evictions amounted to what I label an abolitionist demand. This demand had the potential to problematize gentrification, residential segregation, and other racialized market processes that have limited access to decent jobs and affordable housing, worsened injustices like labor exploitation, predatory lending, and housing discrimination, and thus pushed many borrowers and tenants into situations where they might become victims of foreclosure. It also had the potential to deepen disadvantaged people's desires for a right to housing that ameliorates these processes and lays the groundwork for dismantling them. In addition to supporting this demand, the Bailout Coalition organized in neighborhoods affected by foreclosures, building their constituents' capacity for political engagement and mobilizing a more expansive base of support. However, they somewhat weakened their calls to end foreclosure-related evictions by couching their representational efforts in a misleading color-blind rhetoric. As I will show in chapter 5, this rhetoric obscured some of the very racialized market processes that the demand for a moratorium was meant to address; it also failed to clarify the inadequacy of more moderate anti-foreclosure and anti-eviction measures like mortgage and financial counseling.

On September 24, 2010, the Bailout Coalition hit a proverbial brick wall when FBI agents raided the homes of several of the organization's key members. The raids were part of an investigation into possible "material support for terrorism" among a national network of antiwar activists.[74] The investigation had nothing to do with the Bailout Coalition's efforts. Nevertheless, it repressed these efforts by forcing many of the group's members to devote their energy to publicizing the raids and protecting themselves and their close friends from further threats. The Bailout Coalition continued to organize around foreclosure-related evictions and economic inequality, but it never regained the level of activity it had before the FBI raids. By the end of 2012 it was no longer active.

As the Bailout Coalition's activity waned, I shifted my attention to the North High Coalition, a relatively new organization operating in north Minneapolis that a classmate and an activist friend had mentioned to me. The group was a racially, socioeconomically, and ideologically diverse public education coalition. It was led primarily by civically active members of north Minneapolis's African American middle class—most but not all of whom were men. And it had formed in the summer of 2010 to resist a proposal by the superintendent of Minneapolis Public Schools to close North High School, a public high school in the Near North neighborhood of north Minneapolis. More generally, the group sought to protect and expand access to quality education for northside students. After an initial wave of protest, they eventually settled on supporting a school district–led effort to "redesign" North High, improve its performance on standardized tests, and increase its attractiveness to students around the city.

As I described in the book's Introduction, the demand to redesign and raise the performance of North High—and, implicitly, other schools threatened with closure—was a moderate one. It normalized the system of school choice and privatization that had imperiled schools like North High and compounded oppressive racialized and market-based systems like gentrification and residential segregation. Furthermore, the North High Coalition adopted a misleading school-centered rhetoric that obscured the systemic nature of the problems facing students from north Minneapolis. This rhetoric located students' problems in the school's unresponsiveness to community needs rather than, for instance, the neoliberal governance of both the school and the community. They also adopted a narrow approach to mobilization that relied on highly engaged community leaders to bargain and deliberate with school district officials over the redesign process. This approach reproduced the disengagement of north Minneapolis students and families in debates over education and yielded a somewhat weak constituent base.

The implementation of the effort to redesign North High ultimately ended the North High Coalition. It co-opted most of the group's leading organizers by inviting them to participate in two community advisory committees. These committees worked under the guidance of district officials and supported different aspects of the redesign process, including hiring an external consultant, gathering community input, and developing curricular recommendations. As the coalition's leaders embraced roles as advisory committee members, their attendance at the

	Bailout Coalition	North High Coalition	Welfare Rights Committee
Demands	Abolitionist (moratorium on foreclosure-related evictions)	Moderate (higher-performing school)	Abolitionist (stronger welfare entitlements)
Rhetoric	Conventional (color-blind)	Conventional (school-centered)	Oppositional (class, race, and gender conscious)
Mobilization	Grassroots (outreach to struggling homeowners and renters as well as committed left-wing activists)	Limited (outreach focused only on already committed alumni, activists, and North High supporters)	Grassroots (outreach to welfare recipients and other low-income women as well as committed left-wing activists)

Representational choices of the Bailout Coalition, the North High Coalition, and the Welfare Rights Committee.

organization's meetings declined, and they invested less and less energy into planning independent actions and directly challenging educational inequalities. Eventually, around the end of May 2011—when the redesign process crystallized—the North High Coalition dissolved.

At the start of 2011, as the North High Coalition was shifting more of its energy toward supporting the North High redesign, I began to study the Welfare Rights Committee. This organization—a mainstay on the socialist left in Minneapolis—was a multiracial citywide group composed of current and former welfare recipients and led entirely by poor and working-class women. Its leaders were prominent in the local network of socialist organizers surrounding the Bailout Coalition; they were also among the Bailout Coalition's most active participants. The Welfare Rights Committee formed in 1991, amid an emerging national panic about welfare dependency. Its primary goals were to oppose budget cuts and disciplinary reforms to Minnesota's social welfare programs and to demand that the poor receive greater access to and control over these programs. During my time with the group they continued to pursue these goals. They organized grassroots opposition to multiple bills in the state legislature that reduced spending on public assistance, further restricted access to this assistance, and increased monitoring and policing of welfare recipients. They also exhorted progressive legislators to support bills that would make the Minnesota Family

Investment Program (MFIP, Minnesota's Temporary Assistance for Needy Families program) and other state-funded assistance programs more generous and accessible and, in general, expand poor individuals' rights to income and other goods. One bill, for example, called for the doubling of MFIP recipients' cash grants, which—at the time—the state had not raised since 1986.

The Welfare Rights Committee went the furthest of all three organizations in advancing an abolitionist demand, avoiding strategic missteps, and reaching for their potential as political representatives. Their calls for stronger welfare entitlements, particularly cash assistance, problematized the patriarchal, racial, and market-based systems bearing down on welfare recipients and lower-income people in general. They intimated the possibility of building a world where ordinary people can rebel against job discrimination, labor exploitation, domestic violence, and other oppressions created by these systems without losing the money needed to live. Moreover, they used an oppositional and class-, race-, and gender-conscious rhetoric, which effectively clarified the justification for their demand. Finally, they engaged in extensive and generative constituent outreach campaigns. These campaigns reflected a strong, enduring commitment to grassroots mobilization and building a constituent base with the potential to disrupt politics as usual.

By the time I ended my fieldwork, in the fall of 2012, the Welfare Rights Committee had gained several new members and were as active as they had been throughout my entire study. A few years later, around 2019, their level of activity declined, leaving the organization's future in doubt. However, in contrast to the declines in activity I witnessed in the Bailout Coalition and the North High Coalition, theirs was not due to repression or co-optation. Instead, according to one longtime member, it occurred because several of the organization's members had shifted their energy to working in the socialist wing of the Black Lives Matter movement. Rather than a defeat for the Welfare Rights Committee, this transfer of activity indicated a political victory. It was made possible precisely *because* the group had effectively deepened and expanded its members active desires for freedom and equality—a point I return to in later chapters.

In addition to immersing myself in the Bailout Coalition, the North High Coalition, and the Welfare Rights Committee, I also spent a small amount of time studying organizations that either collaborated with them or worked on similar issues. For example, early in my fieldwork I volunteered for the Minnesota Poor People's Economic Human Rights Campaign (PPEHRC), a small organization led by poor and working-class women. As I previously mentioned, PPEHRC worked closely with the Bailout Coalition to organize home occupations and other anti-foreclosure and anti-eviction actions. I also attended public events hosted by many other social justice organizations, including Take Action Minnesota, Occupy Minneapolis, Centro de Trabajadores Unidos en la Lucha, Council 5 of the American Federation of State, County and Municipal Employees, and several others. Although I did not study these groups closely, paying some marginal attention to them enriched my sense of how the Bailout Coalition, the North High Coalition, and the Welfare Rights Committee compared and contrasted with Minneapolis's broader universe of social justice organizations.

As I further explain in the methodological appendix, the set of cases I studied have four features that help to throw the political hazards and consequences of contentious identity-building into sharp relief. First, all three organizations operated in Minneapolis, a city where the mainstream political landscape is relatively progressive and open to the efforts of social justice organizations (see chapters 2 and 3). Consequently, the political hazards they faced and their responses to them are likely relevant for social justice campaigns in other cities and towns, where the landscape is less inviting. Second, all three organizations claimed to represent segments of Minneapolis's lower-income population, a highly and often intersectionally marginalized group. As a result, in the process of fashioning contentious identities they tended to encounter political hazards and challenges that exemplify those facing other social justice organizations (see chapter 3). Third, their representational efforts differed from one another in several theoretically important ways, such as the issues they addressed, the neighborhoods they based themselves in, and their methods of collective action (see the appendix). Given these differences, the commonalities I found in their efforts to fashion contentious identities are likely relevant for many different types of social justice organizations. Finally, all three organizations had substantial participation from socioeconomically disadvantaged individuals and at least some critical distance from the nonprofit sector (see chapters 4, 5, and 6). This position helped to minimize the direct pressures that unequal participation and the nonprofit sector placed on their representational efforts and thus magnified contentious identity-building's relatively autonomous influence over their representational efforts.

"Organizers and leaders cannot prevent the ebbing of protest, nor the erosion of whatever influence protest yielded the lower class. They can only try to win whatever can be won while it can be won."[75] These statements from Frances Fox Piven and Richard Cloward's foundational book *Poor People's Movements* elegantly frame the egalitarian and emancipatory potential of social justice organizations like the Bailout Coalition, the North High Coalition, and the Welfare Rights Committee. The representational efforts undertaken by these organizations cannot evoke disruptive and influential movements for freedom and equality where the social control of disadvantaged groups remains entrenched, nor can their efforts stop the decline of these movements in response to the restoration of control. However, as representatives, organizers can develop a more democratic and radicalized political environment that helps these movements to "win whatever can be won" when they emerge, eases their emergence when they remain dormant, and, in general, heightens their potential power over time.[76]

The way social justice organizations' representational efforts nurture such an environment is by demanding measures aimed at abolishing systems of oppression. Abolitionist demands, if bolstered by oppositional rhetoric and support for expansive grassroots mobilization, work to problematize these systems and clarify possibilities for building a freer and more equal world. Making abolitionist demands in a forceful way helps to incite and deepen ordinary people's desires for egalitarian and emancipatory social change—the same desires that stimulate the disruptive movements discussed by Piven and Cloward and amplify these movements' effects on electoral behavior and party competition.

The central puzzles of this book are why, on a day-to-day basis, social justice organizers so often make decisions that suppress abolitionist demand-making and undercut the potential power of disruptive left-wing movements, and how they might come to make better decisions. As several scholars have shown, organizers in the neoliberal era have frequently either opposed demands geared toward abolitionist goals or weakened these demands by adopting misleading rhetoric and narrow approaches to mobilization. Instead of developing a political environment that enables, escalates, and empowers movements for freedom and equality, they find themselves reproducing one that enervates these movements and perpetuates many oppressions facing their constituents.

The answers to my questions are multifaceted, but I think they hinge to a large extent on the process through which social justice organizations fashion contentious identities. These identities, which counter stigmatizing perceptions of disadvantaged groups in political and policy debates, are vital for social justice organizations' representational efforts. The problem for organizers is that, to actually assemble, publicize, and legitimate contentious identities, they must traverse a hazardous terrain created by neoliberal capitalism. On this terrain, dominant ideologies constrict aspirations for freedom and equality, audiences have a low baseline understanding of important systems of oppression, and disadvantaged constituents often lack the capacity for sustained independent engagement. The result is that organizers have a much easier time fashioning contentious identities if they are willing to either table abolitionist demands or make choices about rhetoric and mobilization that significantly weaken these demands. To enable themselves to make better choices, organizers must, I argue, learn to treat the hazards they confront as mutable problems rather than fixed constraints and, in turn, take strategic and incremental steps to address these hazards.

The next five chapters tell a story about Minneapolis, the Bailout Coalition, the North High Coalition, and the Welfare Rights Committee that aims to enrich as well as support my central claims about social justice organizations and political representation. This story does not capture the full range of social justice organizing in the United States, or even in Minneapolis. But it does, I hope, illuminate the broad and practical relevance of the ideas outlined in this chapter and provoke readers to ask themselves about how these ideas apply to other organizations. If it is successful, it will not have resolved debates about contemporary social justice organizing and political representation so much as clarified the ground on which those debates take place.

NEOLIBERALISM IN A PROGRESSIVE CITY

In 2009, Minneapolis seemed like an ideal place for social justice organizing, especially on the issue of housing. Local civic and political leaders occupied the forefront of national efforts to enact a progressive response to the nationwide growth in foreclosures. As mortgage defaults skyrocketed, they developed several programs and laws aimed at assisting delinquent borrowers and tenants of foreclosed properties. City officials, for instance, pooled $115 million from the federal government's Neighborhood Stabilization Program, foundation grants, and various local and state agencies; they used this money to provide mortgage financing, down payment assistance, home improvement loans, and other modest supports for a range of borrowers, including first-time homeowners. They also funded mortgage counseling for struggling borrowers and invested in the purchase, redevelopment, and sale of several vacant residential properties.[1]

Neighborhood organizations, social service agencies, and other nongovernmental entities supplemented city officials' efforts by working with developers to purchase and rehabilitate foreclosed homes—especially in north and south Minneapolis, the areas of the city with the highest foreclosure rates. They also made mortgage and financial counseling widely available to struggling borrowers and helped these borrowers pursue loan modifications through the federal government's Home Affordable Modification Program.[2]

Finally, state legislators from Minneapolis supported city officials and advocates by leading successful efforts to strengthen prohibitions on subprime lending and increase lenders' obligations to connect struggling borrowers with nonprofit agencies that provide mortgage counseling. They even led the passage of a one-year foreclosure moratorium for borrowers in possession of predatory and subprime loans (the legislation was ultimately vetoed by the state's then governor, Tim Pawlenty). In addition, they supported statewide protections for tenants living in foreclosed properties. For instance, they successfully pushed for legislation that removes foreclosure-related evictions from tenants' rental records and requires landlords to notify tenants when properties are in foreclosure.[3]

This progressive agenda starkly contrasted the hateful one promoted by many conservative leaders. Rather than assist working-class borrowers and tenants, these conservative leaders sought vengeance. They claimed that struggling borrowers had defrauded banks and behaved foolishly by taking out exorbitant, unaffordable loans, and they concluded that these borrowers should absorb the cost of the crash.[4] Moreover, they treated renters living in foreclosed properties as insignificant collateral damage.[5] To defend their agenda, they deployed long-standing stereotypes about the dysfunctionality of poor and female-led Black families—a group who had borne the brunt of the housing crash and suffered elevated foreclosure and eviction rates since the 1990s.[6] Conservatives also attacked the 1977 Community Reinvestment Act and other federal community reinvestment and fair housing initiatives. Such efforts, they argued, rewarded predatory *borrowers,* incentivized reckless financial behavior, and unfairly restricted creditors and landlords.[7]

Despite opposing this hateful response, progressive decision makers in Minneapolis nevertheless mimicked one of its most central features—namely, its adherence to market rule. Apart from the state legislature's moratorium proposal, each of their efforts—the mortgage counseling and modest aid, the property investment and rehabilitation, the enactment of new consumer protections, and the pursuit of minor loan modifications—assisted ordinary people by encouraging and supporting their participation in the local housing market. Notably absent was any concerted effort to socialize and democratize control over the provision of housing—by, for example, deferring *all* foreclosure-related evictions or building more subsidized and public housing. Even the moratorium proposal was too narrow to really limit the market dependence of people at risk of foreclosure-related eviction—most of whom either did not possess subprime loans (the focus of the moratorium) or were not borrowers but tenants.[8]

The problem with this approach, at least for social justice organizers, was that, among their disadvantaged constituents, overdependence on the local housing market was itself a major *cause* of foreclosure-related evictions. Starting in the early 1990s, that market—which had never supplied enough decent affordable housing for lower-income residents—began to provide even less. Long-standing patterns of residential segregation and disinvestment and newer moves toward gentrification combined to reduce the production and maintenance of low-cost market-rate units.[9] Simultaneously, deunionization and racialized and gendered divisions in the labor market decreased the income that working-class African Americans and other disadvantaged individuals could use to purchase or rent those units.[10] Meanwhile, federal, state, and local governments rolled back support for public and subsidized housing, increasing the demand for decent and affordable market-rate housing, even as the supply dwindled.[11] The result was predictable. Housing insecurity became a larger and more permanent feature of Minneapolis's political economy; for many individuals, borrowing high cost loans—prime as well as subprime—or renting properties purchased with such loans became the most viable options.[12]

Minneapolis's foreclosure response had no answer to the lack of affordability in the local housing market. In fact, aspects of it may have worsened this problem. For example, one part of the local government's efforts involved the demolition of over 250 vacant and "blighted" residential properties, the vast majority of which were concentrated in high-poverty neighborhoods. By 2014 the city had only begun to redevelop twenty of those properties, not necessarily for use as affordable housing.[13]

Consequently, despite their progressiveness, local leaders' efforts to deal with the housing crash yielded massively unequal consequences. On the one hand, these efforts benefited advantaged and typically white middle-class individuals (for whom affordability was a less chronic problem), safeguarded wealthy investors' financial well-being, and helped to ensure that the overall peak in foreclosure-related evictions was less enduring than in other major U.S. cities.[14] On the other hand, among disadvantaged groups, local foreclosure recovery efforts allowed for widespread suffering. Working-class Black families, in particular, continued to experience elevated foreclosure and evictions rates, as did immigrants, families with children, and others.[15] Likewise, processes like gentrification and deunionization continued apace, further diminishing the availability of affordable housing and ensuring future social insecurity.[16]

By the time the U.S. housing market crashed, journalistic and academic observers had long regarded Minneapolis as one of the United States' most well-run and progressive cities.[17] This reputation stemmed from a long-standing commitment among area leaders—initially forged during the New Deal era—to improving the socioeconomic incorporation and well-being of disadvantaged groups.[18] Their comparatively supportive response to the housing crash was just one in a long list of efforts that exemplified this commitment—a list that also included, for example, above-average human services expenditures and a highly participatory system of neighborhood planning.[19]

Minneapolis's progressive regime set it apart from several other cities, where leaders since the 1970s had instead embraced what geographer Neil Smith labeled a "revanchist" agenda.[20] Exemplified by the most hateful responses to the housing crash, urban revanchism prioritizes assailing disadvantaged beneficiaries of government programs and social protections. Far from hoping to more fairly incorporate these beneficiaries into the social order, it demands their expungement. It criminalizes their presence, plunders their already scant resources, and pushes them openly and violently out of personal homes and public spaces to facilitate real estate development. For example, before the Great Recession, housing authorities, developers, and city officials in Chicago and New Orleans pursued aggressive programs of public housing demolition, pushing poor and disproportionately African American and female populations off of profitable land without fairly rehousing them.[21] In Los Angeles and New York, city governments and business owners used "quality of life" and "anti-gang" policing as a pretense to criminalize the homeless, sex workers, and Black youth and to expel them from tourist destinations, public parks, and spaces targeted for redevelopment.[22] And in Phoenix, the county sheriff's office worked with federal immigration agencies and vigilante citizens to harass, arrest, and deport migrant laborers.[23]

Minneapolis certainly had (and has) its own revanchist side. This side emerged most plainly through police killings of poor and working-class African Americans, several of whom also had mental health issues.[24] Furthermore, conservative state legislators regularly encouraged urban revanchism. Just after the housing market crash, in 2012, one infamously compared Twin Cities' food stamp recipients to "animals" in a public park whom legislators "should not feed, as [they] may grow dependent."[25] Yet overall, Minneapolis had avoided the most elaborate instantiations of the revanchist agenda.

For social justice organizers at the time of the Great Recession, there were many benefits to working in a progressive city like Minneapolis.

Because local officials, legislators, businesses, and nonprofit advocates were at least nominally committed to assisting disadvantaged individuals, the overall political landscape was relatively inviting. Each organization I studied regularly collaborated with both local and state-level policy makers. Even organizations that embraced more leftist ideologies and used confrontational methods, such as the Welfare Rights Committee and the Bailout Coalition, were able to form working relationships with a handful of public officials. Policy makers sometimes sponsored and advocated for legislation proposed by these organizations, invited organizational leaders and members to participate in press events, spoke at their protests and rallies, and on rare occasions even coordinated strategy with them.

In addition to collaborating with individual policy makers, the social justice organizations I encountered were able to rely on many public and community institutions. The Bailout Coalition, the Welfare Rights Committee, and the North High Coalition all received support from movement-oriented unions, left-leaning churches, and community-based news sources. These institutions provided meeting and event space, funding, members, and public endorsements. And again, even the more left-wing and confrontational groups were often able to use these resources.

The rub for social justice organizers—as revealed in the local response to the 2007 housing market crash—was that Minneapolis's progressive regime, like the revanchist regimes, also embraced a market-centered form of rule—what most left-wing academics and activists now call neoliberalism. This regime could not, regardless of how supportive it was, realize organizers' most egalitarian and emancipatory aspirations. It held down many of the city's disadvantaged residents and allowed for the growth and uneven distribution of human suffering.

The rest of this chapter and the next trace the broader development and socioeconomic consequences of neoliberalism in Minneapolis and describe the challenging and hazardous political terrain it created for the Bailout Coalition, the North High Coalition, and the Welfare Rights Committee. In this chapter I take on the first task, showing how the city's progressive brand of neoliberalism took shape. I then review its socioeconomic consequences, demonstrating that, under its influence, a large group of disadvantaged residents—including especially poor and working-class African Americans but also, for instance, Native Americans, single mothers, and queer youth—fell further behind while the rest of the city thrived. I conclude by explaining why transforming this type of unequal order requires social justice organizers to go beyond collaborating with progressive leaders and become ardent proponents of abolitionist struggle.

NEOLIBERALISM AND DECONCENTRATING POVERTY

The bona fide merging of progressivism and neoliberalism within Minneapolis occurred in the early 1990s. At that time, local leaders transformed the city's governing regime by embracing a national push for what came to be known as "poverty deconcentration"—a policy initiative centered on the geographic dispersal of public housing residents and other disadvantaged individuals living in high-poverty and disproportionately non-white inner-city neighborhoods.

Poverty deconcentration is actually shorthand for an amalgam of urban planning efforts that have reshaped America's cities. The core of these efforts has focused on dispersing the poor through public and subsidized housing demolition.[26] Since the early 1990s, the U.S. Department of Housing and Urban Development (HUD) and local public housing authorities have either demolished or approved the demolition of more than 20 percent of America's public housing stock. On the ruins of this demolished housing they have developed privately owned "mixed-income" properties meant to attract wealthy investors and middle-class residents to high-poverty neighborhoods. They have also increasingly leaned on Section 8 rental vouchers to provide housing assistance and created mobility programs that counsel and encourage poor families to use their vouchers in middle-income, suburban neighborhoods. Finally, leaders at various levels of government have increasingly favored demolishing and replacing rather than maintaining subsidized units in high-poverty neighborhoods.

While deconcentration efforts have largely hinged on the demolition of public and subsidized housing, they have also touched several related policy areas. For example, government advocates for deconcentration have closed public schools and opened charter schools in high-poverty neighborhoods. Simultaneously, they have instituted school choice programs meant, in theory, to disperse low-income—and, usually, Black and Latino—students into predominantly middle-class white schools.[27] Other deconcentration supporters have instituted community policing programs aimed at removing "problematic elements"—low-income individuals perceived as violent criminals, drug dealers, and prostitutes—from urban neighborhoods.[28] Still others have focused on welfare policy, proposing laws that trim social services and restrict public assistance, particularly for new residents. These laws, they argue, discourage in-migration of low-income families and thus buttress other deconcentration efforts.[29] Finally, deconcentration supporters have fought for tax policies that redistribute city revenues to developers who invest in high-poverty areas. The most notable of these policies is tax increment financing (TIF), which uses future growth in property tax revenues to finance commercial real estate and other higher-end development projects.[30]

Taken together, deconcentration efforts have constituted a neoliberal approach to urban governance. These efforts have cleared out and further commodified space in high-poverty neighborhoods. They have depopulated and privatized the public spaces that sustained these neighborhoods, especially public housing and public schools, and have turned high-poverty neighborhoods into a series of "emerging markets" for well-off families and wealthy investors. Moreover, deconcentration efforts have pressed disadvantaged residents of high-poverty neighborhoods into geographically expansive and competitive markets (or, in the case of school choice programs, market-like arrangements). Before deconcentration's rise, many progressive cities had been pursuing a more social-democratic (if not always perfectly so) "community development" approach to urban planning. This approach supports publicly funding the creation of decent, low-cost housing units and programs that assist disadvantaged families *in situ*.[31] In contrast, the deconcentration model has further encouraged and forced these families to compete for life's necessities in citywide and regional markets.

THE NATIONAL PUSH

The national push for poverty deconcentration crystallized during the first Clinton administration. In the 1980s and early 1990s, Ronald Reagan, George H. W. Bush, and a resurgent right set the stage for this push by reducing federal support for traditional community development. For example, they virtually stopped enforcing federal laws against lending and rental discrimination and eviscerated funding for public housing and other social services that benefit the urban poor, placing much more responsibility for their provision on private actors.[32] They also convinced Congress to authorize the HOPE VI program, which provided financing for the demolition of "severely distressed" public housing projects and the development of lower-density, mixed-income, and privately owned housing in their place. But it was Bill Clinton and his allies who made deconcentration a national priority. For instance, Henry Cisneros—Clinton's first HUD secretary—emboldened HOPE VI by successfully lobbying Congress to repeal the "one-for-one" law, which required public housing authorities to replace demolished units. Freed from this requirement, the program initially targeted 100,000 public housing units for demolition, with a goal of replacing just 60,000 and no plan to publicly fund the development of those replacements.[33]

Clinton, Cisneros, and their neoliberal allies saw HOPE VI and other federal deconcentration efforts as the solution to a decline that beset U.S. cities starting in the late 1960s.[34] By that time, initial fractures in the New Deal regime and its manufacturing base had catalyzed a process of deindustrialization and demographic change that would eventually leave many cities—especially those in the Midwest and the Northeast—with fewer resources, needier populations, and greater inequalities.[35] Firms stripped their assets, employed fewer people, and moved manufacturing plants to expanding suburbs, the U.S. South, and countries with weaker labor protections. Local leaders responded by using city revenues and TIF to further develop their central business districts. These efforts produced massive amounts of new office space and large service sectors, designed to house and support corporate administration. While beneficial for corporations and finance, insurance, and real estate professionals, these developments yielded few decent unionized jobs for workers without advanced education.[36]

White middle-class families followed industry out of the city, just as they had since the start of the postwar era (when the Federal Housing Administration implemented its racially stratified system of mortgage guarantees). These families largely settled in outer-ring suburbs, seeking job opportunities and higher property values. As fair housing legislation weakened racial exclusion in the suburbs, several middle-class African American families joined the exodus—though their final destinations were typically less prosperous than those of whites. Subsequently, urban neighborhoods featured higher concentrations of low-income racial minorities, single mothers, "out" LGBT people, and other disadvantaged groups.[37] Because of redlining, discrimination, and labor market segmentation, these groups remained locked in place and out of the remaining pool of decent jobs; the poorest often found themselves living in segregated and underfunded public housing properties. For numerous cities, the results of this process were devastating: a shrinking tax base, intensifying demands for social services, increased fiscal stress, and growing pockets of extreme poverty outside the central business district.[38]

National supporters of poverty deconcentration misleadingly framed the most visible and distressing *outcome* of post-1960s urban decline—geographic concentrations of poverty and deteriorating public and low-income housing—as its primary *cause.* They dutifully cited academic, government, and nonprofit research suggesting that these concentrations fostered a "cycle of poverty" and "a range of social problems whose whole is greater than the sum of its parts."[39] Furthermore, they argued that such "concentration effects" emerged because high-poverty neighborhoods and their disadvantaged and publicly housed residents were isolated from (rather than pushed to the bottom of) "mainstream" market society.[40]

Backed by this misreading of history, many national policy makers treated poverty deconcentration as the key to renewed urban prosperity. Breaking up disadvantaged communities in high-poverty neighborhoods would open these neighborhoods to profitable investment, and developing mixed-income, privatized communities would allow disadvantaged individuals to learn from "self-sufficient" middle-class neighbors about how to succeed in a market society. Everyone's interests would be served, including, in progressive arguments for deconcentration, those of public housing residents and other disadvantaged groups.

To build public support for deconcentration, Clinton and other neoliberals leaned on images of a dangerous, disorderly, and mostly African American "urban underclass."[41] Grounded in long-standing, racialized, and gendered stereotypes, these images depicted concentrations of poor residents as not just outside of but threatening to "mainstream" society. For example, Ken Auletta, a reporter who helped popularize the underclass notion, described it as follows:

> the arsonists, the chain snatchers, the passive people dependent on welfare, the hustlers rejecting society's values and choosing to make their living illegally, the defeated people . . . who feel "crushed," and lose hope and sometimes steal, the traumatized, whether they become alcoholics, addicts, occupants of mental institutions, harmless shopping-bag ladies, or malignant killers.[42]

By leaning on the disturbing images evoked by Auletta and others, neoliberals associated public housing and low-income tenants with stigmatized behaviors—such as drug dealing, teenage pregnancy, and welfare use—and reduced these behaviors to criminality, promiscuity, dependency, and other social pathologies. In short, they presented deconcentration as a moral as well as economic necessity. Beyond delivering renewed growth and prosperity, it would make cities safe for "normal" people by breaking up "decaying" communities.[43]

THE LOCAL EMBRACE

For the soldiers of urban revanchism, the national push for poverty deconcentration was a godsend. It offered exactly the kind of bipartisan and seemingly evidence-driven policy tool they needed to "take back" valuable spaces from poor African Americans, single mothers, welfare recipients, and other disadvantaged groups. Revanchist coalitions across America vied for HOPE VI funds and endorsed bellicose demolition and deconcentration campaigns. Unsurprisingly, these coalitions tended to rule over cities with especially acute challenges stemming from deindustrialization and especially large and racialized pockets of concentrated poverty—that is, cities run by leaders desperate to attract capital and occupied by easily vilified populations.[44] The most prominent examples in the upper Midwest were Chicago and Detroit.

In contrast to revanchist cities like Chicago and Detroit, early 1990s Minneapolis had a less obvious political-economic basis for embracing deconcentration and the neoliberal shift in governance it portended. The city had largely avoided the economic troubles and demographic changes underlying national calls for public housing demolition and related efforts. While, after the 1960s, other cities struggled to cope with deindustrialization, Minneapolis rode a wave of strong economic growth. Local officials effectively diversified and expanded the local economy, turning the City of Lakes into "the leading corporate and financial center in the upper Midwest."[45] The city's development agency drove this process by leveraging federal assistance, the area's educated workforce, and a significant dose of TIF. It redeveloped aging downtown property and added more than 750,000 square feet of office space per year, the bulk of which housed corporate headquarters and producer services. In addition, local officials financed the development of two major sports facilities, a convention center and several shopping centers on Nicollet Mall, the city's downtown retail hub.[46]

Amid this growth, Minneapolis also retained its majority-white and middle-class populace. To be sure, throughout the 1980s Minneapolis's racial and socioeconomic demographics still shifted in ways that mirrored what happened elsewhere: the white share of the population shrank by over 15 percent while the African American, Native American, Asian, and Latino shares all at least doubled,[47] and both overall poverty and concentrated poverty grew at *above-average* rates, especially among Black and Native American families.[48] Likewise, the reasons for these shifts were largely similar to those found in other metro areas: white and, later, African American middle-class families migrated out of the city while discrimination, suburban opposition to subsidized and affordable housing, and limited job opportunities kept many disadvantaged residents in place;[49] growth in the city's non-downtown neighborhoods—where the poorest people of color lived—benefited less from public investment, suffered from the fallout of ill-conceived "urban renewal" initiatives, and lagged far behind the rest of the Twin Cities region;[50] and an increasing proportion of jobs—especially those few jobs available to working-class people of color—fell in the lower-paying and predominantly non-union service sector.[51] Nonetheless, because of high labor participation and low unemployment among whites—who remained the demographic majority—the city's overall per capita and median household income still climbed after the 1970s and often exceeded national averages.[52] Poverty never reached the levels seen in other midwestern hubs and fell below the average for all major U.S. cities.[53]

In addition to avoiding the economic challenges and demographic pressures facing other cities, Minneapolis in the early 1990s was ruled by a long-standing progressive coalition. At the top of this coalition was a steady stream of white, and sometimes Black and Brown, liberal public officials. Standing alongside these officials was an especially philanthropic and civically engaged business community. And beneath public officials and the business community was a large group of social-justice-oriented nonprofits and community organizations, mostly led by educated professionals.

Between the late 1960s and the early 1990s, this coalition occupied the leading edge of various efforts to strengthen the social incorporation and well-being of America's disadvantaged urban residents. City officials passed the nation's first law banning discrimination against trans individuals, maintained high spending on human services for the poor, prioritized issues like family and child welfare, and created the Neighborhood Revitalization Program (NRP), "the most financially empowered structure of neighborhood governance in any American city."[54] Nonprofit and community organizations supplemented the city's service programs, contributed to the stock of subsidized and affordable housing, monitored the enforcement of national and local antidiscrimination laws, worked through the NRP to support non-downtown development, and helped to place neighborhood activists in elected and appointed government positions.[55] Business leaders, for their part, "established one of the nation's most ambitious corporate philanthropy programs" and developed a reputation for collaborating with officials and activists on programs meant to curb unfairness in the local economy.[56]

It should go without saying that this coalition's support for disadvantaged groups was *not* universal. For example, as in other cities, they allowed law enforcement to aggressively police queer sexual practices and poor African Americans' informal economic activity.[57] Nonetheless, overall, they avoided the extreme revanchism cropping up elsewhere.

Moreover, by the time the national push for deconcentration emerged, Minneapolis's progressive regime already possessed an alternative and more social-democratic model for addressing poverty and uneven regional growth—one that strengthened rather than replaced community development efforts. Instead of dispersing the poor per se, this model focused on redistributing the benefits of economic growth and expanding wealthier communities' responsibilities for providing affordable housing and social services. It largely hinged on the Metropolitan Council, a governing body tasked with coordinating development across the Twin Cities region (including Minneapolis, St. Paul, and their inner- and outer-ring suburbs).

In 1967, Minnesota's state government created the council, making the Twin Cities one of the few metro areas in the country with a highly active regional government. During the 1970s the council enjoyed widespread political support and institutional leverage to ensure that wealthier communities produced their "fair share" of affordable housing and contributed to equitable regional development. It created a formula that showed these communities had not been meeting the fair-share standard, and, to enforce this formula, it "weighed communities' records in producing modest-cost housing as it reviewed their applications for federal infrastructure grants."[58] The council gained even more authority when state legislators passed the 1976 Land Use Planning Act, which required communities to submit comprehensive growth plans for its approval. These plans had to include (among other things) a strategy for producing enough "low- and moderate-income housing."[59]

In addition to the Metropolitan Council, the state government created the Fiscal Disparities Program in 1971, which redistributed growth in the region's commercial-industrial tax base to less wealthy communities. The NRP—approved by the Minneapolis City Council and the Minnesota state legislature in 1990—enacted a similar redistribution within city limits, capturing growth in the downtown tax base to fund community development projects in lower- and middle-income neighborhoods.[60] These efforts did not actually deliver enough resources and power to disadvantaged groups, as evidenced by the persistence of racialized inner-city poverty throughout the 1980s.[61] However, in contrast to poverty deconcentration, they established an institutional framework with at least the potential to yield a more equitable urban political economy.

The upshot is that Minneapolis in 1990 seemed well positioned to resist the turn to deconcentration and neoliberalism. The city's overall socioeconomic outlook was relatively good. Furthermore, in response to the challenges that did exist, members of its progressive governing coalition were working hard to expand government-led and redistributive development efforts. Indeed, several public officials were allying with leaders from St. Paul and various inner-ring suburbs to advocate for granting the Metropolitan Council even more enforcement authority.[62]

Beneath the surface, however, the decision makers and advocates staving off deconcentration were politically weak. Neither Minneapolis's progressive coalition nor the city's disadvantaged residents had any real power to hold the Metropolitan Council accountable to an egalitarian, redistributive development agenda. That power went to the governor, who appointed the council's members. The governor's seat is, of course, not immune to statewide political pressure. From the Great Depression through the New Deal era, Minneapolis's progressive coalition and disadvantaged residents had been attached to a workers' movement with enough organizational strength and disruptive capacity to uphold a statewide social-democratic platform. This movement yielded some of the country's most impactful strikes and demonstrations of the 1930s—including the famous Teamsters' strike of 1934—and formed the base of the Minnesota Farmer–Labor Party, the most successful left-wing state-level party in U.S. history.[63] However, by the late twentieth century, Minnesota's powerful left had long since faded.[64] And the local social justice organizations that might have rebuilt it were too fragmented, professionalized, and moderate to do so.[65]

In truth, the ability of Minneapolis's leaders to promote downward redistribution depended almost entirely on the goodwill of their suburban counterparts. And while, throughout the 1970s, suburban politicians worked with the Twin Cities to keep the governor and Metropolitan Council committed to this goal, in the 1980s they switched positions.[66] As the Reagan administration reduced federal subsidies for social services and low-income housing, they found themselves dedicating far more of their own community's resources to meet fair-share standards and address regional inequities—something voters and local real estate interests were reluctant to do. Furthermore, as the region's poor population became larger, more racialized, and less heteronormative, their majority-white constituencies no longer saw a strong moral justification for tolerating the financial burden of regional cooperation. White middle-class voters throughout the metro area became less likely to accept low-income housing as a necessary evil that, although costly, provided a helping hand for "people like me." And they became more willing to castigate it as a magnet for "those people" and their social problems.

By the mid-1990s, suburban opposition to downward and regional redistribution crescendoed, prompting its downfall. Many suburban officials stopped contributing to the region's affordable housing stock or any other traditional community development efforts. Consecutive governors rewarded this opposition by filling the Metropolitan Council with members who possessed little interest in regional planning.[67] The council, in turn, stopped enforcing fair-share guidelines. It also produced two reports that documented the problems facing high-poverty neighborhoods in Minneapolis and St. Paul, seemingly validating suburban fears about inviting "those people" into their communities.[68] Finally, in 1995, Minnesota governor Arne Carlson brought the era of regional and redistributive development to an end by signing the Livable Communities Act. The act watered down the Metropolitan Council's process for setting and enforcing fair-share development goals, replacing it with one that authorized most communities to *reduce* their affordable housing stock.[69] Although the NRP and the Fiscal Disparities Program continued, the Livable Communities Act ended the region's thoroughgoing commitment to resolving uneven growth and urban poverty through more social-democratic means.

Minneapolis's progressive regime responded by embracing the national push for poverty deconcentration. Theoretically, they could have doubled down on traditional community development, using taxation, the NRP, and other mechanisms to fund subsidized housing, expanded social services, and public employment opportunities for disadvantaged individuals. In practice, however—with social justice organizations incapable of creating a powerful movement to back this approach and in the face of declining state support—deconcentration was their only financially and politically viable pathway forward. It promised to retain the political support of financial and real estate interests, placate activists concerned about poverty and marginalization, and enable public officials to maintain economic growth.

Members of the local governing coalition who led the charge on deconcentration quickly attained prominent positions. One such leader was Sharon Sayles Belton, who was elected city council president in 1990 and, in 1994, became the city's first African American and first woman mayor. She was also a finalist to replace Henry Cisneros as President Clinton's HUD secretary (the job eventually went to Andrew Cuomo, another supporter of poverty deconcentration).[70] As mayor, Sayles Belton partly secured her influence by championing a demolition campaign—described in the next section—that created new opportunities for developers and purported to redress persistent forms of marginalization highlighted by community activists. Likewise, several community-based and nonprofit social justice organizations—including, most notably, the local chapter of the National Association for the Advancement of Colored People (NAACP)—gained greater voice by pushing reforms and remedies that comported with public officials' deconcentration efforts. And real estate investors, landlords, and other development interests attained public financial support and political cover for new projects by attaching them to these efforts. One such project aimed to develop "gayborhoods" that would replace low-income residents with more affluent queer families.[71]

DECONCENTRATING POVERTY IN MINNEAPOLIS

Minneapolis's governing coalition eventually instituted almost every major type of poverty deconcentration effort. In the process, they officiated a marriage between progressive and neoliberal governance that would define the local political economy up through and following the Great Recession. They adapted poverty deconcentration to their progressive ideals by imbuing it with greater supports for disadvantaged residents and reserving its punitive side for a comparatively small group of the most highly stigmatized individuals. For example, in contrast to the leaders of more revanchist cities, they provided much stronger relocation support to tenants displaced by public housing demolitions, and they fought harder to develop privately owned replacement units throughout the region. Likewise, through the NRP they implemented a community-based policing program, in which officers collaborated with residents of high-poverty neighborhoods to carefully single out prostitutes, users of illegal drugs, and other highly stigmatized individuals for arrest.[72] Pointing to these efforts, they cast deconcentration as a remedy for the marginalization of disadvantaged but respectable constituents—one that expanded their housing and economic opportunities and freed them from a small but malignant group of "bad elements" in their communities.

The city's single most important deconcentration effort was the settlement of *Hollman v. Cisneros,* a class-action antidiscrimination lawsuit against HUD, the Minneapolis Public Housing Authority, and other related agencies. The Minneapolis branches of the NAACP and the Legal Aid Society filed the lawsuit in 1992 on behalf of residents of the Sumner Field, Olson, Lyndale, and Glenwood (henceforth, Sumner-Glenwood) projects—a set of adjacent, underfunded, and dilapidated public housing developments in a high-poverty and disproportionately Black and Hmong neighborhood called Near North. NAACP and Legal Aid Society lawyers alleged that the defendants had purposely built the Sumner-Glenwood homes in an area with many low-income racial minorities and also encouraged Section 8 recipients to settle there. The agencies had, thus, intentionally discriminated against the Sumner-Glenwood residents and exacerbated their "isolation" from society.[73]

The *Hollman* settlement, covered heavily by local reporters, signaled the shift to a poverty deconcentration paradigm in Minneapolis. This settlement provided for the demolition of all 770 Sumner-Glenwood housing units; the forced relocation of their more than three thousand residents; the redevelopment of the site into a private mixed-income community; the development of 770 new low-income housing units, to be scattered throughout the region; the creation of nine hundred new Section 8 certificates; and more than $100 million in additional HUD funding—all meant to assist low-income residents by dispersing them into citywide housing and labor markets and attracting developers and middle-class residents to Near North.[74] Despite the anti-demolition activism of Northside Neighbors for Justice—a coalition of social service advocates and northside community leaders—and other organizations, including the Welfare Rights Committee and future members of the Bailout Coalition and the North High Coalition, every provision was eventually implemented.

Beyond the *Hollman* settlement, local policy makers pursued many additional deconcentration efforts throughout the early to mid-1990s.[75] Health officials demolished rather than rehabilitated housing units contaminated with lead, a disproportionate number of which were in Near North and other high-poverty neighborhoods. City agencies switched from mandating to merely incentivizing affordable housing development in middle-income neighborhoods.[76] They also supported public–private development projects aimed at bringing real estate investors and well-off consumers to high-poverty neighborhoods. As I previously stated, police departments developed community-based policing programs in which fearful residents worked with officers to investigate, arrest, and evict "suspicious" low-income renters and racial minorities in the central city. Neighborhood activists repurposed the NRP to encourage the expansion of middle-class homeownership and discourage the development of affordable housing and social services in their communities.[77] Finally, at the state level, in 1991, legislators from the city approved a budget that restricted new and "employable" residents' access to Minnesota's General Assistance program.[78] They also, in effect, reduced welfare cash grants for low-income single mothers by allowing inflation to slowly erode the grants' real value.

Just like other deconcentration supporters, Minneapolis's progressive leaders deployed stigmatizing underclass imagery to sell their efforts to the public. From the 1980s to the 1990s, local news outlets popularized this imagery via stories about gang- and drug-related violence among low-income people of color, especially young African American men.[79] Reports issued by the Metropolitan Council, the University of Minnesota, and local nonprofit organizations validated these stories by pointing to the Twin Cities' "decaying core."[80] The local experts who authored such reports often framed revanchist cities—those with larger Black and Brown populations and greater economic challenges—as harbingers of the dysfunction awaiting Minneapolis if it failed to solve its underclass problem. As one warned:

> What happened in Detroit, Chicago, or Milwaukee is not just the story of a dying metropolitan core; their histories mark the path

> that our community follows today. If we do nothing to change our housing and education patterns and trends, the Twin Cities will join other northern communities whose central cities have decayed.[81]

Residents absorbed this underclass imagery, exhibiting heightened fears of urban crime.[82] When gang-related homicides spiked between 1993 and 1995, the city became popularly known as "Murderapolis."[83]

The most exemplary invocations of underclass imagery occurred, predictably, in debates about deconcentration and housing. In the *Hollman* lawsuit, for example, Legal Aid Society attorneys emphasized the "decay" wrought by decades of race and class segregation. They described not just the housing stock but, at least implicitly, social life in Near North and the Sumner-Glenwood homes as deteriorated and dysfunctional, articulating a clear need to relocate rather than provide resources to low-income residents (many individuals would later use similar descriptions to characterize schools like North High).[84] These descriptions were endorsed by prominent city officials, including Mayor Sayles Belton and Jackie Cherryhomes, a councilwoman representing Near North.[85] They were also referenced by officials and advocates from more affluent city wards looking to block affordable housing development.[86]

Local leaders also used underclass imagery to rationalize other types of deconcentration efforts.[87] For example, in 1996, Mayor Sayles Belton defended restricting new residents' welfare benefits by arguing that the state's allegedly generous assistance programs had attracted "a lot of people . . . who don't share the kind of ethic we expect in Minnesota."[88] And in 1997, the CEOs of Honeywell and other large local employers leaned into sensationalized and racist stories about "Murderapolis," threatening to relocate unless policy makers ramped up policing in high-poverty neighborhoods.[89]

TRANSITION TO THE EARLY 2000S

Poverty deconcentration's national supporters promised that it would bring greater prosperity to U.S. cities. However, as the 1990s became the early 2000s, Minneapolis's solid record of economic growth and security actually waned. Under the leadership of Mayor R. T. Rybak—a white man and former political activist who replaced Sayles Belton in 2002—the city felt the negative effects of a development strategy that had produced a glut of downtown office and retail space and paid little attention to affordable housing needs. Vacancy rates for office and retail units rose fast and remained high throughout the decade.[90] Meanwhile, the entire Twin Cities region experienced a severe affordable housing shortage. Housing vacancy rates in the early 2000s fell well below 2 percent, and from 1996 to 2000 average rent increased by over 30 percent.[91] Rents continued to rise throughout the decade, while rental vacancy rates remained well below the national average.[92] These trends overlapped with national recessions in the wake of the 9/11 terrorist attacks, the bursting of the telecommunications bubble, and the housing market crash. The result was that poverty grew steadily, average incomes decreased, housing insecurity rose, and unemployment reached levels that the city had mostly avoided throughout the 1980s and 1990s.[93]

Starting in this period, a few members of Minneapolis's progressive governing coalition began to question poverty deconcentration and, more implicitly, neoliberal governance. For example, in 1996 the local NAACP experienced a sudden transformation wherein the membership elected a left-leaning and protest-oriented president and adopted a more social-democratic and abolitionist agenda. The new president, Leola Seals—who later participated in the North High Coalition—pressed against the *Hollman* settlement and fought to channel settlement funds more directly to public housing residents and low-income northsiders. Under her leadership, the NAACP also protested the rise of community-oriented policing programs that targeted low-income African Americans.[94]

Similarly, public officials in the state legislature and the city council showed more willingness to question deconcentration efforts. This willingness partly stemmed from community-based opposition to the displacement of low-income families, especially following the *Hollman* settlement. Even more important was the fact that the regional affordable housing shortage had begun to hinder relatively advantaged middle-class individuals and worry business owners who employed these individuals.[95] Facing these new forces, some public officials became more willing to protect and develop affordable housing—at least for a time.

Nonetheless, overall, poverty deconcentration's dominance remained secure. Indeed, the state made substantial cuts to local government aid that only reinforced the turn away from community development.[96] Progressive actors challenging the deconcentration consensus lacked the unity and power needed to break this consensus or stop its spread to other policy arenas; in addition, they mostly targeted particular policies rather than deconcentration and neoliberalism per se. Indeed, many of these actors continued to promote or accommodate some deconcentration initiatives even while opposing others. For example, as I describe next, the NAACP's new left-wing leadership facilitated a school choice initiative—even while opposing public housing demolition and tough policing.

The local policy response to the 2008 housing market crash, which I discussed at this chapter's outset, exemplified the continued dominance of deconcentration. Initiatives pursued by progressive leaders—including consumer protection laws, mortgage counseling programs, public–private rehabilitation projects, "blight" removal, and modest aid packages—generated market opportunities for investors and middle-class families, especially in some of the highest-poverty and hardest-hit neighborhoods. At the same time, they normalized the displacement of poor people of color and other disadvantaged residents, with decision makers either unwilling or unable to develop large amounts of subsidized and public housing, enact a moratorium on all foreclosure-related evictions, or pursue other redistributive and egalitarian measures. The message was clear: even amid a deep recession, those in charge prioritized commodifying space and raising property values in struggling neighborhoods over serving the regular people living in those neighborhoods.

The early 2000s also saw poverty deconcentration efforts reach public education, the one major sphere that had previously gone untouched.[97] In 2001 the state government initiated the first substantial deconcentration effort focused on public education in Minneapolis, the Choice Is Yours program. Like the Sumner-Glenwood demolitions, the Choice Is Yours was the resolution to an antidiscrimination lawsuit filed by the Minneapolis NAACP. The program reserved two thousand seats in predominantly white and affluent suburban schools for low-income students from Minneapolis, with the state covering transportation costs. While ostensibly built to expand low-income Black students' educational opportunities, in practice this program mostly helped to depopulate and weaken high-poverty public schools. It reduced educational inequalities to matters of spatial distribution, stigmatized high-poverty schools as incorrigible failures, and forced these schools to compete with celebrated suburban schools for the best students and most active parents living in poor communities.

Both the state of Minnesota and Minneapolis Public Schools pursued several additional education-focused measures. For example, each entity promoted charter schools, creating new investment opportunities for the wealthy and increasing the flow of students out of public schools in Near North and other high-poverty neighborhoods. MPS began allowing low-income students from Near North to enroll in Southwest High School, a public high school in one of the city's wealthiest neighborhoods. The district also created various "citywide" or magnet programs in middle-income neighborhoods. Simultaneously, they eliminated the guaranteed attendance zone for North High, Near North's only public high school; this change meant that the district would not send Near North students to North High unless they requested it on their formal enrollment applications.

Finally, as choice and competition expanded, MPS closed several "failing" high-poverty public schools. Between 2005 and 2010—when Bernadeia Johnson became superintendent—the district closed eight public elementary and middle schools in north Minneapolis alone.[98] Adding insult to injury, they justified these closures by pointing to the dwindling enrollment and public support that their own policies had helped to create.[99] More generally, proponents of state- and district-level deconcentration efforts asserted incorrectly that downward redistribution could not address the challenges facing high-poverty public schools.[100] They also lent credibility to depictions of these schools as cesspools of underclass dysfunction. By the end of 2010, as the North High saga was playing out, the district's focus on deconcentration remained firm. For instance, a major part of its 2011 state lobbying agenda was a "Proposal to Reconfigure Minnesota School Boundaries to Deconcentrate Poverty," which would have further reduced the number of public schools around the state and increased reliance on charters.

Individual members of the city's progressive regime did not necessarily support every deconcentration effort of the early 2000s. However, in general, progressive policy makers continued to assume that poverty and socioeconomic disadvantage could be addressed mostly by rearranging bodies and expanding market participation. In one of the country's most progressive cities, neoliberalism had found a safe haven.

SOCIAL MARGINALIZATION AND INEQUALITY IN THE LIVABLE CITY

In the years following the Great Recession, Minneapolis boosters liked to point out that, despite its recent economic struggles, the city remained a comparatively "livable" place. It housed more corporate headquarters per capita than any other city in the United States, and its employment rate, labor force participation, educational attainment, and per-capita income all remained above average.[101] Moreover, while its individual poverty rate approached levels more typical of other major U.S. cities, its family poverty rate remained below average.[102] Pointing to these and other statistics, national journalists continuously celebrated Minneapolis as one the country's "hottest cities" and affirmed its popular reputation for being a "nice" and welcoming place. One even dubbed it a "miracle" of smart and equitable urban governance.[103]

Such plaudits and aggregate statistics obscured a persistent and even deepened marginalization that had overtaken disadvantaged residents since poverty deconcentration entered the scene. Just as in other cities, this marginalization was linked to growing income inequality. While the rich captured an increasing share of the economic pie, the average income of working-class families either stagnated or fell.[104] These families experienced increased poverty, housing instability, and an overall intensification of their disadvantages.[105]

As in the past, social marginalization in the city fell especially hard on working-class African Americans. Throughout the early 2000s, Minnesota maintained the largest Black–white poverty gap in the nation.[106] This poverty itself reflected several other socioeconomic challenges. For example, in the leadup to the housing crash, Black borrowers were at least four times as likely as white borrowers at any income level to receive a subprime loan, and borrowers of any color living in heavily Black and lower-income neighborhoods were especially likely to receive these loans.[107] More generally, African Americans in Minneapolis were more segregated than their counterparts in other major cities and less likely to comfortably afford housing or live near traditional banks.[108] After the housing crash, they also faced extreme rates of foreclosure, eviction, and unemployment—to the point that, in 2009, the Twin Cities had the second-highest Black unemployment rate and, by far, the highest Black–white unemployment gap among the nation's largest metro areas.[109] Finally, educational attainment among the city's Black residents was far below that of white residents across Minnesota and of Black communities in other states.[110]

Other disadvantaged groups also faced heightened marginalization. For example, between 2009 and 2011, Minnesota had the third-highest unemployment gap between whites and Native Americans. In addition, for the 2012–13 school year it had the second-lowest graduation rate for Native Americans in the country.[111] Single mothers and women of color were mostly confined to the lowest-paying segments of the labor market and had among the highest poverty rates in the city.[112] The same went for the city's large Somali and Mexican immigrant populations. Somalis, in particular, felt the brunt of the city and state's growing inequality, with over 80 percent living near or below the poverty line in 2008.[113] Moreover, whether from Somalia, Mexico, or elsewhere, foreign-born residents were, like their Black counterparts, overrepresented among foreclosed households after the housing market crash.[114] Finally, both before and after the crash, queer youth were consistently overrepresented in the city's homeless population.[115]

Leading regime intellectuals asserted that this persistent marginalization largely stemmed from poverty deconcentration's *incomplete* implementation. Most notable is Myron Orfield, a University of Minnesota law professor who, in the 1990s, led the push for deconcentration as a state legislator. Working through the university's Institute for Race and Poverty,[116] Orfield authored several widely discussed reports, each of which argued that accelerating the pursuit of deconcentration was the *key* to mitigating inequality and social marginalization in the region.[117] Orfield also presented his reports to local institutions and community groups, a practice he started in the 1990s.[118] His presentations contained an almost dizzying array of colorful charts and graphs—all implying a simple causal relationship between concentrated poverty on the one hand and negative social outcomes on the other. I witnessed one such presentation in the spring of 2012. The audience—including several self-described social justice activists—became captivated as he sped through his slides and concluded that Section 8 vouchers, mixed-income development, and the Choice Is Yours program can reduce inequality simply by bringing middle-income and low-income people together. Even in the wake of the Great Recession, Orfield continued to frame these and other deconcentration efforts as the solution to inequality.[119]

A closer look reveals that, contrary to Orfield's claims, the turn to poverty deconcentration actually enabled rising inequality and social marginalization—a result mirrored in other cities.[120] Even some of the most progressive manifestations of this turn—those focused directly on assisting disadvantaged residents—reinforced the interlocking systems of oppression pushing people to the bottom of the social order. Take the *Hollman* settlement, for instance. While the settlement was intended to improve the life chances of low-income residents in north

Minneapolis, in practice it did nothing of the sort.[121] Over half of the people displaced from the Sumner-Glenwood homes wound up living in other high-poverty, disinvested, and segregated sections of north Minneapolis, as few workable options existed elsewhere. The private housing stock in these areas was often in disrepair and, because it was private, came with increased exposure to landlord abuse and eviction.[122] Post-displacement, Sumner-Glenwood families were no more likely than traditional public housing residents to find decent jobs, and they were less satisfied with their access to services like health care, public transportation, and education. For immigrant families, discrimination and language barriers compounded and exacerbated these patterns. In general, the *Hollman* settlement increased the demand for affordable private housing at a time when the availability of such housing was already declining—thus reproducing conditions ripe for predation, exploitation, and displacement among the disadvantaged.

A similar pattern can be seen in the Choice Is Yours program. Like the *Hollman* settlement, this program was intended to expand opportunities for disadvantaged northsiders. But, again, these opportunities never came. Over half the program participants left each year, and as a group they experienced no consistent improvement in academic performance.[123] Simultaneously, the program diminished support for high-poverty schools in north Minneapolis, undermining the public educational resources guaranteed to many disadvantaged students. These students subsequently found themselves more and more reliant on poorly regulated charter schools, which did not have to accept them and often closed within a few years of opening.

At the same time as poverty deconcentration left disadvantaged residents further behind, it also fostered gentrification and rewarded well-off individuals. Deconcentrated spaces yielded new profits for developers and new residential and recreational opportunities for middle-class, usually white consumers. One such space is the Midtown Exchange, a public–private development project that, in the early 2000s, repurposed a long-abandoned Sears warehouse in south Minneapolis. The exchange now includes condos and apartments, an upscale hotel, office space, and the Midtown Global Marketplace—a gathering of trendy restaurants, cafés, and independent grocers. While most of the development's apartments are marketed as "affordable," in reality they are too expensive for many poor and working-class families.[124] And although the marketplace is theoretically open to anyone, in practice, city officials and building owners have used police to exclude "problematic elements" coming from the surrounding community. For developers, the Midtown Exchange has been a major success, as it has increased area property values and supported profitable businesses. And for more-affluent residents, it has become a great place to relax, especially because it connects to a well-manicured bike and walking trail that reaches many of their higher-end communities. However, for disadvantaged neighborhood residents, it has come with few benefits and a heightened risk of displacement.[125]

Not all deconcentration-fueled development projects have been as profitable as the Midtown Exchange. For instance, Heritage Park—the mixed-income development that resulted from the *Hollman* settlement—has been somewhat of a failure.[126] Nonetheless, on the whole, deconcentration helped to gentrify significant portions of the city, creating unequal communities where socioeconomically advantaged families enjoy new opportunities and many poor and working-class people of color struggle to keep their place.[127] Indeed, since 2000, gentrification in Minneapolis has proceeded at a quicker pace than in most other major American cities.[128]

To sum up, the turn to poverty deconcentration—and, more generally, the integration of neoliberal and progressive governance—did not just fail to mitigate Minneapolis's unequal and racialized social order. It perpetuated and entrenched this order. While affluent and mostly white residents enjoyed the "livable city" praised by the mainstream media, working-class people of color and other disadvantaged groups were (and still are) confined to situations of continuous oppression and intensified social marginality.

This growing inequality was on full display in the summer of 2011 when a tornado ravaged north Minneapolis. In addition to causing several injuries and two deaths, the tornado damaged over thirty-seven hundred properties.[129] Such massive property damage would have devastated any neighborhood, but the problems already facing disadvantaged northsiders magnified its negative effects. Several tenants lacked renter's insurance, forcing them to bear the total cost for any lost belongings. Furthermore, many homeowners were already reeling from foreclosures, which had eliminated what little ability they had to absorb these costs. At the same time, the resulting instability further enabled efforts to promote deconcentration, reinvestment, and gentrification. Much like other recent disasters in the United States, the 2011 tornado laid bare the systemic oppression that poverty deconcentration and neoliberalism have reproduced, even under progressive urban regimes.[130]

In Minneapolis, as in other U.S. cities, the turn to neoliberal governance was embedded within national policy shifts and, more broadly, the collapse of left-wing political coalitions and Fordist economic configurations across North America and Western Europe. The basic outlines of the U.S. story are well known: when the New Deal regime subsided at the end of the 1970s, a coalition of corporate interests, far-right Republicans, and moderate Democrats articulated a new, pro-market (and neoconservative) regime. Centered in Washington, D.C., this federal regime instituted an array of policies that comprise what left-wing organizers and intellectuals now think of as American-style neoliberalism—including poverty deconcentration, free trade, welfare reform, financial deregulation, weakened labor protections, and militarized policing. It rolled back the assistance and social protections available to city residents and used the state to institute market rationality throughout urban society.[131] In one sense, then, the neoliberalism encountered by social justice organizations in Minneapolis had little to do with the city (or the state of Minnesota) per se and everything to do with global economic turbulence and national political conflicts.[132]

Nevertheless, as critical scholars of urban politics have asserted, "The local still matters."[133] Since the 1970s, urban regimes have initiated and accelerated neoliberalism's spread—whether in the form of poverty deconcentration or other related initiatives. Revanchist regimes, in particular, have inarguably catalyzed neoliberalism's advancement. These regimes attacked the very populations whose marginalized presence might otherwise raise concerns about the limits of capitalist market relations. And they framed neoliberalism as a way to "take back" cities from these populations, whom they publicly regarded as the members of a dangerous underclass.

As the example of Minneapolis demonstrates, progressive regimes have also abetted neoliberalism's rise. Yes, the version of neoliberalism that emerged under these regimes has generally been softer and somewhat more focused on assisting (versus attacking) the disadvantaged. But it still reproduces social marginalization and fosters extreme, often racialized inequality between the working class and the affluent. Taking the form of poverty deconcentration, neoliberalism in Minneapolis was much more supportive than in revanchist cities. It included greater consumer protections, social services, and market opportunities specifically targeted for disadvantaged groups. Nevertheless, it still drew on underclass imagery and reproduced the market-based oppression and marginalization of these groups in ways that contradicted progressive leaders' commitments to expanding socioeconomic opportunity.

Progressive regimes in other major U.S. cities have yielded similar results.[134] However, as activists like to say, another world is possible. Progressive urban regimes could resist neoliberal initiatives like poverty deconcentration and instead promote egalitarian and emancipatory reforms. They could develop and rehabilitate rather than demolish public housing. They could expand rent-controlled and community-owned rather than market-rate housing. And they could echo the voices of residents who are opposing discrimination, deunionization, and regressive taxation and calling for more truly public spaces, guaranteed cash assistance, and living-wage work. Of course, cities doing these things could expose themselves to "capital flight" and financial distress, especially if they proceed without proper planning or popular support. But they could also tip the scales toward the disadvantaged, pressure wealthy investors to serve the public in exchange for access to urban space, and expose the contradictions between managing capitalism and achieving a freer and more equal society.[135]

If social justice organizations hope to generate this kind of change, then they must empower movements that prioritize ending systemic oppression over maintaining capitalist markets. Urban geographer Samuel Stein has suggested that, to help build such movements, social justice organizations need three features—each of which corresponds to those I laid out in the previous chapter.[136] First, and most basically, they must support demands that simultaneously problematize and intimate possibilities for dismantling systemic, often market-related oppressions. These demands, which I call abolitionist, could include not only calls for universal rent control and expanded public housing—both of which Stein discusses—but also restorative criminal justice, well-funded public schools, and others. Second, social justice organizations must embrace oppositional rhetoric, which clarifies the systems of oppression targeted by abolitionist demands. One example mentioned by Stein is anti-privatization rhetoric, which underscores the oppression inherent to widely accepted market processes, such as residential segregation or deunionization.[137] Finally, social justice organizations must pursue grassroots mobilization, which focuses on building and activating a broad base of disadvantaged constituents. Focusing on the case of tenants, Stein points out that a large and independent base can advance abolitionist demands by threatening to withdraw their contributions to society and, thus, "make the status quo untenable."[138] Organizations following such a model cannot generate such disruptive movements on their own, but they can expand opportunities for these movements.

Yet, social justice organizations in Minneapolis and other cities have all too rarely adopted this model. Why? The next chapter starts to answer this question. Continuing with the case study of Minneapolis, I demonstrate that the city's embrace of poverty deconcentration and progressive neoliberalism did more than just reproduce the systemic oppression of disadvantaged residents. It also created a hazardous political terrain, which social justice organizers had to traverse as they sought to address such oppression. As I show in chapters 4 through 6, this terrain would encourage organizers to resist underclass imagery and fashion contentious identities in ways that suppress rather than advance abolitionist struggles.

THREE

THE POLITICAL HAZARDS OF CONTENTIOUS IDENTITY-BUILDING

The 2010 midterm elections were a major victory for the American right. Riding a wave of Tea Party anger and post–*Citizens United* corporate spending, a fiercely conservative Republican Party won majority control of the House of Representatives, flipped seven seats in the Senate, gained six gubernatorial seats, and flipped twenty state legislative chambers. What followed was a multipronged campaign to eliminate the last vestiges of American social democracy and push neoliberal capitalism to its revanchist extremes.[1]

In Minnesota, the right's electoral victory was especially pronounced. Republicans flipped both the House and Senate, gaining unified control of the state legislature for the first time in almost forty years. While Democrat Mark Dayton—a longtime member of Minneapolis's progressive coalition[2]—narrowly won the gubernatorial election, the right would set the legislative agenda and guide upcoming negotiations over how to resolve the state's recession-fueled budget deficit. Republican legislators—many of whom had ties to the Koch brothers' donor network, the American Legislative Exchange Council, and other corporate-backed right-wing organizations—approached this moment as their chance to further empower the wealthy. They demanded cuts to social services and income assistance, more intense monitoring of welfare recipients, and reductions in public-sector employment—even while disadvantaged residents were still reeling from the Great Recession.

Against this backdrop, in January 2011 (the start of the legislative session), three members of the Minnesota Welfare Rights Committee and I met with state senator Linda Higgins. Higgins was a five-term incumbent and progressive Democrat who had supported some of the committee's prior efforts. Her district included north Minneapolis, the home of the state's highest concentrations of poverty and low-income welfare recipients. Not coincidentally, she also served on the Senate's Health and Human Services Committee, which heard all legislation related to Minnesota's social welfare programs. In short, she was a strong potential ally. The goal of the meeting was to secure Higgins's sponsorship for two bills. One would have doubled the monthly cash payments for recipients of the Minnesota Family Investment Program (MFIP, the state's welfare program for low-income single parents), which (at the time) had not been raised in twenty-five years. The other would have expanded MFIP eligibility.

Cynthia—a clerical worker at a local university and one of the committee's main organizers—opened the meeting. She introduced our two proposed bills and explained why we were pursuing them, even in the face of a hostile Republican majority and substantial budget deficits. She argued that pushing our bills would create opportunities to counter the stigmas driving public support for Republicans' revanchist welfare proposals. In particular, she pointed to stigmatizing underclass imagery coming from the local ABC-affiliated television station. The station's "eyewitness" news team had recently broadcast an investigative series on "Welfare Waste," which framed the poor as ne'er-do-wells who illegally barter their food stamps and squander their cash benefits on liquor, gambling, tattoos, and beach vacations (a "benefits bonanza," they called it). Leading up to the 2011 legislative session, Republicans propagated the "Welfare Waste" series, citing it as cause for further restricting and regulating income assistance.[3] Cynthia suggested that, while championing MFIP expansion, progressives could rebut the series with accounts of actual problems facing the welfare poor—such as exploitation and racism in the labor market and domestic violence at home. Furthermore, progressives could articulate "what we should be doing in the middle of an economic crisis," namely, granting low-income people more income assistance and, thus, mitigating their exposure to exploitation, racism, domestic violence, and other systemic injustices.

Unfortunately for the committee, the senator promptly dismissed Cynthia's argument. She framed our proposals as infeasible, asserting that the case for welfare expansion simply "doesn't matter when [the state is] billions of dollars in the hole." She added:

> I looked into [raising MFIP payments] several years ago. And raising payments for everyone by even ten dollars would add millions to the budget. . . . And, you know, what's ten extra dollars going to do for anyone really? . . . We'd never see any action on [the committee's proposed legislation]. Not even a hearing.

Pressed further, she concluded that "at this point, I'm not sure how I feel about carrying bills for having a discussion versus going after bills that I really feel passionate about that I know can possibly get passed."[4]

Higgins then revealed one bill she *was* "passionate about" and believed could "possibly get passed." The bill she had in mind would have required welfare recipients to present government-issued photo identification when using their electronic benefit transfer (EBT) cards (state-issued debit cards that recipients use to access their benefits).[5] This requirement, she suggested, would benefit recipients as well as improve the integrity of the state welfare system. She clarified her point by relaying a story about a couple "big guys" who stole an EBT "cash card" from a young woman in her district and "went around town buying like, you know, size 12 shoes with it." Widening her arms to indicate just how imposing and threatening the "big guys" were, the senator impressed her point: "And they could have caught them easily if anybody had asked for an ID."

To the senator's bemusement, the other committee members and I questioned her analysis and opposed her proposed ID requirement. Cynthia, who had the most experience debating legislators, replied for the group. She calmly explained, "Well, you know, there's another side to that as well. Sometimes people send their kids down to the store to get things for them." Higgins widened her eyes and replied, "Really, they give kids their cash cards?" At this point, Jacqueline—an African American woman, longtime committee member, and, at the time, unemployed single mother—jumped in, "Yeah, if you have a thirteen-year-old, sometimes . . . and you don't want to leave your twelve- or thirteen-year-old home alone with an infant." Cynthia added, "And sometimes people are disabled, and they can't easily get out to the store on their own." Higgins's response mixed sincere puzzlement with condescension: "Wow. Really, I didn't realize that. I attribute that to the fact that I don't have kids. Because I'm like, how can you give a kid a cash card?"

By the meeting's end, it was clear that Senator Higgins and the Welfare Rights Committee were operating on different wavelengths. Everyone in the room agreed that, as the senator put it, "tons of people are suffering," and everyone thought the Republican majority's stigmatizing depictions of recipients were, in my words, "disconcerting." However, Higgins saw no reason to pursue a legislative strategy focused on expanding rights to cash assistance. For her, welfare retrenchment was an unfortunate but necessary consequence of recession and being "billions of dollars in the hole"; in such a context, she thought, improving administrative integrity and efficiency were the primary vehicles available for supporting recipients. Moreover, she appeared sincerely confused and slightly put off by our suggestion that her proposed ID requirement would, in practice, further oppress low-income single parents and people with disabilities.

On our way out, Tammy—a white woman, production support specialist at a local firm, and longtime committee member—petitioned the senator to include our organization in future policy discussions and legislative hearings. "We are the experts on welfare, poverty, and human services issues," she asserted. Jacqueline reiterated this point, stressing that the committee was well positioned to help legislators and their staff members understand the interests of "poor and working people" and "make a more informed decision." While the senator's assistant promised to notify us as pertinent bills rose on the legislative agenda, as far as I know, we never heard back.

The representational work of social justice organizations is often summarized as a matter of "giving voice to the voiceless" and "speaking truth to power." But this work is rarely so straightforward. Organizers do, indeed, fight to grant disadvantaged groups more say-so and to replace stigmatizing depictions of these groups with more truthful and contentious public identities. However, as the Welfare Rights Committee's meeting with Senator Higgins illustrates, even for organizers from a progressive city like Minneapolis, this process is rife with hazards.[6] In turn, these hazards encourage organizers to "give voice," "speak truth," and fashion contentious identities in ways that disempower struggles to abolish systemic oppression.

Three hazards (which I described in chapter 1) stand out—in both the scholarly literature and the Welfare Rights Committee's experience. The first is the dominance of ideologies that make abolitionist goals seem infeasible and ridiculous.[7] Higgins's resignation to welfare retrenchment exemplified one such ideology, which the late social theorist Mark Fisher dubbed "capitalist realism."[8] Capitalist realism centers on the belief that capitalist market relations are the only feasible model for organizing a stable and self-sustaining modern society. In Higgins's case, capitalist realism meant accepting that poor individuals must primarily depend on the labor market or employed family members for income, even in the wake of a recession. Yes, of course, this system of market dependence enables a "ton of suffering," especially among the single mothers who use MFIP. But attempting to resolve this suffering by expanding cash assistance—and thereby granting the poor greater independence—would insuperably burden society. Within a capitalist realist lens, achieving the type of freedom desired by the Welfare Rights Committee was both politically difficult and technically impossible.

The second hazard is the prevalence of audiences who remain blind to the systems of oppression targeted by abolitionist demands.[9] Senator Higgins embodied such an audience. Like other Democrats from Minneapolis's state legislative delegation, she—in contrast to her Republican counterparts—clearly understood the formal rules, procedures, and characteristics of Minnesota's social welfare programs.[10] At the same time, her support for implementing a photo ID requirement revealed a limited comprehension of the unjust market relations bearing down on welfare recipients. Following the logic of liberal "identity politics," she framed recipients as a discrete and injured minority group in need of greater legal protection—especially from "big guys" and other threatening figures.[11] This framing understated the oppressions welfare recipients experience as members of a broad heterogeneous working class that relies heavily on exploitative employers for income. As a result, when we suggested that an ID requirement would actually harm many recipients by further restricting their access to cash, she expressed confusion and incredulity.

The third hazard is that many disadvantaged individuals lack the capacity to pursue sustained collective action in support of abolitionist demands.[12] For the Welfare Rights Committee this political incapacitation was a major challenge, suppressing attendance at their meeting with Senator Higgins and undermining their potential influence. The committee's membership was racially diverse and composed of current and former welfare recipients, most of whom were single mothers. Although every one of these members was invited to meet the senator, only three attended; two of these three members were stably employed, had no children, and made enough money that they no longer qualified for means-tested welfare assistance. Many of the absent members were either working, caring for children, searching for employment and fulfilling other MFIP requirements, or resting at home because of disabilities and limited mobility. Furthermore, beyond those members, there were many additional poor and working-class women who likely would have supported the committee's efforts but lacked the necessary resources and sense of efficacy. With such a politically weakened and demobilized constituency, it was unsurprising that the senator never followed up with us. She had little baseline reason to treat the committee as a legitimate player in welfare policy debates.

It is easy for social justice organizers to treat the foregoing hazards as hardwired constraints on their representational efforts, because each one is so widespread. Over the years, members of the Welfare Rights Committee experienced several meetings like the one they had with Senator Higgins. More generally, in the neoliberal era, social justice organizers have had an exceptionally difficult time making abolitionist demands seem realistic (to themselves as well as others), publicly clarifying the justification for those demands, and mobilizing disadvantaged individuals.[13]

Yet to treat the political hazards of contentious identity-building as immutable external constraints would be a mistake. Every good social justice organizer knows that these hazards are, in fact, rooted in contestable (albeit durable) institutional practices—even if she loses sight of this fact in the fog of political struggle. For example, during the postwar era, American political institutions emboldened overly restrictive promarket ideologies by solidifying the market's role (alongside collective bargaining, civil rights, and the welfare state) in ordering the economy and distributing goods.[14] They also obscured the market-based roots of injustice by construing marketization and the pursuit of freedom and equality as compatible forces, and they diminished the political capacity of the working class—that is, the vast majority of disadvantaged individuals—by normalizing this class's expansive dependence on markets for income, housing, and other goods.[15] These types of practices were perhaps more contestable in the postwar era, when influential social-democratic reformers and transnational left-wing movements championed alternatives.[16] But even today, under the specter of neoliberalism, it is possible for social justice organizers to counter the institutional practices that dog their efforts.[17]

The rest of this chapter explains how neoliberal governance has exacerbated the political hazards of contentious identity-building and representing disadvantaged individuals—even in cities like Minneapolis, which are ruled by progressive coalitions. In particular, I explain how, by the time of the Great Recession, Minneapolis's turn to neoliberalism *qua* poverty deconcentration had fostered the dominance of capitalist realism, the prevalence of ignorance about market oppression, and the political incapacitation of poor and working-class people. First, I explain how various political institutions elevated capitalist realism by modeling not just private economic exchange but *public* administration on market principles. Second, I explain how they obfuscated market oppression by not only associating but *equating* marketization with the achievement of freedom and equality. Third, I explain how they diminished the working class's political capacity by not only normalizing but *intensifying* this class's dependence on and participation in markets. I conclude by highlighting the agency that organizers have in how they respond to their hazardous landscape, a central feature of this book's remaining chapters.

THE RISE OF CAPITALIST REALISM

The capitalist realism reiterated by Senator Higgins is by far the most dominant and unifying ideology of the neoliberal era.[18] Whereas postwar consumerism treated the market as a pillar of modern society—one that needed the support of others, especially the Keynesian or social-democratic state—capitalist realism frames it as the only viable foundation. Capitalist realism's dominance is partly reflected in elite defenses of welfare retrenchment, attacks on trade unions, and other attempts to expand market relations and empower the wealthy. Most famously, former British prime minister Margaret Thatcher defended her aggressive pro-market agenda by simply declaring that "there is no alternative."[19] However, more than such outward declarations, capitalist realism's dominance reveals itself through the general public's inability to imagine a world without market supremacy.[20] As Fisher underscored, this inability—common to ordinary people as well as elites, progressive activists as well as their quiescent or conservative neighbors—has driven even individuals with anticapitalist sentiments to behave as if markets are the only realistic basis for social order.[21]

While some commentators attribute capitalist realism's rise to the influence of conservative intellectuals, its dominance in the neoliberal era is more directly rooted in the changing practices of political institutions.[22] Under neoliberalism, American political institutions have promoted capitalist realism by universalizing the market—that is, by shifting from merely solidifying the long-standing marketization of private economic exchange to applying the market as a model for *public* administration as well. For example, in addition to privatizing education, state and local governments have increasingly restructured public education itself as a market enterprise. Open enrollment, high-stakes testing, and the expansion of charter schools have forced public schools to compete with one another for high-performing students and the resources of these students' families.[23] State and city governments have also marketized the administration of other public services. In more and more cases, they have devolved responsibility for providing these services to foundation-backed nonprofits. These nonprofit firms then compete for and retain government contracts on the basis of their (perceived) ability to generate neighborhood investments, reduce welfare participation, and reach other market-centered performance benchmarks.[24] More recently, some states, counties, and cities have resorted to financing public services through "social impact bonds," which promise a return to private investors when the programs being funded meet their benchmarks.[25] Many more have increased their dependence on traditional municipal bonds, which guarantee a return to investors and saddle future generations with unsustainable debt and diminished financial autonomy.[26]

Universalizing the market in these and other ways has circumscribed many people's exposure to more democratic arrangements and encouraged them to accept capitalist realism as common sense. For instance, rather than aspire to a system of inclusive and well-funded public schools, administrators and community activists have focused more and more on improving the brand, test performance, and marketability of schools facing threats of closure.[27] Similarly, disadvantaged parents have increasingly viewed education as customers or investors, seeking the best purchase or return for their individual children—even if that means supporting charter school expansion and other reforms that harm most members of their communities.[28] In the field of public welfare, advocates have largely relinquished hopes for redistributing wealth and expanding social and economic rights; instead, they have focused on securing government contracts to provide services, defending the budget for those services, and meeting their performance benchmarks.[29] The list goes on.

By the time of the Great Recession, the institutionalization of neoliberalism *qua* poverty deconcentration had marketized Minneapolis's public sphere in several ways. Deconcentration initiatives restructured public schools, the Minneapolis Public Housing Authority, the Neighborhood Revitalization Program, and several other public agencies as market enterprises, which must either attract well-off consumers and investors to the city or face institutional discipline. For example, the Choice Is Yours program, charter school expansion, and other education reforms forced high-poverty and stigmatized schools like North High to compete with celebrated middle-class schools for resources and high-performing students. Market principles even overtook the police department, as city officials partly judged law enforcement based on whether it secured profitable developments in gentrifying neighborhoods.[30]

In addition, poverty deconcentration initiatives devolved much of the responsibility for administering public programs onto a growing, and growingly competitive, array of nonprofit service organizations. To be clear, even in the era of community development, nonprofits played an important role in delivering services and governing the city. Under poverty deconcentration, however, that role became much larger and more central. Between 1993 and 2009 the number of nonprofit workers in the Twin Cities region increased from 89,100 to over 150,000, and nonprofit organizations came to employ over 10 percent of the area workforce (by 2016 this number reached almost 15 percent). Most of this sector's revenues came from government contracts.[31] Through the contracting process, state and local agencies leaned on nonprofits—including many staffed by social justice activists—to perform crucial functions related to deconcentration. Some of these functions included researching social problems and development opportunities in the city's "decaying core," relocating displaced public housing tenants, redeveloping properties in high-poverty neighborhoods, reorganizing and managing "failing" schools, reducing welfare participation, and helping the police department to identify "problematic elements" in gentrifying communities.

Finally, poverty deconcentration made public agencies more reliant on private investors. Minneapolis fortunately never acquired the dangerous levels of municipal bond debt seen in cities like Detroit and Chicago, partly because voters approved property tax increases to replace declining state and federal aid.[32] Nevertheless, in general, the city still drifted away from democratically controlled modes of financing. Increased reliance on municipal bonds was not the only form this drift took. During the 1990s and early 2000s, Minneapolis's development agency also increased its use of tax increment financing, which effectively reduces wealthy investors' property taxes and increases the city's need for privately controlled revenue sources.[33] Moreover, by contracting so much of its deconcentration program to nonprofits, the city also increased its reliance on grants from corporate-backed foundations; these grants constituted the second-largest source of nonprofit revenues, behind only government contracts.[34] Faced with the task of simultaneously funding an expansive and progressive deconcentration program and pleasing private investors, city and state officials often fell short. In 2010, 78 percent of Minnesota's nonprofits—most of which resided in the Twin Cities—reported problems with insufficient government payments. To survive, they reduced salaries and rolled back their efforts.[35]

In this context of a marketized public sphere, capitalist realism gained traction across the city. Certainly, this traction was evident among public officials. For instance, just as Senator Higgins dismissed the feasibility of expanding cash assistance and promoting independence from the labor market, members of the local school board dismissed the feasibility of guaranteeing access to decent public schools and rolling back the marketization of education. In the fall of 2010, when members of the North High Coalition asked the board to commit more resources to North High, board members claimed in public meetings that "we don't have enough students" in the school to warrant such a commitment. And when coalition members pointed out that the board itself drove students away—by supporting charter school expansion, removing North High's guaranteed attendance zone, closing its feeder schools, and labeling it a "failing" school—most board members insisted that they had no other realistic options. Creating "the choice to exit," one explained, and threatening public judgment and closure "is how you pressure" high-poverty schools like North High to better serve students and families. Other board members, even if they privately questioned this mind-set, largely accepted it in practice. Indeed, in the same public meeting where they considered the future of North High, the board voted down a proposal to restore the school's attendance zone; at the next meeting they moved to close another one of North High's feeder schools and replace it with a charter school (the charter school itself would close only a couple years later).[36] The truth, for the board, was clear: unless stigmatized, high-poverty schools could improve test scores and compete for students, any additional commitment of resources would be wasteful.[37]

Had capitalist realism only influenced public officials and other local elites, it would have been easier to combat. However, it also took root among non-elites. For example, nonprofit service providers adapted to their marketized environment primarily by working harder to demonstrate their cost-efficiency and retain their government contracts. They exuded this tendency most clearly through their lobbying and advocacy efforts. During the 2011 state legislative session, they came out en masse to oppose the new Republican majority's budget proposal for health and human services, which contained over $1.5 billion in cuts. However, rather than making a collective argument for the protection of social and economic rights, providers focused mostly on defending particular programs and explaining how these programs either served the "truly needy" or transformed disadvantaged residents into "self-sufficient" market actors. In committee hearings—which I attended with the Welfare Rights Committee—one nonprofit representative after another followed this script, acknowledging "the need for difficult cuts" and implicitly conceding the impossibility of more equitably supporting and protecting disadvantaged individuals. One of them—the head of a large coalition of affordable health-care providers—crassly (but honestly) summarized: "This is pie-cutting season. . . . This year we have a smaller pie. . . . Everyone is gonna come to the table and say why their piece of the pie should be bigger than everyone else. And I'm gonna be one of those people." He then argued that it would be "more profitable" to fund the health-care services delivered by his group and, thus, impose cuts elsewhere. Testifiers who dared to question market rule itself and suggest more egalitarian pathways forward were *very* few and far between. These few, including the Welfare Rights Committee, were notable for how big their aspirations seemed in comparison to those of service providers.[38]

In addition to service providers, capitalist realism gained influence among progressive community activists (a number of whom, it should be stated, also worked in the nonprofit industry). As local agencies worked to deconcentrate and gentrify high-poverty neighborhoods, many activists conceded that supporting these neighborhoods' disadvantaged residents via state-led downward redistribution was unrealistic. Instead, they focused on courting middle-class consumers, in the hopes that doing so would bolster neighborhood economies and expand opportunities for upward mobility.

One of the North High Coalition's most committed supporters, Belinda—a retired history teacher and north Minneapolis resident of over forty years—exemplified this approach. In the spring of 2011 she organized a bus tour of north Minneapolis, which essentially served as an advertisement for everything the area could offer liberal middle-class professionals. During the tour, Belinda pointed out old factory buildings, most of which no longer housed industry or employed blue-collar workers but instead gave the neighborhood an aura of authenticity that many liberal professionals crave.[39] She magnified this aura by showing us historic churches, sharing stories of residents' past struggles against discrimination, and detailing long-standing neighborhood connections to Black celebrities—such as Stevie Wonder, Denzel Washington, and Minneapolis's own Prince. Belinda also gestured toward the locations of fallen postwar public housing developments, explaining their historical importance but giving no sense that their current absence was a problem. In turn, she highlighted newer middle-income private developments. Finally, she emphasized the neighborhood amenities available to people with leisure time and spending money. These amenities included multiple public parks, a newly renovated library, and several either historic or recently built restaurants, stores, and entertainment venues. We even concluded with a group lunch at a trendy new café. All said, the tour impressed upon its nearly all white middle-class patrons that the best way to assist north Minneapolis was to consume and enjoy it.[40]

Although the bus tour of north Minneapolis is an extreme example, it reflects an acceptance of market rule that affected many progressive community activists I met. For example, some of North High's community supporters initially approached the struggle to protect the school as a branding exercise—one in which the main objective was to better market the school to middle-class families across the city as well as low-income northsiders. In North High Coalition and school district meetings, these supporters regularly passed over important conversations about the unmet needs of northside students and families and instead focused on developing advertising and recruitment strategies that might boost North High's enrollment. They talked about producing and airing a North High commercial, posting a series of "Why I chose North High" videos on social media, and promoting already existing curricular programs that would "sell" well to students around the city.

Even in the Bailout Coalition and the Welfare Rights Committee—organizations that, as the coming chapters discuss, were led by socialists—activists sometimes drifted toward capitalist realism. For example, Cheryl—a Black and Native American woman, personal care aide, and longtime but infrequent participant in the Welfare Rights Committee—

often slipped into treating the battle over Minnesota's human services budget as a zero-sum game constrained by market fluctuations. On the one hand, in planning meetings she regularly and openly worried that fraud and inefficiency in cash assistance programs inherently shrank the slice of the human services budget that supported her work as an aide. As she put it, "They"—that is, welfare cheats and wasteful administrative practices—"are taking my money."[41] On the other hand, she implicitly treated *overall* reductions to this budget as a natural outcome of the Great Recession—not so much by what she said but by the fact that she never engaged the committee's discussions about "taxing the rich" and growing the budget.

Finally, as marketization spread, disadvantaged and politically disengaged residents also sometimes adopted a capitalist realist mind-set. Most notably, in my experiences this mind-set sometimes informed their responses to social justice organizations' outreach efforts. When—outside a south Minneapolis workforce center—members of the Bailout Coalition and I circulated a petition to extend unemployment insurance, some of the unemployed people we met spoke much like Cheryl. This group opposed potential cuts to unemployment insurance and other welfare benefits. However, they blamed these cuts largely on fraud and inefficiency, and they treated government fealty to market rule as a simple fact of life. When—outside a central Minneapolis human services office—members of the Welfare Rights Committee and I distributed fliers about proposed welfare cuts, some of the welfare recipients we met offered the same type of response. And when—in north Minneapolis—a couple members of the North High Coalition and I knocked on doors to recruit supporters, some of the residents we met looked to school competition and choice as the most realistic hope for educating their community's low-income students. A few agreed with the school board that continuing to fund schools like North High—schools that cannot succeed in a competitive choice-based system—was wasteful. "I think every school that isn't meeting the standards set should be shut down," one person told me. Others did not necessarily oppose North High's continued existence, but were—as I recorded in my notes—"apathetic," treating efforts to support the school as unrealistic.

From the top to the bottom of Minneapolis's social order, poverty deconcentration in particular and neoliberalism in general helped turn capitalist realism into the dominant ideology of the early 2000s. By no means was this dominance evenly distributed. Public officials, service providers, and community activists were, in my experience, much more prone to accepting market supremacy than the disadvantaged groups they all claimed to serve. Nor was capitalist realism's dominance all-encompassing. Individuals up and down the social ladder, including several organizers and activists and even a handful of public officials, cultivated more egalitarian and emancipatory worldviews. Nevertheless, its dominance was sufficient to shape most of the terrain on which social justice organizations pursued their representational efforts—from the hearing rooms and offices of the state capitol to the streets of Minneapolis's historically diverse and working-class neighborhoods.

THE ERASURE OF MARKET OPPRESSION

Alongside the rise of capitalist realism, the neoliberal era has also featured the widespread erasure of market oppression from public deliberation. This is not to say that all systemic oppression has fallen into obscurity. To the contrary, large center-left and progressive audiences have become increasingly aware of the generic and intersecting contours of racism, sexism, heterosexism, and nativism.[42] However, until perhaps recently, even many of these audiences had lost touch with how capitalist markets enable and compound oppression. For example, as socialist feminists emphasize, neoliberal-era progressives have ignored how the labor market exposes working-class women to sexual harassment and domestic violence by making these women dependent on intimate partners and domineering employers.[43] Whereas capitalist realism has made it harder to defend the feasibility of anti-market abolitionist demands, such political erasures have raised the difficulty of communicating the moral justification for these demands.

Left-wing analysts have thoroughly cataloged how social justice organizations contributed to the erasure of oppression's market-based roots (a discussion I take up in chapter 5). Nonetheless, as with the dominance of capitalist realism, it is important to realize that this erasure is grounded first and foremost in changing institutional practices. Neoliberal-era political institutions have obscured oppressive market processes by idealizing market relations. More precisely, they have switched from promising to conjoin markets with freedom and equality to outright equating marketization with the achievement of these ideals. For example, state and local agencies have often designated growth in labor market participation as the benchmark for whether welfare programs are helping the poor become full and independent members of society.[44] They have similarly evaluated low-income housing programs based on whether these programs expand private homeownership or rental market participation; likewise, they have assessed neighborhood revitalization plans based on whether these plans increase real estate investment and property values.[45] Even many of the most progressive neoliberal-era reforms have staked their moral worth on their ability to incorporate disadvantaged individuals into capitalist markets. Everything from the federal Earned Income Tax Credit to state and local subprime lending restrictions have equated freedom and equality with the promotion of market entry, ignoring the challenges that plague disadvantaged individuals upon and because of that entry.[46]

By idealizing marketization, America's political institutions fostered public ignorance about the oppressions and injustices that accompany capitalist markets. Of course, this ignorance has predominated among public officials and right-wing operatives. More tellingly, however, it has also taken root among progressive voters, activists, and professionals. Even those who harbor personal misgivings about capitalism—such as left-wing college professors—have difficulty grappling with market-based systems of oppression in everyday policy debates. Many have instead embraced a crude "identity politics," which ignores working-class market experiences and treats disadvantaged groups as discrete, socioeconomically homogeneous entities. This politics prioritizes seeking cultural recognition, formal legal protections, and other reforms that primarily benefit disadvantaged groups' most prosperous members.[47] Others have taken up "respectability politics," a related framework that depicts disadvantaged groups as "normal" middle-class people and implicitly attributes the marginalization of these groups' poor and working-class members to bad behavior.[48] Both of these political frameworks accept the equation of marketization with freedom and equality and obscure how market relations bolster exploitation, discrimination, sexual harassment, and other interlocking oppressions.

During the 1990s and early 2000s, Minneapolis's neoliberal regime idealized markets in ways that mirrored the rest of the country. Programs at the heart of the city's deconcentration agenda championed market expansion and participation as keys to empowering disadvantaged residents. The *Hollman* settlement implied that converting public housing residents into rental market participants would remediate the long-standing marginalization of low-income African Americans.[49] The

Choice Is Yours program, open enrollment, and charter schools attributed similar powers to the expansion of school competition and choice.[50] Public–private development projects—such as the Midtown Exchange, which I discussed in chapter 2—portrayed the transformation of struggling neighborhoods into "emerging markets" as a boon for disadvantaged residents, and community policing programs affirmed that same portrayal through their efforts to remove "bad elements" and secure these markets. Other deconcentration initiatives—particularly the demolition of the Sumner-Glenwood public housing projects, the closure of northside public schools, and the expansion of welfare restrictions—reinforced market idealization by treating government-led redistribution as a *barrier* to freedom and equality.[51]

In the process of idealizing marketization, Minneapolis's deconcentration regime also redefined progressivism as an effort to better support market participation among disadvantaged individuals. Instead of structuring and using progressive measures to place social-democratic checks on markets, it treated these measures as tools for making marketization's alleged benefits more widely available. For example, the *Hollman* settlement structured and framed Section 8 assistance as a crucial mechanism for securing low-income people's entry into the rental market, rather than a supplemental measure to compensate for the undersupply of public, subsidized and rent-controlled properties. The Choice Is Yours program conceived busing as a way to grant working-class students of color greater school choice, rather than a means to augment their access to educational resources. And the city's response to the housing crash treated subprime lending restrictions as standalone protections for disadvantaged mortgagors, rather than complements to something more egalitarian like a moratorium on all foreclosure-related evictions.

Such institutional practices substantially undermined public deliberation about market oppression and taught, or at least enabled, city residents to simply ignore it. Like Senator Higgins, other progressive officials from Minneapolis often embraced a crude "identity politics" that reflected and reproduced this learned ignorance. For example, following identitarian precepts, members of the local school board tended to frame north Minneapolis's Black students mostly as a discrete minority group in need of protection from underperforming, and often racist, teachers. Chris Stewart—a nonprofit professional, one of two African American school board members, and the board's most vociferous proponent of school choice—took this frame to the extreme.[52] At his last public meeting as a board member—a meeting where he voted to close a north Minneapolis middle school and replace it with a charter school—he stated the following:

> The time of union [that is, public] schools telling African Americans and our community what's good for us is over. It's done. You have put us in a place now where we have to be very clear with you. Your results are unacceptable. And if you don't know that they're unacceptable, maybe you're not right for this job.

Stewart's diatribe contained a big kernel of truth. Much research has, in fact, shown that public school teachers tend to discriminate against Black students.[53] However, his comments also ignored the market processes dragging down Minneapolis's Black students—such as residential segregation, gentrification, and the disappearance of quality unionized jobs.[54] These processes fostered widespread social insecurity and limited working-class Black students' educational resources; they pressured teachers to lower expectations and adopt the very discriminatory pedagogical practices that Stewart maligned.[55]

For their part, many nonprofit service providers embraced "respectability politics." In 2011, during the debates over the state's health and human services budget, service providers frequently assured legislators that their disadvantaged clients were "just like everyone else"—that is, no different from respectable middle-class members of society, save for a disability, a sickness, or a temporary loss of income. All that welfare recipients needed, providers implied, was a set of modest and affordable services. To underscore this point, they sometimes brought one or two of their most successful clients to committee hearings, clients who thrived because of the provider's interventions. These appeals to respectability neglected that many, if not most, welfare recipients need much more than the help of a single service provider. Recipients regularly face exploitation, domestic violence, discrimination, and other oppressions, which are caused at least in part by market dynamics and can only be curbed by robust and truly egalitarian public programs.[56] By neglecting market-based systems of oppression, providers' appeals to respectability also allowed conservatives to frame less successful recipients as members of an undeserving underclass, whose suffering stems as much from bad behavior as disadvantage.[57]

Progressive community activists also sometimes embraced identitarian and respectability politics. For example, several northside community activists depicted North High as a fundamentally good school that would be thriving if not for the racial stigmas and stereotypes it faced. This account all but ignored the negative effects that school choice and competition had imposed on the school and its students, and it attributed those effects almost solely to individual discrimination. In addition, anti-foreclosure activists in the Bailout Coalition and other organizations like Occupy Homes often spoke of foreclosure victims as "normal" people who fell on hard times. They discussed cases where, for example, grandmothers were outright swindled by lenders or gainfully employed individuals experienced a sudden loss of income due to recession or illness. At least implicitly, they also encouraged foreclosure victims themselves to highlight the ways in which they were "just like" advantaged middle-class people who had not lost their homes. Left out of this rhetoric were homeowners and renters with chronic housing problems stemming from the more ordinary and deep-rooted practices of investors, developers, employers, banks, and other privileged market actors.

The public's ignorance regarding market oppression was striking, especially given Minneapolis's progressive credentials. As with capitalist realism, the spread of this ignorance was by no means total or evenly distributed, but it was nevertheless impossible for social justice organizers to avoid. From public officials down to progressive activists, organizers' audiences regularly overlooked the role of capitalist markets in reproducing injustice; for the duration of my study, these audiences usually faced very little social or political backlash for doing so.

THE DECLINE OF WORKING-CLASS POLITICAL CAPACITY

Alongside the rise of capitalist realism and the erasure of market oppression, the neoliberal era has featured the decline of the working-class's capacity for political action. The political incapacitation of the working class is, of course, typical of American capitalism.[58] However, since the 1970s, it has worsened in two notable ways. First, the working class's political resources, both individual and collective, have further contracted. Many ordinary people can only survive by working more hours for less income, leaving them without the energy, leisure time, and surplus money for politics.[59] Furthermore, labor unions have turned away from organizing members and declined in size and clout. So have other civic associations, which now prioritize reliance on donations, grants, and professional staff more than membership dues and widespread participation.[60] Second, working-class people have experienced a decline in political efficacy. Many more of them doubt that taking collective action could increase government responsiveness to their concerns and demands.[61] As a result of these two trends, independent grassroots engagement among disadvantaged people has dissipated, and elites have acquired more power to co-opt the engagement that occurs.[62]

While the working class's loss of political capacity stems from many factors, neoliberalism has been a key contributor. It has reduced this capacity by commanding ever more frequent, active, and compliant market participation from working-class individuals. For example, under the banner of welfare reform, government institutions have reduced income assistance and formally required many welfare recipients to seek and accept low-wage employment. Similarly, as I already discussed at length in chapter 2, they have demolished public housing and embraced tenant-based forms of low-income housing assistance that require recipients to participate in rental markets. These initiatives have intensified the market participation of not only welfare recipients but workers as a whole, who are forced to compete for jobs and housing with a larger and more vulnerable reserve army of labor.[63]

Neoliberal-era political institutions have also more aggressively disciplined working-class individuals who defy the push for market participation. Public and nonprofit agencies have deployed police officers, prosecutors, welfare case managers, and other "street-level" bureaucrats to monitor and reprimand so-called "surplus" populations—those especially marginalized working-class people who occupy the bottom of formal markets and often turn to sex work, the illegal drug trade, and other informal economies for survival.[64] Using arrests, fines, welfare sanctions, and the like, these agencies have increased the negative repercussions of resisting marketization.

The intensification of market participation has deprived poor and working-class people of the requisites of political engagement in several ways. Initiatives like welfare reform have diminished their political resources by entrenching their subservience to employers, landlords, and other powerful market actors. These initiatives have pressed ordinary people to focus more on currying the favor of such powerful actors, thereby, worsening exploitation and weakening unions and other independent civic associations.[65] They have also destabilized the communal networks and ties that working-class individuals had previously used to mobilize one another.[66]

Disciplinary measures have further constricted working-class political resources—by, for example, seizing income via fines and forcing the class's most disadvantaged members to spend their time living "on the run" from the police.[67] These same measures have also diminished working-class individuals' sense of political efficacy by instilling cynicism about government. Through their disciplinary encounters with representatives of the state, many working-class people have learned to see the government as incurably paternalistic and doubt the potential power of collective action.[68]

Despite its progressivism, Minneapolis's neoliberal governing coalition has aided more than resisted the intensification of working-class market participation. By the time of the Great Recession, their embrace of poverty deconcentration had significantly expanded the market demands placed on ordinary people. The *Hollman* settlement pushed several hundred low-income families, especially Black and Hmong families, out of public housing and into the local rental market. Related efforts to demolish private affordable housing have forced working-class residents as a whole, and low-income residents in particular, to become more active and compliant rental market participants.[69] The slow erosion of welfare cash benefits—alongside the implementation of federally mandated work requirements—had parallel effects on working-class participation in the low-wage labor market.[70] In the public sphere, school choice tied working-class students' educational access to their ability to win a market-like competition for spots in predominantly white, higher-income schools.[71] More generally, because so much of the local deconcentration agenda was implemented through nonprofits, it also contributed to a decline in government employment and increased the working class's overall exposure to the vagaries of the private labor market.[72] Not only that, but because this agenda was funded largely through either private or public–private sources, it has made working-class communities more reliant on real estate and financial markets for neighborhood improvement.

In comparison to other cities, Minneapolis's approach to poverty deconcentration has been much less disciplinary. However, the discipline that occurs has been doled out in especially unequal ways. The case of policing is instructive. On the one hand, even as deconcentration overtook the city, the police department was relatively restrained in its efforts to arrest and punish working-class people. It is certainly true that the push for deconcentration included efforts to remove "suspicious" or "problematic" individuals from high-poverty neighborhoods—a fact reflected in the rapid growth of Minnesota's incarceration and probation rates during the 1990s and early 2000s.[73] Nevertheless, available evidence suggests that, overall, policing in Minneapolis remained less severe than in other major cities.[74]

On the other hand, the city's policing *disparities* have been among the most extreme in the nation. Officers came down hard on "surplus" populations entering the central business district and neighborhoods marked for deconcentration. They targeted Black, Native American, and homeless people in particular, stopping and arresting these groups at rates far exceeding their share of the population, for often dubious reasons.[75] Unsurprisingly, African Americans, Native Americans, sex offenders, and other especially marginalized segments of Minneapolis's working class also landed in prison at elevated rates.[76] The pattern is clear: leniency for the majority and severity for the most marginalized and stigmatized minorities. The use of other disciplinary measures, such as welfare sanctions and school suspensions, largely followed the same pattern.[77]

Consequently, by the time of the Great Recession, Minneapolis's working-class residents had experienced major reductions in political capacity. Just like the national working class, their individual and collective political resources substantially declined. For example, as deconcentration shrank the local public and affordable housing stock, working-class residents had to sacrifice much more of their time and income to landlords and lenders. In addition, as it repositioned these residents in a more insecure and demanding labor market, they had to settle for more exploitative employment. Public service workers pursued nonprofit jobs that were lower paying, less likely to be unionized, and less secure than government jobs.[78] Working-class women and racial minorities in high-poverty neighborhoods found themselves trapped in service-sector jobs that were even worse.[79] More generally, working-class people experienced major declines in unionization, wage growth, and access to decent retirement and health benefits.[80] To stay afloat, many households worked more hours.[81] And those with fewer job opportunities, especially working-class African Americans, were forced to either take on large amounts of debt or endure housing, food, and health insecurity.[82] Fines, welfare sanctions, and other disciplinary measures only made this situation worse by further sapping resources from the most vulnerable members of the local workforce.[83] Finally, as deconcentration made working-class communities as a whole more reliant on real estate and financial markets, the organizations representing these communities lost their independence and strength. Organizations that, in the past, might have mobilized poor and working people to demand economic rights and redistribution instead felt pressured to cooperate with banks, developers, and middle-class homeowners to raise the profile of their neighborhoods.[84]

The working class's loss of political resources made a clear imprint on the community outreach efforts of the North High Coalition, the Bailout Coalition, and the Welfare Rights Committee. Indeed, resource deprivation was a constant challenge for these organizations' constituents, including Black students, welfare recipients, foreclosure victims, and other especially marginalized segments of the poor and working class. Many of the individuals whom activists sought to organize lacked a predictable work schedule, dependable transportation, and, if they had young children, affordable day care. Some also lacked a stable phone number and reliable internet access, making it very difficult to even contact them; each time I called petition signees from the Welfare Rights Committee's or Bailout Coalition's constituent outreach efforts, previously working phone numbers were frequently out of service. Furthermore, virtually none of the disadvantaged individuals engaged by each organization were members of unions. And because of public housing demolition, many low-income people had lost access to communal resources that previously facilitated their political engagement.[85] Faced with such a dearth of resources, even lower-income people who showed interest in taking collective action had little baseline propensity and ability to do so.

Beyond just losing political resources, Minneapolis's working class also experienced the same decline in political efficacy that occurred nationwide. While precise estimates of this local decline do not exist, it also made a clear and substantial impact on each organization's outreach efforts. The individuals they sought to mobilize were among the most likely to have endured disciplinary encounters with police officers, welfare case managers, and other "street-level" bureaucrats. These individuals often shared stories of their encounters during conversations with organizers. Welfare recipients spoke of their dealings with paternalistic case managers, who sometimes reduced their benefits because of minor infractions. Foreclosure victims discussed how government and nonprofit officials ignored their concerns, gave them the "run-around," and simply abandoned them to be evicted by judges and the local police. And African American parents and students from north Minneapolis shared how disheartened they felt by the disciplinary actions that district officials took against their neighborhood schools.

To be sure, because of these disciplinary encounters, the individuals contacted by each organization were usually receptive to claims that the state legislature, the school district, and other government institutions "don't care" about their interests. However, these encounters also taught many disadvantaged and working-class individuals that government institutions are incapable of caring more. Few of the individuals I met during outreach activities evinced a strong initial belief that they might improve their lot through collective action. Some commented that they were "glad you guys are doing what you're doing." And a few suggested that their situation might improve if "we . . . get some Democrats elected." Most, though, just took a flier and moved on. As I wrote in my field notes after organizing outside a human services office with the Welfare Rights Committee, even individuals who paused to speak very rarely "seemed . . . excited about the thought of coming to the rally [at the state capitol, which the committee was organizing] or coming to a meeting."

The loss of political capacity was certainly more extreme among the highly marginalized and stigmatized groups represented by the Bailout Coalition, the Welfare Rights Committee, and the North High Coalition. However, as the evidence above suggests, it was almost surely not confined to those groups. Across the city, ordinary people struggled to find the time, money, energy, and motivation to take independent action against systemic oppression. For social justice organizers, this meant that mobilizing a large base of support for abolitionist demands would be, at least initially, very difficult.

In addition to exacerbating the interlocking oppressions facing disadvantaged groups, neoliberalism has yielded an especially hazardous political terrain for organizations representing those groups. Under its influence, American political institutions have turned capitalist realism into common sense by marketizing public administration alongside private economic exchange and sidelining democratic alternatives to the market. These same institutions have fostered public ignorance about market-based systems of oppression by equating marketization with the achievement of greater freedom and equality. And they have diminished working-class political capacity by demanding more frequent, active, and compliant market participation. All three hazards have reinforced one another and inherently hampered struggles to abolish oppression—struggles that usually question market supremacy, underscore the market-based roots of oppression, and rely on the working class, or some segment of it, for grassroots support.

Contrary to what liberal talking heads and Democratic voters might hope, the presence of progressive leaders cannot, on its own, enervate the aforementioned hazards, any more than it could have blocked neoliberalism's emergence in the first place. Minneapolis's progressive regime still reproduced the institutional practices underlying each hazard, even while claiming to support social justice organizers and their disadvantaged constituents. For example, the city's approach to poverty deconcentration still marketized the administration of many public goods and services, even while inviting social justice organizers to participate in this administration as nonprofit workers or volunteers. In addition, local deconcentration initiatives still championed the alleged benefits of marketization, even while aiding disadvantaged residents struggling to realize these benefits—via measures like expanded Section 8 rental assistance and heightened restrictions on subprime lending. Finally, poverty deconcentration in Minneapolis still intensified the market participation of the poor and working class, even while somewhat less aggressively using arrests, welfare sanctions, and other disciplinary measures to uphold this intensification.

Set against such a hazardous political terrain, it can feel like social justice organizers have no choice but to fashion contentious identities in ways that forswear abolitionist ideals. On some level, this feeling is correct. If organizers naively push abolitionist demands without confronting the influence of capitalist realism, then they will fail to attract and unite potential activists. If they call out market oppression without educating people about the processes underlying that oppression, then their message will fail to resonate with key audiences. And if they stake their influence on working-class support without rebuilding working-class political capacity, then their attempts at grassroots mobilization will fail to launch.

However, social justice organizers still have agency over how they respond to their environment. They can treat the hazards they face as immovable barriers, which means assembling contentious identities around moderate pro-market demands, publicizing these identities with misleading market-friendly rhetoric, and legitimating these identities without much working-class engagement. Or they can treat each hazard as a hurdle, which means using contentious identity-building as an opportunity to question market supremacy, teach the public about oppression's market-based roots, and rebuild the political capacity of potential working-class supporters. If they choose the first option they can still give voice to disadvantaged groups and even achieve minor change in favor of these groups, but they also suppress abolitionist demands and hinder disruptive movements for freedom and equality. If they choose the second option, they by no means ensure the advancement of abolitionism and powerful disruptive movements. However, they can incrementally ease that advancement, while still pursuing beneficial egalitarian and emancipatory reforms in the short term. This is not the simple choice between reform and revolution that many on the left wish was in front of them, but one between more and less promising approaches to reform. Nonetheless, the choice is there, and it matters.

Return, for example, to the story of the Welfare Rights Committee, which opened this chapter. Since its founding in early 1990s, the committee had experienced many hazardous encounters like the one I described, with legislators like Senator Higgins, journalists, middle-class voters, and even welfare recipients themselves. They could have easily adapted to these encounters by becoming a professionalized nonprofit service group. And in that role they could have focused their energy on improving the administrative fairness of neoliberal welfare reform (e.g., increasing the cultural sensitivity of case workers, resisting further benefit reductions, etc.). Many progressive antipoverty and welfare activists have followed this trajectory, forsaking more abolitionist goals.

However, the committee took a harder but more productive path. As the coming chapters explain, they represented their constituents in ways that problematized the rule of capitalist labor markets, illuminated the oppression these markets impose on current and former welfare recipients, and built political resources and efficacy among poor and working-class women. In other words, they created opportunities to effectively pursue an abolitionist politics. They were not, of course, able to fully reshape their hazardous political terrain, which the meeting with Senator Higgins demonstrates. But they did develop a group of activists who eventually made key contributions to important emancipatory and egalitarian movements, including the Occupy movement and Black Lives Matter. In addition, they were also able to secure beneficial reforms in coalition with other progressive and left-wing political actors. This included (after my research ended) the first substantial increase to MFIP cash benefits in over thirty years—the very feat that Senator Higgins claimed was impossible.

At the end of the day, most social justice organizations—including the other two I studied—do not perform like the Welfare Rights Committee. They at least partly accommodate rather than challenge the hazards of contentious identity-building. Why do so many organizations choose this path and, thus, suppress demands for abolition? And how could more organizations pursue representational efforts like those of the Welfare Rights Committee? The remaining chapters tackle these questions.

ORGANIZING FOR MODERATION

On November 9, 2010, the board of Minneapolis Public Schools approved a proposal to "redesign" and "turn around" rather than close North High School. The proposal, introduced by Superintendent Bernadeia Johnson, authorized MPS to hire a consulting firm that would lead district employees and "community stakeholders" in designing a "new North High." Their goal would be to raise the school's performance on standardized tests and make it a financially "viable" and attractive "choice" for more students.

By approving this proposal, board members gave the Save North High Coalition a partial but nevertheless clear victory (partial because it protected the system of school competition and choice that imperiled North High in the first place, but clear because it kept the school open for the indefinite future). At the same time, however, the board's action forced the coalition to shift gears, to move beyond "saving" the school and to decide what they actually wanted for the North High "community"—a development they acknowledged by rechristening themselves the North High Community Coalition. Was the board-approved proposal good enough, or should the coalition demand something more?

In considering this question, coalition members raised several concerns. Among these, the most widespread was that the proposal issued broad symbolic support for North High without actually promising to deliver or seek out additional resources—such as assistance enrolling and retaining students, "wrap-around" social and housing services, and a larger and better-trained staff. Following neoliberal principles, Superintendent Johnson implored the coalition to take responsibility *themselves* for helping the school and its students. At the board meeting where her proposal was approved, she pointed to the coalition's supporters and declared that "We [the school district] need people on the other side of the table to do work every day [to "turn around" North High] because we don't have the funds." She even compounded this "work" by adding a provision to her plan that required the school to recruit a 2011 freshman class of at least 125 students, a number almost three times as large as the previous class. If the school fell short of this number, MPS would eliminate the class and force incoming students to enroll elsewhere, perpetuating the educational instability in north Minneapolis.[1]

While every North High Coalition organizer worried about the school district's tepid commitment, they divided over how to respond. Two days before the coalition's next public meeting, Stephen—a white organizer from a Trotskyist group and leader of the Public Education Justice Alliance of Minnesota (PEJAM), the coalition's most left-leaning member organization—circulated the following message, making the case for rejecting the board-approved proposal:

> Last Tuesday the community campaign to stop the closure of North High School won a partial victory when the Minneapolis Board of Education voted 4 to 3 to keep North High open another year if the community could recruit 125 9th graders to the school by March. While this is a far cry from what the community was demanding, it shows that when we organize, we have real power. It also provides a new window of opportunity to continue to organize to save our school![2]

A large, multiracial, and mostly working-class group of coalition members embraced the tenor of Stephen's message. Like Stephen, this group believed that the board and district's actions were still a "far cry" from what the "community" wanted, and they thought the coalition's next step should be to demand a more redistributive plan. Such a plan would relinquish the district's obsession with competition and choice and simply prioritize supporting North High and guaranteeing greater educational resources for northside students.

Another group—led mostly by Black and middle-class alumni and northsiders—disagreed. In fact, they saw Stephen's message and overall tone as detrimental to the North High "community's" interests. Chief among this group was Xavier, an African American northside homeowner who had graduated from North High in the 1990s. Xavier—who, at the time, worked in marketing and employee relations for a local Fortune 500 company—was one of the North High Coalition's founding members and public spokespersons, a frequent chair at the coalition's planning meetings, and a leader of the Friends of North High Foundation (a small nonprofit charity that provided North High with fund-raising and volunteer support). In sum, he was one of the most active and "respectable" members of the organization.

Within hours of Stephen's initial message, Xavier sent a reply, chastising him and promoting a more conciliatory stance:

> I'm not in agreeance with the messaging here. It's [the superintendent's proposal is] not a "far cry" from what we asked for. It [Stephen's "messaging"] has a tone that may keep people on a defensive blame game versus moving forward. Before anyone sends out anything else on the behalf of the group please send to the organizers first. If we aren't on the same page it is going to be difficult organizing more people behind a cause.

Xavier and his allies rejected the notion that the superintendent's proposal and the "community's" interests were irreconcilable. Indeed, they treated this proposal as their best opportunity to secure North High's future and expand educational and economic opportunities for disadvantaged northside students. To succeed, they argued, the coalition would have to maximize their participation in the redesign and "turnaround" of the school. Doing otherwise would only, in Xavier's words, encourage a childish "blame game" and prevent the coalition from truly "moving forward" on behalf of northside families.

In the moment, this conflict—between what I would call abolition and moderation—felt like it could go either way. On the one hand, Xavier and his allies were, as Black middle-class northsiders and North High alumni, treated as the coalition's authentic and natural leaders.[3] Stephen himself confided to other PEJAM members that "we just don't have the organic connection to the neighborhood and the school that someone like [Xavier] does." If division between the two camps erupted, he added, "more people in the room would be willing to stand up and defend [Xavier]."

On the other hand, Stephen's message of resistance tapped into many working-class northsiders' deep-seated anger toward the school district. During MPS meetings about North High, these angry residents jeered board members and district employees for showing even the slightest or most unintentional hint of disrespect. Several of them proudly held up PEJAM's printed signs, imploring the school board

North High supporters at an October 2010 school board meeting. Photograph by Tom Weber. Copyright 2010 Minnesota Public Radio®. Reprinted with permission. All rights reserved.

to "STOP the Privatization of Public Education!" They also repeatedly carped at the district's director of community affairs, a middle-aged Black man and former nonprofit professional who—at Xavier's invitation—attended several of the coalition's meetings. Multiple times during these meetings, neighborhood residents either insinuated or outright claimed to the director's face that his "boss," the superintendent, did not care about northside students.

Ultimately, Stephen balked. In a rejoinder to Xavier's email, he reframed his message and assented to the district-led redesign process. He stressed that "the Board's decision of making North's future contingent on recruiting 125 . . . creates a very uphill battle for us . . . with no formal commitment of resources or support from the District." However, he also granted that "of course we should go all-out trying to" recruit 125 students. And he recast the limits of the redesign proposal as a "tall hurdle for our community campaign to overcome" (rather than, as before, a "far cry" from "community" wants and needs). Within a few weeks, the coalition had shifted the entirety of its energy toward recruiting students and implementing the redesign of North High. Stephen's initial articulation of the "community's" interests lost its foothold in the organization, and the collective will to demand greater educational resources and rights evaporated.

Sometimes consciously and sometimes not, organizers like Xavier and Stephen are always fighting over and assembling contentious public identities, such as "the community." Through these identities, they combat harmful depictions of the disadvantaged groups they claim to represent. They articulate the patterns of injustice facing their constituents, define these constituents' relationship to the status quo social order, and delineate the collective interests that inform their demands for reform and change.

In their most promising moments, organizers assemble contentious identities around demands aimed at abolishing oppression. This includes, for example, demands calling for single-payer health care, a reduced work week, and—in the case of public education—well-funded and inclusive public schools. Like the "non-reformist reforms" described by Marxist philosopher André Gorz or the "radical incrementalism" advocated by political scientist Sanford Schram, abolitionist demands problematize the widely accepted systems of oppression permeating capitalist societies and suggest far-reaching but realistic possibilities for dismantling these systems.[4] If effectively advanced, they provoke disadvantaged individuals' desires for emancipatory and egalitarian change and create a friendlier environment for movements built on these desires.[5]

More typically, however, contemporary social justice organizers have assembled contentious identities around moderate demands, such as those calling for expanded access to private health insurance, increased work supports, and higher-performing schools.[6] Such moderate or reformist demands may, if realized, deliver benefits to disadvantaged groups. However, in contrast to abolitionist demands, they usually temper rather than cultivate disadvantaged individuals' desires for greater emancipation and equality. Instead of challenging widely accepted systems of oppression, they help to naturalize and reproduce these systems; and instead of articulating previously underappreciated possibilities for creating a better world, they diminish what seems achievable.

Why, in the years leading up to and following the Great Recession, did the North High Coalition and so many other social justice organizations define their disadvantaged constituents' interests in opposition to abolitionist demands? And how could today's organizations do better?

Organizers themselves often respond to the first question as if they had no other reasonable choice (and, thus, render the second question moot). For all their differences, Stephen and Xavier agreed on this point. Each implicitly blamed their group's moderation on ideological constraints. In particular, they blamed capitalist realism, a neoliberal-era ideology that treats markets as the only viable basis for ordering public education and other parts of society.[7] According to Xavier, for example, promoting aspirations that contravened capitalist realism—namely, aspirations for a government-led, downward redistribution of educational resources and rights—would lock the coalition and its constituents in a "defensive blame game" with the school district. He argued that associating the "community's" interests with these abolitionist aspirations would only reduce opportunities for "moving forward." Stephen followed a different thought process to the same conclusion. Despite personally embracing a radical push against neoliberal education policy, he avowed that this push could not generate enough support from northsiders to overrule Xavier and other moderate and middle-class leaders.

Much academic research appears to support Xavier's and Stephen's intuitions. Social scientists have published numerous articles and books explaining how "opportunity structures" constrain the alternatives available to social justice organizations.[8] Among these structures' different parts, scholars have consistently cited ideologies like capitalist realism as one of the most important. Because of their overall impact on the political climate, such ideologies tend to influence what most people see as reasonable aspirations for policy and social change.[9] For example, as both Xavier and Stephen discerned, capitalist realism has made calls for social-democratic reform and redistribution seem unworkable to many people—even individuals who privately support these calls.[10] From the "opportunity structures" perspective, this fact inherently limits organizers' chances to effectively fashion pro-abolition identities, which typically challenge market supremacy.

Despite containing much truth, the foregoing explanation is also incomplete. Organizers *do*, of course, regularly confront ideologies that disparage abolitionism. This fact is one of the key hazards they face in attempting to build contentious identities and give voice to disadvantaged groups. At the same time, dominant ideologies are not simply exogenous constraints on organizers' opportunities and choices. Research on American political development has shown that the ascendency of different ideologies is always already grounded in the contestable practices of political institutions—from the U.S. Congress and large national bureaucracies down to mayoral offices and local nonprofit service providers[11]—and a growing body of scholarship has shown that social justice organizations themselves help to mediate the influence of these institutional practices.[12] This mediating role does not enable activists to conjure a world in which problematic ideologies have no influence on their supporters. But it does allow them to act as a countervailing force, steadily challenging these ideologies' underlying assumptions and helping to create new political opportunities.

Certainly, some contemporary organizers have acted as such a force. Moreover, as I explain in this book's conclusion, there is good reason to believe that more and more of them are doing so. Overall, though, they have not. The rest of this chapter explains why this is the case by analyzing the internal deliberations of the North High Coalition and the Welfare Rights Committee and comparing how organizers in these two groups differently assembled contentious identities on behalf of their constituents. It shows how the dissemination of ideologies like capitalist realism leads social justice organizations to assemble contentious identities around moderate demands. It also clarifies how social justice organizations could reverse this trend, creating more opportunities for abolitionist demand-making.

At the center of my explanation is Erving Goffman's and Nina Eliasoph's concept of "footing" or "etiquette"—that is, a group or organization's collectively assumed guide for action.[13] In the world of rough-and-tumble politics, I argue, organizers are more likely to adopt etiquettes that treat capitalist realism and other dominant ideologies as fixed constraints on abolitionist demand-making. The reason for this is straightforward: even among social justice activists, these ideologies often engender skepticism toward different abolitionist goals, threatening to divide organizations and alienate supporters. Although there are methods for minimizing this skepticism, pursuing such methods requires a high level of discipline and commitment.[14] In most cases, it is much easier for organizers to maintain unity and forge ahead by accommodating the resistance to abolition within their ranks. As they do so—as they come to assume ideological constraint as a given—contentious identities that endorse abolitionist demands become near-impossible to assemble, and moderation takes over.

This, I show, is what happened in the North High Coalition. Nevertheless, using the case of the Welfare Rights Committee, I also show that there is hope. I demonstrate that small, committed groups of organizers can alter the drift toward moderation by purposefully developing alternative etiquettes. These alternative etiquettes treat dominant ideologies for what they really are—namely, durable but mutable problems. They push organizers to check the influence such ideologies have on their supporters and, thus, create opportunities to assemble contentious identities that favor abolitionist demand-making.

CONTENTIOUS IDENTITIES AND COLLECTIVE DEMANDS

To explain why organizers so often assemble contentious identities around moderate aspirations, one must first answer a more basic question: What kinds of contentious identities *should* these organizers assemble, if they instead want to unite around abolitionist demands? How, for instance, should organizers like Xavier and Stephen have construed the North High "community"?

The answer is twofold. First, as numerous poor and working-class women of color have long intuited, these identities must be "intersectional."[15] Simply put, in the context of social justice organizing, intersectional identities speak to an interlocking range of injustices or oppressions facing disadvantaged groups. They especially underscore oppressions that cut across particular groups and marginalize large and diverse clusters of ordinary people.[16] For example, an intersectional rendition of the North High "community" would not only address racial discrimination against north Minneapolis's disproportionately Black population; it would also highlight the exploitation, disinvestment, and other injustices that compound Black northsiders' exposure to racial discrimination and harm many non-Black residents around the city and country as well.[17] Such identities stand in contradistinction to those that are unitary—that is, focused solely on the injustices that differentiate marginalized groups from one another. From an abolitionist perspective, intersectionality is crucial because it locates disadvantaged individuals within an interconnected, heterogeneous majority—rather than a series of discrete, homogeneous minorities—and speaks to the harms affecting this majority. It highlights the pervasive oppressions and distressing socioeconomic outcomes that abolitionist demands seek to redress.

	Unitary	Intersectional
Cooperative	Moderate	Moderate
Adversarial	Moderate	Abolitionist

Relationship between contentious identity constructions and collective demands.

Yet, as necessary as an intersectional approach is, it is not enough on its own (indeed, as I will show, the North High Coalition's construction of "the community" *was* relatively intersectional). To support abolitionist demands, contentious identities must also be adversarial.[18] Adversarial identities deride the broader political-economic systems underlying various oppressions. They emphasize how multidimensional systems like mass incarceration, deunionization, and gentrification reliably exacerbate exploitation, discrimination, and other injustices. For example, an adversarial construction would frame the exploitation, impoverishment, and educational challenges of the North High "community" as endemic rather than contingent features of such systems. It would emphasize how these systems deprive low-income African Americans and many other disadvantaged individuals of the prerequisites for healthy learning and socioeconomic advancement. Just as intersectional identities contrast with unitary identities, adversarial identities contrast with those that are cooperative—that is, accommodating toward the systemic processes driving oppression and widespread marginality.[19] The tie between adversarial identity constructions and abolitionist demands is clear; these constructions underscore the broad political-economic shortcomings to which abolition is a response.

Once assembled and conjoined, intersectional and adversarial identity constructions invite and even compel abolitionist demands, such as demands for guaranteed access to a well-funded and inclusive public education. Put differently, the push for abolitionism is a constitutive part of these identities.[20] They suggest an urgent need to counteract and eventually dismantle systems of oppression affecting large numbers of people, and they valorize reforms that take plausible steps toward meeting this need.[21] To ask why Xavier, Stephen, and other social justice organizers suppress abolitionism is to ask why they so often turn instead toward unitary and/or cooperative logics—logics that entrench moderate goals and make the elimination of systemic oppression seem impossible or unimportant. Using the example of the Welfare Rights

Committee as well as the North High Coalition, the next section explains how capitalist realism, the dominant ideology of the neoliberal era, has pressured organizers to embrace these logics.

CAPITALIST REALISM'S OBSTRUCTIVE INFLUENCE

While Xavier and Stephen were wrong to treat capitalist realism as a fixed constraint, they were right to infer that it was an impactful and widespread ideological force. Throughout the 1980s, 1990s, and early 2000s, American political institutions made capitalist realism the dominant worldview of the neoliberal era. They did so by universalizing the application of market principles, modeling not just private economic exchange but public administration on such principles. As I showed in chapter 3, Minneapolis followed this trajectory in the wake of its turn to poverty deconcentration. For example, charter school expansion, cuts to education funding, and the intensification of open enrollment forced the city's public schools into a market-like competition over high-performing students and community support (a competition that schools like North High were bound to lose). Likewise, other deconcentration initiatives forced the local public housing authority, the police department, and other nominally public agencies to act more as market enterprises. These agencies focused less and less on serving the common good and more and more on increasing commercial activity and securing profitable developments, especially in gentrifying neighborhoods.

In combination with changes to national policy, such institutional shifts diminished most people's exposure to democratic arrangements and led many to take market supremacy for granted. To varying extents, this capitalist realist mind-set infiltrated nearly all segments of Minneapolis society. This, of course, included influential decision makers such as school board members and district officials. But it also included ordinary people. Many activists from the diverse, working-class neighborhoods of north and south Minneapolis internalized capitalist realism. These activists conceded the unviability of supporting themselves and their disadvantaged neighbors via downward redistribution and the expansion of basic social rights. They instead pursued entrepreneurial activities, with the hope that, by attracting private investment and commerce to their neighborhoods, they might create more job and housing opportunities.

Capitalist realism's sheer dominance ensured that, as a baseline, many neoliberal-era social justice activists would oppose calls for well-funded and inclusive public schools and a range of other abolitionist appeals. As I will show, this opposition could stem from either activists' own pro-market beliefs or an assumption that such beliefs predominated among their potential supporters. It could also take different forms. For some activists in the groups I studied, opposition to abolitionism centered on its intersectional underpinnings—particularly its tendency to politicize economic injustices like exploitation and disinvestment, which cut across disadvantaged groups and, from a capitalist realist mind-set, are unavoidable. For others, their opposition centered on abolitionism's adversarial side—that is, its assumption that addressing injustice requires the elimination, rather than the perfection, of market rule. Either way, for many of them, desires to curb school choice and competition, decommodify goods and services, and otherwise reduce market supremacy could easily seem overzealous or impractical.

The North High Coalition: "We Can't Pitch Storming the District"

From the jump, multiple factions in the North High Coalition were skeptical of abolitionist calls to redistribute educational resources and guarantee access to well-funded public schools. Some coalition members took this opposition to the extreme, rejecting such calls on all dimensions (intersectional as well as adversarial) and fully embracing the tenets of capitalist realism. These members, typically middle-class professionals, were aware that North High and many northside families had suffered under the school district's neoliberal setup. Early on, the Friends of North High Foundation and the North High Alumni Association—the North High Coalition's most moderate and middle-class member organizations—published a report that clearly connected North High's plight and its students' struggles with the district's increasing emphasis on charter schools and school choice. Those who rejected desires for social-democratic education reform never disputed this report. Nevertheless, like district officials, they treated these desires as misguided. There was nothing wrong, they asserted, with school choice and competition per se; the real problem was simply that the media and the district had stigmatized North High, thereby undermining its ability to thrive in a choice-based system. During strategy meetings, they emphasized the need to overcome this stigma by "mak[ing] the district advertise the school." One of them—a white government official from a nearby suburb and the mother of a North

High student—summarized: "I'm not debating public [versus] private. That's not what I'm here for. I'm here for 'go North.'" Our message to supporters, she added, should be that "this is an excellent school," and "you can help us show that."

While such all-encompassing opposition to abolitionist ideals was present, it was not dominant. Far more opposition came from members who did not personally reject abolitionist aspirations but worried—not unreasonably—that embracing these aspirations could alienate supporters. In particular, they worried about taking an adversarial stance toward choice and competition, despite recognizing that neoliberal education reform had undermined northsiders' access to quality schooling and exacerbated racialized and economic injustices.[22]

One faction worried more specifically that denouncing charter schools, insisting on greater resource commitments for North High, and making associated demands could upset district allies. At the head of this faction were Xavier and other members of the Friends of North High Foundation, each of whom had spent countless hours building rapport with board members, the superintendent, and MPS staff. Their position was clear from the first coalition meeting I attended, in October 2010. At this meeting they argued, accurately, that several district officials were "on the fence" and that what fence-sitters wanted was a plan to make North High "viable" within the existing marketized setup—a plan that would, Xavier said, infuse the school with "high rigor, high standards, and something that is fresh and new." To instead attack school choice and the broader marketization of education would deny this request, possibly driving a permanent wedge between the coalition and the district.

Another faction worried less about the school district and more about alienating the North High "community" itself. This faction included several of the coalition's left-leaning members. These members saw the fight against neoliberal education reform and for egalitarian redistribution as a worthy one. They understood that practices like charter school expansion and public school closures constricted educational access, facilitated gentrification, and worsened the oppression of students and families like those in north Minneapolis.[23] In addition, they supported movements in other cities to reverse these practices. However, they feared that most northsiders, including parents, had little interest in joining such a movement. The "community," many of them stated, simply wanted "something viable" for students within the existing system and would abscond from abolitionist efforts.

During an early meeting about the superintendent's redesign proposal, Daniel—a professional community organizer—clearly outlined this position. He affirmed that the coalition should not simply accept "the next round of gimmicks and initiatives" or "the latest fad" from district officials. At the same time, he asserted, "We can't pitch storming the district and the capitol to parents." Instead, parents needed "incentives" to send their children to North High. Most of the twenty or so individuals in the room nodded in agreement. "The community," one of them added, would not "sign on for a fight against the system." Another, a local professor of African American studies, followed up by suggesting that Daniel's position simply reflected a commonsense organizing principle—namely, that "We have to work with the communities from where they are." And "where they are," she implied, was complacent with school choice and competition.

The Welfare Rights Committee: "You Ain't Gonna Change Anything"

The Welfare Rights Committee was very different from the North High Coalition. As I will show later, the committee effectively suppressed capitalist realism's influence within their organization. Consequently, the ideology had little sway over most of their members. And the baseline wariness it attached to abolitionist appeals was much harder to detect. Indeed, despite having about as many active members as the North High Coalition, the Welfare Rights Committee never experienced a major rift around abolitionist desires to radically expand welfare entitlements and liberate poor women and other disadvantaged groups from the low-wage labor market.

Nevertheless, the pull of capitalist realism was still there and still detectable on the margins. This pull predominantly revealed itself among the committee's newest and most infrequent participants, who sometimes resisted the group's high expectations and sense of entitlement vis-à-vis the welfare state. In most cases, their resistance manifested as a discomfort with abolitionism's adversarial side, which most longtime members took for granted. During meetings, committee veterans comfortably and even boisterously accused politicians of using neoliberal welfare policy to "steal" from "poor and working people" and give to the wealthy; they proposed ending this theft by "taxing the rich" and pursuing decommodification. Newer members, however, did not always follow suit. Despite being surrounded by, and seemingly attracted to, the committee's abolitionist ideals, some of them remained sheepish in expressing their own desires to effect egalitarian and emancipatory change.

One such member was Darlene, a single and highly educated white woman who had fallen on hard times due to a medical emergency. Darlene joined the committee during the middle of my fieldwork and remained active until I moved away. Throughout that period she attended several meetings and public actions. But while she was confident and comfortable in ordinary conversation, she rarely spoke during these events. When she did speak, she only made generic and modest statements about "having a voice" and wanting to "thumb her nose" at politicians supporting neoliberal reforms—a far cry from the others' adversarial desires to take back what had been "stolen." Moreover, in contrast to the committee's veterans, even the way Darlene expressed her desires for change was more diffident and reserved. Her tone of voice remained exceedingly polite and unassuming, indicative of self-doubt about whether expanding rights to cash and other goods was a realistic goal.

In a couple cases, committee members more openly dismissed the group's abolitionist fervor. These dismissals were always unexpected and surprising. The committee's recruitment materials emphasized their unyielding desire to "tax the rich" and defend welfare entitlements, which usually primed recruits to accept these desires themselves (even if only in the passive way exemplified by Darlene). Not always, though.

Cheryl—a Black and Native American mother and personal care aide whom I introduced in chapter 3—somewhat regularly disagreed with the committee's overall bent, especially its intersectional commitments. Cheryl was a longtime but infrequent member of the group. Like the committee's leaders, she expressed righteous anger toward politicians who, in her words, "know that we out here and they in there" and who proposed welfare cuts that were "a bunch of garbage." However, when the time came to discuss priorities and actions, she doubted the group's ideas about downward redistribution and welfare entitlements. She often spoke as if the only viable way to secure resources and halt cuts was to make welfare programs more efficient and exclusive, so that they primarily served the most deserving recipients. She was, for instance, the only member of the committee who supported efforts to restrict and monitor the use of EBT cards. "I don't want to not get paid because people are out using EBT cards illegally," she announced at one meeting, "They're taking my money." When others reiterated the group's commitment to expanding welfare entitlements—explaining how monitoring criminalized and furthered the exploitation of poor women—she was unmoved. "You ain't gonna change anything," she announced at one meeting.[24] Other times, she just stared.

At the end of the day, it is easier for most social justice organizers to accommodate rather than redress such pushback from their base. By treating it as a constraint, by taking capitalist realism's influence for granted, they can—without much additional effort—minimize their risk of alienating supporters and maximize their ability to maintain unity.[25] However, this kind of political etiquette also puts them on a limited path. It requires them to forgo the intersectional or adversarial dimensions of abolitionism that prove controversial with their most active supporters and assemble contentious identities around moderate demands. This is what happened with the North High Coalition.

"BEING POSITIVE" IN THE NORTH HIGH COALITION

North High Coalition organizers could have resisted capitalist realism's obstructive influence and thereby created more opportunities for assembling "the community" on abolitionist terms. They could have minimized its direct sway on their members by highlighting the sweeping inegalitarian consequences of neoliberal education policy and outlining realistic steps toward redistributing educational resources. And they could have diminished its seeming intransigence by presenting situations in which ordinary people defied it while still gaining responsiveness from public officials and maintaining "community" support. Doing this type of work would have been difficult, but it was nevertheless entirely possible.[26]

Moreover, a few coalition organizers actually *did* try to check capitalist realism's influence and build more space for abolitionism. One was, unsurprisingly, Stephen.[27] But there were others, including an ally of Stephen's named Manny. Manny, a middle-aged and working-class African American man, was a self-identified socialist. Just as importantly, he was a longtime northside community activist. He had served on the local NAACP's executive board, participated in prior neighborhood struggles against public housing demolition and other deconcentration initiatives, and engaged in a range of nonpolitical civic activities (several years prior to the coalition he had coached Xavier's youth basketball team).[28] Manny was, in other words, as much a "community" leader as anyone else in the group.

Manny emphasized early on that coalition organizers and supporters had "to be willing to dream big." This meant, for him, devising and embracing realistic and fairer alternatives to the district's neoliberal approach to public education. One alternative, which he actively researched and shared with the coalition, was the "community school model."[29] This model, by Manny's account, focused on converting schools into community hubs where students, their families, and other residents could access social services, health care, legal assistance, and various enrichment activities as well as traditional classes. In meetings he explained how it helped disadvantaged families to access needed educational resources and build the solidarity to fight for further egalitarian and emancipatory reforms. He also stressed that activists in similar situations—in which districts had "orphaned" public schools—had successfully fought for and implemented this model.

Besides Stephen and Manny, Daniel—the community organizer previously mentioned—was the only other coalition leader who worked to counter capitalist realism's influence. Toward that end, his own group, Neighborhoods Organizing for Change (NOC), planned multiple events in coordination with the coalition. The most important of these events was a community forum featuring Zakiyah Ansari—a parent activist from New York City—and Michelle Renée—an academic expert on public education organizing from the Annenberg Institute for School Reform. The forum, titled "Building Community Power to Achieve Excellent Public Schools," centered on how activists in New York and other cities had successfully halted public school closures and secured additional government resources and support for disadvantaged students. It encouraged the audience to embrace similar goals, and used presentations, videos, and conversation to explore strategies for building enough power to achieve those goals.

To some extent, Stephen's, Manny's, and Daniel's efforts were successful. They certainly made *me* feel less unreasonable about rejecting marketization and demanding greater resources for public schools in Minneapolis's diverse, working-class neighborhoods. They also had at least some impact on other North High Coalition members. At NOC's community forum, for example, the coalition members in attendance responded favorably to Ansari's and Renée's presentations and posed incisive questions about how to get students and families more involved, organize public meetings, and engage with teachers and principals. "Is there a particular model you use," one asked, "to educate your parents on how to be successful community activists—how they get to a level with their confidence in their ability to use their own voice, to be their own advocates and to speak on behalf of their children?" Individuals who, in other settings, took market rule for granted were suddenly discussing how to topple it, at least as it relates to public education.[30]

On the whole, however, efforts to refute capitalist realism and enable abolitionist identity-making fell short. Stephen, Manny, and Daniel did not strategically coordinate or build on one another's efforts. And most coalition leaders did not support such efforts at all, treating them as supplemental—if not inimical—to the group's core mission. Even Daniel—someone who openly sympathized with other organizers' concerns about alienating "the community"—could not get the support of most coalition leaders. He communicated with them through every step of the planning for NOC's community forum. He also made the forum as accessible as possible, hosting it at a well-known theater in the heart of north Minneapolis and scheduling it for a Saturday afternoon, when fewer people would be working. But Xavier and other leaders would not get on board. After encouraging Daniel to go ahead with the NOC forum, they organized a separate event for the prior weekend, thus dividing the attention of coalition activists. Moreover, they poorly advertised the NOC forum and, with only one or two exceptions, did not attend it themselves. Consequently, overall coalition attendance was also minimal. Other than PEJAM activists, no more than a handful of supporters participated.

"All Messaging Should Be Positive"

Why didn't the North High Coalition do more to quell capitalist realism's influence? The answer is that almost all of them eventually adopted—or at least accommodated—an etiquette that normalized rather than problematized market supremacy. This etiquette centered on "moving forward" in "partnership" with the neoliberal school district and "being positive" about North High's future. It assumed that, with enough dedication and enthusiasm from the coalition, the district-led effort to redesign and "turn around" the school *would* benefit northside students.[31] And it militated in particular against adversarial constructions of "the community's" interests—precisely those constructions that most worried coalition activists. Organizers could discuss how, in practice, school choice and competition had exacerbated the racialized, educational, and economic inequities facing northsiders. However, conversations about the irremediable flaws of the district's neoliberal approach—not to mention the broader poverty deconcentration project of which it was a part—were too "negative" and, thus, mostly off-limits. The status quo may be imperfect, but according to this etiquette, it could be refurbished to meet the northside's needs.

Leading the charge in support of "being positive" were Xavier and his allies. Especially crucial were the middle-class, middle-aged African American men from the Friends of North High Foundation. And most crucial were two nonprofit professionals: James, the director of a local nonprofit focused on voter outreach and a former member of the local NAACP's executive board;[32] and Reggie, who ran a nonprofit health and wellness program focused on Black teens and safe sex. Like Xavier, James and Reggie were also North High alumni.

It is important to note that the North High Coalition per se was unincorporated and, from the start, had no formal relationship to the nonprofit sector in which these men worked. Moreover, the sole member organization that had paid staff and a highly developed relationship to the sector—Neighborhoods Organizing for Change—was, to my knowledge, formally unconstrained in its ability to question market rule.[33] Nevertheless, people like Xavier, James, and Reggie were able to introduce nonprofitization's moderating influence into the coalition by shaping its etiquette.

This group set the stage for "being positive" by first preempting what Xavier often called "political" talk. Such talk emphasized the need to publicly pressure the district and call for more thoroughgoing change. An example, from an October 2010 meeting, was when a current teacher and union activist stressed that the coalition should be "refusing to relent from strong community pressure," or when another socialist member suggested that "we could stop" a school board vote on an inadequate proposal "by chanting them out of the room." Comments like these invited more adversarial accounts of "the community's" interests, which framed the district-led redesign process as inherently limited and derided how market rule deprived northside students of educational rights and resources. In short, "political" talk was "negative" talk.

Xavier and the other Friends of North High organizers blocked purveyors of "political" talk from controlling or influencing the coalition's meetings. When the coalition was still nascent, they established planning meetings that were largely inaccessible to poor and working-class northsiders—the people most likely to support raising the stakes and publicly pressuring the district.[34] Nobody was formally excluded from these meetings. But Xavier and the other Friends of North organizers insufficiently advertised them. In addition, they held the meetings on weeknights, when many low-income northsiders—especially mothers with young children—were busy with family obligations. Some of these residents also lacked private vehicles and would not walk unattended through their neighborhood after dark. Furthermore, Xavier's group eventually decided to hold the meetings at North High itself, which was an exceptionally inaccessible building; it had no obvious main entrance, and almost all the doors remained locked. On multiple occasions, individuals tried to attend meetings but never showed because they could not enter the school. The result was that—besides Stephen, Manny, and one or two other seasoned left-wing organizers—"political" activists did not participate, quelling their influence over the group's etiquette.

Xavier and his allies also preempted "political" communications outside of meetings. Leading up to the announcement of the superintendent's redesign proposal, they pressured Stephen to, in the interest of maintaining unity, remove calls to stop the spread of charter schools from PEJAM's coalition fliers. In addition, they shut down radical criticisms of the district on the coalition's listserv. In early December 2010, as one neighborhood resident after another sent emails deriding the superintendent and the redesign effort, Xavier—with the support of Reggie, James, and others—responded by asking that supporters "keep the listserv emails to action items" and engage in "political conversations . . . outside of the organizers' listserv." Subsequently, these conversations largely shifted to what Goffman called "backstage" spaces, such as individual emails and private phone calls.[35]

Finally, Xavier's group preempted "political" talk by exacerbating coalition members' already existing fears that this talk would alienate supporters. At a pivotal meeting on November 18, 2010—immediately after the board passed Superintendent Johnson's redesign proposal—Xavier argued that "doing the political thing" would make the coalition look like "immature adolescents" and distract from "the work we have

Rally to Save North High

At the Board of Education Meeting

TUESDAY, OCT. 26TH

4:30pm: Rally Outside School District
5:30pm: March Into Board Meeting

Despite widespread community protests, the School Board has made no commitment to re-invest in North High. They may still vote to close it down on November 9th!

We Demand:

- Withdraw the proposal to close North High and commit to re-investment in the school.
- Reverse the decision to open two "Minneapolis College Prep" charter high schools.
- Re-establish a "home zone" for North High to boost enrollment.
- In partnership with parents, teachers, and students, develop an aggressive, fully-funded plan to boost enrollment at North High.
- Support the efforts of North teachers, parents, and students to address academic and enrollment concerns by re-organizing North as a self-managed "community school."

SAVE NORTH HIGH COALITION

North High Alumni Association |
Friends of North Foundation | · Public Education Justice Alliance of MN |

Updates @ www.PEJAM.org

PEJAM-produced flier, advertising an October 2010 rally.

in front of us." When Stephen asked why the coalition should not be more "publicly distrustful of the district's redesign process" and simply demand greater investment in the school, Xavier replied: "We have to spin [the community's interests] in a way that's not like [shaking his fist and speaking with a nasally voice] 'Oh, look at us down here.'" The message was clear. Assembling "the community" on adversarial terms and opposing marketized education per se would seem whiny and childish to potential supporters. James followed up by submitting that "we have to introduce the community to being a community again," a process of maturation that, according to him, "political" talk would only encumber. Presented with no alternatives—no possibility for changing supporters' perceptions—the other twenty or so people in the room mostly agreed.

As Xavier and his allies preempted "political" talk, they in turn became the chief proponents of "being positive." Especially once the redesign proposal was approved, much of their activity centered on routinizing this etiquette. Xavier opened the coalition's November 18 meeting by underscoring his "personal opinion" "that all messaging [about the redesign proposal] should be positive." The proposal was, he admitted, "not perfect." Still, he emphasized that "we're in a unique position to move the school forward," referring specifically to the opportunity to make North High a "viable" choice in "partnership" with the district and other "community stakeholders." For Xavier, "moving forward [with this opportunity] in a positive light" would do the most to benefit north Minneapolis students.

Beyond just setting the tone of "being positive," Xavier's group used their control over meetings and communications to align the coalition's priorities with this etiquette. At one meeting in October 2010, their most-discussed agenda items included developing "21st century programs" and curricular proposals, identifying "potential donors," "determining methods to recruit new students," and "liaising" with the district to determine what else "the community" can do "to make North High a viable option"—all of which aimed at improving North High's performance and competitiveness *within* a marketized education system. By contrast, the only item involving more "political" concerns was "rally mobilization" outside of an upcoming board meeting. Xavier and James treated this item as an afterthought, raising it at the end of the discussion and only briefly attending the rally that occurred. Once the district's redesign plans emerged, discussion of rallies evaporated altogether. At that time, Reggie also formalized the group's agenda, handing out printed copies before meetings and underlining the need to "hold ourselves accountable" to a "positive" mission.

This etiquette, of course, did not sit well with the organizers who, like Stephen, were committed to dismantling market-based systems of educational injustice and inequality. Before "being positive" became an entrenched norm, they somewhat regularly spoke against it. For example, in the October meeting I just mentioned, Robert—a white, middle-aged PEJAM member and a former president of the Minneapolis Federation of Teachers—implored Xavier and James to focus less on "partnering" with the district and making North High "viable" and more on pressuring the district to commit greater resources to the school. Efforts to placate the district with new curricular proposals and community-run recruitment efforts were, he added, a "waste of time."[36]

Even after Xavier declared that "all messaging should be positive," Stephen, Manny, Robert, and others continued to express their frustration in private. "The fact is," Manny explained in one conversation, "we [the coalition and 'the community'] *are* in opposition" to the district and the neoliberal status quo. At an independent PEJAM meeting, Stephen and Robert excoriated the emphasis on positivity and "partnering" with the district. This approach, they argued, undermined calls for the kinds of reform that northside students and their families needed. It also, they insisted, alienated North High's teachers, who saw continued neoliberal education reform as a threat to their jobs and were, at the time, embroiled in a contract negotiation with the district.

Nevertheless, in the coalition's strategy meetings and internal communications, Manny, Stephen, Robert, and PEJAM ultimately accommodated rather than resisted "being positive." Especially once the rallies stopped and the redesign process started, they substantially minimized their push for a more "political" focus. Without any concerted and coordinated effort to check capitalist realism's influence, they had little capacity to do otherwise. As Robert stated in a smaller meeting with me, Stephen, Manny, and a couple others, an explicit focus on "political" opposition "wouldn't play well," and proponents of redistribution "need[ed] to stay positive" in tone.

Following Robert's advice, they worked to give "political" and adversarial accounts of "the community's" interest a more "positive" valence. Stephen, for instance, took this approach at the previously described November 18 meeting. "Of course," Stephen conceded, the redesign process provided "a real opportunity" to help "the community," one that deserves a "positive vision" and "lots of excitement." But, he continued, "being positive" should not mean "putting false trust in the school board" and district officials. He declared: "We can't be bound by the district['s]" already existing emphasis on test performance, enrollment, and competitive "viability"—criteria that are "designed to make schools [like North High] fail" and "aid privatization." The coalition must "define our own criteria for success" and build a "positive" campaign around those—even if these criteria suggest the need to bolster redesign with downward redistribution.

Try as they might, abolitionists like Stephen, Manny, and Robert could not square "being positive" with adversarial constructions of "the community's" interests. Stephen was right that the coalition could have built a "positive vision" around more adversarial and less market-based "criteria for success." For example, the coalition and other participants in the redesign process could have asserted that "the community" needed more guaranteed public investment (rather than just improved test scores and higher enrollments). However, district officials would have never accepted such an adversarial position. Contrary to the spirit of "being positive"—as established by Xavier's group—advancing this position would have required the coalition to publicly attack rather than partner with the district. By pretending to embrace that spirit, Stephen and his allies only enabled the suppression of adversarial identity constructions.

After the November 18 meeting, "being positive" became the coalition's accepted political etiquette. Email announcements to organizers and supporters began to consistently reflect its influence. The following examples are representative:

> A rare but yet substantial opportunity to mend, balance, and excel is amongst us.
>
> We are all a community, designated to serve the same purpose, to create a refreshing and positive image and perception for North High.
>
> Today was great!!! There was a ton of positive energy and great information given and shared with our community today. I just want to thank all that put in the work to make this event [a "community potluck"] a success. Without each and every one of you we would not be as far as we are and we will need that energy moving forward.

By January 2011, "political" talk felt almost completely out of place. None of this is to say that, henceforth, "being positive" went totally unchallenged. There were times when long-simmering disappointments boiled over and organizers showed a renewed willingness to reconsider their "partnership" with the district.[37] But such moments were fleeting. "Being positive" always won out.

"We Must Speak with One Voice"

The turn to "being positive" erased any possibility that the North High Coalition might unite around abolitionist demands—for reducing charter schools, providing "wrap-around" services, and, more generally, guaranteeing every student access to a well-funded public school. By accommodating capitalist realism's influence on coalition members and suppressing adversarial identity constructions, it rendered such demands off-limits. Consequently, it also marginalized the small faction who ardently supported abolition. Most of them—including PEJAM members, poor and working-class northside residents, and left-wing activists from around the city—reduced their participation. A few, including Stephen, continued to participate for at least a bit longer, hoping perhaps that new opportunities to get "political" would emerge. However, for the most part, they had to moderate their positions to stay involved.

The few moments when individuals tried to push in more abolitionist directions became increasingly uncomfortable. One such moment occurred in late February 2011, when Joanne—a Black northsider and respected "community" elder—unexpectedly showed up to a small meeting, during which coalition organizers brainstormed ideas for the redesigned North High. Toward the end of the meeting, Joanne—who had been an especially angry and "political" voice at the group's 2010 rallies—became frustrated and rose to leave. Out of respect, Xavier interrupted the conversation and thanked her for coming, and Joanne, speaking slowly and with desperation, replied, "You know, I'm just . . . so interested in this whole thing. . . . And I'm just waiting for something to grab me and just show me . . . why so many of these kids are failing." She added, "And you know, you guys are sitting here going through these whole abstract discussions about curriculum. But I really think the students need to be here [to help you understand what they need]."

Xavier and others responded with awkward silence.[38] Those "abstract discussions" were all that the district's redesign process would allow. Directly addressing northside students' material needs would have forced the coalition to acknowledge how negative the situation really was. It would have required them to embrace a more adversarial identity construction, one that positioned the "the community" in a struggle to overturn initiatives like school choice and the pattern of racialized market rule exacerbated by these initiatives.[39]

When Stephen later re-upped his own abolitionist appeals, he was met with far more than awkward silence. In early February 2011, as a response to district officials' continued wavering about North High's future, he sent the following message to the coalition listserv:

> I wonder how much longer the partnership model of working with the District will continue to serve this cause, particularly if partnership comes at the expense of a campaign to relentlessly expose and protest the District, to demand real public statements of commitment to North, including a clear budget plan, infusion of resources, attractive programs, etc. Without all this . . . I don't blame a single parent or student for viewing a decision to attend North with healthy skepticism about its future and viability. I blame the District leadership and their well-financed, politically connected backers.

In short, Stephen argued, without a sustained "campaign" for greater public investment and redistribution, the North High "community" would continue to suffer. Anything less would fail to effectively counter the systemic injustices at the heart of this suffering. He also implicitly accused "District leadership" of actively worsening the situation by continuing to force North High and other high-poverty public schools to compete within a marketized, choice-based arrangement.

The response to Stephen's message was swift and harsh. Xavier wrote a lengthy email, criticizing the ways in which Stephen had violated the coalition's etiquette. It read in part:

> As a member of this group and in charge of sending communications, I want to address an issue that is creating more havoc than good. Using language that disrespects anyone including the district is not appropriate. It's divisive, does not accomplish anything nor does it get us anywhere. . . .
>
> We do not want to squash the opinions of individuals in this group, but as a coalition working to improve the lives and education of this community, we must speak with one voice. The North High

> Community Coalition voice is one of collaboration [with the school district] and positive movement for change. . . .
>
> There is trust our coalition needs to earn within our community and within the district. Division will incubate indecision and inaction. We can't tell district employees how to do their jobs. How would you react to this happening to you? The district leadership . . . have earned their stripes.
>
> If you aren't with the positive movement this coalition has created, there are other opportunities for you get involved in the community.

No other discussion followed, either on the listserv itself or at the next organizers' meeting, which both Xavier and Stephen attended. Certainly not everyone agreed with Xavier's exaggerated defense of district officials.[40] However, on one level he was absolutely and obviously right: In a group that had already assented to building a "positive movement," abolitionist messages like Stephen's could only divide. Anybody who agreed with Xavier's commonsense assertion that "we must speak with one voice" would have had a difficult time coming to Stephen's defense.

As "being positive" undermined coalition support for abolition, it also gave rise to an understanding of "the community" that favored moderation. This understanding framed "the community" as an underachieving—rather than materially deprived—population. It suggested, in particular, that "the community" failed to secure important educational and economic opportunities because of their unsuccessful integration into—rather than overdependence on—markets and market-like arrangements. According to this construction, disadvantaged northsiders lacked the sociocultural skills and dispositions needed to compete for broad necessities like decent jobs and housing as well as education-specific goods like access to quality schools, corporate scholarships, and program support from local businesses. As a result, private actors like employers, lenders, and business owners could easily discriminate against, exploit, and dispossess them, leaving them ill-equipped to support their children's educational access.

Coalition organizers assembled this contentious identity through conversations about "the community's" needs (the "abstract discussions" that had frustrated Joanne). In these conversations they focused very little on material scarcity per se. Instead, they primarily emphasized deficiencies in aptitude, attitude, and ability, affirming the idea that "the community's" educational and economic disadvantages hinged on underachievement. For example, several organizers—particularly the men from the Friends of North High Foundation—spoke of needing to improve "the community's" cultural attitudes. In an early brainstorming session, one supporter—a middle-aged, middle-class, and African American North High alumnus—argued that "the community" needed to approach school and work with a greater sense of "self-value." He expounded his point, asserting that northside adults must, for instance, tell young men to "pull their pants up" and explain to them that if you want to secure a good education and good job "in this society," you must "dress and carry yourself" in professional ways. During a later meeting—the one Joanne attended—Reggie made a similar point:

> Something I've been struggling with ever since this whole thing started and that I still think is very important is that the whole expectation of learning extends to the entire community. So, when a kid is walking down the street, people ask them, "Hey, how is school going, how are your grades?," instead of just asking about sports or music or other things.

Others nodded their heads in agreement. He added, "It would help to have people other than the parents who are tasking the students"—that is, inculcating them with more productive attitudes.

The coalition eventually formalized this emphasis on culture, making it a central part of what they called their "re-vision" of North High. Xavier, for instance, invested countless hours developing a mentorship program that would seemingly correct "the community's" cultural deficiencies by connecting students with economically successful alumni. Beyond improved cultural attitudes, coalition organizers also frequently mentioned needs for educational training geared toward "future"—that is, high-tech—and "green" jobs, greater "parent engagement" in this preparation, and stronger pedagogical collaboration with local businesses.[41]

Meeting such needs, they implied, was key to overcoming a range of injustices facing northside students and families. Improving cultural attitudes toward school and work would combat popular beliefs that northsiders do not care about socioeconomic advancement and would delegitimate widespread discrimination against them. Preparing northside students for high-paying jobs of "the future" would give them a competitive advantage on the labor market and undermine "the community's" reliance on highly exploitative service jobs. And bringing successful neighborhood businesses into the classroom would disseminate strategies for acquiring wealth and help to reverse the disinvestment that tended to follow "the community." In total, the result would be a prosperous cycle in which young, Black, and working-class northsiders acquire important skills and abilities lacking among their neighbors, achieve greater market success, and secure the resources needed to provide future generations with even more expansive opportunities.

The coalition's account of the North High "community" was, thus, relatively intersectional, acknowledging the interlocking racialized and economic injustices that held down northside students and other disadvantaged young people in cities across America.[42] However, this account still favored moderation, because it remained cooperative toward market rule (a reminder that intersectional organizing alone cannot inform robust efforts to abolish oppression). The district failed, the account suggested, not by extending the marketization of U.S. society per se but rather by neglecting to adequately support "the community's" achievement within that society. For example, it implied that, by labeling northside public schools as "failures," the district had discouraged "the community" and made it harder for them to develop and demonstrate improved attitudes toward school and work. Furthermore, it insinuated that, in closing northside schools, the school board removed institutions that, for generations, had done more than any other to instill "the community" with productive attitudes and skills. As organizers from the Friends of North High and the North High Alumni Association summarized in a collective statement, "The district would rather throw out its most valuable assets [that is, its public schools] than do the hard lifting to improve educational outcomes for North's current students and students living on the north side." In other words, the district had abandoned "community" members rather than helped them to develop the wherewithal—what one person called the "leg up"—to succeed as competitive market actors.

Although this account brought some negative attention to the district, it remained "positive," because the problems it highlighted could theoretically be solved by partnering with district officials and redesigning schools like North High. The coalition suggested that an effective redesign could help to meet northside students' sociocultural needs and, ultimately, reduce racialized, educational, and economic inequalities. Doing so would require neither a public challenge to the district's neoliberalism nor a fight against market supremacy.

Building on intersectional and cooperative assumptions, the coalition settled for demanding expansive neighborhood engagement in the district-led redesign process and the conversion of North High into a more socioculturally supportive and higher-performing school. By the start of 2011, most of their key projects and decisions focused on advancing this demand. For example, in January 2011 they hosted a potluck in North High's cafeteria at which neighborhood residents were invited to help "re-vision" the school. Almost every important coalition organizer, a handful of North High teachers, Superintendent Johnson, the district's director of community affairs, and even a few school board members attended. With residents, they worked in small groups to identify the types of "school culture, curriculum, community support, leadership, and faculty and staff" that would support "student excellence" in north Minneapolis.[43]

Similar moments followed. After the potluck, Xavier and other leaders formally added Minneapolis Public Schools as a member of the coalition. This addition—which occurred unceremoniously and without open debate—signified a growing engagement between the coalition as "community" representatives and the district as the manager of North High's redesign. In addition, the coalition helped several "community" members—including some from its own ranks—to secure spots on two district-controlled redesign advisory committees. One was a "hiring committee," formed to advise the selection of the consulting firm that would lead North High's redesign. Another was a "community advisory board," formed to advise the redesign process itself. At the coalition's request, the district assembled both committees as a way to elicit and incorporate more "community" input on the topics like those covered at the potluck.

The district officials' own actions came to reflect the coalition's demand for "community" engagement, sociocultural support, and higher performance. In addition to joining the coalition and assembling the two advisory committees, they used their own contact lists and office supplies to advertise the coalition's potluck and related events. They also conducted a survey and multiple focus groups, both of which aimed to uncover "the community's" impressions of North High and how it might better address the problem of underachievement.

To lead the redesign effort, the district hired the Institute for Student Achievement (ISA), the consulting firm favored by the coalition's leaders. In line with the coalition, ISA embraced the idea of addressing inequities by encouraging sociocultural development and higher academic performance.[44] The company's promotional brochure championed a system of high expectations, close monitoring, and "shared accountability" in which teachers and staff "build close, caring relationships with students and parents," working tirelessly "to ensure that no student falls through the cracks and that each student develops the academic, social and emotional capabilities essential to success in college." In August 2011, district officials distributed a "vision template" to the "community advisory board" that sounded very similar, emphasizing goals like "strengthen community ties/relationships to the school," "strengthen social-emotional supports for students" and "improve the reputation of the school."

Finally, in early 2012 the district and the coalition's leadership endorsed a "school design" document that centered on actualizing such goals. The document envisioned a school whose "mission is to ensure that all students acquire the knowledge, skills, and habits to succeed in a challenging college program and 21st century workforce."[45] As part of reaching this mission, it called for a longer school day; more individualized and emotionally involved relationships between staff, students, and parents; stronger partnerships with locally based corporations; near-constant monitoring of student behavior and progress; and more focus on cultivating productive "habits of mind" and "habits of work." Besides expanding after-school enrichment activities, however, it advocated few if any redistributive efforts, such as reducing competition from charter schools, assembling a larger and less overworked school staff, or providing more expansive "wrap-around" services.[46] In fact, some of its provisions stood to exacerbate "the community's" material deprivation by placing even more demands on the limited time of parents, teachers, and staff.

Ultimately, by "being positive" and focusing on underachievement, the coalition did indeed help several disadvantaged students. They ensured that North High remained open, protecting one of "the community's" most vital educational resources. In addition, the sociocultural supports they called for undoubtedly benefited some students. Building "close, caring relationships with students and parents," cultivating productive "habits of mind" and "work," and teaching the skills needed to compete for higher-paying, "21st century" jobs—these are, generally speaking, good and helpful things to do.

At the same time, the coalition's moderate demands tempered any broader citywide or statewide movement to reduce persistent inequities in access to education and economic opportunity. They naturalized the unjust market processes that deprived disadvantaged students of necessary educational resources (and that no amount of sociocultural development could overcome). And they dismissed realistic possibilities for moving incrementally away from the district's neoliberal model and toward egalitarian reforms that might redress some of this deprivation.[47] In short, the coalition's "positive" campaign gave voice to the "community," but did so in a way that foreclosed longer-term struggles to abolish oppression.

"FIGHTING BACK" IN THE WELFARE RIGHTS COMMITTEE

The Welfare Rights Committee, a self-declared representative of "poor and working people," operated on a similar terrain as the North High Coalition. Both groups, of course, organized out of Minneapolis—a city that, despite its progressive makeup, had embraced neoliberalism and promoted capitalist realism's influence. In addition, their respective constituencies overlapped a great deal. North High's surrounding neighborhood contained the highest concentration of welfare recipients and the highest poverty rate in the city, meaning that many "poor and working people" were also members of "the community." Beyond those obvious similarities, both groups also worked in issue spaces—public education and social welfare—where nonprofits and middle-class professionals like Xavier, Reggie, and James tended to dominate activism.

Despite these similarities, the Welfare Rights Committee followed a much different trajectory. As I describe more below, in contrast to the North High Coalition and most other social welfare organizations, they acted as "radical incrementalists"—putting a great deal of effort into curbing capitalist realism's obstructive influence on themselves and their supporters.[48] Consequently, they also assembled an intersectional and adversarial contentious identity that linked their constituents' interests to an abolitionist demand. Moreover, they did these things while building a membership as large and diverse as—and less socioeconomically advantaged than—the coalition's. They also kept that membership mostly unified and, by the end of my study, had remained active for over twenty years.

The committee's main demand was, as their name suggested, for stronger welfare entitlements, especially guaranteed cash assistance. Whereas most contemporary social welfare advocates have opposed restrictive and disciplinary welfare reforms in a piecemeal fashion, the committee holistically rejected such reforms. They also pushed for social-democratic alternatives, calling on policy makers to do things like "tax the rich," "double the [cash] grants" for state welfare recipients, and "stop the five-year limit on MFIP" (the Minnesota Family Investment Program, Minnesota's TANF program). Through these calls, they problematized market-based, racialized, and patriarchal systems that deprive "poor and working people" of income and, thus, necessitate welfare. They also framed welfare assistance as something that could provide rights and resources needed to attack those systems.

Committee organizers themselves understood and articulated the abolitionist thrust of their struggle for welfare rights. In a printed summary of "What we stand for," they declared that "We see the current [that is, neoliberal-era] attacks on welfare as racist, sexist, anti-poor, and anti-immigrant" and that instituting generous welfare entitlements was crucial to "fighting all these systems of oppression." The same summary asserted that

> WRC works to put out the big picture: What we all really need are living wage jobs, affordable housing, free education, and childcare, and healthcare. This society needs to recognize raising children as valuable work. Until these things are in place for everyone there will be a need for welfare.

For the committee, in other words, expanding welfare rights was not merely an end in itself. It was also explicitly a means toward dismantling "systems of oppression" and securing "What we all really need"—namely, the requisites of a free and dignified life.

"We Cannot Compromise with People's Lives"

How, in the face of the same challenges as other social justice organizations, did the Welfare Rights Committee successfully embrace such an abolitionist bent? The answer is that, instead of treating capitalist realism as a fixed constraint, the committee developed an etiquette that problematized it. Rather than "being positive," this etiquette prioritized "fighting back" against any and all suffering imposed by the existing, neoliberal welfare state. In their opinion, anyone who remained complicit with this suffering should be subject to popular anger. This included progressives who, in the words of one committee statement, sought a "kinder, gentler way to cut welfare" and force "poor and working people" into low-wage jobs and other oppressive circumstances. Such "kinder, gentler" methods, organizers asserted, still unfairly threatened the "blood" and "survival" of society's least well-off. "Fighting back," they often claimed, means that "We cannot compromise with people's lives" and "will not tolerate" those who do so.

One can already see how this type of etiquette would, if taken seriously, compel organizers to challenge capitalist realism's influence, construe "poor and working people" on intersectional and adversarial terms, and embrace an abolitionist demand. It pushes organizers to question any aspect of existing or proposed welfare policy that requires a "blood" sacrifice—whether by treating one group as more worthy than another, making recipients and other working-class individuals more vulnerable to abusive employers and partners, or encouraging similarly oppressive practices. It also pushes organizers to discuss how more social-democratic policies might undermine these oppressions and unearth a pathway toward eliminating them.

As in the North High Coalition, the Welfare Rights Committee had a small group of leaders who took charge in fostering the group's etiquette. At the center of this group were three white, middle-aged, and long-time socialist organizers. Two of them, Cynthia and Sharon, helped to form the committee in 1991. Tammy, who was active in the "new left" as a college student, began working with them shortly thereafter. All three women were former recipients of welfare assistance (with "welfare" defined broadly to include programs like food stamps, disability and unemployment insurance, and Section 8 or public housing as well as MFIP). All three were also employed in clerical or care work—one at a local university, another at a technology firm, and another in social services. In addition to leading the committee, Cynthia, Sharon, and Tammy invested themselves in a broader effort to strengthen the left in Minneapolis and Minnesota politics. They actively participated in a regional Marxist-Leninist group called Freedom Road Socialist Organization, the members of which led several social justice organizations in the Twin Cities, including the Coalition for a People's Bailout.[49] Working with Freedom Road, they also helped to publish a bilingual (English/Spanish) paper, *Fight Back! News,* which reported the efforts of many left-wing groups in the city.

The committee's leaders established a commitment to "fighting back" by, first and foremost, disparaging what they called an "advocacy" model of social justice organizing. Instead of attacking the "blood" sacrifices of the neoliberal welfare state, this model—grounded in the nonprofit sector—emphasized helping economically disadvantaged people to cope with those sacrifices. In the minds of committee organizers, it mostly involved brokering with policy makers and partnering with corporate-backed foundations to improve the delivery of particular, already existing benefits and services. It was, for them, the inverse of "fighting back."

The disparagement of "advocacy" is something that defined the committee from its earliest days. Indeed, the committee emerged out of a split with another social welfare organization that started as one of the most radical in the Twin Cities but eventually embraced a neoliberal model of service provision and self-help. In 1990 and 1991, this organization, Up and Out of Poverty Now, used illegal occupations of vacant buildings to push for government-funded affordable housing development.[50] Its leader, Mark Thisius, was a recovering alcoholic and formerly homeless white man who had abandoned a potential career with Lutheran Social Services—Minnesota's largest nonprofit social service organization. "Within the [social services] bureaucracy," Thisius argued at the time, "the biggest thing that was going on is writing grants and sustaining the bureaucracy and doing nothing at all politically to deal with the problem" of homelessness and poverty; and the solution, he asserted, was to "fight back."[51]

Eventually, however, Thisius shifted from pushing for a transformation of the social services bureaucracy to forswearing that bureaucracy and embracing a privatized alternative. In 1991, he and other members of Up and Out of Poverty Now founded Freedom Place, Inc., a nonprofit organization that purchased and managed properties for use as transitional sober housing. "We realized government was not interested in solving this problem," the Freedom Place website states, "so we set up sober homes without one dime of government funding," raising money from individuals and foundations and primarily employing the poor and homeless to rehabilitate and manage properties.[52] Cynthia and Sharon started the committee precisely to distance themselves from this kind of turn to "advocacy."

From the committee's early years, leaders like Cynthia, Sharon, and Tammy took further steps to suppress the influence of "advocacy"-oriented professionals. First and foremost, they limited their dependence on money and mainstream policy expertise, which these professionals tended to control. The Welfare Rights Committee, unlike Up and Out of Poverty Now, remained all-volunteer, eliminating any need to compensate a paid staff. Likewise, unlike the North High Coalition, Cynthia, Sharon, Tammy, and, eventually, the rest of the group developed their own "bottom-up" policy expertise, decreasing their susceptibility to the expertise of mainstream lobbyists, bureaucrats, and consultants. They often dedicated large chunks of their twice-monthly meetings to developing independent evaluations of negative welfare bills, preparing to propose their own bills, and identifying opportunities to engage the policy-making process. "We analyze current law and policy from our perspective," they wrote in their mission statement. "We, the women, children and men on assistance, are the real experts on poverty and welfare."

The committee's separation from the "advocacy" world was not total. To cover the cost of basic supplies—such as office space, transportation to and from events, and child care and food during meetings—they annually sought and received a ten-thousand-dollar grant from Minnesota's Headwaters Foundation for Justice. Headwaters, in contrast to other liberal foundations, had a history of funding more radical and confrontational social justice organizations.[53] Nevertheless, the committee's leaders treated even their reliance on this small grant as a concession to the status quo that, if handled poorly, could pull their organization in the wrong direction.[54]

In addition to limiting their overall dependence on proponents of "advocacy," Cynthia, Sharon, Tammy, and other longtime committee organizers also castigated these proponents. In meetings, they criticized the members of "nonprofit"[55] or "advocacy groups" who, according to Jacqueline—a low-income single mother and longtime committee organizer—"just sit around and talk about these [systemic] issues." These "poverty pimp groups," Sharon argued in a strategy discussion, "get into all the little details" about specific programs but "usually stay away from the broader picture because they're afraid" of placing too much pressure on the legislators and wealthy interests who fund their efforts. "We can engage in helpful alliances with them to try and stop certain cuts but not when we're trying to introduce legislation and push a [redistributive] agenda."

Lastly, committee leaders strategically built a membership that would more likely mimic and perpetuate their rejection of "advocacy." They formally excluded most of the middle-class individuals who led "poverty pimp groups," requiring from the beginning that all committee members be "welfare recipients (current and former) and/or working poor." Furthermore, they committed themselves to developing future committee leaders who would maintain independence from the "nonprofit" universe. When the time came to identify speakers for public events or choose who would chair and co-chair planning meetings, they primarily encouraged the participation of members with strong anti-establishment proclivities. People whose exposure to capitalist realism had muted these proclivities—people like Darlene and Cheryl, discussed in a prior section—were by no means excluded from leadership roles. But, over time, Cynthia, Sharon, and Tammy guaranteed that, to occupy such roles, these people would have to comport with other members who disliked "advocacy."

Having dismissed "advocacy," committee leaders promoted "fighting back" as the most strategic and righteous way forward. They ensured that the idea of protesting complicit civic and political leaders would have an impact on anyone who entered their sphere. Their fliers and recruitment materials labeled themselves "fighters for justice" and almost unfailingly included specific requests for confrontational action as well as exclamations like "Enough is enough!" and "Not at the people's expense!" Moreover, whenever new members attended committee meetings, the group's most experienced members would open with a round of introductions, in which they not only stated their names but proudly declared their commitment to, in Tammy's words, "fighting against the Republicans" and "getting on the Democrats." At one meeting, Cynthia captured the essence of these introductions in the following way:

> I think the easiest way to put it is just to say that, these politicians, they know that what they're trying to do is eventually going to kill people. And we expose that. . . . We point out the big stuff so that they can't get away with the small stuff.

Other longtime and passionate members followed suit—proclaiming, for example, that they "like to get up in some legislators' faces" and that "When people look back, they'll see that we fought back and that [poor and working] people wouldn't take the crap they were throwing down at us."[56] This kind of talk persisted, and was encouraged, throughout the group's internal communications, from email announcements and substantive policy discussions to side conversations and text messages.

Committee leaders matched this internal discourse to an agenda that was itself almost singularly geared toward "fighting back." At the start of meetings, after introductions, chairs typically invited members to summarize any recent "actions" through which the group had directed popular anger toward neoliberal decision makers. Organizers almost always described these "actions"—such as rallies, press conferences, or legislative testimonies—as raucous events, where the committee and its supporters "look[ed] them in the eyes" or "look[ed] at their faces" and "basically called them scum." They especially enjoyed recounting moments when their members encountered "intimidation" but, in Sharon's words, "refused to give in." For example, one such moment in April 2012 involved what Cynthia called a "tussle with the cops," during which state capitol police tried to confiscate one of the committee's large banners and, in response, various members held firm, "got in their faces," and declared, "This is our capitol!"[57] After summarizing "actions," meeting chairs also invited "updates" on proposed legislation. While "updates" existed partly to share basic information, they also reminded members why "fighting back" was so necessary. According to these "updates," Republicans usually pressed "evil-spirited, idiotic" plans and Democrats lacked an egalitarian and emancipatory "vision." The committee was, thus, impelled to, as Jacqueline put it, "get into shaming them publicly." Finally, after "updates," every meeting ended by either preparing an "action" or planning "outreach" at welfare offices to build support for "action."

Surrounding all this discussion and agenda-setting—what made it work—was a consistent and coordinated effort to check capitalist realism's influence. In other words, to actualize their commitment to "fighting back," committee leaders had to show themselves and their supporters that flouting market supremacy was, in fact, a plausible alternative.

A skeptic could have easily claimed the opposite by pointing to a few basic facts. First, they could have stressed that "fighting" neoliberal welfare policy pressured governments to deploy revenue that, because of a series of economic downturns, they did not actually have. During the years I studied the committee—2010, 2011, and 2012—state and local officials were continually dealing with recession-fueled budget deficits, which seemed to *require* sacrifices from ordinary people. Second, revenue questions aside, a skeptic could have pointed out that "fighting" against complicity with market rule turned off potential supporters, who simply took the neoliberal welfare state for granted. During my time studying the committee, one state official—a progressive who represented one of Minnesota's poorest districts—openly reported that "some [legislators in the Democratic Party] feel like they can't work with you"; in particular, he claimed, many Democratic legislators felt that Sharon's attacks on mainstream welfare politics were "too forceful." Within the committee itself, individuals like Cheryl—who clung to capitalist realist assumptions—usually became frustrated with "fighting back" and either disappeared or limited their activity.

Leaders like Cynthia, Tammy, and Sharon doggedly preempted the foregoing claims. To thwart claims about budget deficits, they reiterated over and over (and over) that, although actually existing government revenue was paltry, potential revenue was much larger. "Look at the facts," they argued in one 2011 press statement:

> If the [Democratic] governor's original proposal to raise taxes on 5% of the population with the most income results in over $3 billion, this signifies just how much the State of Minnesota has been losing in tax income, year after year because the rich have not paid their fair share and because of the massive tax breaks they have benefitted from.

Such "facts," they (correctly) argued, proved that welfare "cuts" instituted during the early 2000s were unnecessary.[58] "Fighting back" was, thus, an eminently reasonable and appropriate response.

To ward off concerns about alienating supporters, committee leaders also regularly presented (what they considered to be) successful examples of people "fighting" pro-market welfare policy. Most of these examples came from the committee's own history. Organizers maintained a timeline of all they had completed—every "action" from their founding to the present—and once a year they distributed it to both longtime and potential members at a community "Celebration" of their "Fight for Justice." Just for the 1990s, this timeline contained over six single-spaced pages of events, many of which, by their account, altered government policies and practices. They presented this history as proof that the committee's "fighting" approach made liberal policy makers more, rather than less, supportive. "We got [Democratic] politicians to . . . do our bidding," Tammy explained at the 2011 "Celebration," "because we shamed them against doing really horrible things to us." Ashley, another former welfare recipient and longtime member, added:

> Throughout the eighteen years that we've been fighting . . . we have managed to stop the complete stoppage of welfare and health-care programs. And that's [by] doing exactly what we're doing now . . .

Date	Event
3/7/96	Statewide rally - MOD-Squad from Duluth, Women for change, Winona, Feminist single moms of Mankato.
3/29/96	Stood outside house chambers with giant checks comparing AFDC yearly income to governor's yearly income. $6314 vs. $114,506. Brought checks to Governor's office.
4/1/96	Deb K was on Jason Lewis show, with Goodno and Samuelson (oddly, it was Lewis against the 3 of them!)
4/1/96	MNJOBS bill passed. We were mad.
4/1/96	National "Stand for children"
4/13/96	Community forum: "Today's worker could be tomorrow's welfare recipient"
5/1/96	Mothers Day benefit at Riverside Café
5/1/96	Telling people to call Clinton and demand a veto
6/1/96	Packed Wellstone's office. Demanded he press Clinton for a Veto. Also demanded that the bill benefitting Hmong veterans be stand alone and not attached to an immigrant bashing bill. Don't know date.
6/1/96	Protest at Special Session against new twins stadium. Don't know date
6/1/96	Statewide MN Welfare Rights Coalition formed.
6/4/96	MOD/Duluth protest at St. Louis County
7/12/96	Boycott Wisconsin campaign - against WI's welfare reform, W-2.
7/31/96	National day of action against federal welfare reform. WRC organized actions in 40 cities. We had a march in downtown St. Paul and duct-taped dozens of signs to Dem HQ. We were on ABC news.
8/1/96	Hunger strike begins
8/7/96	Hunger strike ends Aug. 7
8/22/96	Press conference at St Paul federal building against Clinton signing bill
9/1/96	Community meeting on welfare reform
9/2/96	Letter to acting DHS commissioner John Petraborg about closed door meetings
1/7/97	March on Capitol - Demand MN make up for federal cuts.
1/7/97	Opening day rally.
1/28/97	Pack the Senate hearing
2/7/97	Pack the Senate hearing, again
2/26/97	Capitol protest with arrests.
2/28/97	Duluth MOD demands end to secret welfare hearings.
3/7/97	Protest at Capitol - Give state surplus to the poor!
3/26/97	Statewide protest
4/30/97	Protest at "Arne's BBQ". Same day, also had a protest at Arne's office as he got ready to sign bad welfare bill.
5/7/97	Protest at Capitol - part of national day of action to undo SSI and food stamp cuts to immigrants. turn over $2.3 billion surplus to the poor
5/15/97	Protest at HC-WO demanding education, end to sanctions, childcare, etc
6/1/97	"Wanted posters" against Berglin and Greenfield
6/1/97	Protest against Sen. Neuville (the white devil) in Northfield, MN
7/1/97	Statewide day of protests against start of 5-year clock. We went to HC-WO

4

Sample page from the Welfare Rights Committee's timeline of past actions.

> organizing, getting people to fight with us. . . . The Welfare Rights Committee is not a lobbyist group. . . . We do it ourselves.

Longtime members also flaunted their personal histories of "action" as proof that "fighting back" actually *drew* low-income supporters to the group. One after another, they recalled how, despite initially hesitating to get involved, they embraced the group, because it delivered what Cynthia called "opportunities" to "speak the truth" and "see the power you have." "You might resist for awhile, but we'll keep bugging you," explained Jacqueline. "And once we bug you and you come and you check us out, you get hooked."[59]

The committee, of course, never fully eliminated capitalist realism's obstructive influence within their ranks. However, they kept it at bay. All of their core members accepted in practice—even if they disagreed in private—that "fighting back" was more sensible than "advocacy." On the surface, this unity was strong and consistent enough that it could easily seem natural. But it was built and maintained through the disciplined organizing of a core group of leftists. Their careful efforts to shape the committee's discourse, agenda, and membership made "fighting back" seem as logical to those around them as "being positive" seemed to much of the North High Coalition.

"That's Just a Principle We Follow"

"Fighting back," in the Welfare Rights Committee, ruled out moderate demands—such as those calling for smaller reductions in benefits, increased job training and work supports, or greater administrative fairness and efficiency. Whether by implying the existence of a potentially cooperative relationship between "poor and working people" and the existing welfare state or by ignoring the intersecting "blood" sacrifices affecting "poor and working people," these demands contravened the goal of assailing complicity with the neoliberal status quo. From the perspective of "the fight," they could only appear like calls for a "kinder, gentler" version of this status quo.

As a result, appeals for moderation were almost entirely absent from the committee's meetings and internal deliberations. And whenever such appeals emerged, most members dismissed them. Many of these instances involved Cheryl. For example, during a July 2011 meeting, Cheryl expressed her willingness to accept increased policing of "welfare fraud," if doing so would improve program efficiency and forestall greater spending reductions. At the time, Minnesota was in middle of the government shutdown that pitted the state's progressive Democratic governor against a right-wing Republican-led legislature. Committee leaders wanted the governor to refuse any budget deal that included, among other things, new "fraud"-prevention measures. But for Cheryl, this stance was untenable. She was incredulous that the committee would defend individuals who, she thought, abused welfare when "people are losing jobs" because of the shutdown. "I see people selling food stamps and getting high," she complained, "I work and bust my hump every day. . . . I care about folks on welfare but . . ." The implication of her comment was that opposing "fraud" prevention actually undermined the interests of "poor and working people" by shielding wasteful practices. The committee would be better off seeking to make anti-"fraud" measures smarter and fairer.

The response to Cheryl's appeal for moderation was overwhelmingly negative. As typically occurred in these instances, several other members began to grumble and show their displeasure. Cynthia—who was chairing the meeting—took the lead in articulating this displeasure. She first criticized the notion that groups like the committee were causing people to lose jobs by pushing the governor to hold strong. "They'll lose those jobs permanently," she argued, if the defenders of "poor and working people" give up and neoliberal legislators win. More to the point, Cynthia condemned Cheryl's moderate position for ignoring the injustices engendered by "fraud" prevention and, thus, violating the group's etiquette. She asserted that "lots of rich folks are addicted [to drugs] and gaming the system too" and reminded everyone that "one of our principles is that we don't attack our brothers and sisters," because doing so undermines "our fight." "That's just a principle we follow," she concluded. Nobody pushed back. As with Stephen in the North High Coalition, it is possible that some committee members privately agreed with Cheryl's moderate stance. Nevertheless, to the extent that "fighting back" already structured their interactions, it would have felt inappropriate to express this agreement.

Instead, committee organizers assembled a contentious identity that favored abolitionist demands for stronger welfare entitlements. Rather than construe "poor and working people" as an underachieving population—or even a materially deprived population—this identity treated them as a variegated and embattled class. More precisely, it treated them as a large, heterogeneous group who cannot secure their fair share of the good life, or sometimes meet their basic needs, because they are under the thumb of economic elites. According to the committee, public officials, lobbyists, and advocates allow these elites to take for themselves through capitalist markets, leaving everyone else to suffer. By reproducing overlapping processes of exploitation, predation, discrimination, and disinvestment, mainstream political leaders help "the rich" to enhance their social position and oppress "poor and working people." For the latter, "fighting back" was the only option available.

Committee organizers assembled this identity through their conversations about the problems with mainstream, neoliberal welfare policy. In these conversations, like any left-wing or progressive group, they emphasized the direct harms effected by welfare austerity and discipline. But, unlike many other groups, they also stressed the extensive political-economic protection and clout such policies gave to "the rich"—protection and clout that, they argued, enabled a multifaceted "attack" on "poor and working people."

For example, organizers repeatedly underscored that state-level welfare "cuts" protected "the rich" from having to incur costs for engaging in exploitation and other unjust practices. Because of such "cuts," they asserted, policy makers were able to keep taxes unnecessarily low for high-income earners, wealthy individuals, and large corporations—even as those groups benefited from deunionization, racialized divisions of labor, and other market systems that impoverished disadvantaged people like single mothers and women of color. "We wouldn't be talking about cuts," Sharon often liked to say, "if the rich had been paying their fair share [in taxes] for all these years." Committee leaders also linked "cuts" to subsidies for powerful and oppressive companies. When Minnesota's legislators began planning to subsidize a new Minnesota Vikings stadium, organizers framed it as a giveaway to Zygi Wilf—billionaire real estate developer and Vikings owner—and an "attack" on "poor and working people," enabled partly by welfare austerity. "It's just deplorable," explained Stacy, a newer committee member, African American mother, and former welfare recipient:

> [State legislators] are trying to hand down cuts to poor women and children, without any additions to education. . . . It's just crazy that they're trying to build a stadium. Meanwhile, we're being attacked. So, I'm here and ready to fight.

These sentiments carried over into the committee's "action" planning. For example, one of the committee's largest events each year was a "Tax the Rich!" rally, held on the steps of the state capitol. They were also the only social welfare organization to actively protest the Vikings' stadium subsidies.

In addition to "cuts," committee organizers outlined how "workfare" and anti-"fraud" measures reproduced the domination of "the rich" over "poor and working people." They argued that "workfare," alongside "cuts," not only put the pinch on poor women and other lower-income individuals; it bolstered employers' overall capacity to exploit these individuals, compounding the effects of oppressive labor market processes like deunionization. "What it is," Tammy said in a 2011 meeting, "is that they just want to force us to work for the most meager wages possible, or even work for free." Jacqueline affirmed her point, equating "workfare" measures with the promotion of "slave labor."

Anti-"fraud" measures, they contended, validated efforts by "the rich" and other powerful actors to discriminate against, stratify, and divide "poor and working people." When, in 2011 and 2012, Republican legislators proposed mandatory background checks for welfare recipients, new residency requirements for General Assistance, and more restrictions on the use of EBT cards, organizers underlined that these measures supported discrimination against lower-income groups associated with welfare programs. Regarding the EBT restrictions, Cynthia argued in one meeting that "we should emphasize that it's discrimination." She added, "You know, all the representatives get government checks too, and nobody is harassing them about every little thing they spend their money on." Jacqueline—who was chairing the meeting—followed up, emphasizing the damaging political-economic consequences of allowing such discrimination: "I think we need to be careful about saying they know who the people are that are doing wrong with their EBT cards, or saying, you know, oh we aren't with those people, because that's a slippery slope. We have to stay united."

This construction of "poor and working people" as an embattled class followed both intersectional and adversarial logics. It attended to interlocking injustices that prevent low-income and working-class individuals from accessing income and leading healthy lives, and it targeted these injustices' systemic roots. It particularly derided any system of extensive market rule wherein "the rich" get to dictate the terms on which "poor and working people" participate in society. And it suggested that promoting the well-being of their constituents would require the drastic circumscription of such rule.

For committee members, demanding stronger welfare entitlements and limiting market dependence became part and parcel of representing their embattled constituents—demonstrating the importance of bringing intersectional and adversarial logics together. Virtually all of their "fight back" centered on this abolitionist demand. In legislative committee hearings, they testified against any and all bills that promoted "cuts," "workfare," and "fraud" prevention. They also worked with friendly legislators to produce alternative bills, which moved incrementally toward expanding welfare rights. Some of these bills would have raised income taxes for the wealthiest Minnesotans, doubled the cash grants for MFIP recipients, and loosened the federally instituted five-year limit on MFIP participation. In addition to working on legislation, the committee used rallies, protests, and other—often confrontational—public events to advertise "poor and working people's" need for entitlements. For example, they organized a "die-in" outside the governor's office, interrupted legislators' press conferences, and disrupted legislative committee votes.

Construing "poor and working people" as a variegated and embattled class and demanding welfare entitlements was not enough on its own to make the committee a potent force for equality and freedom. However, doing these things put them on the path toward becoming such a force. Moreover, it is important to note that the committee's dedication to abolitionist demand-making did not preclude them from achieving short-term policy success. They never came close to meeting their overall demands or policy goals—simply because these goals were much more aspirational than those embraced by groups like the North High Coalition. However, the committee operated as the "radical flank" in a number of successful, left-leaning legislative alliances.[60] Each of these alliances stopped Minnesota from descending further down the hole of neoliberal welfare reform and moved the state incrementally toward a more redistributive and social-democratic approach.

Most importantly, in 2019 they helped to secure a one-hundred-dollar increase to MFIP recipients' monthly cash payments—the first such increase in over thirty years.[61] In the few years prior, members of the committee prepared the ground for this change by serving on an MFIP task force for Minnesota's Department of Health and Human Services and working with progressive legislators to push their own, more transformative bills—which would have doubled MFIP cash payments, expanded state-funded General Assistance to cover families who had passed MFIP's five-year time limit, and instituted a COLA (cost of living adjustment) for all future MFIP cash payments. Their efforts, though too strident and left-wing for many of their allies, weakened support for simply continuing to make the neoliberal welfare state more progressive and strengthened the case for pursuing egalitarian and emancipatory reform.

Until a society emerges that effectively prioritizes human flourishing, social justice organizers will continue to confront ideologies like capitalist realism—that is, ideologies geared toward the perpetuation of inequality and unfreedom. These ideologies will yield substantial opposition to abolitionist politics. Potential supporters and activists, from a variety of backgrounds, will question the wisdom of construing disadvantaged constituents' interests on intersectional and adversarial terms and demanding far-reaching egalitarian and emancipatory reforms. And organizers will, as a result, feel pressure to discipline vocal proponents of abolitionist demand-making and assemble contentious identities around moderate demands—all in order to maintain unity and dedication among themselves and the majority of their followers.

Nevertheless, as I have shown, the turn away from abolitionism and toward moderation is preventable. Organizers in the North High Coalition and the Welfare Rights Committee responded to the pull of capitalist realism in contradistinctive and revealing ways. Whereas even some of the coalition's most progressive members accommodated this pull and moderated accordingly, the committee mitigated it, creating new opportunities to pursue abolitionist demand-making. Led by women like Cynthia, Sharon, and Tammy, committee members assuaged reservations about challenging market rule and construed the "poor and working people" they represented as an embattled, heterogeneous class. This construal—that is, the contentious identity they assembled—attended to the interlocking injustices facing their constituents. It also derided the market-based, racialized, and gendered systems that drove these injustices. In total, it underwrote their support for the protection and expansion of welfare entitlements—a demand that problematized much of the oppressive status quo, challenged the neoliberal logic underlying poverty deconcentration, and laid out an ambitious and realistic path toward something better. When all was said and done, the Welfare Rights Committee united around this demand for over two decades, while remaining as large and active as the North High Coalition.

The key to explaining the differences between organizations like the North High Coalition and the Welfare Rights Committee lies in their political etiquettes. These etiquettes set the boundaries of appropriate engagement. They can be codified or informal, conscious or unconscious. In any case, they place real limits on negotiations and agendas.[62] The coalition's etiquette, centered on "being positive," treated market supremacy as a fact of life and required organizers to partner with district officials, the administrators of a neoliberal education regime. This etiquette allowed for discussions of the discrimination, exploitation, and disinvestment facing "the community," but it suppressed attacks on the market processes underlying these injustices and made school choice and competition seem like a workable, or unavoidable, approach to public education. As Xavier and his allies effectively marginalized "political" talk and championed "being positive," any possibility of resisting capitalist realism, assembling an adversarial contentious identity, and embracing abolitionist demands evaporated.

In contrast, the committee's etiquette—centered on "fighting back"—treated the acceptance of market supremacy as an immoral and unnecessary compromise and required organizers to condemn neoliberal legislators. This etiquette encouraged their awareness of the myriad and interlocking injustices—the "blood" sacrifices—holding down "poor and working people." It also drove their holistic opposition toward restrictive and disciplinary welfare policies. "Fighting back" meant treating all civic and political leaders who tolerated the existing welfare regime as a threat—whether these leaders sought to push this regime to ever more revanchist extremes or give it a "kinder, gentler" facade. In the process of normalizing such conduct, committee organizers pushed themselves to counter capitalist realism's influence, made intersectional and adversarial depictions of "poor and working people" seem commonsensical, and solidified their commitment to abolitionist demand-making.

The foregoing observations suggest that the battle to improve how social justice organizations assemble contentious identities and make demands must start at the level of intra-organizational relations. Without changing the etiquette through which group members relate to one another, without orienting that etiquette against capitalist realism or whatever future ideology takes its place, organizers pushing for abolitionism cannot succeed. Stephen's experience in the North High Coalition exemplifies this point. His depictions of "the community" as a materially deprived population and his arguments for redistributing educational resources were thoughtful, forceful, and clear. They spoke to concrete challenges facing Black northside students and—based

	North High Coalition	Welfare Rights Committee
Etiquette	"Being positive" about "partnership" (normalized capitalist realism's influence)	"Fighting back" against "blood" sacrifice (problematized capitalist realism's influence)
Assembled Contentious Identity	Intersectional-cooperative ("the community" as underachieving population)	Intersectional-adversarial ("poor and working people" as variegated and embattled class)
Demand	Moderate (higher-performing school)	Abolitionist (stronger welfare entitlements)

Assembling contentious identities: North High Coalition and Welfare Rights Committee.

on the reactions I witnessed at rallies and school board meetings—resonated with many North High supporters. But what they did not, or could not, do was accord with "being positive." To make abolitionism less divisive and more unifying, Stephen and his allies would have needed to rework this etiquette, especially its underlying faith in "partnership" over "political" pressure.

In addition, the experiences of the North High Coalition and the Welfare Rights Committee suggest that tipping intra-organizational relations toward abolitionism requires a militant and typically leftist collective. This collective—what labor scholars sometimes call the "militant minority"—need not be especially large. But it must work intentionally, strategically, and independently to establish more radical etiquettes.[63] In socialists like Cynthia, Sharon, and Tammy, the Welfare Rights Committee had such a collective. By influencing the group's structure, agenda, rules, and norms, these women incorporated "fighting back" into its day-to-day life. As I showed, the North High Coalition also had organizers—Stephen, Manny, and Daniel—who tried to push beyond "being positive." However, they did so in relatively fragmented and uncoordinated ways. They were unable to act as a united and disciplined force, incapable of either holding the coalition's leaders accountable to something like "fighting back" or building an alternative group around such an etiquette. For social justice organizations to become faithful proponents of abolitionist demands, more leftists like Stephen, Manny, and Daniel must develop this capacity.

MISLEADING THE PUBLIC

In the fall of 2009, as the United States was still reeling from the 2007 housing market crash, anti-foreclosure and anti-eviction activism in Minneapolis was building steam; its momentum was due in no small part to the efforts of the Minnesota Coalition for a People's Bailout.[1] By occupying foreclosed homes and pushing for a two-year statewide moratorium on home foreclosures and evictions from foreclosed rental properties, the Bailout Coalition was galvanizing the debate about housing issues in a major way. Moreover, they brought "poor and working people" to the center of this debate, working most closely with lower-income African American women. Their efforts starkly contrasted with those of Minneapolis's progressive leaders, most of whom presumed to address foreclosures through moderate measures like mortgage counseling, public–private housing rehabilitation projects, and strengthened consumer protections.[2] Though helpful, these measures did little to directly challenge the city's neoliberal and racialized political economy, and they left behind many of the foreclosure victims who had been most harmed by that political economy. In contrast to calls for moratorium and a redistribution of economic resources and power, they mostly accommodated market rule, lowered expectations for a better world, and provided insufficient assistance to the city's most disadvantaged residents.

To publicize and build support for their efforts, the Bailout Coalition held multiple community forums. One such forum took place at an Urban League branch in north Minneapolis, a high-poverty and disproportionately Black area that also had, by far, the city's highest foreclosure rate.[3] Speakers from the Minnesota Tenants Union, the Welfare Rights Committee, and other member organizations introduced the Bailout Coalition and overviewed its efforts to address what they called "the housing crisis." They shared the stories of multiple working-class female homeowners, all of whom had been victims of predatory lending and/or recessionary layoffs and were working with the coalition to halt foreclosures on their properties. Coalition representatives also enjoined those in attendance to aid the defense of these properties and support their campaign for a moratorium on foreclosure-related evictions.

Much of the audience clapped in agreement throughout the forum. However, when meeting organizers opened the floor for discussion, they experienced pushback from a handful of attendees. Though left-leaning, these individuals strongly opposed using either home occupations or moratorium legislation—the pillars of the coalition's efforts—to stop evictions. The most vocal among them, a white homeowner named Jeff, was also the housing director for the Hawthorne Neighborhood Council, a progressive community-based nonprofit in north Minneapolis. In his position as housing director, Jeff had spearheaded and championed market-friendly efforts to prevent foreclosure-related evictions, especially mortgage counseling. His comments are worth quoting at length:

> JEFF: In my neighborhood, we've got a lot of houses right now sitting vacant, nobody in them. We've got an absentee owner, and the only thing . . . that's gonna get that house, aside from forcible takeovers and squatting—which my neighborhood has officially passed a motion, we do not support that. . . . The only thing that's gonna get that house out of that status and into a good owner-occupant or a good landlord and good tenants is a foreclosure. And . . . I can take you over to the area right behind Kemps. You all know what I'm talking about with all the rampant drug dealing that happens at a couple of the houses right there. You know what, if those houses were foreclosed on and those drug dealers, those prostitutes were out of our neighborhood because of a foreclosure, nobody would shed a tear on that block.
>
> AUDIENCE MEMBER: That's right.
>
> JEFF: And, if there's a moratorium that blocks those things from happening, that freezes, that puts my neighborhood into something that's stagnant that doesn't allow things to get better, then that's not something that I can support. That's not something that my neighbors are gonna support.

This message was one I had heard from other progressive middle-class northsiders. It depicted many of the city's poorest foreclosure victims as members of an irresponsible, mostly Black underclass; it framed foreclosure and eviction as potentially *helpful* instruments for removing this underclass and deconcentrating poverty; and it dismissed moratorium proposals as misguided policies that would ultimately harm rather than benefit upstanding working and middle-class residents. As Jeff summarized, a moratorium would "freeze" poverty deconcentration efforts and harm the "good owner-occupant," the "good tenants," and the "good landlord" trying to improve their struggling neighborhoods. The best way forward, he suggested, was to expand the consumer protections and counseling available to lower-income homeowners and tenants.

Deb—a social service worker and a founding member of the coalition—tried to allay Jeff's concerns, leading to the following exchange:

> DEB: The moratorium on home foreclosures was not for investment properties, it's for "owner-occupied."[4] It wasn't on . . .
>
> JEFF: I can take you to some owner-occupied problem properties if you want to see them. We can sit there and watch the drug dealers come and go.
>
> DEB: Our issue is there's a housing crisis. People are suffering, and that's what we're gonna take care of. The big issue is the big issue—of housing crisis, our families that are being thrown into the street.
>
> AUDIENCE MEMBER: When I live next to a house where drugs are being dealt openly, that's a big issue for me.

Deb ardently defended the coalition's position. At the same time, she (unintentionally) accepted the premise of Jeff's comments—namely, that foreclosure policies should primarily or only protect respectable homeowners and tenants, the supposedly true victims of the "housing crisis." Put differently, her response conveyed that the coalition's efforts would *not* protect "drug dealers" and "prostitutes" living in disreputable "investment properties."

The problem for Deb was that the coalition's proposed moratorium *would,* in fact, assist members of Minneapolis's alleged underclass. By pausing *all* foreclosure-related evictions for two years, it would help many "poor and working people" whose housing problems extended beyond the "crisis" and stemmed from causes other than predatory and subprime lending or recession-driven layoffs; a disproportionate share of these people were undoubtedly drug dealers, sex workers, ex-convicts, and, generally speaking, individuals living on society's stigmatized margins.[5] Not only Jeff but Deb herself and probably everyone at the forum knew this. By attempting to distract from it, she *undermined* rather than strengthened the argument for a moratorium. More precisely, she obscured the broader market-based systems of injustice—such as gentrification, residential segregation, and deunionization—that diminished good job and housing opportunities for "poor and working people," especially African American northsiders; encouraged some of these people to accept dangerous jobs like drug dealing and prostitution; pushed many of them to obtain expensive mortgages (prime as well as predatory and subprime) or enter precarious rental agreements with financially unstable landowners; and necessitated bold redistributive responses. She also allowed Jeff and his allies to mark her as an ignorant outsider, someone with half-baked ideas and no understanding of how the presence of "problem properties" complicated the foreclosure response in north Minneapolis. Ultimately, without an alternative account of the realities facing lower-income northsiders, especially those of color, Deb could only reiterate that the city was facing a "housing crisis" and that the crisis was a "big issue"—points that neither Jeff nor anyone else in the audience actually contested.

The previous chapter examined how social justice organizers assemble contentious identities like "poor and working people" or "the community." It explained why they have so regularly oriented these identities against struggles to abolish oppression and how they could reverse this trend. However, organizers do not just assemble contentious identities among themselves. They also reconstruct and publicize these identities for broader audiences, such as policy makers, advocates, and the general public. Often, the rhetoric they use to achieve this publicity simply reflects the shared assumptions informing their demands. But not necessarily. As Deb's exchange with Jeff illustrates, even proponents of abolitionist demands can deploy rhetoric that unintentionally favors moderation.[6]

In the best of worlds, organizers publicize contentious identities using oppositional rhetoric that strengthens the moral justification for abolitionist demands. Such rhetoric condemns the systems of oppression targeted by struggles for abolition. It attacks the processes and relations that constitute these systems, and it underscores the unwarranted disadvantage they have imposed on masses of people. An example would be the class-, gender-, and race-conscious rhetoric that the best welfare rights organizers use to publicize welfare recipients' interests and justify demands for greater assistance. As Rose Ernst demonstrated in her national study of welfare rights organizations, this rhetoric condemns the widespread disadvantages produced by exploitative, discriminatory, and predatory market processes and stresses the ways in which ragged safety-net programs support these processes.[7] It transcends concerns about the behavior of poor individuals and articulates a public need for expanding ordinary people's rights to cash assistance and other benefits.

Unfortunately, research suggests, organizers more often deploy conventional rhetoric that misleads the public and weakens the case for abolitionist demands.[8] This rhetoric obscures or naturalizes systems of oppression facing large numbers of people. Rather than attack the processes that make up these systems and underscore the disadvantages they create, it partly or wholly ignores both, enabling opponents of abolition to defend the status quo more easily. Deb's ill-conceived disavowal of the "drug dealers" and "prostitutes" in Jeff's neighborhood exemplified this type of rhetoric. Her disavowal implicitly endorsed Jeff's moral condemnation of these individuals and obscured the systems that, in fact, pushed them into dangerous work, foreclosure-related evictions, and other forms of financial and housing insecurity. Moreover, it missed an opportunity to explain how, by addressing those systems, social-democratic policies like a moratorium could also *reduce* crimes associated with drug dealing.[9]

As with their tendency to embrace moderate rather than abolitionist demands, many organizers attribute their use of misleading rhetoric to forces beyond their control. Most commonly, they blame societal ignorance about the injustices facing disadvantaged groups. As political scientist Sanford Schram has explained, when organizers like Deb encounter such ignorance, they often conclude that they have no choice but to work around it.[10] So they try to make their constituents seem more relatable, more like individuals whose experiences their audiences *do* understand. In Deb's case, she encountered an audience of liberal northsiders who—like many neoliberal-era progressives—did not fully understand the unjust market processes affecting their lower-income neighbors, particularly those of color. And she concluded that the most sensible response was to talk as if these lower-income people were actually no different from "good" middle-class tenants and homeowners—

except that they had been victimized by predatory lending and cyclical unemployment.

Social movement research about "discursive opportunity structures" tends to confirm Deb's instincts.[11] This research suggests that dominant public discourses determine the rhetoric organizers can effectively use to reach audiences and articulate disadvantaged groups' interests. It also implies that discourses marked by ignorance about widespread injustices will prove especially limiting.[12] As this ignorance spreads, it enervates potentially important arguments and justifications for change. For example, the ignorance about market injustice embodied by people like Jeff has made rhetorical attacks on many of capitalism's very real moral disasters sound confusing and unintelligible.[13] According to the theory of discursive opportunity structures, this ignorance denies organizers like Deb the chance to successfully deploy such attacks, though they might want to.

This explanation—like the similar one for why organizers assemble contentious identities around moderate demands—is insightful but incomplete. It is true that public audiences are frequently ignorant about systemic injustice and that, in the neoliberal era, they have been especially ignorant about the market-based roots of that injustice.[14] This ignorance is an unignorable hazard of contemporary efforts to represent disadvantaged groups. Left uncorrected, I will show, it leads people to misunderstand and reject oppositional rhetoric. Nevertheless, the claim that this fact on its own blocks effective attempts to deploy such rhetoric is too strong. At their best, organizers can countervail societal ignorance about injustice.[15] They can label this ignorance, educate audiences, and slowly—albeit never easily, perfectly, or indefinitely—*expand* opportunities to publicize contentious identities using oppositional rhetoric. Indeed, as scholarship from multiple fields has shown, educating the public about systemic oppression is one of the main contributions that social justice organizations can make to movements for freedom and equality.[16]

So, then, why don't they do that more often? The rest of this chapter seeks to answer this question. It shows how, in practice, societal ignorance about oppression leads social justice organizations—even some that, like the Bailout Coalition, support abolitionist demands—to publicize contentious identities using misleading rhetoric. It also clarifies how organizers can instead push themselves to embolden oppositional rhetoric that identifies the failures of the status quo and clarifies the need for abolitionism. To get at these questions, it analyzes the public activities of the Bailout Coalition and the Welfare Rights Committee, comparing how they differently publicized contentious identities on behalf of their constituents.

Again, the heart of my argument has to do with the political "etiquettes" that guide organizers' collective actions. I contend that, in carrying out public activities like protests and community meetings, neoliberal-era organizers feel great pressure to treat societal ignorance about market oppression *as if* it were immutable, thereby predisposing themselves to deploy misleading rhetoric. The reason for this is that this ignorance affects not only conservatives and centrists but also progressives, whose assistance social justice proponents desperately need; while educating such ignorant progressives is possible, the easiest way to avoid confusing them is to accept their ignorance as given.

I demonstrate that the Bailout Coalition followed this process, undermining their ability to deploy oppositional rhetoric and defend their abolitionist calls for a moratorium on foreclosure-related evictions. At the same time, returning to the case of the Welfare Rights Committee, I also demonstrate that organizers can foster etiquettes that weaken the draw of misleading rhetoric. These etiquettes prioritize long-term struggles to redress societal ignorance. They encourage organizers to educate rather than appease their audiences and, thus, create opportunities to publicize contentious identities in ways that bolster, rather than obscure, the case for abolitionist demands.

ABOLITIONISM'S RHETORICAL UNDERPINNINGS

What, in general, does effective oppositional rhetoric look like? What kinds of contentious identity constructions does it tend to invoke? In a nutshell, oppositional rhetoric invokes the same kinds of contentious identities as abolitionist demands themselves. More precisely, it articulates identities that are both intersectional (rather than unitary) and adversarial (rather than cooperative).[17] They are intersectional because they speak to injustices that cut across as well as differentiate disadvantaged groups, and they are adversarial because they rationalize challenges to, instead of participation in, the social systems that enable and drive these injustices.

In the case of the Bailout Coalition, oppositional rhetoric would have gone beyond addressing the predatory lending practices and recessionary layoffs that most easily differentiated many "poor and working" foreclosure victims (a highly unitary frame). It would have also addressed longer-term, market-based, and racialized systems of labor exploitation, neighborhood disinvestment, and housing discrimination. Under the rule of neoliberalism and poverty deconcentration, these systems became more extreme, decreased access to decent jobs and housing, and, in fact, enabled the later spikes in predatory and subprime lending and cyclical unemployment.[18] They also pushed substantial numbers of "poor and working people"—disproportionately African Americans, Native Americans, and Latinos—into foreclosure-related evictions as early as the 1990s, well before high-cost lending reached its peak and the Great Recession began.[19]

By invoking intersectional and adversarial logics, oppositional rhetoric strengthens the case for abolitionist demands. It broadcasts the moral failures to which measures like a moratorium on foreclosure-related evictions or subsidized and public housing development are a rational response. It cannot, on its own, provoke a widespread and winnable political conflict around these measures, but it provides what political scientist Murray Edelman called the "language of resistance" needed to articulate and organize such a conflict.[20] Organizers who use it well can fitfully loosen public resistance and sow public openness to their most abolitionist aspirations, whereas organizers who abandon it rescind their capacity to do either.[21]

With the foregoing insights in mind, it becomes important to ask why so many social justice organizers nevertheless drift toward rhetoric that fails to publicize contentious identities on intersectional and adversarial lines. The next section picks up this question. It explains how societal ignorance about market oppression pressures contemporary organizers to fall back on rhetoric that either ignores important, crosscutting economic injustices or obscures the broader, market-based roots of these injustices. Specifically, it explains how this ignorance creates conditions in which users of oppositional, anti-market rhetoric can easily sound unintelligible or overly radical to important audiences, including progressive advocates, policy makers, and voters. Organizers, thus, face strong incentives to moderate themselves and weaken the public case for abolitionist demands.

THE DANGER OF BEING MISUNDERSTOOD

Ignorance about market oppression, as I will show, does not inherently constrain how social justice organizers publicize contentious identities. Nonetheless, organizers are correct to treat such ignorance as a major political hazard. Since the onset of the neoliberal era, American political institutions have successfully promoted its spread by idealizing marketization—that is, by equating market expansion and market rule with the achievement of freedom and equality. In Minneapolis this idealization occurred largely through the pursuit of poverty deconcentration. Neoliberal deconcentration initiatives—like the *Hollman* settlement, the Choice Is Yours program, and the promotion of public–private development projects in high-poverty neighborhoods—implied that intensifying low-income individuals' market participation could remediate long-standing and racialized economic inequalities. A subset of these initiatives—such as the demolition of the Sumner-Glenwood public housing units and the slow erosion of state welfare benefits—went even further, treating redistributive programs as *barriers* to freedom and equality and thus limiting the scope of progressivism to bolstering market participation with various protections and supports.

Throughout the 1990s and early 2000s, the foregoing process of idealization helped to erase market oppression from public deliberation and consciousness. This erasure affected not only conservative individuals but also social justice organizations' potential allies, including everyone from progressive government officials to nonprofit advocates and community activists. As I demonstrated in chapter 3, leaders in all of these groups adopted discourses that perpetuated market oppression's erasure, and until economic inequality became a bigger issue in the mid-2010s they typically faced little if any serious recourse for doing so. For example, many of Minneapolis's progressive officials unreflectively deployed a crude "identity politics" discourse, which ignored the oppressive consequences of market-based systems like gentrification, deunionization, and the city's racialized and gendered divisions of labor. This discourse treated constituencies such as foreclosure victims and welfare recipients as discrete minority groups in need of legal protection from chiselers, bigots, and other unscrupulous individuals. It lacked any conception of disadvantaged individuals as members of a heterogeneous working class who are perpetually in thrall to powerful market actors and in need of downward redistribution.

In addition to crude identity politics, advocates and activists also perpetuated a "respectability politics" discourse, which had similar effects. The *truly* disadvantaged, this discourse suggested, were virtually the same as "normal" middle-class people, except that they had endured an exceptional injustice or misfortune. Jeff offered such an account during the Bailout Coalition's community forum when he framed the *true* foreclosure victims as "good" people who had fallen on hard times and casted those with sketchy employment histories and chronic housing problems as miscreants.

In conjunction with the dominance of capitalist realism, overall ignorance about market oppression predisposed many people to misunderstand oppositional rhetoric, regardless of how well articulated it was. As I will show, these misunderstandings could—like people's overall hostility toward abolitionist demand-making—take different forms. Sometimes, in my research, they centered on oppositional rhetoric's intersectional trappings—particularly its tendency to blame disadvantaged groups' problems on crosscutting economic injustices such as labor exploitation and housing discrimination. For individuals ignoring market oppression, attacks on such economic injustices could easily sound like attempts to excuse the bad behavior of society's dregs. At other times, misunderstandings of oppositional rhetoric centered on its adversarial side—particularly its tendency to frame ending market supremacy as a necessary step toward redressing all injustice (economic or otherwise). To the ears of someone wrapped up in identitarian or respectability politics, calls to end market supremacy could easily sound like the rantings of a crazy radical, a person hell-bent on attacking political-economic norms that are *not* fundamentally inimical to social justice. Whatever the case, organizers' target audiences were often unprepared to appreciate pro-abolition rhetoric and identity constructions.

Both types of misunderstanding were legion among the centrist and right-wing politicians faced by groups like the Bailout Coalition and the Welfare Rights Committee. One such politician was Joe Atkins, a white lawyer and centrist Democrat. From 2003 to 2016, Atkins served in the Minnesota House, representing a mostly middle-class and suburban area to the south of St. Paul. More importantly, in 2009 and 2010 he chaired the House Committee on Commerce and Labor, a committee that the Bailout Coalition needed to approve their moratorium proposal. As chair he professed great concern for lower-income foreclosure victims, but he dismissed any rhetorical suggestion that widespread foreclosures reflected an endemic failure of market rule and a need for more socialized and democratic control of housing. He interpreted these suggestions as unnecessarily radical and used this interpretation to justify blocking the coalition's moratorium proposals.[22] Prior to becoming chair, in October 2007, he told a meeting of the Minnesota

Bankers Association—a statewide lobbying group representing 95 percent of Minnesota's banks—that proponents of a moratorium and other social-democratic interventions were ignoring "what the market can do on its own."[23] Moreover, at the start of his chairmanship in 2009, as foreclosures and unemployment continued to climb, he reaffirmed this position, telling a local reporter that "I think banks are getting a bad rap" from left-wing activists.[24]

When the Republican Party gained control of Minnesota's legislature in 2011, centrist committee chairs like Atkins were replaced by right-wing ideologues with even less awareness of the market forces holding down disadvantaged groups—and even more propensity to misunderstand rhetorical opposition to neoliberal capitalism. For example, one of these ideologues was Steve Gottwalt, a white corporate consultant who took over as chair of the House Committee on Health and Human Services Reform (which hears all proposed legislation related to social welfare programs). From the chair position, Gottwalt—who also had ties to the pro-business American Legislative Exchange Council—pushed several bills that Welfare Rights Committee members saw as unjust. In 2011 he pushed a bill that would have prevented welfare recipients from withdrawing more than twenty dollars in cash assistance from ATM machines, required them to present photo identification when using their EBT cards, and restricted new residents' access to state welfare programs for ninety days. Put simply, the bill would have further stigmatized and limited poor individuals' access to cash outside the labor market. In doing so, it would have also made poor and working-class people as a whole more vulnerable to exploitation at the hands of employers, landlords, and lenders. Furthermore, it would have validated discrimination against the groups associated with cash welfare assistance, such as women of color, single mothers, people with disabilities, and women fleeing domestic violence.

To Gottwalt's ears, though, anyone highlighting or hinting at these facts was trying to protect welfare cheats. During the bill's hearing, he expressed disbelief toward legislators and testifiers—including a member of the Welfare Rights Committee—who suggested that it would contribute to social injustice.[25] When one testifier, a Legal Aid attorney named Jessica Webster, claimed that bill supporters were using the bad behavior of a few to justify "punishing" all low-income families, Gottwalt interrupted her—something he did to no one else—and initiated the following exchange:

GOTTWALT: I need to ask you for clarification on this. You mentioned that it's punishing people. Um, I'm not hearing that. I'm hearing that this is more akin to saying everybody will . . . stay between the lines. . . . Help me understand how that's punishing people, by limiting [their access to cash benefits]?

WEBSTER: . . . My view of punishment is not being able to access a federal benefit that you have been given. Um, I guess I could ask you, Mr. Chair, if you could no longer get your salary in cash, but you could only get twenty dollars of your salary and the rest of it had to be on a card, would *you* view that as a punishment?

GOTTWALT: I'm not sure that that's the model we're talking about here . . . frankly.

In posing his question, Gottwalt maintained a puzzled look on his face; when Webster challenged him, he and other GOP legislators began to chuckle, as if her challenge was so preposterous that it did not merit a serious response.[26]

The ignorance and misunderstandings of centrist and right-wing politicians were certainly hazardous for social justice organizers. However, regardless of what these politicians knew or understood, most of them were never going to support abolitionist proposals in any case. As leaders of both the Bailout Coalition and the Welfare Rights Committee would attest, the far more frustrating patterns of ignorance and misunderstanding were those that predominated among progressives—that is, people who could potentially support policies like a two-year moratorium on foreclosure-related evictions or an expansion of welfare benefits.

In this chapter and chapter 3, I have given examples of progressive officials and nonprofit advocates with little awareness of market oppression and a high propensity to misunderstand oppositional rhetoric. One is obviously Jeff, who challenged Deb and the Bailout Coalition's anti-eviction efforts. To reiterate, Jeff was not a conservative or even a moderate nonprofit professional. He probably would have described himself as an advocate for racial and economic justice; beyond his work in mortgage counseling, he had also served as an anti-predatory-lending organizer for the Minnesota branch of ACORN, which—before right-wing attacks brought it down 2010—was the country's best-known progressive community organization.[27] At the same time, though, his ignorance about market oppression predisposed him to hear serious attacks on market rule as too radical. It also led him to treat complaints about market-based discrimination and exploitation as excuses for poorly behaved residents of his neighborhood.

State senator Linda Higgins, whom I introduced at the outset of chapter 3, is another example. As a reminder, Higgins represented north Minneapolis, a position she held from 1997 until 2012. Any fair observer would have considered her one of the state's most important progressive legislators. In the early stages of the housing crash, she worked with nonprofit advocates like Jeff to pass the country's strongest anti-predatory-lending and foreclosure-prevention laws. She also spearheaded legislative efforts to reduce the spread of toxic waste, a major concern for north Minneapolis's low-income residents.[28] However, as I demonstrated in chapter 3, she sometimes embraced a crude identity politics that ignored the oppressive market conditions facing her disadvantaged constituents; consequently, she was also prone to misunderstanding rhetorical attacks on economic injustice and market supremacy. In January 2011, when the Welfare Rights Committee met with her to discuss the upcoming legislative session, she actually *endorsed* the idea of requiring welfare recipients to present government-issued photo identification when using EBT "cash cards." From her identitarian perspective, this legislation would have protected deserving welfare recipients from thieves—what she called "big guys"—trying to steal their cards and pilfer the benefits. When committee members complained that, in practice, an identification requirement would have worsened the market-based harms facing single mothers and people with disabilities, she responded with confusion and incredulity.[29]

The ignorance and misunderstandings coming from progressive leaders like Jeff and Higgins extended down to community activists from the lower-income areas of north and south Minneapolis. For example, throughout my research I met multiple progressive and middle-class homeowners in north Minneapolis who shared Jeff's perspective. One of them—another white man and liberal activist—told me that "the foreclosure crisis helped us out" and improved the neighborhood by "clear[ing] out" some of the "riff-raff"; he thought that the oppositional rhetoric surrounding the crisis went "too far." Another—a Black man, nonprofit professional, and antiracism activist—thought that left-wing organizers placed too much blame on housing, lending, and job markets and not enough on the fact that "a lot of people bought a lot of shit they couldn't afford."

Other activists reiterated Higgins's perspective and, like her, had trouble understanding criticisms of market processes holding down the city's poorest residents. One such activist was Stevie, a middle-aged African American woman with whom I had knocked on doors for the North High Coalition. She was a longtime northsider and frequently volunteered for progressive community organizations. Yet she shared Higgins's mistaken tendency to blame neighborhood criminals, whom she called "slicksters," for the harm incurred by her community. She even dabbled in a long-standing and racist myth that most of these "slicksters" were socially dysfunctional individuals migrating to Minneapolis from majority-minority cities. One day she told me:

> I'm going to give you the dirty low down. . . . A lot of people around here are slicksters. . . . And it's mostly people who came into the north side from other places. You know, the number of people who are natives, north Minneapolis natives, is not that many. It used to be the case around here that if someone was acting up, you'd tell that someone's family and they would tell that someone to get in order. But when these new people came here from everywhere else, they'd usually be without their extended family. . . . And these people coming in were from St. Louis, New Orleans, Chicago, some fast cities. . . . And they'll try to take you for a ride. And, see, when these people came and started doing their thing here, people in this city did not know what to do. And everybody was just running around from about, oh, the 1980s to 2000.

Stevie's perspective was infused with sincere care for her community and a profound desire to address its problems. However, it also erased the racialized market processes behind those problems, which had harmed "slicksters" and "north Minneapolis natives" alike. Moreover, it left her unable to appreciate criticisms of such processes. When, in response to her comment, I mentioned the poverty deconcentration programs that had worsened the market oppression facing African American northsiders, she mistakenly thought I was trying to *commend* these programs for removing what she called "the bad element."[30]

Such misunderstandings place a great deal of pressure on social justice organizers. Especially because these misunderstandings come from potential allies as well as opponents, it is usually easier for organizers to just work around them. Doing so—taking societal ignorance about market oppression as a given—is the most straightforward way to avoid looking like crazy radicals or defenders of immoral behavior. Such an etiquette, however, also requires organizers to silence intersectional and adversarial claims against market oppression. It pushes them to publicize contentious identities on more conventional and misleading terms, thereby, shoring up the neoliberal status quo and weakening abolitionist demands. The next section shows that the Bailout Coalition, despite its valiant and impressive efforts, fell into precisely this trap.

MISLEADING THE PUBLIC

Organizers in the Bailout Coalition could have redressed instead of accommodated public ignorance about the market-based roots of "poor and working people's" oppression. In other words, they could have done what the best organizers have always done: educate.[31] They could have debunked false stories told by activists like Jeff—explaining, for example, that mortgage counseling and other market-friendly efforts actually *failed* to help even the lion's share of "good" foreclosure victims. More importantly, coalition organizers could have developed alternative stories that illuminated the causal links between market processes like deunionization and segregation and the spread of foreclosure-related evictions. These stories would have clarified how such processes constricted access to decent jobs and fairly priced housing, compelling many individuals—particularly Black individuals—to either use risky mortgages to buy "a lot of shit they couldn't afford" or rent from financially unstable landlords. They would have challenged the assumption that capitalist markets can uphold social justice, and by teaching people to see the overthrow of market supremacy as a moral necessity, they would have emboldened oppositional rhetoric.

There were moments when coalition organizers adopted such an educative role. In particular, they often debunked myths about the efficacy of market-friendly foreclosure policies and programs. For example, at the Urban League forum, one of them, Peter—an elderly white man and volunteer lawyer with the Minnesota Tenants Union—cogently established that mortgage counseling in Minnesota had been an abysmal failure. "In 2008," he explained, "twenty-six thousand foreclosures were not stopped [and] five thousand were through mortgage counseling. That's 16 percent." As he pointed out in other settings, this failure occurred even though both Minnesota in general and Minneapolis specifically had relatively well-funded counseling programs.[32] After Peter, Deb established that the state and city's formal protections for tenants of foreclosed properties had also failed. This was, again, even though tenant protections in Minneapolis and Minnesota were comparatively robust.[33] "Poor and working" renters, Deb argued, continued to lose money and experience displacement through the foreclosure process. They "put down damage deposits, first month [payments]" without "even knowing [the property] is in foreclosure," and "then all of a sudden" found themselves "out on the street."

When confronted with these facts, even Jeff had to concede that the state's progressive but neoliberal approach to preventing foreclosure-related evictions was leaving behind many "good" people. He admitted outright that "we"—the proponents of mortgage counseling—"need to do better" at stopping home foreclosures. He also acknowledged that "there really isn't a good way to track [landlord behavior] and enforce" the city's and state's evolving (and somewhat complicated) protections for tenants of foreclosed properties.

By debunking myths about mortgage counseling and formal tenant protections, the coalition went part of the way toward boosting their audiences'—especially their progressive audiences'—appreciation of market oppression. The problem was that they never moved beyond debunking myths. They never publicly developed counternarratives that clarified why market-friendly measures were *bound* to fail many "poor and working people." They never showed how market dynamics unleashed by years of poverty deconcentration had exacerbated their constituents' vulnerability to exploitation, discrimination, and predation at the hands of employers, landlords and lenders—a setup that, as early as the 1990s, placed many people at risk of foreclosure-related eviction.[34]

As a result, their audiences continued to ignore market rule's inherently oppressive consequences. Rather, for example, than blame the failures of mortgage counseling and tenant protections on the broad racialized patterns of job insecurity and housing unaffordability wrought by marketization, progressive advocates like Jeff could instead point their finger at technical issues. At the Urban League forum, Jeff suggested that these measures failed simply because he and other advocates were not effective enough at contacting at-risk homeowners and renters. In committee hearings at the state capitol, progressive officials similarly implied that counseling could succeed at a larger scale if they better identified and disseminated "best practices." These suggestions were wrong. No matter how well conceived, neither counseling nor consumer protections could get at structural problems with the labor and housing markets. Nevertheless, the coalition stopped short of forcefully and effectively making this point.

"Make the Rich Pay for Their Crisis!"

Why didn't the Bailout Coalition do more to redress the public's ignorance? The answer is not that its leaders lacked the general knowledge or desire to do so. Most of them were dedicated poor or working-class leftists who had long opposed capitalism and possessed an overall sense that socioeconomic disadvantage resulted from the entwinement of unjust market processes and other interlocking systems of oppression. Moreover, several of them participated in a cadre group, Freedom Road Socialist Organization, which had meticulously outlined and defended their ideas about market oppression in a number of collective statements.[35] Some of these statements spoke directly to the political-economic underpinnings of foreclosure-related evictions.[36] One of them even declared that, in the wake of the housing crash, "Opportunities for educating people about the true nature of [capitalist markets] are growing."[37]

Nor was the coalition was constrained by foundations or other donors. Like the Welfare Rights Committee, the Bailout Coalition had an intentionally weak and combative relationship with the nonprofit sector. Its only real grant-based funding came from the Headwaters Foundation, which—as I explained in chapter 4—was one of the very few foundations that supported radical and abolitionist politics. In addition to the Welfare Rights Committee, a handful of the coalition's member organizations regularly received Headwaters money. Beyond that, however, they worked independently of foundations, nonprofit leaders, and the like.

Nevertheless, the Bailout Coalition neglected to educate because, in practice, they assumed the public's overall ignorance was incorrigible. They adhered to an etiquette that, as I explain next, normalized this ignorance and encouraged them to work around it. On the surface, this etiquette was quite similar to that of the Welfare Rights Committee. It centered on "fighting back" against mainstream legislators, lobbyists, and socioeconomic elites. But whereas the Welfare Rights Committee's "fight"—introduced in chapter 4—was about political leaders' complicity with the "blood" sacrifices of the neoliberal welfare state, the Bailout Coalition's "fight" focused more specifically on their complicity with the ongoing economic "crisis." This "crisis," as the coalition described it, was a situation in which extremely high numbers of "poor and working people" were threatened with or experiencing job insecurity and foreclosure-related evictions, while society's well-to-do continued to thrive.

The emphasis on "fighting" for a resolution to the "crisis" permeated the coalition's collective actions and deliberations.[38] The very first sentence of their founding unity statement called on lawmakers to "Make the rich pay for their crisis," which "is condemning tens of millions of people [in the United States] to poverty, hunger, and homelessness." On one side of this crisis, they declared, was "a rising tide of home foreclosures, evictions, and layoffs." On the other side was a "host of politicians" looking to "enact legislation that serves the self-serving interests of corporations and the wealthy" and "push the burden of the crisis onto [poor and working people's] backs." Their guiding purpose, the statement concluded, was to "[come] together to meet the effects/challenges of this crisis head on." This sense of purpose carried into their strategy meetings, where organizers at least implicitly determined how much energy to spend on different agenda items by evaluating how directly each one related to the "crisis." It also found its way into their proposed moratorium legislation, which formally declared a state of "economic emergency" to justify halting foreclosure-related evictions.

Within the Bailout Coalition, this "crisis"-centered etiquette allowed organizers to construe "poor and working people's" interests on intersectional and adversarial terms and endorse a two-year moratorium on foreclosure-related evictions. Because of their familiarity with leftist thought, most of them intuited that the "crisis" stemmed from a range of crosscutting injustices, including not just short-term spikes in predatory lending and recessionary layoffs but also deep-rooted patterns of racialized discrimination and exploitation on the part of lenders, landlords, and employers. The coalition's leaders also understood that these crosscutting injustices largely derived from broader market processes that, under neoliberal governance, had reduced "poor and working people's" access to decent employment and affordable housing, most excessively impairing racial minorities at the bottom of Minneapolis's social order. Consequently, in their collective mind, ending the "crisis" required nothing less than a series of inclusive and democratic impingements on market supremacy, beginning with something like a sweeping moratorium proposal. In determining their agenda, they did not necessarily lay out this thought sequence explicitly.[39] But they did not need to. It was implied by the anticapitalist perspective they shared. Moreover, in 2009 and 2010 it was carefully articulated in a series of Freedom Road statements about the "crisis," which at least a few coalition leaders read.[40]

In public, however, the Bailout Coalition's focus on "fighting" to "make the rich pay for their crisis" had much less abolitionist consequences. Unlike coalition organizers, members of the public tended—because of their ignorance—to see the rise in foreclosure-related evictions as an exceptional event with exceptional causes, rather than one connected to longer-term, racialized market processes. In progressive circles, leaders and commentators reduced the foreclosure-related evictions happening among lower-income people almost entirely to post-2000 spikes in predatory lending and recessionary layoffs. In legislative hearings, op-eds, and other public venues they typically made one or both of these issues their sole focus, ignoring the foreclosure situation's link to other injustices and market processes.[41] During a January 2010 committee hearing about the coalition's moratorium proposal, one of Minnesota's most progressive state senators encapsulated this view, matter-of-factly summarizing the moment as one in which "sometimes people got scammed into bad mortgages"—or, for renters, leases on properties purchased with bad mortgages—and "sometimes it's just the recession and they lost their job, and they can't pay it." At the time, this reductive view was so accepted among progressives and leftists that nobody thought to question or push beyond it.

The coalition's "crisis"-centered etiquette accommodated and affirmed the public's tendency to treat the rise in foreclosure-related evictions as an exceptional event. It also pushed organizers to indulge this tendency when communicating with different audiences. At every public event I attended they presented themselves as a group trying to protect "poor and working people" from the fallout of predatory high-cost lending and cyclical unemployment. When organizers spoke, they framed the "crisis" as more of a transitory than inherent feature of market rule. They referenced "having our houses pulled out from under our feet" and being "thrown out into the streets" because people were "trapped into bad, bad loans that are becoming these balloon payments," hit with "layoffs," and pulled into agreements with landlords "who don't even tell us" about being in foreclosure; consequently, they defined their appropriate role as being "on the street," "at the [state] capitol," "in the politicians' faces," and "at the doors where houses are being foreclosed on" so that "poor and working people" can "get through" the temporarily bad times without "slipping" or "falling behind." The goal of "making the rich pay" and pursuing a "people's bailout," they implied, was to alleviate these surface-level issues and achieve some sort of return to normalcy (as opposed to, say, enacting a durable expansion of affordable housing rights and redistribution of economic power—their actual goals).

To be sure, the coalition, as a "fighting" organization, typically presented the "crisis" on much more impassioned terms than their mainstream progressive counterparts—employing words like "insane," "crazy," and "criminal" to describe its effects. Nevertheless, they built their etiquette around the same basic story, about ordinary people losing their shirts due to the momentary collapse of the lending, housing, and labor markets. Moreover, they did so despite privately understanding as well as any Marxist economist that the "crisis" also derived from the normal and racialized workings of those markets.

At times, coalition leaders gestured toward a broader and more transformative vision of their "fight." Peter, at the Urban League forum, made one such gesture. Toward the beginning of his presentation, as a way of connecting to northsiders in the audience, he referenced the Minnesota Tenants Union's efforts in the 1990s to resist the *Hollman* settlement and defend the Sumner-Glenwood public housing units. After reviewing these efforts, he offered the following comment as a segue to the coalition's organizing around foreclosure-related evictions:

> It seems to me every decade has its particular way—the status quo finds a way to be particularly harsh and oppressive to low-income and working people. And what the *Hollman* resistance was for the mid-nineties, it seems to me the foreclosure crisis is to our age. And it is up to us to be finding ways to be putting our shoulders together to find ways to resist that kind of oppressive pushing around.

Peter's comment hinted that the housing problems during the Great Recession stemmed from Minneapolis's turn to poverty deconcentration and neoliberalism in the 1990s ("the status quo"); in particular, it took aim at the disappearance of public and affordable housing that this turn portended.

The most left-wing politicians working with the Bailout Coalition sometimes made similar gestures. One such politician was Scott Dibble, a white man and left-wing state legislator from St. Paul. Dibble—himself a former organizer for ACT-UP (AIDS Coalition to Unleash Power) and other progressive groups—sponsored the coalition's moratorium bill across multiple legislative sessions. Toward the end of one of the bill's hearings, almost as an afterthought, he made the following comment:

> People's credit has been devastated . . . because Congress hasn't gotten its act together and enacted health-care reform, in large part, [and] because Minnesota hasn't gotten its act together and established some aggressive approaches to economic development and keeping our incomes up and keeping jobs coming. . . . So, people are losing their jobs, they're encountering bankruptcy circumstances for reasons that are way beyond their own control and the response is important to be a public policy response. That's why we have representative democracy and government in the first place. When the market fails people, when the systems fail people, we need to even the playing field somehow. Because there's no way to overcome . . . powerful corporate forces and overarching economic forces that just kind of sweep people around in their tide.

This comment was remarkable for how directly it criticized neoliberal-era political institutions for reproducing long-term market oppression and, in doing so, generating the mortgage and employment "crisis."

Mostly, however, such gestures received little attention and consideration. Peter's comment, as I said, was more of a segue or an aside than an invitation to explore the racialized and oppressive market processes underlying foreclosure-related evictions. Its implications were never spelled out for the audience, by Peter or anyone else. The same was true of comments like Senator Dibble's. The most remarkable feature of these comments was how infrequent they were and how little discussion they generated. To an average observer of the coalition, "fighting back" against complicity with the "crisis" simply meant alleviating the harms done by predatory and subprime lending and recessionary layoffs.

"They Were Lied to" after "Working for Years and Years and Years"

The Bailout Coalition's "fight" to end the "crisis" left little room for publicizing "poor and working people's" interests using oppositional—that is, intersectional and adversarial—rhetoric. By normalizing the public's ignorance about structural and racialized market oppression, they unintentionally helped to ensure that such rhetoric would remain unintelligible. None of the coalition's leaders would have actively silenced a supporter who used it, but as a group they could not prioritize it. Their most pressing need, rhetorically, was to establish that "poor and working" foreclosure victims were sympathetic casualties of aggressive high-cost lending and spiking unemployment—the definitive "crisis" issues.

To meet this need, the Bailout Coalition deployed a generic populist, or anti-elitist, rhetoric. This rhetoric positioned "poor and working" foreclosure victims as an embattled and homogeneous class who had been purposefully driven into high-cost loans and mass layoffs by "banks," "the rich," and "billionaires" looking to turn a profit. For example, Linden—a white working-class woman and coalition founder—kicked off the group's Urban League forum with, among other things, a statement about how "banks" had pushed "poor and working people" toward "crisis" by "kicking [victims of subprime lending, including tenants] out of their homes" and "denying credit to our businesses and making us lose our jobs"—all while taking "trillions" in "bailout" money from the federal government. The coalition's call for a "people's bailout" was, she explained, a response to this situation. So was the group's main chant, "Bail out the people, not the banks!"—different versions of which appeared on most of their fliers.

Other coalition activists built on the rhetorical frame outlined by leaders like Linden. "[Poor and working] people, we didn't do this to ourselves," one activist undergoing foreclosure insisted during a summer 2010 rally. "The banks did this to the people in pursuit of big big bucks! And now it's time to rise up against these parasites!" Standing in front of her foreclosed home—the site of the rally—this activist insisted that economic elites caused evictions among "poor and working people" by fomenting "this darn [subprime] mortgage crisis." In a media interview, another coalition activist emphasized that "banks" were taking "trillions" of "our tax dollars" while refusing to "bail out" the "millions of [poor and working] people" they had subjected to "dire straits" involving risky loans and cyclical unemployment.

The coalition's populist rhetoric was overtly adversarial. It suggested that a broad and corrupt system or set of systems had allowed banks and other "parasites" to unscrupulously and sometimes even criminally push "poor and working people" into foreclosure-related evictions. And it implied that defending those people would require somehow transforming the status quo. At the same time, however, their

Occupy the Capitol Rally

on Opening Day of MN State Legislature

Stop the Attacks on the 99%

STOP Foreclosures!

Housing is a right!

Get ready to fight for our bill to put a **2-Year Moratorium (a halt) on Foreclosures and Evictions** in MN. We will also have a bill to **Tax the Rich**! It's time to make the politicians do something for the PEOPLE!

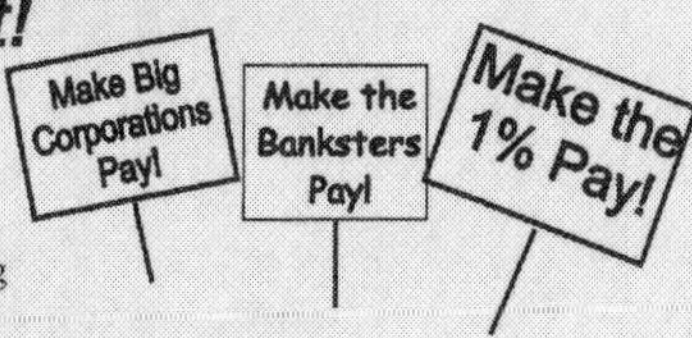

Make the RICH pay for their Crisis: Tax the Rich!

Bail Out People, Not the Billionaires!

Protest

Tuesday, Jan. 24

12 noon to 1 pm

St. Paul State Capitol

Organized by the Minnesota Coalition for People's Bailout and the Welfare Rights Committee.
Initial endorsers include: ADAPT MN, AFSCME Council 5, AFSCME Local 3800, Anti-War Committee, Communities United Against Police Brutality, General Assembly of OccupyMpls, Marriage Equality Minnesota, MN Immigrant Rights Action Committee, MN Neighborhoods Organizing for Change (NOC), MN Nurses Association (MNA), MN Tenants Union, MN Peace Action Coalition, Occupy the Hood, Occupy Saint Paul Tactical Working Group, Poor Peoples Economic Human Rights Campaign, Saint Paul Regional Labor Federation, Students Association for the Advancement of Children as People (SAACP), Students for Democratic Society (SDS), Twin Cities Peace Campaign, United Food And Commercial Worker Union Local 1189, Universal Health Care Action Network of MN, Women Against Military Madness (WAMM)

MN Coalition for a People's Bailout -
Welfare Rights Committee - - *Look for us on Facebook*

Bailout Coalition outreach flier.

rhetoric could not truly be oppositional toward the systems of oppression holding down "poor and working" foreclosure victims, because it reduced those systems almost entirely to rapacious lending practices and the Great Recession per se. It obscured the longer-term and racialized market processes that presaged and transcended the "crisis." It was, in a word, color-blind.[42]

The color-blindness—and, thus, unitary logic—of the coalition's rhetoric showed in how it ignored the experiences of many "poor and working" people of color, who often fell into foreclosure problems for reasons beyond the widely recognized "crisis." For example, Deb's response to Jeff at the Urban League forum ignored that many lower-income and non-white foreclosure victims had *not* been caught up in predatory lending schemes or laid off from decent jobs during the recession. Because of long-term and racialized market oppression, at least some of the "drug dealers" and "prostitutes" mentioned by Jeff had never been adequately employed or in possession of enough income to afford either a traditional home loan or a lease on a decent and well-managed rental property.

This rhetorical pattern was not confined to impromptu remarks like those made by Deb. It also occurred in more prepared communications. One such communication was a media interview with five working-class women—two white, three Black—who were trying to stop foreclosures on their homes. The interview was twelve minutes long and produced by the Minnesota Poor People's Economic Human Rights Campaign, a group that the Bailout Coalition had teamed up with in defense of low- and moderate-income borrowers undergoing foreclosure. During the entire twelve minutes, the only time you hear the interviewer—a local Green Party politician and coalition supporter—speak, she says the following:

> It sounds that, um, many of you are working women or had a job but were working for years and years and years. And, you know, the stereotype out there is that, oh why don't they just get a job and pay off their mortgage. Well, first of all, we are working, number one. And number two, if we're not working, we were working but our economy went down and now it's difficult to find a job.

Like Deb's response to Jeff, the interviewer's comment sought to reassure ignorant audiences that "poor and working" foreclosure victims were respectable people who had simply fallen prey to the "crisis"—particularly the recession. It also ignored the experiences of constituents of color who, because of deunionization, racial divisions of labor and other market processes, had not been "working" as steady wage earners "for years and years and years."

The Bailout Coalition's populist rhetoric was not only color-blind in the sense that it ignored the experiences of non-white (and also white) foreclosure victims who suffered primarily from non-"crisis" injustices. It also mischaracterized the experiences of "poor and working" people of color who *had* suffered from these injustices. A good example is Tecora Parks, a lower-income resident of south Minneapolis whose home the coalition was defending. Tecora—a Black woman and retired hospital worker in her mid-sixties—had owned and occupied her home, a duplex, for over twenty years, living in the downstairs unit and renting the upstairs to her adult daughter Leslie. In 2009, however, she fell behind on her payments and entered foreclosure. This moment stemmed back to 2005, when she refinanced her standard fixed-rate mortgage with an adjustable-rate mortgage to pay for window upgrades and other repairs ordered by the city as part of its rental licensing process. Both Tecora and her daughter claim she was duped into signing the mortgage, which not only had an adjustable rate but was also negatively amortizing.[43] By the summer of 2010 she owed over $315,000 on a $288,000 loan, and as her interest rate adjusted her payments grew from less than $1,000 to almost $2,000. She and Leslie—a logistics coordinator for a local manufacturer—could not keep up.

In narrating Tecora's foreclosure experience, and in line with their overall rhetoric, coalition organizers mostly emphasized that a predatory lender had fraudulently sold her a subprime mortgage. As Deb summarized during a legislative hearing, "They [Tecora and Leslie] were lied to" and given a bad loan they did not want—even though, according to coalition statements, Tecora had "perfect credit." Leslie Parks herself, who spoke on her mother's behalf at public events, told a similar story. "This particular loan officer," she stated in one media interview, "was a total crook . . . because that mortgage that he wrote was an absolute crime." The long and the short of it, she concluded, was that her mother "got this goofy ARM that just basically put her in foreclosure." Organizers repeated this same "crisis"-centered narrative in their printed communications about the Parks family home.

Save the Parks Family Home!

Be READY to call IndyMac/OneWest

6-8-2010: Thanks to all of our work in the past and in gathering here today, IndyMac/OneWest is sounding like they want to come to the table. The Parks family is clear about what they need. IndyMac/OneWest is aware of their just demands. Now we'll see what really happens.

So, be READY to make these calls. When action is needed, we will send out emails, tweets and post info on our websites. If you are want to get a phone alert, call [redacted] to be put on the phone list. We very well may call for another action here at Leslie's.

Wait for the word to call

Terry Laughlin - CEO: [redacted]
Dave Garrett - VP of Corporate Customer Service: [redacted]
Steve Mnuchin - Chairman of the Board: [redacted] to leave a message

Be ready to Demand of IndyMac/OneWest...

1. Keep your promise! Rescind the foreclosure & sheriff's sale!
Even though IndyMac/OneWest stated in a letter dated Nov. 25, 2009, "*...we have started the process of rescinding the Trusteed Sale...*" they still have not done so!
Tell them to rescind the sheriff's sale and give Tecora Parks the title to her home!

2. Give the Parks family an affordable loan modification!
IndyMac/OneWest is trying to force the Parks to scramble for outside financing. This is wrong. IndyMac/OneWest was complicit in the fraudulent/scam ARM mortgage; they should be the ones to make it right to the Parks family.
The Parks need a 30-year fixed rate mortgage at an affordable rate, based on the home's current value.

Leslie Parks lives in south Minneapolis. Her family has owned the building for over 20 years. Because of needing to pay for city-ordered storm windows, the Parks family was swindled into getting an ARM (adjustable rate mortgage). The man from Allied Mortgage who sold the scam ARM lied and insisted it was a conventional loan. The Parks had perfect credit and qualified for a conventional loan hands down. But they were lied to, got swindled into an ARM (that particular kind of ARM is now illegal), and after months of trying to keep up, both Leslie and her mother lost their good credit and went into foreclosure.

The FDIC stepped in to bail out the IndyMac investors and gifted the bank to OneWest. They are reaping a corrupt "benefit" from the fraudulent practice of a mortgage broker that sold Tecora Parks on an ARM on behalf of IndyMac. They are making money off of a swindle. IndyMac thought it could make big bucks trying to steal this home, but it won't, because Leslie Parks has no intention of giving up!

"The banks messed up the system so bad and we the taxpayers bailed the banks out, with an expectation that the banks would help save people's homes. They took our money but refuse to modify people's loans so we can stay in our homes and save our communities!" says Leslie Parks.

We are sick of banks wrecking our communities. The banks were greedy gamblers. They should be the ones to pay.

Stop Foreclosures NOW!

MN Coalition for a People's Bailout: [redacted] **mn-peoples-bailout.org**
Poor People's Economic Human Campaign: [redacted] **mnppehrc.wordpress.com**

Bailout Coalition flier about the Parks family home.

What this narrative left out—what the coalition mentioned but barely discussed—was the reason *why* Tecora Parks needed a subprime mortgage in the first place: in an era of market rule, she could not otherwise afford necessary repairs on her home (she had to "buy a lot of shit" she "couldn't afford"). A combination of deunionization and racialized and gendered divisions in the local labor market had ensured that she and her daughter would lack the income to pay on their own.[44] And there was no community development or social-democratic government program to cover the cost for them.[45] In addition, while it is surely true that Tecora's lender—an unconventional broker—had scammed her into a subprime mortgage, the overall lending market did not necessarily grant her stellar options. Years of residential segregation and disinvestment had conspired to block families like the Parks from accessing conventional fixed-rate mortgages. They lived in a racially diverse and lower-income part of the city, where residents—especially Black residents—had less immediate access to banks offering such mortgages.[46] Moreover, even if Tecora's lender had given her a conventional fixed-rate mortgage, the interest rate probably would have exceeded what she could afford. During the year she refinanced, the average interest on thirty-year fixed-rate mortgages hovered close to 6 percent, which was about the same rate that her loan reached when she defaulted.[47]

Because of its color-blindness, the Bailout Coalition's rhetoric weakened and muddied their case for a moratorium on foreclosure-related evictions and expanded rights to affordable housing (a reminder that abolitionism needs intersectionality, not just adversarial critiques of political-economic arrangements). This rhetoric obscured the systemic injustices to which their moratorium proposal and other abolitionist measures were a justifiable response. And it underscored issues that could be addressed with much more moderate measures—such as mortgage and financial counseling, bans on high-cost subprime loans, a foreclosure deferment *only* for homes purchased with these loans, and increased consumer protections for tenants. If, as the coalition's rhetoric suggested, predatory lending and recessionary layoffs were the penultimate injustices facing "poor and working" foreclosure victims, then there was little reason to push beyond the foregoing measures. Furthermore, there was little reason to demand more aggressive action by the progressives in Minneapolis and the Minnesota state legislature—who, by 2009, had already implemented or backed all of these measures.

By insisting on their moratorium proposal anyway, Bailout Coalition organizers ran the risk of appearing disingenuous. Advocates like Jeff could easily point out that, although the coalition's rhetoric centered on "good" people harmed by the "crisis," their proposed moratorium served a much broader, more diverse, and seemingly less reputable constituency. And the only response organizers could offer was to insist, using ever more fervent terms, that halting all foreclosure-related evictions was simply the right thing to do. As Deb said at the forum, a moratorium was the only way "we're gonna take care of . . . the big issue—of housing crisis, our families that are being thrown into the street." When asked to publicly elaborate their thoughts, other organizers and activists issued some version of the same appeal. "They [banks and politicians] have to do the right thing" and support a moratorium, one of them commanded during a media interview, "or things will get worse and worse even for them." At a state legislative hearing, another coalition leader testified that the moratorium was "just plain common sense." "It doesn't cost the state a dime, saves the state money, saves the social fabric of our communities, and," she concluded, "it just makes sense." Such comments excited the proverbial choir but meant little to people for whom a moratorium did not already "make sense."[48]

In sum, the Bailout Coalition's "fight" to "make the rich pay for their crisis" led them into a counterproductive representational strategy. On the one hand, in the process of building this "fight" within their ranks they assembled an intersectional and adversarial contentious identity that commanded unwavering support for a sweeping moratorium and other abolitionist demands. On the other hand, in taking their "fight" to the public they used a homogenizing populist rhetoric that invoked a color-blind vision of "poor and working people" and made such demands seem unnecessary. By misleading rather than educating their ignorant audiences, they unintentionally weakened the laudable movement for affordable housing and against evictions that they so courageously supported. Today, although foreclosures have significantly declined, the market-based systems obscured by the coalition's rhetoric continue to push lower-income Minnesotans into risky home financing and rental arrangements—such as land installment contracts and rent-to-own schemes.[49] Furthermore, although—as I discuss in this book's conclusion—more and more local activists are starting to question market oppression, the coalition's rhetoric played a suboptimal role in raising those questions.

EDUCATING THE PUBLIC

As I have stated elsewhere, the Welfare Rights Committee was a close partner of the Bailout Coalition. In addition to being formal members of the coalition, several of the committee's organizers were also among the coalition's most active participants. At least one or two of them showed up to every coalition meeting (other organizations had one at most).

Committee organizers also regularly spoke at the coalition's rallies and protests. Indeed, the two groups regularly co-hosted these events. And perhaps most tellingly, the leaders of both groups were members of Freedom Road Socialist Organization, the regional network of Marxist-Leninist organizers I previously introduced. The connections between the two groups were so multitudinous that a casual observer could be excused for thinking they were the same. When I first started volunteering with the committee, one of its members even joked that the two groups were somewhat indistinguishable.

However, despite its connections to the Bailout Coalition, the Welfare Rights Committee publicized "poor and working people's" interests in a much different and more oppositional way. This difference germinated from the group's distinct approach to "fighting back," which focused less on economic "crisis" and more on the "blood" sacrifices perpetrated by the neoliberal welfare state.[50] As I demonstrated in chapter 4, "fighting back," for the committee, meant building popular anger toward political leaders who accepted and reproduced these sacrifices. Internally, their etiquette pushed them to check capitalist realism's influence so that they could more effectively rationalize such anger to themselves and their supporters. It also, thereby, allowed them to more easily unite around an abolitionist vision of "poor and working people's" interests and demand stronger welfare entitlements.

Similarly, on the public stage the committee's "fighting" etiquette prioritized incrementally but doggedly correcting societal ignorance about market oppression. Whereas the Bailout Coalition could pursue their "fight"—building anger around the economic "crisis"—without addressing this ignorance, the Welfare Rights Committee could not. It needed audiences to see marketization per se as a major source of injustice and a threat to many individuals' "blood" and "survival." Otherwise, the scope of their anger toward neoliberal welfare policy—including what they called the "kinder, gentler" versions of this policy—would seem unjustified. Progressive as well as conservative audiences would see no reason for the "fight," and pursuing it with any efficacy would be near impossible.

Committee leaders themselves underscored education's importance to winning their "fight" and advancing their demands. As one of their communications to potential members asserted, "The politicians have no idea what our lives are like." A crucial way to "join the fight," it added, was to publicly "Tell your story" about "how this [welfare] system has failed us, our family members or friends." In line with the Bailout Coalition, one goal of telling "your story" might be to highlight the "system's" unresponsiveness to the predatory lending and recessionary "crisis." But just as—if not more—important was highlighting the steady disappearance of decent unionized jobs and other deep-rooted, market-based threats to survival. They often called it giving "the big picture." "We're the only group," one of them stated, "that is willing to bring that big-picture perspective" about the constraints of market rule "and show why it's really not acceptable to do any cuts" or restrict access to cash and in-kind welfare benefits.

Giving "the Big Picture"

The Welfare Rights Committee exercised their commitment to giving "the big picture" in different ways. It began in strategy meetings, where committee leaders trained themselves and other activists to use public actions as instructional opportunities. Most of this training involved learning how to critique Minnesota's welfare policy landscape. As I covered in chapter 4, meeting chairs devoted substantial amounts of time to discussing the ways in which neoliberal welfare policies reproduced market-based and other systems of oppression. Throughout each discussion, committee leaders tacked back and forth between allowing members to share their own thoughts and linking these thoughts to general lessons—the "big picture"—that legislators, nonprofit advocates, journalists, and the general public needed to hear.[51] The biggest lesson—which came up over and over—was that "cuts" to cash and in-kind welfare assistance empowered "the rich" to more aggressively exploit "poor and working people."[52] But there were other lessons about the ways in which "fraud prevention" and "workfare" as well as "cuts" reproduced market-based (and also racialized and gendered) systems underlying labor exploitation, domestic abuse, and other injustices.

Subsequently, in public communications, committee members applied their training. As in the Bailout Coalition, part of this application involved debunking pro-market myths. One especially important myth—which had been used to justify all manner of neoliberal welfare restrictions—was that Minnesota's welfare programs were too generous and permissive. This myth featured prominently in the 2012 state legislative session, as politicians and advocates debated "Welfare Reform 2.0"—a pair of welfare bills geared toward limiting access to assistance and promoting labor market participation. The bills proposed a series of changes, such as restricting participation in the Minnesota Family Investment Program to a total of three years, lowering the amount of income a family can earn while collecting MFIP assistance and, in various ways, making it easier to disqualify individuals from receiving *any* state-funded welfare assistance. Their most vocal proponents—many of whom had ties to the American Legislative Exchange Council (ALEC)—asserted that Minnesota offered a "Cadillac plan" of welfare assistance, which attracted "a certain criminal element" from majority-minority cities like Chicago (Stevie's "slicksters") and undermined efforts to deconcentrate and eliminate poverty.[53] And the bills' primary sponsor, first-term legislator Kurt Daudt, argued that by "bringing our benefits in line with the state's around us"—that is, by restricting benefits—Welfare Reform 2.0 would create a "more cost-effective government" for "the taxpayer" and help to "protect [welfare] resources for people that really need them."[54]

In flier after flier, speech after speech, testimony after testimony, Welfare Rights Committee members debunked the myth of over-generosity and over-permissiveness. During one of Welfare Reform 2.0's legislative hearings, Angel—a working-class Black woman, mother of four, and longtime committee member—emphasized that state legislators had not increased MFIP cash payments since 1986. "For a family of three," she explained, "the cash MFIP grant is $532 per month. That is 60 percent below the poverty level. You try to find an apartment that will take a family of three for that kind of money." In a later hearing she described the "stress of trying to keep up with paperwork, trying to maneuver through each hoop to get through everything" while participating in programs like MFIP—something she knew from personal experience. She pointed out that recipients could receive sanctions—reductions in assistance—for the most minor mistakes, like missing a meeting or forgetting to submit a form. Against such facts, claims about generosity and permissiveness appeared completely fallacious.

Committee organizers also challenged many other market-friendly myths. One worth mentioning, because it was common among progressives, asserted that welfare recipients primarily needed greater opportunities for education and job training (the welfare policy equivalent of claiming that people at risk of foreclosure-related eviction primarily needed more financial counseling). Democratic officials and progressive advocates often framed training as the logical alternative to punitive reforms—the more empowering way to promote labor market participation and "self-sufficiency." In one of the Welfare Reform 2.0 hearings, Jessica Webster—the Legal Aid lawyer I introduced earlier—offered this perspective:

> It's not a nuclear secret anymore as to how to help people get off of assistance, which I think is the goal of probably everyone in this room. And it's education and training. The way that we turn $9-an-hour jobs into $17- and $18-an-hour jobs is education and training.

According to her and many other progressives, these statements were not only true but obviously so.

Committee organizers, however, regularly demonstrated their falsity. Angel, at the same hearing where Webster spoke, stressed that "tens of thousands of people with even degrees and high-level skills are having difficulty finding jobs." In addition, Darnella—a single Black mother and longtime committee member—explained how, even years after completing job training and leaving MFIP, she still found herself working for poverty-level wages. "I've been employed [in] various" low-end occupations, she explained, "including [jobs] like trash removal"; her most decent job, as a personal care attendant—which she had been doing for about ten years—barely allowed her to get by. At a small press conference the next day, Darlene—a low-income white woman and newer committee member—echoed these sentiments, announcing that "I actually have a master's degree, okay" but "wound up on MFIP because I had a medical crisis." She concluded, "Now I'm off and I'm . . . trying to make it with some part-time work." The message of all these comments was the same: for many people, education and training were not enough to deliver "$17- and $18-an-hour jobs" and end poverty.

Clearly, debunking pro-market myths was crucial to giving "the big picture." But the Welfare Rights Committee did not stop at that. They also replaced the myths with a counternarrative. More specifically, they acquainted audiences with the reality that post-1960s capitalist labor markets have not, as general rule, produced enough decent living-wage jobs—particularly for working-class women of color.[55] And they told a story about how the lack of decent work—not of discipline or training—was the main reason "poor and working people" in Minnesota and other states needed assistance.

This story was a prominent part of the committee's response to Welfare Reform 2.0. For example, Ebony, the very first committee member to testify at one of the bill's hearings, criticized legislators for ignoring the unavailability of good jobs. Speaking as, in her words, "a single mother of four kids in north Minneapolis" and "a domestic abuse survivor as well," she commented toward the start of her testimony that "I am one of many people that's been laid off, for the third time, and I have yet to hear anybody talk about livable wage jobs." She later added: "Most people that I know that are on welfare are working, but guess what? The jobs that are out here, they're only paying six, seven dollars an hour." And, unlike Bailout Coalition organizers, she neither stated nor implied that the lack of decent employment was strictly due to recession and economic "crisis."[56]

Angel—the second Welfare Rights Committee member to speak—elaborated Ebony's point, highlighting that, in boom or bust, adult welfare recipients tend to be people for whom decent jobs are least available.[57] Low-income single mothers are, she explained, the people who are "last hired at a workplace, which means they are the first fired" when the demand for labor shrinks. They are also the people, disproportionately Black and female, who—when they do find work—"have been working temp [and seasonal] jobs" and, as a result, usually make low wages and "don't have the right number of work quarters in the right time period to qualify for unemployment insurance." "Welfare," she concluded, "*is* the unemployment assistance for poor families."

Other committee organizers and activists told a similar story about welfare and work, not only in the debates over Welfare Reform 2.0 but throughout all their campaigns. In telling it, they did not usually label particular market-based processes that drove the unavailability of good jobs. But they did establish that this unavailability was one of the labor market's structural features and an unavoidable challenge for current, former, and potential welfare recipients. They also sometimes highlighted that the housing market—in conjunction with reductions in housing assistance—reinforced the inadequacy of work by forcing families to pay increasingly high prices for decent shelter.

Through their story about the lack of decent jobs, committee members showed audiences exactly why any neoliberal approach to welfare—including the "kinder, gentler" approach—would threaten the "survival" and "blood" of ordinary people. Lowering assistance levels and pressing low-income single mothers and other recipients onto the labor market meant forcing them into a sphere devoid of opportunity. Most of them would be left without adequate income and find themselves more vulnerable to experiencing injustice. And so would other disadvantaged individuals who are forced to compete with them over lower-end jobs and housing.[58]

Most commonly, committee activists pointed out the extreme labor and, in some cases, sexual exploitation that single mothers, women of color, and other disadvantaged groups would experience at the hands of landlords and employers, including unconventional employers like procurers and gang leaders. Darnella stressed this point in her testimony against Welfare Reform 2.0:

> I actually would like for [Minnesota legislators] to implement a system where [my family] could get back on assistance, not off forever. . . . Because there's no one to talk to. There's no one to help us. There's nothing out here for us. . . . It hurts, it does, when you're standing there fighting for your kids and you know for a fact there is no other way. Either you sell your body, or you sell your drugs, or you sell your soul.

Later committee testimony gave a more concrete example what "selling your soul" could look like, especially as it relates to low-income single mothers:

> As a parent you will do anything to protect your child. If a landlord offers to give you reduced rent if you give him some special favors, you compromise yourself to give your child a roof over his or her head—and believe me we have heard repeated stories of landlords who will take advantage of women in poverty trying to keep their kids alive.

Unfortunately, sociological research has shown all these claims to be true.[59]

In addition to exploitation, committee activists also spoke to non-economic injustices that occurred because welfare programs encourage participation in capitalist labor markets. For example, they sometimes mentioned the domestic violence that occurs as low-income women without job prospects and government assistance come to rely more on intimate partners.[60] "If you are in a domestic violence situation with an abusive partner," one of their legislative testimonies explained, "you stay there, or you go back to it, because your life is about your child and if you have to get beaten up to keep a roof over your kids head, you do it." The testimony continued, "Statistics show that around 60 percent of the mothers who need to be on welfare come from abusive situations. Minnesota's welfare grants force women to go back to these abusive men." Again, during the hearings about Welfare Reform 2.0, multiple committee members at least gestured toward these facts. Darnella, for instance, mentioned both how she fell into an abusive relationship after leaving MFIP and how returning to MFIP helped her to leave.

Amazingly, but unsurprisingly, very few progressive legislators and advocates mentioned the enduring constraints of the labor market as a reason for welfare participation. Among these few, only one discussed these constraints as consistently and clearly as the Welfare Rights Committee, detailing the sheer lack of decent jobs available to low-income single mothers and other economically disadvantaged groups. And nobody besides committee activists so forcefully discussed how, because of the lack of decent work, neoliberal welfare policy inherently reproduced oppression. As political educators, they were in a league of their own.

"Jobs or Income Now!"

The Welfare Rights Committee's efforts to "fight back" and give "the big picture" undercut the misleading rhetoric coming from their opponents. More specifically, the stories committee members told about welfare and the labor market revealed the blind spots inherent to such rhetoric—whether it focused on demonstrating accountability to "taxpayers," protecting benefits for the "truly needy," or promoting "self-sufficiency." They highlighted the racialized and gendered patterns of market oppression that misleading rhetoric usually obscured. And they confounded progressives and conservatives who used this rhetoric to justify neoliberal welfare policy. Just as normalizing ignorance about market oppression made these people hard to criticize, chipping away at it put them on the defensive.

I saw the committee's educational efforts cause this shift on multiple occasions. I saw it, for example, in their exchanges with progressive leaders like Senator Higgins. Higgins's rhetoric about using photo identification requirements to protect EBT card users from "big guys" could not account for the problems raised by committee members. Once these members explained how her proposal would cause *more* market oppression—by, for example, preventing single or disabled parents from sending their kids to the store—she had no answer. As I reported in chapter 3, "How can you give a kid a cash card?" was the best response she could muster.

I also saw committee's educational efforts weaken conservative proponents of misleading rhetoric during the Welfare Reform 2.0 debates. Once activists like Ebony, Angel, and Darnella illuminated the oppressive consequences of promoting labor market participation, these conservatives' pretensions about protecting "taxpayer dollars" and preserving benefits for the "truly needy" lost all credibility. And, in virtually every case, their responses to the committee implicitly conceded as much. Several of them, for instance, accused committee members of unfairly attempting, in Representative Daudt's words, to "villainize" them. It is "very disingenuous and unfair," another ALEC-associated legislator claimed, to "accuse [supporters of Welfare Reform 2.0] of wanting to deliberately not help the poor and put them out in the street." "I would never stoop to that level," he added. Others accused committee activists of getting "off topic" rather than discussing the technical details of the legislation. What *none* of their responses did is challenge the substance of the committee's claims about the labor market and welfare policy.

In the process of undermining the rhetoric used to justify neoliberal welfare policy, the Welfare Rights Committee also created opportunities to deploy more oppositional rhetoric—opportunities that the group eagerly seized. The specific rhetoric the committee used to publicize "poor and working people" was in some ways quite similar to the Bailout Coalition's. Whether directed at legislators, the media, or the general public, it depicted "poor and working people" as members of an embattled class—used, abused, and held down by "the rich" and their allies. A typical press release in 2011 asserted that, with the help of politicians, "the wealthiest in Minnesota . . . have gotten richer and richer at the expense of poor and working Minnesotans." A later speech asserted that "in recent years, the rich got richer through outright theft." And "the bashing of welfare," another press release declared, "is just a smokescreen to take attention off the fact that the majority of people are getting worse off, while the wealthiest are getting richer and richer." In all these statements, the committee's rhetoric sounded indistinguishable from the Bailout Coalition's.

The difference was that committee's rhetoric addressed a more all-encompassing variety of ways in which economic elites and their political backers held down "poor and working people." Their rhetoric did not just condemn, for instance, how the greediest banks had driven respectable working-class families into a temporary "crisis," or how right-wing, business-friendly politicians failed to respond to that "crisis." It also condemned how broad constellations of economic elites persistently diminished the labor market's supply of good work, and how bipartisan legislative coalitions ignored and reproduced that undersupply. More specifically, their legislative testimonies, press releases, and other public statements chastised capitalists for, among other things, "busting unions," "driving down wages," giving many people (especially African Americans and women) "no choice but to work seasonal and temporary jobs," and devaluing those jobs by driving up housing costs. They also attacked politicians for reproducing these processes—by either promoting "racist, bumper-sticker hate" or creating programs to "fix people in poverty" that mostly "benefit the non-profit industry" and "make liberals feel good about themselves." All these actions, they argued, ignored what—according to "the big picture"—"poor and working" families really needed: living-wage jobs or generous income entitlements. Or, in their parlance, "Jobs or Income Now!"

The Welfare Rights Committee's rhetoric was unquestionably adversarial. Its attacks on the "the rich" pointed to various systems of injustice facing "poor and working people" and justified pursuing an egalitarian reordering of political-economic relations. In addition, it invoked a class-, race-, and gender-conscious—that is, intersectional—vision of those systems. More precisely, it attended to the market-based systems that they had illuminated through their educational efforts—deunionization, gentrification, and the like—which pushed all "poor and working people," but especially low-income women and people of color, into oppressive circumstances.

Just as the Bailout Coalition's color-blindness was revealed by the experiences they ignored, the Welfare Rights Committee's class, race, and gender consciousness showed through the experiences they acknowledged—namely, the experiences of employable adults who, even outside the Great Recession or some other "crisis," could not find decent work. For example, their rhetoric spoke to the experiences of the "drug dealers" and "prostitutes" in Jeff's north Minneapolis neighborhood—those who, to use Darnella's language, must "sell their drugs" or "sell their bodies" because the labor market denied them more dignified jobs. It also acknowledged the low-income single mother whose "life is . . . a miserable struggle, 24/7"—as many of their statements asserted—because the labor market undervalues her work as a parent. The committee framed all of these groups and more as "poor and working people" who suffered so "the rich" could "get richer" and for whom—in the words of a 2013 letter to the state legislature—"welfare is the last stop to receive any type of help." All of them, as well as families thrown into "crisis," needed "Jobs or Income Now!"

The impact of the committee's oppositional rhetoric was most noticeable among progressive leaders. With "the big picture" as its backdrop, it provided these leaders with a strong and intelligible justification for strengthening welfare rights. And, over several years, some of these leaders began to adopt that justification, including a number who at first treated the committee's rhetoric as confusing or objectionable. Drawing on the committee's arguments, they undermined the statewide neoliberal consensus on welfare policy and, perhaps unintentionally, incrementally expanded the prospects for abolitionist demand-making.

For example, state and local progressives increasingly—more than ever before—came to treat calls for revanchist measures like those found in Welfare Reform 2.0 as politically toxic. Senator Higgins, for one, dropped her advocacy for requiring EBT card users to present photo identification—as did several other progressives in the state House and Senate who had initially cosponsored a bill that would have instituted this requirement. They never discussed or championed their support for this bill in speeches, interviews, or press releases. And, weeks later, when Republican-sponsored proposals to require photo identification came up in hearings, they joined committee members in expressing opposition. During one of these hearings, Higgins herself partly mimicked the committee, suggesting that EBT card restrictions were already too burdensome for low-income and working-class families. Another legislator, in the House, directly cited Ebony's testimony in explaining her opposition to not only increased EBT card restrictions but the entirety of the Welfare Reform 2.0 agenda. This legislator—a white woman and former nonprofit manager from Rochester, Minnesota—was far less progressive than Higgins, having, by her own admission, supported multiple prior efforts to further restrict and regulate welfare participation.

In addition to informing progressive opposition to revanchist proposals, the committee's rhetoric informed emergent progressive efforts to go beyond "education and training" and expand welfare assistance. Most progressive leaders never came to support the committee's abolitionist calls to, for instance, double the MFIP cash payments or create a more generous statewide general assistance program. However, many of them did come to accept the committee's argument that education and training programs on their own are unhelpful—that focusing solely on education and training was akin to trying to "fix" "poor and working people." One person who changed was Jessica Webster, the Legal Aid attorney who, during the Welfare Reform 2.0 hearings, had unreservedly framed "education and training" as the solution to poverty.[61] By 2015, Webster had become one of the state's most vocal proponents of increasing MFIP cash payments.[62] And in 2016 she published a report that reiterated and elaborated many of the Welfare Rights Committee's arguments in favor of an increase—arguments that, in prior years, *only* they had consistently and publicly articulated.[63] At the end of the day, advocates like Webster still framed increased assistance mostly as a means to improve the efficacy of education and training programs (rather than redistributing economic power). But their shifting priorities and policy arguments were hard to miss.[64]

The committee's rhetorical appeals were, unsurprisingly, less impactful among conservative and center-right audiences. In general, it did not really matter what the committee or any other social justice proponents said to these audiences. They continued to insist that neoliberal welfare proposals were showing accountability to "taxpayers" and preserving state-funded assistance for the "truly needy." Moreover, they continued to misinterpret the committee's rhetoric as an effort to "villainize" them and defend welfare cheats—even as, in doing so, they appeared increasingly out of touch with reality.

Nevertheless, even on the right there was movement. The most notable shift came from Mary Franson—a Republican legislator who, in 2012, had cosponsored the Welfare Reform 2.0 bills and, in a video to her constituents, compared food stamp recipients to wild animals. In 2015, Franson became the chief author on a bill to increase MFIP cash payments by $100, a proposal that came directly from a legislative task force in which the Welfare Rights Committee participated, was championed by the legislature's most progressive members, and eventually passed in 2019. Franson also secured cosponsorship for the bill from Glenn Gruenhagen, a Republican legislator who had previously argued that Minnesota's welfare programs were overly generous and thus a "magnet" for a "criminal element" from other midwestern states.

It is hard to say much about why these legislators came to support the increase or how the Welfare Rights Committee's rhetoric may have informed their thinking. Neither Franson nor Gruenhagen issued press releases or made sustained public comments about it. But, when they did discuss the increase, both treated it as common sense—a view that, just a few years prior, only the committee publicly defended. Franson, commenting to a local reporter, framed the bill as a "good start," pointed out that "cash assistance has remained flat since 1986," and added that "the buying power in 1986 isn't exactly the same as in 2015." In a 2019 committee hearing about raising the MFIP cash payments, Gruenhagen asked rhetorically, "What was the resistance?" "I mean thirty-three years," he continued, "all different types of administrations, and this is the first time we're looking at an increase."

The upshot is that, by coaching themselves to educate the public, the Welfare Rights Committee created opportunities to maintain and advance their commitment to abolitionist demand-making. As with the Bailout Coalition, this commitment started within the organization, as they assembled a view of "poor and working people" that favored demands for stronger welfare entitlements. But unlike the Bailout Coalition, the Welfare Rights Committee was able to maintain this commitment as they engaged in public action and confronted audiences with little apparent knowledge or awareness of market oppression. Their "big picture" prepared these audiences—most importantly, those with progressive leanings—to hear condemnations of neoliberal welfare policy for its role in reproducing injustice. And they deployed an adversarial and intersectional rhetoric that provided those condemnations, creating a strong justification for strengthening welfare entitlements that these audiences could then reiterate.

Today, as United States approaches the second quarter of the twenty-first century, many of its political institutions continue to adhere to neoliberal tenets and idealize market processes underlying the oppression of disadvantaged groups. In addition, much of its populace continues to exhibit ignorance about these processes. Critical observers of the American left have shown that even many self-identified progressives still insufficiently attend to various forces of injustice, particularly those that are market-based.[65]

Until this situation changes, contemporary social justice organizers will face the same rhetorical challenges as the Bailout Coalition and the

Welfare Rights Committee. They will have to deal with the reality that many of their audiences—including important progressive audiences—are predisposed to misunderstand rather than embrace rhetorical opposition to many widely harmful systems of oppression. And they will feel pressure to publicize contentious identities like "poor and working people" using rhetoric that reproduces societal ignorance and thus weakens the pursuit of abolition.

However, just like their ability to unite around abolitionist demands, their capacity to reach audiences with oppositional rhetoric is not inherently constrained by their hazardous political environment. The experiences of the Bailout Coalition and the Welfare Rights Committee show that organizers have a choice: They can work around that environment, appeasing audiences and treating societal ignorance as a given, or they can work through it, educating audiences about the injustices targeted by abolitionist demands. The Bailout Coalition, like most social justice organizations, chose the first option. They largely accepted their audiences' ignorance about the market oppression facing lower-income foreclosure victims, especially those of color. And they publicly constructed "poor and working people" using a misleading and color-blind rhetoric that reproduced this ignorance. The Welfare Rights Committee, on the other hand, chose the second option. They educated their audiences about poorly understood market-based systems of oppression facing Minnesota's welfare recipients, and they publicly constructed "poor and working people" using a class-, race-, and gender-conscious rhetoric that was more oppositional toward those systems. In contrast to the coalition, they provided a much clearer justification for their abolitionist demands and thus laid the basis for building a more powerful movement around those demands.

As with chapter 4, the main lesson of this chapter is that, to take the abolitionist path, social justice organizers must intentionally adopt political etiquettes that prioritize it. The Bailout Coalition's etiquette—which centered on "fighting back" against decision makers' complicity in the housing and financial "crisis"—did not. It affirmed the public's tendency to ignore the deep-rooted market oppressions causing foreclosure-related evictions and focus solely on temporary "crisis" issues—namely, subprime lending and cyclical unemployment. And it pushed activists to construe such high-profile issues as the most fundamental injustices facing "poor and working" foreclosure victims, so that these victims

	Bailout Coalition	Welfare Rights Committee
Etiquette	"Fighting back" against "crisis" (normalized ignorance about market oppression)	"Fighting back" against "blood" sacrifice (problematized ignorance about market oppression)
Publicized Contentious Identity	Unitary-adversarial ("poor and working people" as homogeneous and embattled class)	Intersectional-adversarial ("poor and working people" as variegated and embattled class)
Rhetoric	Conventional (color-blind)	Oppositional (class, race, and gender conscious)

Publicizing contentious identities: Bailout Coalition and Welfare Rights Committee.

might appear more sympathetic. By adopting this "crisis"-centered etiquette, they discounted potential opportunities to illuminate a broader range of injustices, publicize "poor and working people" on intersectional as well as adversarial terms, and strengthen the rhetorical defense of their moratorium proposal.

The Welfare Rights Committee's etiquette—which centered on "fighting back" against decision makers' willingness to sacrifice the "blood" of ordinary people—took them in a much different direction. It problematized societal ignorance about the market-based systems of oppression through which such "sacrifices" took place. It encouraged them to teach audiences about deunionization, racial and gendered divisions of labor, and other market-based systems pulling down "poor and working people," so that rhetorical attacks on these systems might become more intelligible. Moreover, it did these things despite their overlapping membership and collaboration with the Bailout Coalition. Through their "fight" against "blood" sacrifice, they generated opportunities to address the full range of injustices associated with welfare participation, publicize "poor and working people" using oppositional rhetoric, and bolster demands for stronger welfare entitlements.

A second important lesson is that, in pursuing abolitionist demands, social justice organizers must be careful to avoid political etiquettes that have contradictory effects. The same etiquette that leads them to internally assemble contentious identities around these demands can also lead them to publicize identities using misleading rhetoric. The Bailout Coalition's emphasis on "fighting" to "make the rich pay for their crisis" was one such etiquette. In strategy meetings and internal deliberations, this etiquette, much like the Welfare Rights Committee's, led them to construe their lower-income constituents as part of an embattled and heterogeneous class and embrace their abolitionist demand for a moratorium. But in front of public audiences, it led them to deploy rhetoric that obscured oppressive market processes and muddied the case for their demand.

The Welfare Rights Committee's etiquette lacked this contradiction, because it issued a much more expansive challenge to organizers. Whereas the coalition's focus on a narrow "crisis" allowed them to get away with accommodating the public, the committee's focus on ending "blood" sacrifice writ large pushed them to expand the public's as well as their own understanding of how market supremacy had conjoined with other oppressive forces. For them, it was not enough for their members to see "poor and working people" on intersectional and adversarial terms; their audiences had to as well, such that oppositional rhetoric and the case for strengthening entitlements would start to seem like common sense. To effectively defend as well as support abolitionist demands, more social justice organizers must develop etiquettes that issue such expansive challenges.

SEEKING LEGITIMACY WITHOUT MOBILIZATION

During the summer of 2011, elected officials in Minneapolis began debating proposals for the public financing of a new Minnesota Vikings football stadium. Like other professional sports franchises, Vikings team ownership and their allies justified the request for public monies by promising economic growth, job creation, and a bolstering of the city's "big league" reputation.[1] In particular, they promised that the stadium would generate new development opportunities in Elliot Park, a high-poverty and disproportionately nonwhite neighborhood adjoining their proposed site.[2] They also endorsed an "equity plan," devised by local officials in partnership with a statewide coalition of labor and civil rights nonprofits.[3] The plan—which designated about one-third of stadium-related construction jobs for nonwhite city residents—aimed to assure progressives that public funds would reach the disadvantaged.

Belying these assurances and promises was the immovable fact that the bulk of any stadium-related benefits would actually go to team owners and the already well off. Any development it brought to Elliot Park would disproportionately center on higher-income residents and contribute to gentrification, which the neighborhood was already experiencing. And any jobs it created would be a negligible compensation for draining hundreds of millions of dollars from public accounts.[4]

Almost as soon as public financing for the Vikings stadium was proposed, the Welfare Rights Committee began to organize against it. They highlighted the paltry levels of public assistance offered to state welfare recipients and demanded that elected officials use "money for human needs" and "not a rich man's stadium!" Members transcribed their demands onto signs and hosted a series of demonstrations at the state capitol and city hall, where much of the stadium funding debate occurred.

The immediate response to these demonstrations was chilly to say the least. Stadium proponents had built a sizable and active base of

Members of the Welfare Rights Committee protest the Vikings stadium deal. Photograph by John Doman. Reprinted with the permission of the *St. Paul Pioneer Press*.

support, including several students from a nonprofit vocational school who hoped to obtain work constructing the stadium. Several of the students—virtually all men—accosted the Welfare Rights Committee, castigating them as opponents of growth, equity, and "hard work" and accusing them of disregarding the true interests of the poor.[5] Vikings fans fed on these criticisms, dismissing committee members as misguided and disrespectful outsiders who should, in one person's words, "just go away." While such sentiments were far from universal, neither were they initially contested by local journalists, officials, and other onlookers.

Committee members defended their position as best they could. They chanted and held signs declaring that "Our kids can't eat footballs!" and calling for "Housing, not stadiums!" They also explained in press releases, public statements, and one-on-one conversations that the proposed stadium deal would exacerbate growing regional and state inequalities. To bolster their presence they worked to mobilize as large of a constituent base as possible. For years they had organized outside welfare offices, communicating their overall concerns and demands with other poor women and recruiting potential activists. They continued this organizing in the months leading up to and during the stadium debate. In addition, they arranged carpools to meetings and protests, provided bus fare for people they could not pick up, and took other steps to support the engagement of their low-income constituents.

All said and done, the Welfare Rights Committee and other opponents of public stadium financing came up short. The committee could only mobilize, at best, about fifty supporters to their protests. Proponents of the stadium deal, on the other hand, received the enthusiastic backing of several progressive officials, including then Minnesota governor Mark Dayton and Minneapolis mayor R. T. Rybak.[6] By the end of May 2012, both the state legislature and, just barely, the city council had approved the deal.

Throughout the stadium debate, however, committee organizers were able to establish themselves as an important voice for "poor and working people." Even after the deal was approved, they successfully pushed reporters, elected officials, and other bystanders to acknowledge and address—rather than simply dismiss—their representational claims.[7] Indeed, one could argue that the "equity plan" touted by stadium proponents was itself evidence of this acknowledgment.[8] Moreover, although the committee did not succeed in recruiting the massive grassroots base necessary to stop the stadium deal, some of the low-income women they did mobilize went on to become regular activists. These women subsequently participated not only in the Welfare Rights Committee but also in broader movements to redress Minneapolis's growing and racialized inequalities.

As social justice organizers assemble and publicize contentious identities like "poor and working people," they must also, like all political representatives, achieve democratic legitimacy—that is, an overriding sense among supporters and other audiences that they are accountable to their constituents. Without it, their contentious identity constructions and claims about disadvantaged groups' interests come off as empty or imprudent assertions. Absent legitimacy, they cannot effectively give voice to their constituents; they cannot, in any consequential sense, *be* representatives.

Elected officials in the United States, including those with low approval ratings, usually receive some modicum of legitimacy as a matter of fact.[9] However, social justice organizers—as unelected and nongovernmental actors—have no such privilege. Indeed, as the experiences of the Welfare Rights Committee suggest, their legitimacy is rarely presupposed, and their contentious identity constructions are frequently challenged, regardless of how well they articulate these constructions.[10] Throughout its campaign against public stadium financing, the committee encountered accusations, often bipartisan, that their representational efforts reflected a misguided ideology rather than a true concern for the poor.

Most successful organizers as well as progressive scholar-activists agree that the best response to these types of accusations is grassroots mobilization.[11] One reason for this agreement is that grassroots mobilization—by which I mean the recruitment and activation of a broad constituent base—adheres to basic democratic norms for how representatives *should* establish their legitimacy. Well-functioning democratic institutions traditionally expect representatives to prove their legitimacy according to what Jane Mansbridge calls a "promissory" model.[12] Representatives bound by this model must appear accountable to a constituency that actively sanctions demands—promises—made on its behalf. And to meet this expectation, representatives must mobilize a large base to whom they can attribute the sanctioning role. Part of why elected officials can so easily assume their legitimacy is that democratic elections, by their nature, produce such a base. But organizers must build one from the ground up. Thus, to the extent that they care about democratic norms, grassroots mobilization is simply the right thing to do.[13]

Beyond its normative benefits—and, for my purposes, more to the point—grassroots mobilization is also the most empowering tactic that organizers can use to legitimate contentious identities.[14] More precisely, it is the only tactic capable of forging winnable political conflicts around abolitionist demands.[15] It does so by preparing the ground for and, when the time comes, maximizing the intensity of disruptive egalitarian and emancipatory movements.[16] Through majority strikes, mass civil unrest, and other defiant actions, disruptive movements unsettle popular compliance with oppressive systems and radically expand possibilities for advancing demands against these systems.[17] But as Frances Fox Piven explains, for disruption to work, many disadvantaged individuals must be willing and able to break rules and withdraw their contributions to society.[18] Sustained grassroots mobilization helps to develop these individuals.

Despite the foregoing benefits, organizers in the twenty-first century—including many self-avowed radicals and abolitionists—have tended to forswear grassroots mobilization. Instead, they have pursued and relied on much less empowering legitimation tactics, which only require the engagement of professional staff or a handful of already committed activists.[19] For example, many organizers settle for accentuating the descriptive traits—such as race, gender, sexuality, or income level—that they share with their constituents.[20] This tactic implies that organizers are accountable and legitimate primarily because they have backgrounds or experiences similar to those of the people they represent. Rather than require the presence of a broad and engaged base, it calls for the elevation of particular activists who can plausibly claim to stand in for this base.[21] Organizers who solely use this and similar tactics may, in the short term, secure their status as representatives and achieve some amount of influence. However, they also treat disadvantaged individuals as an inherently passive bunch, reproducing the disengagement of these individuals and weakening long-term abolitionist struggles.

If the benefits of grassroots mobilization are so clear, why do social justice organizers often veer elsewhere? Why do they legitimate themselves and their contentious identity constructions in ways that have little potential to empower abolitionist struggles? One major explanation suggests that social justice organizers avoid grassroots mobilization simply because they have to; the disadvantaged individuals they represent are too hard to mobilize.[22] In the wake of neoliberalism's emergence, poor and working-class people in particular have lost much of their capacity for independent political engagement—especially their sense of political efficacy and access to political resources.[23] For example, "poor and working people" represented by organizations like the Welfare Rights Committee have endured stagnating or declining incomes, a loss of leisure time, and an increased sense that they do not matter to public officials.[24] Given such trends, this explanation insinuates, organizers would be foolish to hinge their legitimacy on grassroots mobilization; instead, they must act as what one study calls "rational prospectors," building their legitimacy around the selective mobilization of professional staff, committed activists, and other individuals with an already high propensity for political engagement.[25]

Yet, contrary to the foregoing explanation, the Welfare Rights Committee's anti-stadium campaign shows that it is neither necessary nor—from an abolitionist perspective—especially rational to simply abandon the pursuit of grassroots mobilization altogether. To be sure, from the start of their campaign, committee organizers understood that most "poor and working people" had few resources and little motivation to protest public stadium financing. Like "rational prospectors," they relied heavily on legitimation tactics that only required the selective mobilization of already committed activists. For example, they used chants, such as "Our kids can't eat footballs," that framed themselves and the rest of their midsized base of low-income activists as a stand-in for "poor and working people" in general. Nevertheless—unlike "rational prospectors" and more to the benefit of abolition—the committee also used its campaign to slowly rebuild the political capacity of their low-income constituents, particularly poor women, expanding future opportunities for grassroots mobilization and developing activists who would participate in disruptive movements. Through their organizing, they educated politically dispirited constituents about how to effect policy change and provided avenues and resources for these constituents to increase their political engagement.

The rest of this chapter explains why so many contemporary social justice organizations forgo the pursuit of grassroots mobilization as a legitimation tactic (above and beyond what is "rational"). It also clarifies how some organizations, like the Welfare Rights Committee, buck this trend. To answer these questions, I analyze the overall activities of the Welfare Rights Committee, the North High Coalition, and the Bailout Coalition, assessing how each group legitimated the contentious identities at the heart of their representational efforts.

As in chapters 4 and 5, my answers center on social justice organizers' political "etiquettes." I argue that, in the process of legitimating contentious identities, organizers tend to adopt etiquettes that normalize the loss of working-class political capacity, treating it as a fixed constraint on their efforts and predisposing themselves to avoid grassroots mobilization. This loss, I show, forces all organizers—even those in groups like the Welfare Rights Committee—to find short-term ways to defend their legitimacy in the absence of mass engagement. Consequently, as they do so—that is, as they develop successful low-engagement tactics—it becomes easier and easier for them to simply take that loss for granted.

Unless they intentionally develop alternative etiquettes that problematize the loss of working-class political capacity, they wind up acting primarily as "rational prospectors," reproducing the suppression of grassroots mobilization, and weakening abolitionist struggles.

LEGITIMACY CHALLENGES

The depiction of mobilization-weary organizers as constrained "prospectors" is—though ultimately misleading—correct in one important sense. These organizers *are,* in fact, contending with a long-term and enduring decline to the political capacity of the poor and working-class. And while this decline is not indelible, it is certainly stubborn and widespread. As I showed in chapter 3, neoliberal-era political institutions have thoroughly diminished working-class political capacity by compelling ordinary people to become more active and compliant market participants and increasing these people's subservience to employers, developers, lenders, and other powerful market actors. Even in a progressive city like Minneapolis, for instance, neoliberal poverty deconcentration efforts intensified the market participation and dependence of working-class residents and disciplined those who resisted this intensification, especially people of color. The result has been a net loss of individual and collective political resources—such as money, leisure time, and union strength—as well as a diminished sense of political efficacy.

Social justice organizers faced with such a politically incapacitated working class are bound to encounter legitimacy challenges. Regardless of how much effort they put into grassroots mobilization—and regardless of how effectively they articulate and rhetorically defend abolitionist demands—they cannot, on their own, generate the kind of constituent engagement needed to decisively silence their critics.[26] The organizers in the Welfare Rights Committee, the Bailout Coalition, and the North High Coalition were no different. All three organizations represented poor and working-class constituents with few political resources, often cynical views about politics and government, and little baseline propensity to join in collective action.[27] And all three found that recruitment and outreach efforts only slightly mitigated this problem. Activities such as petitioning outside welfare offices or door-knocking in high-poverty neighborhoods often yielded, at best, one or two engaged constituents for every two hundred people encountered.[28] Indeed, most of the poor and working-class individuals who joined each group did so because of social or familial connections with existing members rather than connections formed through community outreach. Moreover, few of these individuals hailed from the high-poverty, disproportionately African American, and heavily policed neighborhoods in north Minneapolis—a testament to the especially high barriers to political engagement facing residents of these neighborhoods.

Unable to immediately build and mobilize a commanding base, the organizers I studied found their democratic legitimacy—or, more precisely, the legitimacy of their contentious identity constructions—vulnerable to challenges.[29] Their opponents and other actors castigated them as troublemakers, deviants, and threats to civic life. Rather than democratically represent disadvantaged individuals, the story goes, they *mis*represented these individuals and corrupted the political process for the sake of their own misguided causes.

I frequently observed such challenges in my fieldwork. A telling example occurred during one of the Welfare Rights Committee's actions at the state capitol. Approximately fifteen members of the group and I confronted a high-ranking Republican state senator during a press conference. The press conference followed a round of budget negotiations and debates between Republican leaders and the state's progressive Democratic governor—negotiations and debates from which the poor had almost entirely been excluded. While the senator attempted to answer reporters' questions about the negotiations, we displayed signs and began chanting "Tax the rich!" We also questioned his support for cuts to social welfare programs and accused him of lying about how those cuts would affect "poor and working people."

Reporters and other bystanders immediately gave us "a good scolding," in the words of Tammy, a white woman, clerical worker, and longtime Welfare Rights Committee organizer. Rather than treating the group's representational claims as a legitimate part of the policy debate, they almost uniformly told us to "be respectful" and "quiet while we're having a press conference!" One of the senator's staffers went further, telling the woman doing most of the shouting to "shut the fuck up." No observers within earshot defended her, but someone did call the state capitol police to chase us away.

Later that day, when Tammy and I entered the capitol press room to distribute printed statements, reporters once again dismissed the committee's efforts as illegitimate. One reporter from a major news outlet stated the following:

> We realize you guys are trying to get your point across. But when we're trying to have a press conference, it's entirely inappropriate to interrupt like that. . . . You need to respect the process and the senator as he's trying to answer our questions.

Comments like this one construed the Welfare Rights Committee as group of troublemakers who spoil "the [democratic] process" (rather than enhance it) and push a narrow "point" (rather than a broad constituent interest). If the committee had mobilized hundreds of poor and working-class individuals rather than a handful, such challenges to their legitimacy would likely have failed to resonate so automatically and so widely among the news media and other onlookers.

Others might argue that the Welfare Rights Committee's and other social justice organizations' legitimacy issues stem more from their use of confrontational methods than their difficulties mobilizing constituents. According to this argument, confrontational methods—such as interrupting a press conference—undermine legitimacy by demonstrating a lack of civility that audiences expect of democratic representatives.[30] Although such a civility-based explanation is plausible and often repeated in popular discourse, it cannot account for other findings from my study.

For example, the North High Coalition *never* used confrontational methods but still encountered harmful legitimacy challenges because of their inability to mobilize a large constituent base. One such challenge occurred at a November 2010 school board meeting. By that point, the coalition had persuaded the school district to pull its recommendation to close North High, and the district superintendent had proposed her plan to "redesign" the school.[31] Coalition organizers responded by mobilizing supporters to attend the board meeting and respectfully ask for firmer commitments and greater investment from the school district. One by one, these supporters used the time allotted for public comments to voice this and other requests. While some of them were residents of North High's high-poverty and disproportionately Black surrounding neighborhood, many also hailed from other parts of the city.

Several of the citywide supporters were members of the Public Education Justice Alliance of Minnesota (PEJAM), a mostly white and working-class socialist organization that had joined the North High Coalition in the fall. During the meeting, school board member Chris Stewart—an

African American man and nonprofit professional who sometimes presented himself as *the* Black voice on the board—used PEJAM's outsized presence to challenge the North High Coalition's democratic legitimacy:

> This is what I want to say about the community, alright. Some of you are the community. And some of you aren't. Some of you are people from other places that are pushing a socialist agenda and exploiting the community. And I want you to be aware of that. . . . Some of you are coming from other parts of the city to attach your issue and your agenda to the valid agenda of the community. So, for those of you that really care about North High, welcome. I'm glad to see you at the table. . . . For the people that are coming with their worker's party agenda and what not, stop exploiting the community.

This comment alluded to an actual tension in the North High Coalition: whereas the organization's socialist-led faction—which included several northsiders as well as PEJAM—wanted to link the North High battle to a broader movement against the "privatization of education," many of its other members—especially middle-class alumni—did not. However, rather than framing this tension as evidence of a legitimate debate about the "community's" interests, Stewart accused socialists of "exploiting the community" and using the North High Coalition to manipulate this community's "valid agenda." His remarks provoked a handful of jeers, including some from north Minneapolis students and families. But these jeers from a few constituents were not enough to obviate his challenge. Among the other board members and bystanders, his comments met little resistance.

A civility-based explanation for social justice organizers' legitimacy issues also fails to account for the experiences of a statewide council of the American Federation of State County and Municipal Employees (AFSCME), whose public actions I occasionally observed. This AFSCME council maintained a relatively large, engaged, and diverse base of rank-and-file workers and at least sometimes relied on confrontational methods similar to those used by the Welfare Rights Committee.[32] Both of these facts figured prominently during a rally they hosted at the state capitol on the final day of the 2011 legislative session. The rally's purpose was to contest proposed budget cuts that threatened public services and jobs. During the event, at least several hundred working-class Minnesotans crowded outside the House chamber, where last-minute budget negotiations were occurring. They shouted at

Republican legislators to "do your job," providing no noise abatement for lobbyists, staffers, and other groups of people attempting to quietly converse with one another. Several of them gathered behind Republican leaders who were holding a press conference and displayed placards to the media.[33] And the crowd as a whole unleashed its loudest chants of the night when the group I was with, the Welfare Rights Committee, unfurled a banner made of fourteen king-size bedsheets that obstructed movement on the first floor of the capitol rotunda. Yet, no onlookers effectually accused the rally's attendees of violating "the process" or manipulating the "valid agenda" of Minnesota's public workers. Some probably tried, but their challenges received no visible or audible support from other bystanders, including the media. The lack of civility displayed by the AFSCME council and their working-class base did not meaningfully hinder the legitimacy of their representational claims.[34]

LEGITIMACY WITHOUT MASS ENGAGEMENT

Because of their constituents' lack of political capacity, and in response to challenges from other actors, social justice organizers must find ways to provisionally legitimate their representational efforts without mass political engagement. The organizers in my study mounted their defense by deploying a combination of four tactics, each of which opened an alternative pathway toward "proving" their accountability to constituents. In contrast to grassroots mobilization, these tactics only required the selective recruitment and activation of already committed activists.

Magnification

The first tactic was to *magnify* the appearance of supportive and engaged constituents beyond their actual presence. Magnification, like grassroots mobilization, appeals to a traditional, promissory understanding of democratic representation—that is, one in which accountability hinges on whether constituencies appear to sanction demands made on their behalf.

This tactic required organizers to complete three simultaneous steps. The first step was to maximize the visibility of already engaged and supportive constituents. Stella, a retired employee of Minneapolis Public Schools and respected member of the North High Coalition, reflected on this step several months after the November 2010 school board meeting recounted previously:

> Most of the people at those [board] meetings when we were protesting the closing of the school were not from the north side. So, I don't mean any offense to you all [pointing to two socialist organizers from south Minneapolis]. But they need to see teachers, parents, students, and people from the neighborhood.

Other organizers made similar points throughout my time studying the coalition. They followed Stella's advice and increased constituents' visibility by encouraging many of them to testify—at press conferences, public hearings, and other similar events.

The second step toward magnification was to fashion engaged constituents' voices in ways that comport with the organization's contentious identity constructions. Most often, this fashioning occurred through organizers' efforts to craft public statements. For example, in the Welfare Rights Committee, a few key organizers almost always had a hand in drafting and revising constituents' testimonies and public statements. On one occasion I directly experienced this fashioning process. During a planning meeting, Marissa—a welfare recipient and one of the committee's newer members—expressed frustration about a series of articles on food stamp "fraud" that a local newspaper had published. I suggested that she and I coauthor an op-ed on the committee's behalf offering a "bottom up" perspective on the issue. After brainstorming a series of arguments, I drafted the op-ed, molding it to fit Marissa's preferred framing of the issue (one that acknowledged marginal efforts to "game" the food stamp program and recast them as survival strategies). She then approved the draft. However, when I emailed it to the rest of the committee, Sharon, one of the key organizers, revised multiple passages to better fit a framing of the issue that she and other organizers favored (one that denied the existence of "fraud" and primarily emphasized the low levels of assistance and scarce job opportunities available to the poor). As she stated in an email, "I tried to maintain the points you were making in a different way [and] respond in *keeping with how we usually respond* to their BS on fraud" (emphasis added).

The third step toward magnification was to create the impression that the voices of highly visible and supportive constituents denoted a much broader base. Engaged constituents helped to accomplish this step through their public statements, which often labeled their concerns in terms of "we" rather than "I." For example, Rosemary, a woman working with the Bailout Coalition to occupy her foreclosed home, stated the following during a press conference: "There's a whole big picture. There's so many people in the movement. Ann here she's fighting for her house. Leslie and her mother couldn't be here. Linda's at work couldn't be here. We're all fighting to keep our property, and beyond us there's millions." Organizers then defended such impressions, citing whatever evidence they could to show that the "millions" were real. As one organizer asserted in response to Rosemary's statement:

> Every single day there's a letter that comes in from somebody saying what do I do [about my foreclosure]? . . . And we got to start doing like Rosemary says. Whenever Rosemary talks, Rosemary doesn't just say Rosemary, but she says Rosemary, the Donnas, the Lindas, the, you know, all of the other people that are being impacted. . . . Rosemary is in foreclosure, but she's got other people that are in foreclosure over here supporting this fight. And Rosemary is going over to their homes and helping them. And so, that's just the reality of the situation.

In sum, by maximizing the visibility of engaged and supportive constituents, fashioning these constituents' voices, and creating an impression that they reflected a broad base, organizers sometimes magnified what they could not mobilize. In the words of Manny, one of the North High Coalition's leaders, they were able to "create a buzz" of constituent support, effectively hiding the fact that "we're just a few people sitting in a room." They thus constructed and "proved" their accountability and legitimacy within a promissory understanding of democratic representation.

Description

The second and third legitimation tactics used by the groups I studied displaced traditional promissory understandings of democratic representation. Rather than trying to mobilize or magnify an engaged constituent base, each tactic implied that constituents' collective concerns simply aligned with those informing organizers' contentious identity constructions. The second tactic—which I discussed in this chapter's introduction—was for organizers to highlight the *descriptive* characteristics they share with constituents. This tactic evoked a "surrogate" understanding of democratic representation.[35] In this understanding, a political actor's accountability appears to stem from an *experiential* knowledge of constituents' concerns.

The low-income organizers I met frequently used this tactic. For example, Angel—a Welfare Rights Committee organizer, former welfare recipient, and low-income African American mother—often implicitly appealed to descriptive connections and claimed experiential knowledge of "poor and working people's" concerns. The following quote is from testimony she delivered at a 2011 state legislative hearing. Her testimony was opposing a bill that expanded restrictions on how and where participants in the MFIP could withdraw cash from ATMs using their EBT cards:

> The Welfare Rights Committee would like to state that this bill is not based in any common sense or fiscal responsibility. It appears to be based on knee-jerk, ignorant bias and a desire to stigmatize the poor. First, we would like to address the provision that makes it illegal for MFIP families to withdraw cash from the cash portion of the MFIP grant—and in fact, appears to make it illegal for MFIP families to have any type of money at all in their pockets. . . . Not every place we shop at takes the EBT card, and that is why it is necessary for us to be able to pull cash out of the teller machine. . . . You can't pay a parking meter . . . do laundry, ride the bus, set up a bank account, or pay your medical co-pays without cash. . . . Next, the part of the bill that makes it illegal to withdraw MFIP benefits out of state. This puts burdens on families who are forced to leave Minnesota to attend funerals, [visit] sick relatives, visit family members in the military, hunt for jobs and all the other things we have to leave home for. It is a restriction on our constitutional right to travel from state to state. . . . We are angry that this bill would even be considered. We see the hate-mongering in so-called "news" reports in the media. . . . This bill appears to come from there, since it doesn't come from a human or fiscally responsible standpoint.

Speaking as both a low-income mother and an organizer, Angel used assertions of "we" to link the Welfare Rights Committee's representational efforts ("The Welfare Rights Committee would like to state that this bill [lacks] common sense") to experiential knowledge of welfare recipients' concerns ("Not every place *we* shop at takes the EBT card"). Furthermore, she also magnified the presence of a sanctioning base ("*We* are angry that this bill would even be considered").

More socioeconomically privileged organizers also sometimes

claimed a descriptive relationship with their disadvantaged constituents. This occurred frequently in the North High Coalition. In contrast to North High's mostly poor students and families, only a handful of the coalition's main organizers were low-income. However, several of them could and did emphasize other significant descriptive traits they shared with this "community" of students and families—as North High alumni, north Minneapolis residents, and, more implicitly, African Americans. Reggie—a middle-class African American, north Minneapolis resident, North High alumnus, and key coalition organizer—captured this tactic during a meeting when, in response to a question about our "relationship to the community," he simply stated that "We [the coalition organizers] *are* the community." The other organizers in the room nodded in agreement.

Identification

Social justice organizers cannot always effectively or faithfully claim to stand for their constituents by way of description. Many members of the organizations I studied occupied social positions that were much different from those of the individuals they claimed to represent. These organizers instead asserted a strong and principled *identification* with their constituents—the third tactic for construing themselves as accountable and legitimate representatives. This tactic evoked a "gyroscopic" or "internal" understanding of democratic representation.[36] In this understanding, accountability rests on the presumption that organizers have internalized and identified with their constituents' concerns, such that their contentious identity constructions reflect these concerns. While similar to description, identification is distinct because it asserts a *learned* rather than experiential knowledge of constituents' wants and needs.

North High Coalition organizers most frequently used this tactic. Among their ranks were socialists, public school teachers, university students and professors, and ordinary residents from around the city who were generally committed to defending public education. These individuals regularly emphasized their special learned knowledge of the North High "community's" concerns. For example, Robert—a former president of the Minneapolis Federation of Teachers and co-founder of PEJAM—used this tactic in an op-ed published by the *Star Tribune,* Minneapolis's newspaper of record:

> I have worked with teachers, parents, students, and community members of north Minneapolis who have simply said to the board, "Let us help you." Rather than perpetuating divisions and abandoning an entire community, the Minneapolis school board must keep North High open and work to rebuild it. The community stands ready to help.[37]

Speaking as a member of the North High Coalition, Robert suggested that, by having "worked with" the North High "community," he came to identify with their perspective on what the "school board must" do.

Organizers with descriptive connections to their constituents sometimes used those connections to buttress other organizers' identification claims. During one of the coalition's planning sessions for an upcoming public meeting, a new member from south Minneapolis explicitly raised the question of identification: "Now, I know that I'm not actually from the north side. But can I speak as a proxy for someone who can't come to the meeting, for those people who can't make it?" Without hesitation, several organizers from north Minneapolis replied in succession:

> ORGANIZER 1: Sure, you can do that. And, more than that, you can come to speak for yourself.
>
> ORGANIZER 2: We have a lot of supporters in southwest. I know that for a fact.
>
> ORGANIZER 3: I think we all know and operate with the presumption that what we're doing is bigger than this building [North High School]. This is about public education and making sure kids get educated.

These comments reiterated that coalition "supporters" had internalized "bigger" concerns with "public education and making sure kids get educated" held by north Minneapolis's poor students and families.[38]

Projection

The fourth legitimation tactic reached back to the notion that constituents confer accountability and democratic legitimacy by sanctioning representatives. However, instead of mobilizing or magnifying a supportive and engaged constituency in the present, this tactic *projected* it into the future. In other words, projection forecast that a supportive constituency would eventually emerge in response to each organization's representational efforts. Organizers using this tactic appealed to an "anticipatory" rather than promissory understanding of democratic representation—one in which their contentious identity constructions must anticipate and appear accountable to emergent constituencies.[39]

Projection operated in two steps. The first step was for organizers to explain why the broad base to whom they claimed accountability was emergent rather than already present and engaged. They typically answered this question in one of two ways. The first way emphasized structural barriers to political engagement, especially the resource scarcity and diminished feelings of efficacy produced by neoliberalism. Welfare Rights Committee and Bailout Coalition organizers highlighted the effects of resource scarcity in particular. For example, after poorly attended public actions, organizers usually asserted that the turnout was "actually quite good" given various factors that heightened costs of participation for their most resource-poor constituents. Some of these factors included bad weather, short notice, or a lack of drivers for transportation.

Organizers across the board also underlined their poor and working-class constituents' lack of political efficacy, usually attributing this lack to the disciplinary practices of police officers, case managers, and other "street-level" bureaucrats.[40] For instance, the North High Coalition's most left-leaning organizers expended a lot of energy explaining how school district officials discouraged poor and working-class "community" members from participating in debates surrounding North High. They publicized stories about the school district sending demoralizing letters to the school's current families and showing an overall disregard for the opinions and agency of poor individuals. Manny, a coalition organizer I previously mentioned, unpacked this disregard and its effects at a district-organized community meeting:

> I heard [a woman in the audience] talk about parents not showing up and people not taking part in the PTA. . . . Imagine some poor person who works two jobs and can barely get home in time to make it to a PTA meeting. They bust their butt coming to meeting after meeting. And then the folks who wear . . . business suits, they come out saying pretty much that "we know better than you." So after all the time we put in and all the ideas we thought out, it gets tossed out and we just go along the route [the school district] planned on going all along. So [to] the folks who like to beat up on parents—understand that this is why a lot of poor folks don't get

involved. Okay, this is why they don't come to meetings. They don't come because they know that they'll pour their hearts out and some sharp-looking cat in a suit will say "No, this is the way we're gonna go." And it's not right.

The second way organizers explained low constituent engagement emphasized more secondary and subjective factors—namely, different forms of "false" or diminished consciousness. Perhaps because these subjective explanations had the potential to support conservative arguments that disadvantaged individuals are responsible for their own marginalization, organizers used them less eagerly.[41] The organizers who did use these explanations most often underlined the demobilizing effects of a "passive" or "victimized" consciousness among the poor. For example, in a heated debate about why the Welfare Rights Committee did not have more active low-income and Black members from north Minneapolis, Jen—a longtime member and herself an African American northsider—stated that "the problem is that people need to stand up and fight back, but our people don't do that." Carmella, another African American woman and longtime committee organizer, affirmed the spirit of Jen's comment, suggesting that northside residents "are being victimized and won't stand up for themselves." While nobody explicitly mentioned race, references to "our people," north Minneapolis, and passivity were clearly race-coded.[42]

Left-wing organizers also sometimes argued that a "reactionary" consciousness suppressed political engagement among their constituents. Organizers in the Bailout Coalition and the Welfare Rights Committee used this argument to account for individuals who opposed their representational efforts, such as the working-class men who opposed the Welfare Rights Committee in the story that opens this chapter. Lou, an organizer in the Bailout Coalition, described these "reactionaries" as people who say, "I actually deserve [public assistance]" but do not like being associated with "other people" who "abuse the system."

Having explained the low engagement of their constituents, the second step of projection was for organizers to proclaim a coming wave of mass constituent support. This wave would, the story goes, bring their emergent constituency to a state of full presence, sanctioning their representational claims and punishing their opponents. As Cynthia, one of the Welfare Rights Committee's founders, stated in a legislative testimony:

> If you [legislators] think that bashing on the poor will make you more popular with regular working people, think again. The times are changing. If you don't know what is going on, you really have not been paying attention. People in this state and all around this country are fed up. We are fed up with the way we are being treated. We are fed up with politicians protecting the corporate elites and the one percent while you slash away at the few programs left to help poor and working families.

Similarly, Bailout Coalition organizers declared that "this movement is going to continue to grow and grow" and "build with the passage of time," and North High Coalition organizers proclaimed that "the community" was getting "fed up."

ACHIEVING LEGITIMACY WITHOUT BUILDING POWER?

Through the foregoing tactics, organizers in the Welfare Rights Committee, the Bailout Coalition, and the North High Coalition gained an ability to provisionally defend their legitimacy—even if they could not firmly establish it. That ability—that is, the legitimating potential of magnification, description, identification, and projection—is evidenced by how local news media such as the *Star Tribune* covered each organization.[43]

Like most major newspapers, the *Star Tribune*'s baseline tendency was to dismiss social justice organizers' status as legitimate representatives, especially given these organizers' inability to produce a large and imposing base.[44] This usually meant that the paper simply did not report on their efforts. And when the paper did cover the Welfare Rights Committee, the Bailout Coalition, or the North High Coalition, it sometimes questioned their claims to accountability and reinforced challenges to their democratic legitimacy. For example, one article suggested that the North High Coalition's efforts were largely out of step with poor students and families in north Minneapolis—who, according to the reporter, had "lost confidence in the school" and saw it as "the smelly kid in gym class."[45]

Nevertheless, by linking their tactics to newsworthy events and pressuring reporters to cover these events, each group sometimes achieved better results. Indeed, when the *Star Tribune* reported on their efforts it usually validated their claims to accountability and conferred their democratic legitimacy. For example, because of pressure from the

North High Coalition, the reporter who had previously questioned their accountability later validated it by supporting their appeals to descriptive association. He quoted North High Coalition organizers as members of the North High School "community" who can therefore speak to its "needs," and he cited public officials acknowledging that "the North High [Coalition] has valid concerns" for the "community."[46] Coverage of the Welfare Rights Committee supported not only their appeals to descriptive association but also their attempts to magnify the engagement of "poor and working people." For example, one article from the 1990s juxtaposed a quotation in which an organizer described the organization as a large group of poor individuals ("We see a bunch of legislators tinkering with our lives") with a magnifying account of how they had "packed" a legislative hearing.[47] Finally, coverage framed the Bailout Coalition as "advocates for" a broad group of ordinary people "fighting" against foreclosure, thereby supporting their attempts at magnification. It also framed them as experts who had sufficiently internalized this constituency's concerns to "negotiate" with banks on their behalf, supporting their appeals to identification.[48] On a few occasions, the *Star Tribune* also published op-eds written by organizers, allowing them to directly affirm their claims to accountability.[49]

But this success also came with dangers. By allowing social justice organizers to become democratic representatives without the support of a broad constituent base, it enabled them to forgo the pursuit of grassroots mobilization altogether and disempower long-term struggles for abolition. It allowed them to adopt etiquettes that take the low political capacity of their poor and working-class constituents for granted and thereby limited any pressure they felt to rebuild that capacity. Such etiquettes uphold magnification, description, identification, and projection as the only necessary tactics for legitimating contentious identity constructions. They lead organizers to underestimate the need and potential for disadvantaged individuals to become more politically engaged. They turn organizers into "rational prospectors."

The North High Coalition as Rational Prospectors

The North High Coalition exemplified how easily social justice organizations can descend down such a path. Coalition organizers were neither unaware nor completely dismissive of grassroots mobilization as a tactic. During planning meetings, a handful of them sporadically discussed how they wished they could "get more folks [from the commu-

A North High Coalition organizer speaking with a school board member. Photograph by Tom Weber. Copyright 2010 Minnesota Public Radio®. Reprinted with permission. All rights reserved.

nity] involved." And a few, usually the most left-wing organizers, even tried to move in this direction, planning actions that might improve the "community's" political capacity and, in Manny's words, "light a fire under people to where they start recognizing that they need to take a stand." For example, Manny and two of PEJAM's leaders tried to plan outreach meetings with North High students. PEJAM activists also organized phone-banking efforts to expand communication with school supporters about rallies and other public events. Similarly, Daniel—the NOC organizer I introduced in chapter 4—tried to jump-start a sophisticated door-knocking campaign in North High School's surrounding neighborhoods, with carefully prepared scripts, maps, and literature for anyone who wanted to participate.

However, these efforts mostly went nowhere. Having secured its representational status, the coalition adhered to an etiquette that normalized the low political capacity of its poor and working-class constituents. This etiquette—as I explained in chapter 4—emphasized "being positive" about what the coalition could accomplish by "partnering" with neoliberal district officials and "redesigning" North High. In addition to ruling out adversarial identity constructions and abolitionist demand-making, it led organizers to deprioritize mass political engagement. In particular, its emphasis on "partnership" encouraged organizers to focus their energy on behind-the-scenes bargaining and collaboration with district officials—activities that only required the engagement of a few highly active, and usually male middle-class, leaders. The rest of "the community," their etiquette assumed, could rely on these leaders to articulate their interests and had no *real* need to actively participate and sanction claims made on their behalf.

As a result, coalition organizers dedicated very little of their energy to rebuilding the political capacity of poor and working-class "community" members. Especially when pressed for time—which was almost always—they turned away from actions geared toward enabling future grassroots mobilization. For example, Manny and PEJAM's efforts to reach out to students and phone-bank supporters received little to no support from other organizers. Likewise, Daniel's door-knocking campaign quickly dissolved, primarily because Xavier—the coalition organizer I introduced in chapter 4—and other leaders did not prioritize it. They offered a great deal of rhetorical praise to the campaign, thanking Daniel for setting it up and advertising it to members over email. In practice, however, they invested their energy elsewhere, skipping door-knocking events and never really pressuring members to participate. The one event I attended was well organized but included only me, Daniel, and another "community" supporter; from what I heard, attendance at the others was just as sparse.

The North High Coalition as a whole also put very little effort into encouraging and supporting the presence of poor and working-class northsiders at their meetings. Indeed, as I already explained in chapter 4, the group's leaders organized these meetings in ways that surely lowered the participation of low-income residents. Meetings were held at an inconvenient time and location—weeknights (during dinner time) in the North High cafeteria, which was housed in a mostly locked building. They were also poorly advertised to the general public, usually receiving only a brief announcement over the organizers' listserv, which never included specific instructions about how to enter the cafeteria. Furthermore, coalition organizers gave virtually no attention to how individuals without access to reliable transportation would make it to meetings. And not once during my time with the group did anybody ask or mention how they might include single parents of school-age children from the neighborhood, many of whom could not easily find or afford a babysitter.

Instead of figuring out how to engage the majority of "the community," coalition leaders used most of their energy collaborating with board members and administrators and bargaining over the details of the redesign process—that is, building their "partnership" with the school district. As far as I could tell, people like Xavier regularly spent several hours a week either getting in touch or meeting with district officials. Eventually, he and several others even stopped coming to coalition meetings, because they were spending so much time working on a district-run "advisory committee" for the redesign process.

Through all this activity, the coalition maintained their legitimacy as purveyors of "the community's" interests, using various low-engagement tactics. But they never laid a path for pursuing an expansive approach to mobilization and converting their legitimacy into more substantial power. They were content to treat the "community" as a group that was already engaged enough in the political process. In the fall of 2011, one woman—a working-class northsider who also served on the redesign "advisory committee"—captured this point well. "Nobody is really reaching out to the community to get them involved with the school," she complained. "The coalition dropped the ball on that too, even though most of them don't want to own up to it."

The Welfare Rights Committee as Base Builders

This outcome, although likely, was far from inevitable. Even under neoliberal rule, organizers can develop etiquettes that balance their short-term need to secure legitimacy in the absence of mass constituent engagement with long-term, "radical incrementalist" efforts to rebuild the working class's lost political capacity, expand opportunities for grassroots mobilization, and sow the seeds of abolitionist disruption.

The Welfare Rights Committee crafted such an etiquette. This etiquette emphasized "fighting back" against the "blood" sacrifices perpetuated by the neoliberal welfare state and building popular anger toward civic and political leaders who are complicit with those sacrifices. As I showed in chapters 4 and 5, it encouraged committee members to resist the influence of capitalist realism and rectify societal ignorance about the oppression of "poor and working people." In addition, and more relevant for this chapter, it pushed committee members to redress the neoliberal-era decline in their low-income constituents' political capacity. Its emphasis on popularizing anger encouraged them to treat this decline as an ongoing problem in need of resolution rather than a normal constraint to be accommodated. It suggested that, without a sustained commitment to rebuilding poor and working-class political capacity and pursuing grassroots mobilization, the "fight" would fail.

The committee intentionally adopted routines that underscored the foregoing suggestion. Most of these routines were symbolic. One occurred at the start of most strategy meetings, when members performed introductions for each other. In contrast to the North High Coalition, the Welfare Rights Committee encouraged their members to perform highly elaborate and personal introductions. During these introductions, longtime members not only shared their names; at the bequest of the meeting chair, they also explained why they "keep coming back." Their explanations both affirmed their overall commitment to "fighting back"—a point I covered in chapter 4—and usually emphasized the idea that, as one member put it, "our [that is, poor and working people's] power [to win the fight] is in our bodies." For example, different members stated that they "keep coming back" because "who knows what would happen if we [poor women] didn't go get in their [politicians'] faces all the time," because "if we [as poor women] don't stand up for ourselves, nobody is going to," and because, in the committee, "you [as a poor woman] learn how to express yourself to people who are trying to do you wrong." They also clapped for and praised these statements, implicitly encouraging newer members to explain their presence in similar ways. This routine reinforced the presumption that, to effectively "fight back," the committee needed to continually develop their base of constituent supporters and build toward grassroots mobilization. As I explain next, leaders subsequently leaned on this presumption to cajole members into supporting outreach campaigns and other movement-building efforts.

Other routines went beyond the symbolic and produced material evidence of grassroots mobilization's long-term importance for winning the "fight." One such routine occurred at the state capitol when the organization's low-income members testified at legislative committee hearings. These members almost always pushed their testimonies beyond the time allotted by legislative committee chairs and raised issues that overstepped the committee's approved agenda. If chairs tried to silence them, the rest of the group jeered and complained, creating greater disorder and usually preventing the chair from halting the testimony. These routines not only challenged the institutionalized

A Welfare Rights Committee organizer speaks before the Minnesota House of Representatives' Health and Human Services Reform Committee. Photograph by Andrew VonBank. Copyright 2012 Minnesota House of Representatives.

inequalities of political voice that work against poor women in legislative settings;[50] they also generated stories that demonstrated, on a small scale, the positive relationship between grassroots mobilization and success. Later on—for example, during strategy meetings—committee members then used these stories to champion grassroots mobilization's potential long-term benefits and justify devoting greater energy to building poor and working-class political capacity.

Consequently, of the three organizations I studied, the Welfare Rights Committee put by far the most effort into strategically building and mobilizing a broader base of disadvantaged constituents. Much more so than the North High Coalition and even the Bailout Coalition, they deliberately provided their low-income members with basic resources needed for political engagement. For example, all their planning and strategy meetings included a free (albeit modest) potluck meal, including items like sandwiches, chips and salsa, and fruit. They also provided informal day care, typically led by one of the longtime member's older children. Furthermore, all their meetings also occurred at a relatively convenient time—Saturday afternoons—and in more open and accessible spaces, such as the basement of a south Minneapolis community church. Likewise, committee organizers never scheduled future meetings and public actions without considering how the group would transport its members, usually via carpool. The organization also, as much as it could, reimbursed its poorest members for the transportation and meal costs they incurred while organizing.

In addition, the Welfare Rights Committee organized the most extensive and generative constituent outreach campaigns. Everyone contributed to these campaigns at least a little bit. Indeed, it is not an exaggeration to say that participating in outreach at local welfare offices was the group's equivalent of paying dues. Committee leaders expected all members to do it, and anybody who refused would have been viewed skeptically. During meetings, when planning outreach efforts, chairs would often start by saying something like, "So, as you all know, we're always trying to build our movement and get more people involved [in the fight]. And to do that, we must go to the streets." Subsequently, they often *called on* people to ask when they could meet at different welfare offices, rather than wait passively for volunteers. And in the meeting after an outreach event, they would ask those who participated to describe their experience, praising them for their contributions.

Through their outreach campaigns, committee members combated the demobilizing effects of their constituents' past disciplinary encounters with government bureaucrats. Without denying enduring political inequalities, they provided evidence that low-income women and other "poor and working people" could secure beneficial reforms by actively supporting the committee's "fight." For example, organizers distributed fliers that not only listed current policy threats but also recounted past victories under headings such as "When We Fight Back, We Win!" and "Here is what we STOPPED." Similarly, in planning meetings, seasoned organizers often shared stories with new members about how the group had successfully "beat back attacks from Republicans" and "brought Democrats in line." These stories, while not entirely inaccurate, typically overemphasized the group's influence to instill greater feelings of political efficacy and motivation among constituents.[51]

Despite facing the same short-term challenges as other groups, the Welfare Rights Committee effectively committed themselves to sowing the seeds of future grassroots mobilization. They still needed to legitimate their contentious identity constructions amid relatively low constituent engagement and, consequently, had to frequently rely on suboptimal tactics. However, they also emphasized the potential of "poor and working people" to engage in powerful collective actions. As scholars like Hahrie Han and Jane McAlevey would predict, their strategic outreach and recruitment activities enabled them to more successfully mobilize their constituents and prepare the ground for powerful egalitarian and emancipatory movements.[52] At times they were able to turn out enough supporters to do things like disrupt legislative hearings and press conferences where harmful legislation was being discussed. More generally, they accelerated the activism and political engagement of several poor women, all of whom were current or former welfare recipients and many of whom were women of color and victims of domestic violence. In fact, virtually the only women in the group for whom this was not the case were the committee's founders, who were highly engaged in left-wing movement politics from the start. After joining the committee, most members went on to become participants if not key local players in a variety of noteworthy movements, such as the Occupy movement, Black Lives Matter, the George Floyd uprising, and multiple left-wing electoral campaigns.[53]

Despite their importance to disadvantaged groups, social justice organizers can rarely take their status as political representatives for

No Cuts! Tax the Rich!

Stop Attacks on the Poor!

Republicans at the MN State Capitol are going nuts in their attacks on poor and disabled people. The Welfare Rights Committee worked to stop the cuts and we won a few things (so far). But there are ***ton*** of attacks that we still need to fight. Join us!

This is what the enemy is trying to do right now:

--Get rid of Medical Assistance and replace it with paid insurance

--Cut $150 per month from the MFIP grant if we have a family member on SSI. If there are two on SSI, they want to cut $300 per month from the rest of the family's MFIP.

--Get rid of speech, occupational and physical therapies for the disabled.

--Get rid General Assistance, Emergency General Assistance and Emergency MN Supplemental aid for disabled people.

Plus many, many other terrible cuts.

Here is what we STOPPED:

They wanted to make it so we could get no cash from our EBT cards! They wanted to make it so we could only use EBT as a debit card at EBT terminals - no cash for rent, laundry, bus...nothing! Because the Welfare Rights Committee and other spoke out at the hearings in the State House of Representatives, that part is dead. For now.

Tax the rich and use the money to help poor, disabled and working people!

Tax the Rich Rally

Friday, April 15

12:00 noon

@ MN State Capitol

Say NO to Hate!
Say NO to Attacks on the Poor!
Say YES to Saving Our Families.

Welfare Rights Committee [redacted]

Welfare Rights Committee outreach flier.

	North High Coalition	Welfare Rights Committee
Etiquette	"Being positive" about "partnership" (normalized loss of working-class political capacity)	"Fighting back" against "blood" sacrifice (problematized loss of working-class political capacity)
Legitimated Contentious Identity	Quiescent ("the community" is engaged enough)	Activist ("poor and working people" can and need to be more engaged)
Mobilization	Limited (outreach focused only on already committed alumni, activists, and North High supporters)	Grassroots (outreach to welfare recipients and other low-income women as well as committed left-wing activists)

Publicizing contentious identities: North High Coalition and Welfare Rights Committee.

granted. Because of the difficulties they usually face in mobilizing constituents and, thus, demonstrating accountability, these organizers are vulnerable to attacks on their democratic legitimacy; to immediately defend this legitimacy they must usually pursue tactics that rely only on the engagement of professional staff or already committed activists. Organizers in the Welfare Rights Committee, the North High Coalition, and the Bailout Coalition pursued four such tactics. These tactics either accommodated traditional promissory understandings of democratic representation in the absence of a large constituent base (magnification) or replaced these understandings with others that social justice organizers could more reliably uphold (description, identification, and projection). Although each tactic helped to legitimate organizers' accounts of their constituents' interests, they also enabled the adoption of political etiquettes that normalize the political incapacitation of these constituents and, in doing so, suppress disruptive movements.

As the example of the Welfare Rights Committee shows, it is possible for social justice organizations to resist the foregoing tendency and to maintain a commitment to rebuilding the political capacity of poor and working-class people, pursuing expansive grassroots mobilization, and growing the base of support for abolitionist demands. (The Bailout Coalition also successfully maintained a commitment to grassroots mobilization.) But they will not do so automatically. So long as the political etiquettes of social justice organizations normalize low constituent engagement, efforts by individual members of these organizations to promote grassroots mobilization will likely fall flat. Other organizers and group members may vocally agree with calls for more recruitment and outreach. However, especially when the going gets tough—when time and energy are scarce—they will not prioritize it.

This, as I explained, is what happened in the North High Coalition. The coalition's lead organizers did not actively oppose grassroots mobilization. They sometimes discussed and called for greater political engagement among poor and working-class "community" members. Some of them even sketched plans for building this engagement. However, those plans failed to launch, because "being positive" and "partnering" with the school district made high "community" involvement seem unnecessary. Their etiquette only drove them to pursue low-engagement legitimation tactics that reflected this assumption.

To avoid attaining democratic legitimacy at the expense of growing the base for abolitionist demands, social justice organizers must instead adopt etiquettes that problematize the low political capacity of their poor and working-class constituents. These etiquettes, such as the one I found in the Welfare Rights Committee, push organizers to rebuild that capacity and underscore grassroots mobilization's long-term importance for achieving their goals. They encourage organizers to, as much as they can, legitimate contentious identities in ways that affirm disadvantaged groups' potential for mass engagement, even in situations where doing so is not immediately necessary. The result is that the political environment becomes more conducive to disruptive movements, which can force abolitionist demands to the center of political and policy debates.

CONCLUSION

AFTER GEORGE FLOYD

On May 25, 2020, four police officers responded to a 911 call regarding an African American man outside Cup Foods, a family-owned grocery store in south Minneapolis's historically low-income but redeveloping Powderhorn community.[1] The man, forty-six-year-old George Floyd, had allegedly purchased cigarettes using counterfeit money. He was one of the store's regular customers and, like at least forty million other Americans, had recently lost his job due to the economic fallout of the coronavirus pandemic. In response to Floyd's alleged crime, the responding officers threatened him with a gun, pulled him from his car, cuffed him, and eventually pinned him facedown on the ground—at which point one of them, Derek Chauvin, pressed a knee into his neck. During the incident, Floyd was clearly distressed, repeatedly stating "I can't breathe" and begging Chauvin to relent. After a few minutes Floyd lost consciousness, and the officers called for emergency medical assistance. But Chauvin continued using his knee as a restraint, leaving it on Floyd's neck for a total of over nine minutes. By the time paramedics arrived, Floyd's body was virtually lifeless. They loaded him onto an ambulance, drove him away from the scene, and, shortly thereafter, pronounced him dead.

The officers who killed George Floyd were among the most recent agents of Minneapolis's now decades-old neoliberal regime of poverty deconcentration. From the time this regime crystallized in the early 1990s, it has tasked police with removing "problematic" individuals like Floyd—a large Black man with a criminal record—from Powderhorn and other redeveloping, working-class communities.[2] By and large, officers have heeded the call. A 2015 report from the American Civil Liberties Union showed that Minneapolis police have aggressively used low-level offenses as a pretense to stop, detain, and all-too-frequently abuse individuals whose presence frightens developers and middle-class residents.[3] They have also worked with and sometimes forced local business owners—including Mahmoud Abumayyaleh, the owner of

Cup Foods—and other "respectable" community members to identify potential arrestees.[4] The putative goal of all this community policing has been to revitalize struggling neighborhoods and improve the city for everyone. However, in practice it has facilitated gentrification and mass incarceration, exacerbated inequality, and destroyed lives like Floyd's.[5]

The killing of Floyd sparked a national wave of urban protest and rebellion. Minneapolis itself experienced its most significant uprising since at least 1967, when young African Americans, enraged by continued racism and destitution in their communities, protested and damaged several properties in the high-poverty Near North neighborhood. This time around, for several days, residents from communities *across* the Twin Cities took to the streets, putting local officials and business owners in a scramble to restore order. Some of the demonstrators vandalized, looted, or burned properties in south Minneapolis, including the police department's Third Precinct. Thousands more marched, including many who had previously protested the police killings of Jamar Clark and Philando Castile, and others—especially working-class African Americans and Somalis—who had directly experienced or witnessed police brutality in their neighborhoods. Together, they decried injustices perpetrated by local law enforcement, rejected the underclass imagery used to rationalize these injustices, and called attention to racialized economic inequalities that have long plagued the city.

For social justice organizers, the uprising that followed Floyd's death marked the emergence of what political scientists call a critical juncture—a period of uncertainty in which their choices have a heightened potential to effect long-term change.[6] At the heart of this juncture—which began sometime after the Great Recession and still exists today—is a growing web of cracks in popular acquiescence to neoliberalism.[7] In Minneapolis, by the time George Floyd was killed, many ordinary residents were already active in an expanding sequence of movements against tough policing and other inegalitarian, neoliberal-era policies and practices. For example, local activists played substantial, nationally influential roles in both the Occupy and Black Lives Matter movements.[8] They also energized several lower-profile movements—against, for example, exclusionary zoning, wage theft, and the privatization of public housing.[9] Their choice to defy public health guidelines and protest the murder of George Floyd denoted a continuation and heightening of the righteous opposition they had already articulated through these prior movements.

Local officials have, perhaps unwittingly, encouraged this opposition by trying to accommodate or forestall it. Even before the Floyd protests, Minneapolis's progressive officials had enacted several reforms that gingerly rolled back the deconcentration mind-set and implicitly affirmed popular displeasures with the neoliberal status quo. This rollback certainly included reforms directed at police brutality, such as the expanded use of body cameras, the creation of implicit-bias workshops for officers, and the banning of "warrior-style" training.[10]

But it also touched several other policy areas. For example, since 2015 the school board and district have stopped authorizing new charter schools and, alongside the state government, modestly expanded funding for the provision of medical support and other "wrap-around" services in public schools.[11] In 2019 the city council made Minneapolis the first major locale in the country to wholly eliminate single-family zoning, a long-standing impediment to the development of affordable multi-family housing.[12] Moreover, they significantly expanded financial support for affordable housing development, increased city-funded legal assistance for renters facing eviction, and enacted an inclusionary zoning law that incentivizes developers to build up the city's affordable housing stock.[13] A few years prior, the council had passed laws raising the minimum wage to fifteen dollars and mandating paid sick leave. The shift in governance also extended to the state level, where, for example, legislators from the Twin Cities ushered the first major increase to TANF benefits for low-income single mothers in over thirty years. More recently, they worked with Governor Tim Walz to push for another increase.[14] And, in response to the Covid-19 recession, they helped to enact a temporary state-level ban on evictions for unemployed residents.

After the Floyd protests, Minneapolis's progressive officials either took or considered several additional steps, many of which challenged oppressive approaches to policing and further validated calls for egalitarian and emancipatory change. The school board, for instance, rescinded its contracts with the Minneapolis Police Department—a nationally unprecedented move.[15] The University of Minnesota did the same.[16] The Hennepin County attorney and, subsequently, the Minnesota attorney general, Keith Ellison, charged officer Derek Chauvin with the murder of George Floyd—a charge that resulted in Chauvin's conviction.[17] And most notably, the city council pledged to replace the existing Minneapolis Police Department with "community-oriented, non-violent public safety and outreach."[18] Their subsequent actions have come nowhere near to enacting such a decisive shift.[19] However, the fact that they even framed it as a laudable goal was remarkable.

Despite these cracks in support for neoliberal governance, its death is by no means imminent; nor is its replacement by a more humane alternative—even in a leading-edge, progressive city like Minneapolis. For example, as urban-planning scholar Ed Goetz has noted, the city's recent housing reforms have offered mostly *symbolic* or *modest* concessions to opponents of neoliberalism and poverty deconcentration.[20] Inclusionary zoning laws, legal assistance for renters, and increased affordable housing subsidies all underscore the need to redistribute power and resources away from developers, landlords, and other private real estate interests. On their own, however, they neither require such a redistribution nor halt the gentrification of the city's historically poor and diverse neighborhoods.[21] In fact, while enacting these reforms, local officials have also further privatized Minneapolis's public housing stock, placing it more at the mercy of investors who often stand to profit from the displacement of low-income residents.[22] If proponents of housing equality fail to appreciate the symbolic or modest nature of recent reforms—and, thus, find themselves placated—then neoliberalism, or some revamped version of it, may yet define their city's future.

Similar things could be said about most other recent reforms and challenges to neoliberalism in Minneapolis. The school board's turn away from charter schools and modest embrace of "wrap-around" services are important. However—even as charter schools continue to populate the city and many students' basic needs continue to go unmet—the board's most ambitious and controversial plans have still tended to focus more on rearranging bodies than redistributing opportunity and expanding rights.[23] Furthermore, the state's increase to TANF benefits, while substantial, was nowhere near big enough to meet poor mothers' needs or meaningfully increase their leverage against exploitative employers, predatory landlords, and abusive partners.[24] Finally, while the city council's 2020 pledge to transform Minneapolis's system of public safety was rightly celebrated as unprecedented, it is doubtful that they will follow through on this pledge—especially given waning public support for the idea.[25] And if they ever do follow through, there is no guarantee that what comes next will ultimately serve a more egalitarian function.[26]

As Minneapolis and the rest of the United States move through this critical juncture, how social justice organizers fashion contentious identities such as "poor and working people" or "the Black community" will matter a great deal. More precisely, whether these organizers support the continued expansion of powerful left-wing movements will help to determine how public officials and other leaders reconsolidate local and national governance. No matter how progressive the leaders of Minneapolis or any other city are, they cannot mount a substantial rejection of neoliberal capitalism and its attendant oppressions on their own. They need the support of active and often disruptive movements—that is, movements capable of checking the corporate and wealthy interests that have defended neoliberalism and dominated American politics for over forty years.[27] As I showed in chapter 2, the absence of such movements helps to explain why Minneapolis's progressive brand of neoliberalism became so entrenched in the first place.

Social justice organizers cannot sow disruptive movements out of whole cloth.[28] However, as I explained in chapter 1, they can help create a political environment that is more conducive to these movements, easing their emergence, multiplying their force, and slowing their decline.[29] By working to assemble contentious identities around abolitionist demands, publicize these identities using oppositional rhetoric, and legitimate them through grassroots mobilization, groups like the Welfare Rights Committee have incited and deepened ordinary people's desires for egalitarian and emancipatory reform. They have developed activists who possess the wherewithal to break rules and build majorities in support of such reform.[30] The more organizers follow this abolitionist path, the greater the chances are that already existing opposition to neoliberalism will continue to grow and force a reckoning with the intersecting systems of injustice that precipitated George Floyd's death.

The odds, as always, are stacked against those who would promote abolitionist struggles. Just as neoliberal governance remains mostly in place, so do the neoliberal-era political hazards that pressure organizers to delink contentious identity-building from abolition—to give voice without power. For instance, even as calls to "defund the police" have gained traction among progressives, capitalist realism continues to stigmatize or foreclose the most truly abolitionist versions of these calls. Many progressives endorse a market-friendly approach to "defunding" that primarily entails replacing police departments with various "community-based" and privatized alternatives—an approach that would likely *reproduce* extreme inequalities in exposure to violence and physical insecurity.[31] And many at least implicitly assume that creating more restorative *but still* government-run institutions of public safety and strengthening national welfare programs—a far more egalitarian and promising approach—is unworkable.[32]

In addition, ignorance about market oppression continues to influence the terms on which many people embrace something like the "defunding" of police. Progressives often embrace it within a crude "identity politics" framework, which primarily underscores the need to redress racism and other forms of discrimination in policing.[33] This framework helpfully calls attention to the abuses that police departments disproportionately enact on people of color and other disadvantaged groups. However, by focusing exclusively on discrimination, it also ignores gentrification and other broad market-based systems of disinvestment, exploitation, and financial predation that such abuses have helped to shore up. It *understates* the true extent of the damage inflicted by police violence and obscures the reasons why abolitionist and anti-neoliberal approaches to public safety are necessary.

Finally, the political incapacitation of poor and working-class people continues to depress engagement around abolitionist calls for restorative criminal justice, stronger welfare entitlements, and other aspirational reforms. Events like the George Floyd uprising show that extreme and widespread anger can temporarily override this incapacitation. But such intense anger is hard to sustain for long periods of time.[34] In addition, the violent police backlash to these uprisings can further exacerbate ordinary people's loss of political capacity. Over the course of the Floyd uprising, police arrested over ten thousand protesters across the United States and committed countless acts of abuse and brutality.[35] In the short term, these arrests and abuses may have amplified working-class engagement by further stoking popular anger.[36] In the long term, however, they saddled large numbers of ordinary people with criminal records, legal fees, and other costs that further diminished their political resources. They also probably left these people with an even firmer sense that state institutions are incurably corrupt and thus further weakened feelings of political efficacy among the poor and working class.[37]

The foregoing hazards discourage abolitionism by influencing organizers' political etiquettes, or guides for action—a point I drove home in chapters 4, 5, and 6. As organizers work through exhaustion and navigate strategically difficult situations, they simply have a much easier time adopting etiquettes that treat the dominance of capitalist realism, societal ignorance about market-based oppression, and the political incapacity of poor and working-class people as fixed constraints. These etiquettes construe abolitionist demand-making as a fool's errand; they drive organizers to fashion contentious identities around moderate demands, publicly accessible but misleading rhetoric, and narrow and selective approaches to mobilization.

Only groups who intentionally build alternative etiquettes stand a chance of avoiding this outcome. Such etiquettes push organizers and their followers to treat the political hazards of contentious identity-building as what they actually are—namely, as I showed in chapter 3, the product of enduring but contestable institutional practices. Once organizers make this shift in perspective, they can begin the "radically incrementalist" work of redressing the ideologies, ignorance, and incapacities that make abolitionist demand-making seem so implausible.[38] More broadly, they can become vehicles for expanding, rather than constricting, disruptive movements for freedom and equality.

Especially since the 1970s, social justice organizations that have followed the abolitionist path have been few and far between. However, their numbers are growing. In the wake of movements like Occupy Wall Street, Black Lives Matter, and Bernie Sanders's presidential campaigns—and in response to a series of escalating socioeconomic catastrophes—more and more organizers have experimented with strategies that mirror those I found in the Welfare Rights Committee.[39] In Minneapolis specifically, a growing community of organizers have learned how to successfully embrace and defend abolitionist demands for reforms like restorative criminal justice and expanded public housing. They have also learned how to deploy the rhetorical and mobilization strategies needed to strengthen such demands.

These new abolitionist organizers work or have worked in a wide array of community and labor groups. One such group—until its activity declined in 2018—was Neighborhoods Organizing for Change, which in its early days participated in the North High Coalition but did not really adopt an abolitionist footing until after the coalition disbanded.[40] Another is AFSCME Local 3800, which participated in the Bailout Coalition and has since that time developed a more thoroughly abolitionist approach to representing "poor and working people."[41] Other important groups, such as the Defend Glendale and Public Housing Coalition, have only emerged in the last few years.

The organizers in these and other groups around the country are a major—though certainly not the sole—reason why popular acquiescence to neoliberalism has already declined as much as it has. Those in Minneapolis developed the community of activists who enabled the George Floyd uprising and other recent movements against inegalitarian neoliberal-era policies.[42] (As I explained in chapter 6, some of these activists came from the Welfare Rights Committee; one of them was Floyd's niece.) They also helped to elect policy makers who, through legislative action, have further validated and encouraged opposition to neoliberalism. Some of these policy makers have even come directly from their ranks, including Jeremiah Ellison—a racial and economic justice activist—and Steve Fletcher—a former progressive community organizer.

Insofar as more social justice organizers can follow the lead of groups like the Welfare Rights Committee, they will be well positioned to seize, escalate, and sustain future moments like the George Floyd uprising. But if, due to the hazards of contentious identity-building, most of them continue to suppress abolitionist demands, then they will enter these moments as a problematic force, diminishing ordinary people's radical desires for freedom and equality at precisely the time when these desires have the greatest potential to influence American political development. Either way, their representational efforts will play an important role. Those of us who care about creating a world in which all people can live full and dignified lives should do what we can to support these organizers and encourage them to choose wisely.

ACKNOWLEDGMENTS

Numerous individuals have supported the completion of this book. The most important are the activists and organizers who allowed me to observe and write about their tireless efforts in pursuit of social justice. Hearing their insights and witnessing their collective actions, challenges, successes, and failures transformed my perspective on American politics. Without them, this book could not have existed. To the extent I critique their efforts in these pages, it is only in the spirit of finding ways to better achieve the laudable goals for which they struggle.

This book also owes much to the assistance and friendship I received from colleagues and coworkers at four different academic institutions—the University of Minnesota, the University of California Irvine, Arizona State University, and Oberlin College. At the University of Minnesota, Joe Soss and Dara Strolovitch advised the dissertation on which this book is based. Both are exemplary scholars, superb writers, and awesome mentors. I am extremely fortunate to have benefited from their advice and wisdom. In more recent history, Dara (whose book *Affirmative Advocacy* is foundational for my own) provided formative comments on key chapters and aspects of my argument. Beyond Joe and Dara, several other faculty members at "the U" helped me develop this project. Lisa Disch exposed me to crucial insights about political representation. Teresa Gowan taught me about the ins and outs of immersive fieldwork. Antonio Vazquez-Arroyo pushed me to think more critically about political economy. And Will Craig advised me about making my work more readable for a lay audience.

Many of my fellow graduate students at Minnesota also supported this project. In our erstwhile writing group, led by Joe and Dara, Azer Binet, Adam Dahl, Ashley English, Matt Hindman, Zein Murib, and Libby Sharrow all shared helpful feedback on very early iterations of my argument. And in various other settings, Arjun Chowdhury, Brooke Coe, Logan Dancey, Ralitsa Donkova, Mark Hoffman, Andrew Lucius, Geoff Sheagley, and Adriano Udani kindly listened and responded to my ideas. In addition, I benefited from the support of an amazing administrative staff, especially Alexis Cuttance, Kyle Edwards, Judy Iverson, and Judith Mitchell.

While at Minnesota I received valuable grants from two organizations, without which my fieldwork might have been impossible. In the 2011–12 academic year, the university's Center for Urban and Regional Affairs awarded me a dissertation fellowship. And in 2012–13, the Department of Political Science awarded me the David and Janis Larson Graduate Research Fellowship. I am eternally grateful to the individuals overseeing these fellowships for seeing value in my work.

At the University of California Irvine, where I spent a year as a visiting fellow in the Center for the Study of Democracy, I was lucky to receive support from several more colleagues and coworkers. Most important, David Meyer, the center's director, sponsored my visit, giving me a space to write and develop my thoughts. And Shani Brasier, the center's administrative assistant, made sure I had everything I needed to hit the ground running. Others at Irvine who supported me include the members of David's Social Movements/Social Justice Workgroup and Alfredo Carlos, Lukáš Linek, and Sierra Powell.

At Arizona State University, where I spent three years as an assistant professor, several people helped me transform my dissertation research into a book idea. My fellow political scientists in the School of Social and Behavioral Sciences (Natasha Behl, Julie Murphy Erfani, Jennet Kirkpatrick, and Amit Ron) all provided important feedback on my writing and/or pushed and motivated me to sharpen my thoughts. Natasha was a particularly valuable source of support, as our methodological and intellectual proclivities overlapped a fair amount. Jennifer Keahey, Kristin Koptiuch, Carol Mueller, Luis Plascencia, Julia Sarreal, Matt Simonton, and Suzanne Vaughan also provided encouragement and various forms of intellectual and professional assistance. And, once again, I benefited greatly from the expertise and labor of an excellent administrative staff, particularly Ellen Burgess and Gloria Sawrey.

Finally, in my current position at Oberlin College—where I actually wrote almost all of this book—many more people came to my aid. Sarah El-Kazaz was an especially uplifting colleague, even after she departed for London. Toward the end of the process, she joined me for weekly chats on Zoom, holding me accountable to my writing goals and talking me through various challenges and anxieties. Pablo Mitchell also provided crucial assistance. In my first years at Oberlin, he generously volunteered his time to lead a writing group for junior faculty, which helped several of us to maintain steady progress on our book projects. Josh Sperling spent many hours with me at the Slow Train and the Local, listening and responding to wandering thoughts that informed this book in one way or another. He also provided constructive feedback on an early draft of the book's Introduction. Other current and former Oberlin colleagues for whose insights and support I am thankful include Rick Baldoz, Marc Blecher, Charmaine Chua, Steve Crowley, Harry Hirsch, Chase Hobbs-Morgan, Chris Howell, Wendy Hyman, Ron Kahn, Evan Kresch, Sonia Kruks, Shelley Lee, Kristina Mani, Mike Parkin, Eve Sandberg, Jade Schiff, Cortney Smith, Chris Stolarski, Harlan Wilson, and Elizabeth Wueste. And last but not least, Tracy Tucker, the politics department's administrative assistant, was indispensable to the completion of this project, offering copious moral as well as professional support.

Outside the institutions where I have worked, many more colleagues generously gave their time and effort to this project. Molly Riley and Betsy Haugen from the Minnesota State Legislature's Legislative Reference Library kindly located important documents for me. At various workshops and conferences, Kevin Bruyneel, Victoria Hattam, Nancy Love, Ron Schmidt, Peri Schwartz-Shea, Sophia Wallace, and Dvora Yanow provided beneficial advice. Jay Arena and an anonymous reviewer for the University of Minnesota Press shared constructive and productively challenging feedback on the entire manuscript. Jenny Tan at the University of Pennsylvania Press also gave me valuable feedback on a full draft of the manuscript and kindly shared two reviews she solicited on my behalf. Likewise, Angela Chnapko at Oxford University Press shared a review that improved the book. Finally, Pieter Martin, my editor at the University of Minnesota Press, has been helpful in many ways. From our first conversation, it was clear that he really understood and appreciated what I was trying to accomplish. His guidance and enthusiasm, not to mention the support of his assistant, Anne Carter, and the entire University of Minnesota Press staff, greatly improved this book.

Several friends, confidants, and family members also deserve acknowledgment simply for helping me to get through the process. At different moments and in different ways, Jen Idziorek, Chris Kark, Jake Killion, Ilana Kresch, Amy Larson, Cassie McMahon, Mike Scantlin, Justin Sjulson, Abby Stoddard, Corey Vane, and probably many others I am forgetting were all good buddies. Griffith Dye, an amazing therapist, helped me through an especially hard time in this project's development. My family members provided steadfast encouragement and plenty of welcome distractions. Before he died, my dad, Mike, was my biggest champion; and my grandma Pat—who passed around the time I finished this book—was always an inspiring example. My mother, Jo, my stepmother, Bonnie, Bonnie's husband, Dale, my sister, Darcie, and my niece, Daylen, watched after me and kept me grounded. And my family-in-law—Maggie, Manuel, Mo, and Rachel—often did the same. Maggie deserves special thanks for being such a wonderful babysitter as well as cooking meals, doing yardwork, walking the dog, and helping me out in many other ways.

I am so grateful to everyone I have mentioned in these acknowledgments. However, my biggest thank-you goes to my wife and fellow political scientist, Jennifer Garcia. As a colleague, her support for this book was unparalleled. In addition to reading and commenting on many parts of the book, she listened attentively to all my talks and conference presentations, helping me clarify my most central arguments. Furthermore, she reviewed the important emails I sent to mentors, editors, and others and spoke with me at length about everything from chapter structures to reviewer comments, contract negotiations, and so much else. Her contributions as a friend and companion were also unmatched. When things went well, she always made time to celebrate me; and when I was depressed and could not write, she made sure I felt loved. She also brought into the world our son, Benjamin, who made the past couple of years of writing much more pleasant. I dedicate this book to her.

RESEARCH METHODS

Many studies have examined how social justice organizations represent disadvantaged constituents and fashion what I call contentious identities. However, very few have closely examined this process from the position of the organizers and activists who navigate it.[1] Most have instead relied on surveys, interviews, archives, and secondary sources to reconstruct it from a distance. These types of studies are valuable for helping to outline the general contours and consequences of contentious identity-building. But as scholars of culture and organization have long shown, the tacit assumptions and contingent practices that drive such a process are difficult to analyze without immersing oneself among key actors for a sustained period.[2]

In this book I primarily developed my argument by drawing on immersive fieldwork that I conducted among community-based social justice organizations in Minneapolis. My fieldwork took place in the wake of the Great Recession and focused on three organizations: the Coalition for a People's Bailout, the Save North High Coalition, and the Minnesota Welfare Rights Committee. The rest of this appendix further explicates this fieldwork, focusing on how I gathered and analyzed evidence and how this evidence granted me leverage to answer my research questions about social justice organizing, contentious identities, and the political representation of disadvantaged groups. The explanation I provide here is meant to supplement the discussion of research methods in chapter 1.

I gathered most of my evidence about the Bailout Coalition, the North High Coalition, and the Welfare Rights Committee by attending several of their planning and strategy meetings—including those with public officials—and public events, such as protests, legislative hearings, and town halls. In total, I attended more than 120 of these meetings and events (Table 1 reports the number I attended for each organization). The planning meetings typically lasted anywhere from ninety minutes to two hours. The public events varied in length; whereas protests and

Table 1. Number of Meetings and Events Observed

	Bailout Coalition	North High Coalition	Welfare Rights Committee
Planning Meetings	11	25	24
Public Events	18	17	27

press conferences were often as short as an hour, legislative hearings and public meetings could go on for several hours. After each observation period, I spent several hours transforming my records and experiences into field notes. Ultimately, I produced around one thousand pages of typed and handwritten field notes.

During meetings and events, I engaged with each group through a mix of traditional participant observation and what João Costa Vargas calls "observant participation." As Vargas explains, "While participant observation traditionally puts the emphasis on observation, observant participation refers to active participation in the organized group, such that observation becomes an appendage of the main activity."[3]

Where possible and respectful, I leaned toward the participant observation side of Vargas's distinction. As a participant observer I occupied the role of an academic witness in each organization, creating detailed jottings and audio recordings in the field. For example, in many planning meetings I spent most of my time writing rather than providing substantive input on agenda items as a more active participant might. This approach benefited my study in several ways. It enabled me to maintain a critical distance from each organization's efforts, increasing my opportunities for reflection and analysis; to mark myself as a researcher, cultivating a general honesty and transparency about the reasons for my presence; and to collect more detailed observations, helping to ensure the trustworthiness of my analysis.

However, despite these well-known benefits of participant observation, observant participation was equally important for my study. As an observant participant I occupied the role of a highly engaged but less influential volunteer, putting down my pen, taking direction from leaders and other members, and performing low-profile but necessary tasks. Some of these tasks included holding banners at rallies, following up with petition signees, engaging in community outreach, and making occasional contributions to strategy discussions. As an inexperienced organizer, a newcomer to the communities I studied, and someone whose social position (white middle-class male graduate student) often marked me as a relative outsider, I mostly avoided trying to assume influential or high-profile roles. Had I tried, I likely would have been prevented from assuming such roles.

Observant participation benefited my study in at least two ways. First, it allowed me to develop a mutual respect with each organization's members and, thus, helped me to maintain access and assemble a rich set of observations. Indeed, my willingness, as a researcher, to "take sides" played a major role in enabling my research. On one occasion, a longtime member of the Welfare Rights Committee confirmed this point, describing how the group had required past researchers to "give our members [many of whom lack reliable transportation] rides to meetings." I supported her inclination, arguing that:

> Something about this kind of work is inherently exploitative. . . . I am using what I observe to write a dissertation and get a job. . . . Basically, the organization gets very little in return. So, you should require people to contribute something if they are going to study the group.

Looking back, I realize that this comment was a bit myopic. Observant participation, or "taking sides," is not always possible or appropriate as an approach to fieldwork.[4] Nor is it the only way to mitigate the exploitative tendency of social science research. Nevertheless, my experiences showed me that its ability to foster mutual respect *can* be vital when studying social justice organizations. The second benefit of observant participation was that it deepened my experiences in each organization and guided my fieldwork. Through this approach, I often learned *what* to observe. For example, it was by helping to craft messaging strategies in two of the organizations that I first noticed how societal ignorance about various oppressions—one of the hazards I examine—informed their efforts to fashion contentious identities.

In addition to relying on participant observation and observant participation, I conducted many informal interviews with each organization's leaders, members, and supporters. These interviews occurred in the interstices of my fieldwork—on bus and car rides, over meals, on the phone, during side conversations, and, in a couple cases, while helping people move. They allowed me to gather additional information about each group and its members. They also helped me to get a sense of how particular individuals were understanding and responding to various occurrences and exchanges.

Finally, I collected documentary evidence about each organization. This evidence came from a wide range of sources, such as press releases, organizational listservs, mainstream and movement newspapers, event fliers, and secondhand video and audio recordings. I used documentary evidence to corroborate and refine my firsthand observations. I also used it to broaden my exposure to the multiple, overlapping, and sometimes divergent practices through which each organization fashioned contentious identities and pursued their representational efforts.[5]

To bolster my immersive fieldwork, I also conducted secondary and primary research about Minneapolis in general. I read several scholarly books and articles focused on the city's political-economic development since the 1960s. I also reviewed several newspaper articles and reports produced by various public and nonprofit agencies. These articles and reports addressed myriad topics, from the contours of the foreclosure crisis to disciplinary practices in the education system to neighborhood development plans. My research on the city helped me to contextualize the actions of groups like the Bailout Coalition, the North High Coalition, and the Welfare Rights Committee.

I analyzed all the evidence I gathered using an "abductive" approach.[6] Abductive analysis, as opposed to inductive or deductive analysis, proceeds by identifying and resolving tensions between theoretical expectations and a researcher's discoveries in the field. As Peregrine Schwartz-Shea and Dvora Yanow explain, "abductive reasoning begins with a puzzle, a surprise, or a tension, and then seeks to explicate it by identifying the conditions that would make that puzzle less perplexing."[7] In this study, my analysis developed as an effort to resolve the tension between, on the one hand, a theoretical expectation that the organizations I studied would suppress abolitionist demands primarily because of unequal participation, the nonprofit sector, and other external forces, and on the other hand, my discovery that their strategic missteps as representatives often went above and beyond what the pressures created by these forces seemed to require. I ultimately realized that their tendency to suppress abolitionist demands was at least partly a by-product of their struggle to fashion contentious identities and give their constituents greater voice in political and policy debates. The central chapters of this book contextualize and clarify this struggle, explain how it leads social justice organizations to fall short of their potential, and consider how these organizations could better navigate it.

As a set of cases, the Bailout Coalition, the North High Coalition, and the Welfare Rights Committee have four features that make them especially useful for unpacking the relationship between the contentious identity-building process and the suppression of abolitionist demands. First, all three organizations claim to represent different segments of the Minneapolis's poor population, a highly and often intersectionally disadvantaged group. In fashioning contentious identities, organizations representing the poor encounter political hazards that exemplify those facing most other organizations in capitalist societies: dominant ideologies almost always normalize the institutional arrangements, especially the market arrangements, that must be challenged in order to free people from poverty; many audiences associate poverty with behavioral deficiency and thus have an especially difficult time understanding critiques of its relationship to systemic oppression; and the poor themselves possess few resources and frequently experience state-sponsored discipline, both of which substantially diminish their capacity for political engagement.[8] Some social justice organizations may encounter less intense versions of these hazards. Nonetheless, to some extent, all of them must negotiate problems—representational or otherwise—that stem from the political hazards encountered by the organizations in my study.

Second, all three organizations had several active socioeconomically disadvantaged members and at least some capacity to work outside the nonprofit sector. While many social justice organizations—especially those based in Washington, D.C.—almost totally exclude socioeconomically disadvantaged people, the organizations in my study were all based in poor and working-class communities and featured patterns of participation that at least partly reflected this fact: the Welfare Rights Committee was completely run by poor and working-class women and had a diverse membership composed of current and former low-income welfare recipients; the Bailout Coalition was mostly run by working-class women, worked closely with multiple poor and working-class Black women facing foreclosures, and had a socioeconomically diverse membership; and the North High Coalition included a racially diverse group of community and citywide supporters from poor and working-class backgrounds.

Similarly, while many large and/or national social justice organizations are deeply tied to the nonprofit sector, the organizations in my study had the ability to maintain some critical distance from this sector. This ability partly stemmed from the simple fact that the costs of local organizing are lower and create less pressure to turn to the nonprofit sector for massive amounts of resources.[9] In addition, although some individual members of the Bailout Coalition, the North High Coalition, and the Welfare Rights Committee had ties to the traditional nonprofit sector, the organizations themselves received much institutional support from labor unions, regional or national activist networks, and/or truly progressive foundations that support—or at least do not block—abolitionist demand-making. For example, the Bailout Coalition was backed by a local chapter of AFSCME, Freedom Road Socialist Organization (a regional network of left-wing organizers), and multiple organizations with grants from the Headwaters Foundation, which supported a handful of more radical groups in the Twin Cities. In conjunction with their more socioeconomically diverse membership, each organization's sources of institutional support cut against the pressures of unequal participation and the nonprofit sector and magnified contentious identity-building's relatively autonomous role in shaping their efforts.

The third benefit of studying the Bailout Coalition, the North High Coalition, and the Welfare Rights Committee is that they all based themselves in Minneapolis, a city where the political scene is relatively progressive and thus open to representational efforts on behalf of the poor and other disadvantaged groups. The city features a well-documented and active tradition of citizen involvement in social justice organizations, many of which have strong partnerships with local leaders and public officials.[10] In the wake of the Great Recession, when my research occurred, local attention to social marginality grew, and possibilities for social justice organizing expanded further. Indeed, the Bailout Coalition and the North High Coalition formed partly because of these expanded possibilities. Yet, as I show in chapter 3, even in this progressive context the organizations I studied encountered serious political hazards that affected how they fashioned contentious identities. Thus, these hazards and their responses to them likely carry relevance across other U.S. cities and towns, many of which have less inviting political landscapes.

Finally, while all three organizations represented poor individuals, their representational efforts differed from one another in several theoretically important ways. They worked on different issues, including welfare, public education, housing, and taxes. They repre-

	Bailout Coalition	North High Coalition	Welfare Rights Committee
Issue Area(s)	Housing, taxes, unemployment	Education	Social welfare, taxes
Primary Constituents	Foreclosure victims	Black families in north Minneapolis	Low-income women
Sites of Activity	Minnesota State Capitol, south Minneapolis homes under foreclosure, unemployment offices, AFSCME Local 3800 office	North High School, Minneapolis Public Schools headquarters, north Minneapolis community centers (North Commons, Zion Baptist Church)	Minnesota State Capitol, welfare offices, south Minneapolis community centers (Walker Methodist Church, Sabathani Community Center)
Tactics	Home occupations, protests, rallies, lobbying, community meetings	Lobbying, community meetings, some rallies	Protests, rallies, lobbying, community meetings

Organizational differences between the Bailout Coalition, the North High Coalition, and the Welfare Rights Committee.

sented different segments of the poor population, including welfare recipients, Black families, domestic violence survivors, people facing eviction, and others. They based themselves in different neighborhoods, including the working-class and racially mixed neighborhoods of south Minneapolis and the high-poverty and disproportionately African American neighborhoods of north Minneapolis. They organized across several different sites, including the state capitol, welfare offices, the Minneapolis Public Schools headquarters, North High School, and various community centers and churches. They engaged with different types of audiences, including other activists and organizers, public officials, journalists, and the general public. And they used different methods of collective action, ranging from highly confrontational methods like occupation and obstruction to more peaceable methods like lobbying and petitioning. Given these and other significant differences, the commonalities that emerged across each organization's representational efforts are likely relevant to many social justice organizations.

NOTE ON CONFIDENTIALITY

Much of the information discussed in this book is a matter of public record. This public information includes, for example, the names and collective opinions of each organization I studied and the content of statements made during protests and press conferences. The parts of my analysis that draw on public information make no attempt to protect confidentiality. In fact, activists and organizers in most social justice organizations *want* attribution for their public statements and actions.

I also, however, gathered a great deal of information in contexts where each organization's members had a reasonable expectation of privacy and confidentiality. This information includes, for example, the content of statements made during strategy meetings and personal details shared during informal conversations. The parts of my analysis that draw on private information use pseudonyms and omit details that members of the general public could use to determine individuals' identities.

NOTES

INTRODUCTION

1. Brandt 2013a; Waldman 2019.

2. T. Collins 2013.

3. B. H. Johnson 2010.

4. Indeed, district employees distributed materials promoting Minneapolis College Prep at a community meeting about the proposal to close North High. Minneapolis College Prep was part of the Noble network of charter schools, which gained national infamy for its extreme disciplinary practices, such as fining students for "not sitting up straight," "being as little as a minute or less late to school," and other minor infractions (Ahmed-Ullah 2014).

5. In 2015, NCLB was replaced by the Every Student Succeeds Act, which also promotes efforts to discipline public schools with low test scores but weakens federal enforcement of these efforts.

6. Weber 2010.

7. See, for example, Bale and Knopp 2012; Uetricht 2014.

8. See, for example, Weber 2010; Panning-Miller 2010.

9. A guaranteed attendance zone is a district-defined area surrounding a community school, in which students who do not enroll elsewhere are guaranteed to attend that school. Without a guaranteed attendance zone, vilified schools like North High have difficulty building enrollment, retaining funding and support, and, thus, effectively serving neighborhood students who lack access to other stable and dignified educational opportunities.

10. Hawkins 2011.

11. Lipman 2011.

12. Raghavendran 2016.

13. Magan 2017.

14. Piven and Cloward 1977; Clemens 1997.

15. Berry 1977; Boyte 1980; Strolovitch 2007.

16. Frymer 1999; Hacker and Pierson 2010.

17. Weldon 2011; Gillion 2013.

18. Strolovitch 2007; Strolovitch and Forrest 2010; Forrest and Strolovitch 2017. Throughout this book, I use the terms *oppression* and *injustice* as generic labels for the "bad things" that routinely limit the freedom and status of disadvantaged groups in capitalist societies—such as discrimination, exploitation, domestic abuse, and the like. Political theorists have, of course, debated more technical and precise definitions of these terms (for a helpful summary, see chapter 5 of Bohrer 2019). However, for my purposes here, it is unnecessary to weigh in on those debates.

19. See, for example, Forrest 2013; McAlevey 2016; Cedric Johnson 2017.

20. A. Davis 2005. To be clear, an abolitionist demand—as I define it—is not

necessarily the same as a call to "abolish" or "dismantle" a particular institution. In the words of Cedric Johnson (2017), it must be oriented toward "abolishing the conditions" of oppression that various institutions engender. For example, calls to "abolish" sex work do not in any sense fit my definition, as they feed into the over-policing and stigmatization of marginalized groups (Bernstein 2010). Likewise, calls to "abolish," "dismantle," or "defund the police" may or may not fit the definition of what I call abolitionist demands. Sometimes, activists making these calls are simply demanding the replacement of existing police departments with privatized or "community-based" public safety institutions. Such a demand does not fit my definition, as it points toward a world in which physical insecurity and exposure to violence would be even more unequally distributed (Lancaster 2020). However, other activists are demanding the creation of a stronger welfare state and restorative—rather than punitive—*but still* government-run public safety institutions. This demand does fit my definition, as it points toward a world in which all people, and especially disadvantaged people, would have greater access to safety and security.

21. For more information, see the descriptions of my research methods in chapter 1 and the appendix.

22. The Welfare Rights Committee was also an active member of the Bailout Coalition, a point I discuss more in later chapters.

23. See, for example, Arena 2012; Schlozman, Verba, and Brady 2012; Skocpol 2003; Beam 2018.

24. Schneider and Ingram 1993; P. H. Collins 2000; C. J. Cohen 1999; Strolovitch 2007.

25. Schram 2015, chap. 3.

26. The *contentious* identities fashioned by social justice organizations are related to but distinct from the *collective* identities underlying broader movements (Polletta and Jasper 2001). They are related to the extent that contentious identities shape the assumptions that inform movement participants' collective identities (see, for example, C. J. Cohen 1999; Murib 2015). For example, contentious identities may encourage movement participants to embrace a sense of "linked fate" or solidarity with some individuals more than others (Strolovitch 2007). However, contentious and collective identities are also distinct because they answer different questions. Whereas organizers and activists craft collective movement identities to answer the question "Who are we?," they construct contentious public identities to answer the question "Whom are we representing?"

27. Lipsky and Levi 1972; Choi-Fitzpatrick 2015.

28. See, for example, Strolovitch 2007; Ernst 2010; and Murib 2015.

29. See, for example, Cedric Johnson 2007; Arena 2012.

30. Gaventa 1980; Jackman 1996.

31. Schram 2002; Sparks 2003.

32. Piven and Cloward 1977; Soss 2000.

33. Soss, Fording, and Schram 2011, 21; see also, for example, Hindman 2018. By following these authors in framing neoliberalism as a mode of governance, or a set of institutional arrangements, I am distancing myself from prominent commentators who instead frame and critique it as an ideology or worldview. As

Michaele Ferguson (2017) has shown, when scholars discuss neoliberalism as an ideology they too often make it seem like an overpowering "blob" that simply absorbs everything in its path. In doing so they undermine our ability to think more concretely about how, in practice, it shapes politics and society.

34. Fisher 2009.

35. E. Goffman 1979; Eliasoph 1998.

36. See also Strolovitch 2007, 235–38.

37. Schram 2002.

1. SOCIAL JUSTICE ORGANIZATIONS AND THE STRUGGLE TO ABOLISH OPPRESSION

1. See, for example, Austin 2010a; Fishbein and Woodall 2006; Immergluck 2009; Fitzpatrick and Golab 2013.

2. See, for example, Bennett, Scharoun-Lee, and Tucker-Seeley 2009; Lovell and Isaacs 2008.

3. See also Strolovitch 2013.

4. Schram 1995; Hancock 2004; Sparks 2003.

5. J. L. Collins and Mayer 2010; Lipman 2011; Soss, Fording, and Schram 2011; Goetz 2013.

6. Institute on Race and Poverty 2009a.

7. Allen 2011.

8. Fight Back staff 2008, 2009.

9. Dahl 1961; Berry 1999.

10. Piven and Cloward 1977; Clawson, Neustadtl, and Weller 1998; Hacker and Pierson 2010.

11. Strolovitch 2007, 17.

12. Samsaraic 2009.

13. C. J. Cohen 1999; Strolovitch 2007; Cedric Johnson 2007; Beltrán 2010; Hindman 2018.

14. See, for example, Strolovitch 2007, 66–74.

15. See Strolovitch and Forrest 2010; Forrest and Strolovitch 2017.

16. See, for example, Gaventa 1980; Boyte 1980; and Skocpol 2003. These and other studies reflect Saul Alinsky's conviction that "if [working- and middle-class] people have the power to act, in the long run they will, most of the time, reach the right [that is, the most socially just] decisions" (Alinsky 1971, 11).

17. Strolovitch 2007, 98–100; N. J. Kelly and Enns 2010; Gilens 2012.

18. Disch 2012; Hindman 2018.

19. See also Olson 2004; A. Davis 2005; Weeks 2011.

20. McAlevey and Ostertag 2012.

21. Weeks 2011.

22. Nadasen 2005; Kornbluh 2007.

23. See, for example, C. J. Cohen 1999; Cedric Johnson 2007; Arena 2012.

24. Weeks 2011, 68–69.

25. See, for example, C. J. Cohen 1999; Kim 2000; Schram 2002.

26. Ernst 2010.

27. Schram 2002.

28. See, for example, Skocpol 2003; Han 2014; and McAlevey 2016.
29. Piven 2006; Arena 2012; McAlevey 2016.
30. McAlevey 2016.
31. Fantasia and Voss 2004; McAlevey 2016.
32. Schneider and Ingram 1993; Strolovitch 2007; Murib 2015.
33. Schattschneider 1960, 35.
34. Schlozman, Verba, and Brady 2012; see also, for example, Abzug and Galaskiewicz 2001; O'Regan and Oster 2005.
35. Gaines 1996; C. J. Cohen 1999.
36. Young 2000.
37. Ernst 2010.
38. Hall 2016; McKeever 2015.
39. McKeever and Gaddy 2016.
40. Walker 1983; Roelofs 2003; INCITE! Women of Color against Violence 2007.
41. Piven (1970) 1974, 47.
42. Berry and Arons 2003.
43. Roelofs 2003; Arena 2012; McQuarrie 2013; Beam 2018.
44. Weldon 2011; Arena 2012.
45. See, for example, INCITE! Women of Color against Violence 2007.
46. Moreover, it ignores that even some groups with, for instance, *stronger* ties to the nonprofit sector have been able to maintain more transformative political commitments. I do not discuss such a case in this book; but see, for example, the 501(c)(3)'s discussed in Samantha Majic's *Sex Work Politics* (2014).
47. Gaventa 1980; Schram 1995; Jackman 1996.
48. L. Cohen 2003; Wolff 2005.
49. Crenshaw 1992; Schram 2002; Sparks 2003.
50. Ernst 2010; Schram 2002; Forrest 2013.
51. Piven and Cloward 1977; Soss 2000; Lerman and Weaver 2014.
52. Schlozman, Verba, and Brady 2012, 459–63.
53. See, for example, Arena 2012; Kurtz 2002; Strolovitch 2007.
54. Eliasoph 1998; E. Goffman 1979.
55. Strolovitch 2007, 233–38.
56. Lindblom 1982.
57. See, for example, J. Stein 1998; L. Cohen 2003.
58. Piven and Cloward 1971; Gaventa 1980.
59. See, for example, T. F. Reed 2020, ch. 1.
60. L. Cohen 2003.
61. J. Stein 2010.
62. Soss, Fording, and Schram 2011; Osborne and Gaebler 1992.
63. Lipman 2011.
64. Fisher 2009.
65. Schram and Soss 2001.
66. Goetz and Sidney 1994; McQuarrie 2013.
67. Brown 2015.
68. Soss, Fording, and Schram 2011.

69. Goetz 2003.

70. See, for example, Lerman and Weaver 2014; Hertel-Fernandez 2018; Lee, McQuarrie, and Walker 2015.

71. McElwee, Green, and McAuliffe 2018.

72. See, for example, The Movement for Black Lives 2016; Bruenig 2019; Carlock and Mangan 2018.

73. One activist in the Save North High Coalition was a paid organizer for one of the coalition's primary member organizations.

74. To date, the FBI's investigation has resulted in no formal charges against the activists whose homes were raided. All indicators suggest that the investigation was primarily a fishing expedition. It involved, among other troubling activities, the use of an undercover agent who posed as an antiwar activist and befriended many socialist organizers during protests surrounding the 2008 Republican National Convention in St. Paul, Minnesota. For a helpful summary of the FBI's investigation, see Wallsten 2011.

75. Piven and Cloward 1977, 37.

76. Because social justice organizations are political participants as well as representatives, they can also, of course, directly contribute to egalitarian and emancipatory movements by engaging in disruptive collective action. This point has been widely discussed among left-wing scholars and organizers. See, for example, Piven 2006; Arena 2012; and McAlevey 2016.

2. NEOLIBERALISM IN A PROGRESSIVE CITY

1. City of Minneapolis Residential and Real Estate Development Work Unit 2015.
2. K. Nelson 2009.
3. Crump 2008.
4. McLean and Nocera 2010.
5. Crump et al. 2008; Creola Johnson 2010.
6. Fishbein and Woodall 2006; Crump et al. 2008; Strolovitch 2013.
7. See especially Wallison 2011.
8. Allen 2011; Picker 2015.
9. National Community Reinvestment Coalition 2007; Institute on Race and Poverty 2009a; Hartley 2013; Goetz et al. 2019.
10. B. Lewis 2015; Kaul 2017.
11. Goetz 2003.
12. Institute on Race and Poverty 2009a.
13. City of Minneapolis Residential and Real Estate Development Work Unit 2015, 6.
14. Streitfeld 2009; Buchta 2016b.
15. Allen 2011.
16. Kaul 2017; Goetz et al. 2019.
17. Nickel 1995; Rietmulder 2015.
18. Delton 2002.
19. Nickel 1995; Fagotto and Fung 2006.
20. N. Smith 1996.

21. L. Bennett and Reed 1999; Arena 2012; Goetz 2013.
22. M. Davis 1990; N. Smith 1996; Duneier 1999.
23. Weisberg 2009; Romero 2011.
24. Hargarten et al. 2018.
25. Rupar 2012.
26. For evidence of the claims in this paragraph, see Goetz 2003, ch. 3; Goetz 2013.
27. Orfield 2006; Lipman 2011.
28. Goetz 1996; Goetz 2003, 117–22.
29. Schram and Krueger 1994.
30. Lipman 2011, 34–36.
31. Goetz 2018.
32. As Dreier (2011) reports, "By the end of his [Reagan's] second term, federal assistance to local governments had been slashed by 60 percent."
33. Goetz 2003. During the Obama years, HOPE VI was largely replaced by Choice Neighborhoods, a similarly structured program.
34. Under Clinton the federal government also financed aggressive community policing in high-poverty neighborhoods, increased the ability of local public housing authorities to evict public housing residents, turned welfare into a work-promotion program, and supported several other laws that served HOPE VI's neoliberal objectives.
35. J. Stein 1998, 2010.
36. See, for example, A. Schwartz 1995.
37. Quillian 1999.
38. A. Reed 1999.
39. Goetz 2003, 3, 26–27; Arena 2012.
40. L. Bennett and Reed 1999; Goetz 2013.
41. A. Reed 1999.
42. Auletta 1981, 105–6.
43. Forrest 2013, 27–28.
44. Goetz 2013.
45. A. Schwartz 1995, 166.
46. Nickel 1995; A. Schwartz 1995.
47. Sidney 2003, 78.
48. Metropolitan Council 1992; United Way of Minneapolis Area 1995.
49. Goetz 2003, 92–93.
50. As Goetz (2003, 92) reports, in 1990 "the Twin Cities region had the sixth highest level of wealth disparity between central cities and wealthy suburbs when compared with the 25 largest metropolitan areas in the country."
51. A. Schwartz 1995, 167; United Way of Minneapolis Area 1995, 22. From 1980 to 1988 the city lost over 14,000 manufacturing, construction and wholesale trade jobs and gained over 16,500 jobs in the service sector. These service jobs were more likely to include low wages and irregular or part-time hours.
52. A. Schwartz 1995, 165; United Way of Minneapolis Area 1995.
53. Metropolitan Council 1994, 17.
54. Fagotto and Fung 2006, 638; Nickel 1995; Margolin 2016.

55. Hertz 1981; Nickel 1995; Sidney 2003.
56. A. Schwartz 1995, 167–68; Sidney 2003.
57. Murphy and Urquhart 2010; Goetz 2003.
58. Goetz 2003, 96.
59. Goetz 2003, 97.
60. A. Schwartz 1995.
61. Nickel 1995.
62. Goetz 2003, 106–7.
63. Koch 1968; Valelly 1989.
64. Delton 2002. One exception—which I discuss in chapter 4—was Up and Out of Poverty Now, an affordable housing organization. The founding members of the Welfare Rights Committee were participants in this organization before striking out on their own.
65. See, for example, the description of Minneapolis's fair housing activists in Sidney 2003. In my own research I was often shocked at how much fragmentation existed in Minneapolis's community of social justice organizers. For a variety of reasons, organizers who mostly agreed with one another on key issues either did not work together or, in many cases, did not even know each other.
66. Goetz 2003, 98–99.
67. Goetz 2003, 98, 101–5.
68. Metropolitan Council 1992, 1994.
69. Goetz, Chapple, and Lukermann 2003.
70. Diaz 1996, A1.
71. Murphy 2010.
72. Goetz 2003, 120–21. To be clear, the leaders of revanchist cities also structured policing around a dividing line between the respectable and stigmatized residents of high-poverty neighborhoods. However, in Minneapolis the share of residents included on the respectable side of that dividing line was much larger. As I discuss more in chapter 3, the city's overall policing of poor and working-class people was comparatively less severe. But the severity that did exist was imposed on the most marginalized individuals in especially targeted and unequal ways.
73. Crump 2002.
74. Goetz 2003, ch. 6; Crump 2002.
75. See Goetz 2003, 120–26. From 1991 to 1998 the number of demolished housing units outpaced newly built units by more than 2,250.
76. In making this move they followed the federal government, which, in 1986—as it drew down funding for public housing—enacted an alternative program (the Low Income Housing Tax Credit) that incentivized private investors to take on the responsibility of affordable housing production.
77. Goetz and Sidney 1994.
78. Minnesota State House of Representatives 1991, 7728–29; Minnesota State Senate 1991, 4844; Pinney 1991. The law restricting General Assistance for new state residents was later struck down for violating their constitutional right to interstate travel; see Gustafson 1992; Schram and Krueger 1994.

79. "Body Count" 1995.
80. For a complete list, see Goetz 2003, 99–100.
81. Institute on Race and Poverty 1997, 40.
82. An annual regional survey showed that from 1987 to 1993 the percentage of area residents listing "crime" as "the single most important problem" facing the Twin Cities quadrupled, going from less than 15 percent to 61 percent (Metropolitan Council 2010, 11).
83. D. Johnson 1996.
84. Goetz 2003; Crump 2002.
85. Crump 2002; Diaz 1995a, A1; Diaz 1996, A1.
86. Diaz 1995b, A1; Goetz and Sidney 1994; Goetz 2003.
87. See, for example, Schram and Krueger 1994; Kerr 2012; Goetz 2003, 121–22.
88. Murphy 2010, 247.
89. Walsh and Graves 1997.
90. Office vacancy rates in the Minneapolis central business district rose from only 6.8 percent in 2000 to 20.2 percent in 2004. Over the next several years the rate remained above 13.5 percent for all but three quarters, and it rose again to 17.9 percent in the wake of the Great Recession; see Minneapolis Department of Community Planning and Economic Development [CPED] 2006, 2007, 2008, 2009, 2010. Vacancy rates for retail space trended similarly.
91. Goetz 2003, 109.
92. Goetz et al. 2019, 10.
93. Minneapolis Department of CPED 2006; City of Minneapolis 2010a, 2010b.
94. Goetz 2003, 158.
95. Goetz 2003, 110–11.
96. Wirtz 2013.
97. In 1990, the state government laid the groundwork for this emergence by enacting the nation's first charter school law and statewide open enrollment program. However, a somewhat complicated application system for open enrollment, a lack of interdistrict transportation, limited capacity in high-performing suburban districts, and a commitment in Minneapolis Public Schools to maintaining neighborhood schools initially stopped either of these "firsts" from affecting education in high-poverty inner-city neighborhoods. See Corson 2000; Orfield and Wallace 2007.
98. Overall, the district closed twelve schools between 2005 and 2011, matching the per-student closure rate of more revanchist cities like Chicago and Detroit (Mitchell 2011c).
99. McCallum 2007.
100. See, for example, Orfield and Wallace 2007. To prove that greater resources cannot help low-income schools in north Minneapolis, proponents of school choice pointed to the fact that per-pupil spending at these schools was, on average, higher than for the local school district or the state as a whole. However, such per-pupil spending figures are misleading in at least two senses. First, they do not control for the fact that low-income schools are more likely to enroll high-

needs or special-needs students, who require more resources. Second, and more importantly, they do not reflect the significant amount of private funds that affluent parents spend on supplies, tutoring, and other educational resources for their children.

101. City of Minneapolis 2010a, 2010b.
102. Minneapolis Department of CPED 2010.
103. Schmickle 2010; Thompson 2015.
104. Biegler and Madden 2012; Van Wychen 2016.
105. Van Wychen 2017; Goetz et al. 2019.
106. Bernardo 2015.
107. Institute on Race and Poverty 2009a, 23–25; Crump 2007.
108. National Community Reinvestment Coalition 2007.
109. Austin 2010b.
110. Post 2015; Nickrand 2015.
111. Austin 2013; Post 2015.
112. Office on the Economic Status of Women 2008.
113. Dunbar 2010; L. M. Kelly and Egbert 2011.
114. Allen 2011.
115. Wilder Research 2017.
116. Now called the Institute on Metropolitan Opportunity.
117. See, for example, Orfield 2006; Institute on Race and Poverty 2007; Orfield and Wallace 2007; T. Collins 2008.
118. Goetz 2003, 106–7.
119. See, for example, Institute on Race and Poverty 2009b; Institute on Metropolitan Opportunity 2014, 2015; Callaghan 2015.
120. See, for example, L. Bennett and Reed 1999; Arena 2012; S. Stein 2019.
121. See Goetz 2003, ch. 8.
122. B. Lewis 2019.
123. Regan 2011.
124. The Midtown Exchange's "affordable" housing is priced for people making 60 percent of the *regional* median income—which includes the high incomes found in affluent urban and suburban enclaves and is thus much higher than the median income for the exchange's surrounding, higher-poverty neighborhood. As Samuel Stein (2019, 96) points out, developers regularly use regional median incomes to market housing units as "affordable" when, in fact, they are too pricey for most working-class families.
125. Murphy 2010.
126. Brandt 2012.
127. Goetz et al. 2019.
128. Hartley 2013.
129. Roper and Furst 2012.
130. Frymer, Strolovitch, and Warren 2006; Cedric Johnson 2011.
131. Fairbanks 2009; J. L. Collins and Mayer 2010.
132. R. Brenner 2002; Hacker and Pierson 2010.
133. Arena 2012, xxi; N. Brenner and Theodore 2002; Lyon-Callo and Hyatt 2003.

134. New York City under the de Blasio administration stands out as an important recent example (Richman 2019; S. Stein 2019).

135. Akuno and Nangwaya 2017; S. Stein 2019, 159–69.

136. S. Stein 2019, ch. 5.

137. S. Stein 2019, 186.

138. S. Stein 2019, 178. Stein, like me, draws on the scholarship of Frances Fox Piven and Richard Cloward. See Piven 2006.

3. THE POLITICAL HAZARDS OF CONTENTIOUS IDENTITY-BUILDING

1. Lafer 2017.

2. Dayton's great-grandfather established a local department store chain that later became the Target Corporation, one of Minneapolis's most influential and philanthropic business interests. By the 2010 midterms he had already been active in progressive politics for over thirty years. From 2001 to 2007 he was a U.S. senator.

3. Baran 2011.

4. Unless otherwise indicated, uncited quotations such as those contained in this paragraph come from the author's personal sources and notes.

5. At the time we interpreted her proposal as being focused explicitly on EBT cards. However, the bill she introduced—which was cosponsored by several other progressive Democrats—would have required users of *all* financial transaction cards to present a government-issued photo ID.

6. See also Alcoff 1991–92.

7. Gaventa 1980; Jackman 1996.

8. Fisher 2009.

9. Schram 2002; Sparks 2003.

10. During a hearing at the start of the 2011 state legislative session, Republicans on the Senate Health and Human Services Committee betrayed their ignorance about even the most basic elements of state welfare programs—such as eligibility rules and the general characteristics of recipient populations.

11. See also Brown 1995.

12. Soss 2000; Schlozman, Verba, and Brady 2012.

13. See, for example, Arena 2012; Beam 2018; and Hindman 2018.

14. Gaventa 1980; L. Cohen 2003.

15. J. Stein 1998.

16. Rhonda Williams 2005; Elbaum 2018.

17. McAlevey 2016; Blanc 2019; Estes 2019.

18. Harvey 2005; Fisher 2009.

19. Flanders 2013.

20. Fisher 2009; Phillips-Fein 2019.

21. Fisher 2009, 12–14.

22. My point here is not that intellectuals had no role in disseminating capitalist realism. However, as Kim Phillips-Fein (2009, 2017) has shown, their eventual influence was contingent on the restoration of pro-corporate institutional arrangements.

23. Lipman 2011.

24. Hasenfeld and Garrow 2012.
25. Schram 2015.
26. Hackworth 2002, 712; Kirkpatrick 2016.
27. Cucchiara 2008; DiMartino and Jessen 2016.
28. Zernike 2016; A. Reed and West 2019; Shapiro 2019.
29. Marwell 2004; Hasenfeld and Garrow 2012.
30. See also S. Stein 2019, 76–77.
31. Macklin and Pratt 2002; Wessel, Sonam, and Pratt 2010.
32. Pew Charitable Trusts 2013.
33. Nickel 1995; Kriz 2003, 3; Fagotto and Fung 2006, 641. At one point, the Minnesota government also approved a $10 million social impact bond program. However, it failed to attract investors (Temple 2015).
34. Wessel, Sonam, and Pratt 2010.
35. Boris et al. 2010a, 32; Wessel, Sonam, and Pratt 2010, 6.
36. Brandt 2013b.
37. The Bailout Coalition encountered similar manifestations of capitalist realism in their efforts to represent foreclosure victims. In the fall of 2009 the coalition and two women undergoing foreclosure occupied the office of then mayor R. T. Rybak. During the occupation, they spoke at length with one of the mayor's senior policy aides. When they asked if the mayor would help struggling homeowners by refusing to enforce eviction notices, the aide demurred by saying "that's a legal issue"—meaning, a matter of private property rights and, therefore, out of the mayor's hands. And when they asked why the mayor would not support calls for a foreclosure moratorium, she referred us to "research" claiming that a moratorium would *reduce* access to housing by harming creditors and disincentivizing future lending (this claim is questionable if not wrong; see J. M. Collins and Urban 2018). It seemed, from her perspective, that any challenge to the dictates of the mortgage market would result in social decay or disorder.
38. One proponent of a more egalitarian approach, a Catholic bishop, openly acknowledged the distance between his aspirations and those of service providers: "I suspect you know what I'm gonna say before I say it. You're going to say the religious guy wrings his hands, says we can't pull back any services to the poor and elderly and disabled and the sick folks. And you're thinking, that's easy for him to say because he doesn't have to do the math. . . . That is what I'm gonna say." In response to this comment, much of the room chuckled and laughed, enjoying the fact that even the bishop conceded the infeasibility of governing against market rule.
39. Zukin 2008.
40. Afterward, as I waited for the city bus, a Black homeless man asked me for change and struck up a conversation. There is just "nowhere to go for a single dude like me," he stated. Given what I had just witnessed, I could not disagree.
41. This quote and the context surrounding it are discussed further in chapter 4.
42. For example, since 2014, white liberals have experienced a "Great Awokening," marked by a sharp leftward turn in their opinions about race, gender, sexuality, and immigration (Yglesias 2019).
43. Arruzza, Bhattacharya, and Fraser 2019.

44. Schram and Soss 2001.
45. Goetz 2013; Taylor 2019; McQuarrie 2013.
46. See, for example, Battle et al. 2016; Alstott 2010.
47. Brown 1995; J. M. Schwartz 2008.
48. C. J. Cohen 1999; Spence 2015.
49. Goetz 2003.
50. See, for example, Orfield and Wallace 2007.
51. Ironically, as scholars such as Vincanne Adams (2013) have shown, when redistributive public programs fail under the weight of neoliberal cuts and reforms, it often *reinforces* the idea that the idea that these programs are barriers to progress.
52. Stewart was at one point a staff member at the Headwaters Foundation for Justice, a progressive nonprofit that provided grants to social justice organizations in Minneapolis. Some of these organizations included the Welfare Rights Committee, the Bailout Coalition, and Neighborhoods Organizing for Change, a key member of the North High Coalition.
53. See, for example, Hayward 2000; Carter 2005; A. E. Lewis and Diamond 2015.
54. Goetz 2003; Goetz et al. 2019.
55. Hayward 2000. Other board members were not as crude as Stewart. Nonetheless, in practice, most of them similarly framed Black students primarily as victims of bad teaching.
56. J. L. Collins and Mayer 2010; Desmond 2016.
57. C. J. Cohen 1999; A. Reed 1999.
58. See, for example, Piven and Cloward 1971; Gaventa 1980.
59. Mishel et al. 2012.
60. Lichtenstein 2002; Skocpol 2003.
61. Norris 2015.
62. Soss and Jacobs 2009; Lee, McQuarrie, and Walker 2015; Hertel-Fernandez 2018.
63. Piven 2000; J. L. Collins and Mayer 2010.
64. Soss, Fording, and Schram 2011; Wacquant 2009.
65. See, for example, Piven 1998, 2000; Bronfenbrenner 2000; McQuarrie 2013.
66. L. Bennett and Reed 1999; Arena 2012.
67. A. Goffman 2014; E. Jones 2018.
68. Soss 2000; S. Bruch, Ferree, and Soss 2010; Lerman and Weaver 2014.
69. Goetz 2003.
70. McDonnell 2004.
71. Institute on Metropolitan Opportunity 2017.
72. Wirtz 2013.
73. Goetz 1996, 2003; Aiken 2017; Mannix 2017.
74. Frase 2009; Wagner and Sawyer 2018.
75. American Civil Liberties Union 2015; Busker, Gorsuch, and Rho 2018.
76. Frase 2009; Sakala 2014.
77. McDonnell 2004; Minnesota Minority Education Partnership 2013.

78. Wessel, Sonam, and Pratt 2010, 7; Boris et al. 2010b, 56.
79. Chaudhuri 2018.
80. Winkler 2014; Kaul 2017; Minnesota Department of Health 2018.
81. Madden and Macklin 2001, 4–6.
82. Human Impact Partners and ISAIAH 2016.
83. Simms 2014.
84. Goetz and Sidney 1997; Goetz 2003.
85. The Sumner Field, Olson, Lyndale, and Glenwood public housing projects—which were demolished because of the *Hollman* decision—served as a key site for social justice organizers' recruitment efforts. By organizing in these projects, the Welfare Rights Committee was able to mobilize large numbers of Black and Hmong welfare recipients to their protests in the early to mid-1990s. According to one organizer, after the projects were demolished the committee's outreach efforts never regained the same level of efficacy.

4. ORGANIZING FOR MODERATION

1. The provision was unavoidable, she argued, because North High needed over one hundred students per incoming class to remain "cost-effective" and "viable." She ignored that MPS's promotion of school choice and competition was itself partly responsible for the school's enrollment problems.
2. The first statement in this passage was technically false. According to the approved proposal, North High would remain open not "if" but regardless of whether "125 9th graders" enrolled. Stephen was stoking concerns, shared by many, that the school would likely close if it lost its 2011–12 freshman class.
3. In U.S. urban politics there is a long-standing tradition of elevating middle-class "race leaders"—pastors, nonprofit directors, and other (often male) professionals—as the authentic voice of "the Black community" (A. Reed 1999; Cedric Johnson 2007; Arena 2012).
4. Gorz 1967; Schram 2002.
5. Strolovitch 2007; Disch 2011; Weeks 2011.
6. See, for example, Cedric Johnson 2007; Arena 2012; Hindman 2018; Beam 2018.
7. Fisher 2009.
8. Meyer 2004; Meyer and Minkoff 2004.
9. Gamson and Meyer 1996.
10. See chapter 3.
11. Orren and Skowronek 2004; Berkman 2018.
12. C. J. Cohen 1999; Strolovitch 2007; Arena 2012; Majic 2014; Hindman 2018.
13. E. Goffman 1979; Eliasoph 1998.
14. Strolovitch 2007; Majic 2014; McAlevey 2016.
15. C. J. Cohen 1999; Springer 2005; Strolovitch 2007.
16. C. J. Cohen 1997; Keating 2005.
17. Ironically, one of the most eloquent defenses of this point comes from Adolph Reed Jr., who presents himself as a critic of intersectionality (Reed 1999; Forrest 2016, 17–18).

18. Schram 2002; Hindman 2018.

19. Schram 2002.

20. In recent history some authors have suggested that intersectional and adversarial identity constructions actually work *against* one another (see, for example, Michaels 2018). According to these authors, intersectional constructions primarily attribute injustice to individual acts of discrimination and abuse and thus undermine adversarial critiques of its systemic and political-economic roots. Their argument is, in my opinion, only partly correct. On the one hand, they are no doubt right that, in some cases, intersectional constructions of injustice have given short shrift to political-economic critique. On the other hand, they are wrong to argue that appeals to intersectionality *inherently* discount such critique. Many scholars, for example, have successfully tied an intersectional vision of the injustices facing disadvantaged groups to an adversarial account of the political-economic arrangements behind those injustices (see, for example, Taylor 2019 and Gilmore 2007).

21. These points are illustrated well, for example, by Premilla Nadasen's (2015) account of the Black women organizers who built America's domestic workers movement. In the 1960s and 1970s these women coordinated a national effort to redress the poor treatment of household labor. Together, they rejected gendered and racialized images of domestic workers as strong, content, and loyal "mammies." And they reconstrued these workers as "household technicians"—that is, skilled professionals deserving of generous compensation, strong workplace protections, and societal respect (Nadasen 2015, 10–13, 77–81). This identity, as they fashioned it, followed both intersectional and adversarial logics. It called attention to interlocking patterns of discrimination, legal exclusion, and exploitation, which prevented most domestic workers and service workers from achieving the same standing as other skilled professionals. It also at least implicitly blamed these injustices on America's patriarchal and capitalist wage system, which devalues household and care labor to suppress overall wages and subsidize corporate profits (Nadasen 2015, 133–42).

As part of building and committing to the "household technician" identity, organizers embraced an abolitionist call for the universalization of basic labor rights. Their abolitionism, in other words, was built into how they understood the plight of their constituents. The rights they called for included generous minimum-wage requirements, strong workplace safety regulations, and other protections and benefits that policy makers had previously only granted to a partial, disproportionately male segment of the labor force. Organizers (accurately) believed that by extending such rights to everyone, policy makers could lay the groundwork for a revaluation of care labor, a confrontation with the broader wage system, and a longer-term struggle to eliminate the myriad oppressions facing domestic workers.

Had domestic worker organizers construed "household technicians" on more unitary and/or cooperative terms, demanding universal labor rights would have seemed nonsensical or unnecessary. For instance, imagine if, in a unitary fashion, they had reduced the oppression of domestic workers to discrimination—that is, to the fact that discrimination kept many women, especially Black women, out of more prestigious occupations. Even if paired with an adversarial account of discrimination's systemic roots, the demands emanating from such an identity would have focused on rearranging who performed devalued household labor rather than challenging the overall wage system. Alternatively, imagine if, in a cooperative fashion, organizers had attributed domestic workers' oppression to the bad behavior of employers—that is, to these employers' tendency to treat "the help" as servants rather than skilled professionals. Even if assembled on intersectional terms, such an identity would have primarily motivated demands to discipline, shame, or renegotiate with individual employers—again, rather than eliminate the wage system that contextualizes and drives their behavior.

22. Intersectional approaches did not generate the same worry among the coalition's organizers. Explaining why this was the case is beyond the scope of my project. But my general sense is that, for most coalition members, the economic injustices facing "the community" were hard to ignore. Even a cursory examination revealed that racial discrimination could not possibly account for all the problems facing northside students.

23. See chapter 2 and Lipman 2011, 65–69.

24. Cheryl's cynicism about the viability of redistribution also stemmed from a diminished sense of political efficacy. When politicians hear the committee speak, she once said, they "laugh and go in their offices and drink . . . Grey Goose." As I discuss in chapter 6, this diminished sense of efficacy undermined all social justice organizers' efforts to mobilize their constituents.

25. See also Strolovitch 2007, ch. 6.

26. See also, for example, Strolovitch 2007, ch. 7; McAlevey 2016; Kurtz 2002.

27. Stephen often circulated to coalition members articles that highlighted successful efforts to defend public schools in other cities. In addition, he and other PEJAM activists organized an event with Karen Lewis, then president of the Chicago Teachers Union and a leading figure in the national movement to end neoliberal education reform.

28. Manny's tenure on the executive board of Minneapolis's NAACP chapter occurred under the leadership of Leola Seals, the protest-oriented president I mentioned in chapter 2. Seals also participated in the North High Coalition, albeit somewhat infrequently.

29. Manny shared an article about the community school model with the group (Kirp 2010). A few years later, this model would garner more support among local and state progressive leaders (Hinrichs 2018).

30. One of these people was Belinda, the retired teacher who—as I discussed in chapter 3—organized a bus tour that essentially framed north Minneapolis as an attractive commodity for middle-class consumers.

31. This emphasis on positivity mirrored a broader set of fatuous ideas about the "power of positive thinking" (Ehrenreich 2009).

32. James's tenure at the NAACP came after Leola Seals was ousted in a hotly contested—and some say rigged—election.

33. Neighborhoods Organizing for Change was a 501(c)(4) and, thus, did not have to disclose its donors on tax forms. However, my understanding from talking to members of the group was that—at the time—the bulk of their revenue

came from either the labor movement or institutions like the Headwaters Foundations, which were willing to fund radical efforts at social change. Furthermore, a few years later the organization itself awarded a grant to Occupy Homes Minnesota, an avowedly left-wing organization that used home occupations to stop foreclosures and evictions.

34. This statement is based on the behavior I observed among the individuals who *did* attend meetings and participate in the coalition's efforts. It was consistently the case that poor and working-class activists were more likely to engage in "political" talk than middle-class leaders like Xavier.

35. E. Goffman 1959.

36. The teachers at North High had previously developed a plan for reorganizing the school, which the school district ignored.

37. At a meeting in February 2011 even Xavier questioned his commitment to "being positive." In that meeting it became clear that the superintendent had misled the coalition about an important part of North High's redesign process and was wavering on her commitment to the school. Reluctantly, Xavier agreed with a suggestion made by Stephen to release a public letter to the superintendent and the school board. The letter demanded that the superintendent hold a press conference and publish an op-ed, unequivocally stating her commitment to keeping North High open. It also demanded that the school board expand its support for the school, by, for example, restoring North High's "home zone," "so that the hundreds of neighborhood students who don't choose another school are placed into North High." The overall tone was very "negative." Yet, within three days of sending the letter and after a private conversation with one board member, Xavier was already talking over email about how to continue "partnering" with the district.

38. I similarly encountered an awkward silence when—around the same time—I emailed some of the more active members of the coalition, emphasizing that "North High supporters need to remain aware that a 'redesign' can never substitute for the political mobilization and policy changes needed to create an equitable public education system." Nobody, even those to whom I was most familiar, responded or engaged.

39. Once Joanne exited the meeting, someone quickly reset the conversation, asserting that "We need teachers that are going to prepare students for the twenty-first century."

40. In a private conversation, another lead organizer called Xavier's email "bullshit."

41. There were moments when organizers tried to supplement the focus on underachievement with more straightforward discussion of "the community's" material needs. However, such moments never endured. Organizers either returned to discussing sociocultural rather than material needs or unconsciously reconfigured comments about material needs on sociocultural terms. For example, when one person argued for "greening the classroom," several organizers equated this goal with preparing students to compete for "green jobs" rather than constructing healthier learning spaces.

42. The coalition's intersectional approach was not uncontested. As I have

stated elsewhere, some organizers and supporters pushed a more unitary construction, which focused only on discrimination. In discussing the district's redesign process, they emphasized, above all else, needing to rebrand North High as a "good" school. Implicit in their statements was a belief that "the community" and its schools could thrive, if only the school district, the local news, and the public stopped denigrating them. In the same way that "being positive" marginalized adversarial appeals, it also mitigated such unitary ideas about "the community." The coalition's etiquette, as most members understood it, was not simply about crafting a positive image. It was about *actually* redesigning the school, addressing "the community's" manifold oppressions, and achieving a more positive future. When some of them lost sight of this, others issued prompt course corrections. For example, in a small district-led meeting about the redesign, Mary—the African American studies professor previously mentioned—implored those focused on rebranding the school to "be real about the community we're working in." "We need something that's going to give these kids a leg up," she added, receiving nods of agreement from the other meeting attendees. Citing this attitude, coalition organizers nixed several rebranding ideas, such as producing a North High commercial and creating a series of pro-North YouTube videos.

43. To emcee the potluck, the coalition enlisted Verna Price, an education professional from north Minneapolis. Though not a coalition member, she shared the coalition's intersectional and cooperative view of "the community." In 2005 Price founded a nonprofit, Girls in Action, "to address the rise in violent, destructive, and delinquent behavior being exhibited by the female students at Minneapolis' North High School." The nonprofit—which now operates in multiple cities and is supported by 3M, Wells Fargo, and several other large corporations—works from a belief that *all* disadvantaged girls' educational opportunities can be expanded by "providing them with role models, mentors, experiences, and knowledge" ("Dr. Verna Price").

44. ISA's president at the time, Gerry House, was a former chair of the board of directors for the Educational Testing Service (ETS), the world's largest nonprofit developer of standardized tests. In 2013, under House's leadership, ISA became a division of ETS.

45. Elsewhere, the "community advisory board" particularly recommended "educating students about green and sustainable practices to prepare them for college and careers in STEM [science, technology, engineering, and mathematics] fields."

46. The document included a heading that mentioned "Wrap-Around Services." However, the only fully accessible service discussed under that heading was very basic health care, which was already available to North High students prior to the redesign.

47. Tellingly, among the coalition activists I met, few if any of them left the group more engaged in egalitarian and emancipatory movements than when they started.

48. Schram 2002.

49. Freedom Road Socialist Organization is one of several groups that emerged out of the "new communist movement" of the 1970s (Elbaum 2018).

50. Despite facing an emergent neoliberal regime, the group was marginally successful. See, for example, Diaz 1990; Leyden 1991.

51. Hennessey 1996.

52. Freedom Place, Inc. 2020.

53. Roelofs (2003) refers to organizations like Headwaters as "social change" rather than "liberal" foundations, because of their willingness to support more radical politics.

54. Committee leaders' worries came through in their reflections about Headwaters "site visits." One organizer described these visits in the following way: "They send two people out," one of which is a board member, "who may or may not know shit about what you're doing." She continued, "We've had a couple years where the people were kind of backward."

55. Technically, the Welfare Rights Committee was also a nonprofit organization. However, in their discourse only "advocacy" groups were called "nonprofits."

56. Members promoted "fighting back" not only through their own introductions but also through their responses to those of others. The most critical statements about mainstream political leaders often received applause and exclamations of "Yes!" and "Alright!" And tamer statements evoked less praise. For new and existing members alike, these contrasting responses created a subtle pressure to adopt the group's etiquette. Indeed, after several months with the committee, I realized that I had unconsciously altered my own introductions in order to emphasize the "fight" and gain the group's approval.

57. In truth, most "actions" were fairly tame events. However, by describing them as highly confrontational, organizers reaffirmed "the fight" as an ideal toward which members should strive.

58. See also Hinck, Pearson-Cater, and Schmickle 2011.

59. Committee leaders also regularly discussed (what they framed as) successful examples of "fighting back" occurring in other states and countries—such as the Wisconsin Uprising, the Arab Spring, and Occupy Wall Street.

60. McCammon, Arch, and Bergner 2014.

61. Serres 2020.

62. Eliasoph 1998.

63. Blanc 2019; Uetricht and Eidlin 2019.

5. MISLEADING THE PUBLIC

1. See, for example, Baran 2009a, 2009b; Brunswick 2009; Shah 2009.

2. See chapter 2.

3. Crump 2007; Allen 2011.

4. While the Bailout Coalition's proposed legislation allowed tenants to continue living in foreclosed investment properties under a fair lease—thereby, avoiding eviction—it did nothing to actually stop those properties from being foreclosed on and taken over by banks. Only owner-occupied homes could benefit from a stay on the foreclosure process.

5. Even during the "crisis," the sympathetic constituency that progressives most typically associated with foreclosures—longtime homeowners who had

been steered into refinancing their homes with subprime loans—constituted a minority of foreclosure victims (Foote, Gerardi, and Willen 2012; Ferreira and Gyourko 2015).

6. Kurtz 2002; Schram 2002.

7. Ernst 2010, ch. 5.

8. Strolovitch 2007; Ernst 2010; Cedric Johnson 2017; Hindman 2018.

9. See, for example, Clegg and Usmani 2019.

10. Schram 2002.

11. Koopmans and Statham 1999; McCammon et al. 2007.

12. McCammon 2013.

13. See chapter 3.

14. Other types of ignorance have also influenced American politics; see, for example, Charles Mills's (2007) discussion of "white ignorance" about racial oppression.

15. Kurtz 2002; Strolovitch 2007; Majic 2014.

16. See, for example, M. E. Warren 2001; Schram 2002; Sangtin Writers and Nagar 2006.

17. Schram 2002; Strolovitch 2007; Ernst 2010. See also chapter 4.

18. See chapter 2.

19. Cotterman 2002.

20. Edelman 1977, ch. 7.

21. Schram 2002; Ferree 2003; Woodly 2015.

22. When the moratorium bill was referred to his committee, Atkins never granted it a hearing or a vote.

23. Sandin 2007.

24. Serres 2009.

25. Sitting alongside Gottwalt were several first-term GOP legislators who shared his ignorance and near complete inability to appreciate oppositional rhetoric. There was, for instance, Mary Franson, a white woman and licensed child-care provider who later became infamous for comparing welfare recipients to wild animals (Rupar 2012). There was also Glenn Gruenhagen, a white male insurance agent and small business owner who praised restrictive welfare legislation for supposedly discouraging welfare cheats from migrating to Minnesota. Other first-term GOP committee members argued that the bill protected assistance for people who *really* needed it.

26. In 2013 Gottwalt resigned from the state legislature in response to allegations that he violated ethics rules (Scheck 2013). During his time on the Health and Human Services Reform Committee he accepted employment at two firms that lobbied the state on health-care legislation. In one case he joined the firm only months after sponsoring a bill for which it had lobbied extensively.

27. Swarts 2008.

28. Kimball 2011.

29. See chapter 3.

30. Another group of community activists who ignored market oppression and had trouble understanding oppositional rhetoric were some of the northside pastors. For example, a well-known Baptist pastor and civil rights activist told

a Welfare Rights Committee member that people blaming poverty on the labor market were just "encouraging people to stay on welfare." See also Spence 2015, ch. 3.

31. Strolovitch 2007, 62–65; M. E. Warren 2001, 70–82.

32. Grover 2011.

33. Crump 2008.

34. Cotterman 2002.

35. See, for example, Freedom Road Socialist Organization 2001.

36. See, for example, Freedom Road Socialist Organization 2010a, 2010b.

37. Freedom Road Socialist Organization 2010a.

38. Space restrictions prevent me from describing the process through which leaders of the Bailout Coalition established their etiquette. It suffices to say, however, that this process closely mirrored those of the North High Coalition and the Welfare Rights Committee, which chapter 4 outlined in detail.

39. Sometimes they did, though. For example, at one meeting, Lou—a Bailout Coalition founder—asserted that even before the Great Recession the labor market had consistently failed to produce enough decent work. The result was that many "poor and working people" unnecessarily fell victim to things like job insecurity and foreclosure. The "crisis," by his account, was just an escalation of this dynamic.

40. One of these statements explicitly asserted that "The problem is not just the misbehavior of the bank owners. The problem is the system of boom and bust—capitalism" (Freedom Road Socialist Organization 2010b). This "system," another argued, disproportionately hurt African Americans and other "oppressed nationalities" and required "struggle" toward "a system based not on the profit of privately owned corporations, but one based on serving the needs of the working people through government and collective enterprises" (Freedom Road Socialist Organization 2010a).

41. See, for example, Kiel 2012.

42. See also Ernst 2010.

43. At a legislative hearing, Leslie testified that her mother "told the mortgage broker, 'I want the same kind of mortgage I always had.' That was a conventional fixed-rate mortgage she could afford. . . . But what she got was an option ARM [adjustable-rate] mortgage. . . . She didn't even know she had this ARM mortgage until a financial planner . . . told her [much later]."

44. Kaul 2017; B. Lewis 2015.

45. In fact, at the time, many local leaders saw their licensing process as a way to *drive out* owners of rental property who could not make repairs (operating under the assumption that most of these owners were slumlords who refused to make—rather than could not afford—the repairs) (Weinmann and Mannix 2009).

46. National Community Reinvestment Coalition 2007; Institute on Race and Poverty 2009a.

47. Bailout Coalition organizers used similarly color-blind terms in telling the story of Rosemary Williams, another lower-income Black woman, whose home they very publicly defended and occupied. They framed Rosemary mostly as the

victim of predatory lending, as she had been sold an adjustable-rate loan when she refinanced her home around 2005. But, like Tecora, the roots of her foreclosure were much deeper and more entwined with long-run market processes. She initially refinanced with a subprime mortgage because she could not otherwise afford, in her words, to "pay off some bills and help my daughter finish college." She lived in the same area as Tecora, faced similarly limited job prospects, and, by all accounts, had worse credit.

48. I most directly observed the limits of the Bailout Coalition's rhetoric through my efforts to gather signatures on a petition supporting their moratorium proposal. Because I was a graduate student at the time, I mostly reached out to other graduate students with offices near mine. Every person I engaged was liberal or progressive, and in each case I presented the proposal using the coalition's talking points about the predatory lending and unemployment "crisis" facing "poor and working people." Nonetheless, most of them expressed some sort of skepticism toward the proposal—asserting either that the proposal was too radical or that it would help too many irresponsible people who, in fact, had not been scammed by lenders or laid off during the recession. Like the coalition as a whole, the only response I could muster was to emphasize the sheer size of the "crisis" and insist that a moratorium was "the right thing to do."

49. Meitrodt 2013; Battle et al. 2016.

50. One might argue that the differences between the Bailout Coalition and the Welfare Rights Committee simply stemmed from their different issue foci—housing and welfare. However, on several occasions, activists representing the coalition spoke at legislative hearings on welfare policy, and during those hearings those activists typically clung to their focus on "crisis."

51. Occasionally, meeting chairs also led an exercise in which someone would pretend to be a neoliberal but Democratic legislator, and members would have to convince that person to support their "fight." I never personally witnessed such an exercise. However, I heard a committee leader describe it during one of the Bailout Coalition's meetings.

52. Piven and Cloward 1971.

53. The quote about "a certain criminal element" came from Glenn Gruenhagen, a white male, first-term legislator, and small business owner, who also had ties to ALEC.

54. Daudt 2012. Notably, even some of the center-left politicians and advocates who opposed Welfare Reform 2.0 did not challenge the idea that Minnesota's welfare programs were too generous or permissive. In hearings about the legislation, some of them said that they had supported past efforts to restrict access to assistance and conceded that, if properly tailored, they would support future restrictions. According to their statements, the main reason they opposed the bill was that it would have blocked many "truly needy" people, especially young children, from receiving assistance.

55. Benanav 2019; J. L. Collins and Mayer 2010.

56. In a later testimony, Ebony explained that "they won't hire us," meaning working-class African Americans and people with long histories of job instability.

"So, how are . . . especially women with children, how are they supposed to go look for a job . . . when the private sector refuses to hire us in the first place?"

57. J. L. Collins and Mayer 2010.

58. Piven 2000.

59. See, for example, Tester 2008.

60. Scott, London, and Myers 2002.

61. To be fair, Webster also supported the idea of increased welfare cash payments in 2012. But, in contrast to the committee, she was not yet publicly advocating for such an increase.

62. Simons 2015.

63. Webster 2016.

64. It is also worth noting that, during the committee hearings about raising MFIP payments, multiple longtime advocates and legislators cited the past efforts of the Welfare Rights Committee as an important factor in shifting the conversation toward more egalitarian reform.

65. See, for example, Burden-Stelly 2020; Pan 2020.

6. SEEKING LEGITIMACY WITHOUT MOBILIZATION

1. In cooperation with Vikings ownership, the Metropolitan Sports Facilities Commission—a public body charged with managing the acquisition and betterment of sports facilities in the Twin Cities—hired a consulting firm to project the benefits of building a new Vikings facility in downtown Minneapolis (Conventions Sports and Leisure 2009). As Delaney and Eckstein (2003) report, this sort of collaboration is common in efforts to promote public–private stadium development projects.

2. Elliot Park, one of the city's greatest sources of well-managed affordable housing, had long been marked for redevelopment and was already undergoing a government-sponsored process of poverty deconcentration and reinvestment (Elliot Park Neighborhood, Inc. 2002; M. Bruch 2008; Minnesota Compass 2011). Vikings owners promised that a new stadium would accelerate this process by attracting new developers and business owners (Melo 2012).

3. HIRE Minnesota 2012.

4. Goetz et al. 2019, 23; Buchta 2016a; Gose 2018; Goldstein 2012. In general, public–private stadium development projects yield few economic benefits for poor and working-class people (Delaney and Eckstein 2003; Noll and Zimbalist 1997). This trend has held true for the Minnesota Vikings' publicly financed stadium, which opened in 2016 (Draper 2018).

5. These stadium supporters were organized and coordinated, with many of them sporting similar construction vests and hardhats.

6. Roper 2012.

7. See, for example, Nord 2012; D. Davis 2012; T. Nelson 2013; *Star Tribune* 2013.

8. Progressive officials regularly brought up the "equity plan" as they sought to respond to the committee's criticisms. See, for example, T. Nelson 2013.

9. Strolovitch 2007, 57.

10. See also Dreier and Martin 2010; Kim 2000.

11. See, for example, Piven and Cloward 1977; M. R. Warren 2001; Bradbury, Brenner, and Slaughter 2016; McAlevey 2016.

12. Mansbridge 2003.

13. M. R. Warren 2001.

14. Scholars disagree about which approaches to grassroots mobilization are most efficacious. Nevertheless, virtually all of them agree that social justice organizations need widespread constituent engagement to amass significant power. See, for example, M. R. Warren 2001; Ganz 2009; McAlevey 2016.

15. Here and throughout this chapter, I define *tactic* in the same way as Michel de Certeau (1980)—that is, as a practice that weaker groups use to navigate and resist existing sociopolitical arrangements.

16. Arena 2012; McAlevey 2016.

17. Piven and Cloward 1977.

18. Piven 2006, 26–31.

19. Skocpol 2003; Arena 2012; McAlevey 2016.

20. See, for example, Ernst 2010, 53–62.

21. Mansbridge 2003.

22. Rosenstone and Hansen 2003; Schlozman, Verba, and Brady 2012.

23. Mishel et al. 2012; Norris 2015.

24. J. L. Collins and Mayer 2010.

25. Schlozman, Verba, and Brady 2012, ch. 15.

26. Some scholarship seems to imply otherwise (see, for example, Han 2014). However, as scholars like Piven and Cloward (1977) have long shown, the short-term prospects for grassroots mobilization are always already socially structured.

27. See chapter 3.

28. This estimate was reported by a longtime organizer who volunteered in both the Welfare Rights Committee and the Bailout Coalition.

29. See also Choi-Fitzpatrick 2015.

30. Sugrue 2018.

31. See the opening of chapter 4.

32. One of the largest AFSCME locals in this council was also a member of the Bailout Coalition.

33. Orrick 2011.

34. The broader implications of my findings can be summarized using Charles Tilly's concept of "WUNC displays"—that is "public enactments of worthiness, unity, numbers, and commitment" (Tilly 2008, 120). My findings suggest that social justice organizers' ability to decisively establish their democratic legitimacy depends more on producing "unity, numbers, and commitment" among their constituents than on adopting political methods that strictly fit dominant standards of "worthiness."

35. Mansbridge 1999, 2003.

36. Mansbridge 2003.

37. Panning-Miller 2010.

38. The speaker later clarified that her actual question was, quite literally, whether she could speak on behalf of a friend from north Minneapolis who could not make the meeting. That coalition organizers would so easily misinterpret the

scope of her question reveals just how much salience they attached to issues of description and identification.

39. Mansbridge 2003.

40. Lipsky 1980.

41. As I discussed in prior chapters, even these subjective factors are—to the extent they exist—largely rooted in neoliberal-era institutional practices that have engendered the rise of capitalist realism and public ignorance about various systems of oppression.

42. Inasmuch as debates about "false" consciousness remain internal to organizations, they are irrelevant for defending their democratic credentials to the general public. However, such debates can be critical for defending these credentials to another key audience: their membership.

43. As many studies have shown, the news media play an especially significant role in mediating social justice organizations' claims to democratic legitimacy (Dreier and Martin 2010; Gitlin 1980; Rohlinger 2002).

44. Gamson and Wolfsfeld 1993.

45. Mitchell 2011a.

46. Mitchell 2011b.

47. Hopfensperger 1994.

48. Simons 2009.

49. Panning-Miller 2010; Konechne and Molina 1996.

50. See, for example, Sparks 2003.

51. Meyer 2006; Polletta 1998.

52. Han 2014; McAlevey 2016.

53. For example, Loretta and Angel—two low-income African American women who initially became involved in politics through the committee—went on to help form the Twin Cities Coalition for Justice for Jamar, a socialist organization that actively participated in local Black Lives Matter protests.

CONCLUSION

1. Since the 1930s the Powderhorn community has been a key destination for low-income people of color locked out of the region's more affluent neighborhoods—especially African Americans and, more recently, immigrants from Mexico and other Latin American countries (Burnside 2017; Goetz et al. 2019, 41).

2. Goetz 2003.

3. American Civil Liberties Union 2015.

4. Prior to Floyd's death, Abumayyaleh had maintained relatively good relations with the Minneapolis Police Department and contracted with off-duty officers to patrol his business on weekend nights. Moreover, the city's nuisance abatement law required his employees to report the use of counterfeit bills and other suspected criminal activity to the police. In response to the protests and his own anguish, Abumayyaleh—who was not at Cup Foods on May 25 but later recognized Floyd as one of his regular customers—has vowed to avoid police involvement at his store outside of extreme situations (Chapin 2020; Bayoumi 2020).

5. Simms 2014; Goetz et al. 2019. See also chapter 2.
6. Capoccia 2016.
7. Fraser 2019.
8. Knafo 2012; M. Smith 2016.
9. Chen 2018; Howard 2019; Trickey 2019.
10. Mannix 2019.
11. Lahm 2018.
12. Trickey 2019.
13. Ibrahim 2018; Navratil 2019.
14. Serres 2020, 2021.
15. Hensley-Clancy 2020.
16. H. Jones 2020.
17. Montemayor and Xiong 2020.
18. Fletcher 2020.
19. In December 2020, as part of a compromise with the city's mayor—Jacob Frey, a white man and employment and civil rights attorney—the council shifted about $8 million of the police department's budget to other public safety services (Navratil 2020).
20. Goetz quoted in Martin 2019.
21. H. Jones 2018; Ostfield 2020.
22. Moylan 2019; Howard 2019.
23. Feshir 2020; Mervosh 2021.
24. Bierschbach 2019.
25. Oladipo 2021.
26. Lancaster 2020.
27. Piven 2006.
28. See especially Piven and Cloward 1971, 1977.
29. Piven and Cloward 1977, 36–37; Minkoff 1997.
30. McAlevey 2016; Han 2014; Arena 2012; Nadasen 2005.
31. Lancaster 2020.
32. Guastella 2020.
33. Cedric Johnson 2017.
34. Phoenix 2020.
35. Sainato 2020.
36. Day 2020.
37. Lerman and Weaver 2014.
38. Schram 2002.
39. See, for example, Blanc 2019.
40. Tigue 2016.
41. See, for example, Horazuk 2020.
42. See, for example, Han 2020; Jaffe 2020.

APPENDIX: RESEARCH METHODS

1. Exceptions include Kurtz 2002 and Majic 2014.
2. See, for example, Fantasia 1988; Eliasoph 1998; Lichterman 1996; Blee 2012.

3. Vargas 2008, 175.

4. Consider, for example, Blee's (2002) research on organized racism or Wood's (2006) study of civil conflict.

5. On this point, see also Schwartz-Shea and Yanow 2012, 84–89.

6. Schwartz-Shea and Yanow 2012; Timmermans and Tavory 2012.

7. Schwartz-Shea and Yanow 2012, 12.

8. Piven and Cloward 1971; Schram 1995; Sparks 2003; Hancock 2004; Wacquant 2009; Soss, Fording, and Schram 2011; Schlozman, Verba, and Brady 2012; Lerman and Weaver 2014.

9. Berry 2010.

10. Gilman 2012.

BIBLIOGRAPHY

Abzug, Rikki, and Joseph Galaskiewicz. 2001. "Nonprofit Boards: Crucibles of Expertise or Symbols of Local Identities?" *Nonprofit and Voluntary Sector Quarterly* 30 (1): 51–73.

Adams, Vincanne. 2013. *Markets of Sorrow, Labors of Faith*. Durham: Duke University Press.

Ahmed-Ullah, Noreen S. 2014. "Chicago's Noble Charter School Network Has Tough Discipline Policy." *Chicago Tribune*, April 7. https://www.chicagotribune.com.

Aiken, Joshua. 2017. *Era of Mass Expansion*. Northampton, Mass.: Prison Policy Initiative. https://www.prisonpolicy.org.

Akuno, Kali, and Ajamu Nangwaya, eds. 2017. *Jackson Rising: The Struggle for Economic Democracy and Black Self-Determination in Jackson, Mississippi*. Ottawa: Daraja Press.

Alcoff, Linda. 1991–92. "The Problem of Speaking for Others." *Cultural Critique* 20:5–32.

Alinsky, Saul D. 1971. *Rules for Radicals: A Practical Primer for Realistic Radicals*. New York: Vintage.

Allen, Ryan. 2011. "Who Experiences Foreclosures? The Characteristics of Households Experiencing a Foreclosure in Minneapolis, Minnesota." *Housing Studies* 26 (6): 845–66.

Alstott, Anne L. 2010. "Why the EITC Doesn't Make Work Pay." *Law and Contemporary Problems* 73 (1): 285–313.

American Civil Liberties Union. 2015. *Picking Up the Pieces*. New York: American Civil Liberties Union. https://www.aclu.org.

Arena, John. 2012. *Driven from New Orleans: How Nonprofits Betray Public Housing and Promote Privatization*. Minneapolis: University of Minnesota Press.

Arruzza, Cinzia, Tithi Bhattacharya, and Nancy Fraser. 2019. *Feminism for the 99%: A Manifesto*. New York: Verso.

Ashton, Philip. 2010. "CRA's 'Blind Spots': Community Reinvestment and Concentrated Subprime Lending in Detroit." *Journal of Urban Affairs* 32 (5): 579–608.

Auletta, Ken. 1981. "A Reporter at Large: The Underclass—I." *New Yorker*, November 16.

Austin, Algernon. 2010a. *Different Race, Different Recession*. Washington, D.C.: Economic Policy Institute. http://www.epi.org.

Austin, Algernon. 2010b. *Uneven Pain: Unemployment by Metropolitan Area and Race*. Washington, D.C.: Economic Policy Institute. http://www.epi.org.

Austin, Algernon. 2013. *Native Americans Are Less Likely to Be Employed than Whites in Nearly Every State*. Washington, D.C.: Economic Policy Institute.

Bale, Jeff, and Sarah Knopp, eds. 2012. *Education and Capitalism: Struggles for Learning and Liberation*. Chicago: Haymarket.

Baran, Madeleine. 2009a. "Foreclosed Home Auction Draws Protestors, Bargain Hunters." *Twin Cities Daily Planet*, March 30. https://www.tcdailyplanet.net.

Baran, Madeleine. 2009b. "Taking It to Court in Minneapolis: Fight against Foreclosure and Eviction." *Twin Cities Daily Planet*, May 27. https://www.tcdailyplanet.net.

Baran, Madeleine. 2011. "Misuse of Welfare Money Is Minimal, Data Show." *MPRNews*, March 15. https://www.mprnews.org.

Battle, Jeremiah, Jr., Sarah Mancini, Margot Saunders, and Odette Williamson. 2016. *Toxic Transactions: How Land Installment Contracts Once Again Threaten Communities of Color*. National Consumer Law Center. https://www.nclc.org.

Bayoumi, Moustafa. 2020. "Why Did Cup Foods Call the Cops on George Floyd?" *New York Times*, June 17. https://www.nytimes.com.

Beam, Myrl. 2018. *Gay, Inc.: The Nonprofitization of Queer Politics*. Minneapolis: University of Minnesota Press.

Beltrán, Cristina. 2010. *The Trouble with Unity: Latino Politics and the Creation of Identity*. New York: Oxford University Press.

Benanav, Aaron. 2019. "Automation and the Future of Work—I." *New Left Review* 119:5–38.

Bennett, Gary G., Melissa Scharoun-Lee, and Reginald Tucker-Seeley. 2009. "Will the Public's Health Fall Victim to the Home Foreclosure Epidemic?" *PLOS Medicine* 6 (6). http://www.plosmedicine.org.

Bennett, Larry, and Adolph Reed Jr. 1999. "The New Face of Urban Renewal: The Near North Redevelopment Initiative and the Cabrini-Green Neighborhood." In *Without Justice for All: The New Liberalism and Our Retreat from Racial Equality*, edited by Adolph Reed Jr., 175–211. Boulder: Westview Press.

Berkman, Matthew. 2018. "Coercive Consensus: Jewish Federations, Ethnic Representation, and the Roots of American Pro-Israel Politics." PhD diss., University of Pennsylvania.

Bernardo, Richie. 2015. "2015's State with the Highest and Lowest Financial Gaps by Race/Ethnicity." *WalletHub,* February 3. https://wallethub.com.

Bernstein, Elizabeth. 2010. "Militarized Humanitarianism Meets Carceral Feminism." *Signs* 36 (1): 45–71.

Berry, Jeffrey M. 1977. *Lobbying for the People.* Princeton: Princeton University Press.

Berry, Jeffrey M. 1999. *The New Liberalism: The Rising Power of Citizen Groups.* Washington, D.C.: Brookings Institution Press.

Berry, Jeffrey M. 2010. "Urban Interest Groups." In *Oxford Handbook of American Political Parties and Interest Groups,* edited by L. Sandy Maisel and Jeffrey M. Berry, 502–15. New York: Oxford University Press.

Berry, Jeffrey M., and David F. Arons. 2003. *A Voice for Nonprofits.* Washington, D.C.: Brookings.

Biegler, Caitlin, and Nan Madden. 2012. *Income Inequality Grows in Minnesota.* St. Paul: Minnesota Budget Project. http://www.mnbudgetproject.org.

Bierschbach, Briana. 2019. "Minnesota Families in Need Celebrate Long-Awaited Boost in State Aid." *MPR News,* June 10. https://www.mprnews.org.

Blanc, Eric. 2019. *Red State Revolt: The Teachers' Strike Wave and Working-Class Politics.* New York: Verso.

Blee, Kathleen M. 2002. *Inside Organized Racism: Women in the Hate Movement.* Berkeley: University of California Press.

Blee, Kathleen M. 2012. *Democracy in the Making: How Activist Groups Form.* Oxford: Oxford University Press.

"Body Count." 1995. *City Pages,* July 5.

Bohrer, Ashley J. 2019. *Marxism and Intersectionality: Race, Gender, Class, and Sexuality under Contemporary Capitalism.* Berlin: Transcript.

Boris, Elizabeth T., Erwin de Leon, Katie L. Roeger, and Milena Nikolova. 2010a. *Human Service Nonprofits and Government Collaboration: Findings from the 2010 National Survey of Nonprofit Government Contracting and Grants.* Washington, D.C.: Urban Institute. https://www.urban.org.

Boris, Elizabeth T., Erwin de Leon, Katie L. Roeger, and Milena Nikolova. 2010b. *National Study of Nonprofit-Government Contracting*. Washington, D.C.: Urban Institute. http://webarchive.urban.org.

Boyte, Harry C. 1980. *The Backyard Revolution: Understanding the New Citizen Movement*. Philadelphia: Temple University Press.

Bradbury, Alexandra, Mark Brenner, and Jane Slaughter. 2016. *Secrets of a Successful Organizer*. Detroit: Labor Notes.

Brandt, Steve. 2012. "An Unfinished Project on the North Side." *Star Tribune*, July 27.

Brandt, Steve. 2013a. "Teach for America Effort Stalls in Minnesota." *Star Tribune*, June 21.

Brandt, Steve. 2013b. "Minnesota School of Science Charter School Closes." *Star Tribune*, August 22.

Brenner, Neil, and Nik Theodore. 2002. "Cities and the Geographies of 'Actually Existing Neoliberalism.'" *Antipode* 34 (3): 349–79.

Brenner, Robert. 2002. *The Boom and the Bubble: The US in the World Economy*. London: Verso.

Bronfenbrenner, Kate. 2000. "Uneasy Terrain: The Impact of Capital Mobility on Workers, Wages, and Union Organizing." https://hdl.handle.net/1813/74284.

Brown, Wendy. 1995. *States of Injury: Power and Freedom in Late Modernity*. Princeton: Princeton University Press.

Brown, Wendy. 2015. *Undoing the Demos: Neoliberalism's Stealth Revolution*. New York: Zone Books.

Bruch, Michelle. 2008. "Plans for Sober Housing in Elliot Park Spark Debate among Neighbors." *The Journal*, September 29. https://www.journalmpls.com.

Bruch, Sarah, Myra Max Ferree, and Joe Soss. 2010. "From Policy to Polity: Democracy, Paternalism, and the Incorporation of Disadvantaged Citizens." *American Sociological Review* 75 (2): 205–26.

Bruenig, Matt. 2019. *Family Fun Pack*. People's Policy Project. https://www.peoplespolicyproject.org.

Brunswick, Mark. 2009. "Legislature Getting Down to Business." *Star Tribune*, August 14.

Buchta, Jim. 2016a. "Kraus-Anderson Apartment Project Is Turning Point for Elliot Park in Downtown Minneapolis." *Star Tribune*, October 13.

Buchta, Jim. 2016b. "Minnesota's Foreclosure Rate Is Now One of the Nation's Lowest." *Star Tribune*, April 13.

Burden-Stelly, Charisse. 2020. "Caste Does Not Explain Race." *Boston Review*, December 15. http://bostonreview.net.

Burnside, Tina. 2017. "Southside African American Community, Minneapolis." *MNopedia, Minnesota Historical Society*. http://www.mnopedia.org.

Busker, Nicole, Marina Mileo Gorsuch, and Deborah Rho. 2018. *American Indian Women Were Disproportionately Stopped, Searched, and Arrested by Police in Minneapolis in 2017.* Minneapolis: Federal Reserve Bank of Minneapolis. https://www.minneapolisfed.org.

Callaghan, Peter. 2015. "Why Are the Twin Cities So Segregated? A New Report Blames Housing Policies—and Education Reforms." *MinnPost.com*, March 5.

Capoccia, Giovanni. 2016. "Critical Junctures." In *Oxford Handbook of Historical Institutionalism*, edited by Karl Orfeo Fioretos, Tulia Gabriela Falleti, and Adam D. Sheingate, 89–106. Oxford: Oxford University Press.

Carlock, Greg, and Emily Mangan. 2018. *A Green New Deal*. Data for Progress. https://www.dataforprogress.org.

Carter, Prudence L. 2005. *Keepin' It Real: School Success beyond Black and White*. Oxford: Oxford University Press.

Chapin, Angelina. 2020. "If I Would Have Been Here, George Floyd May Still Be Alive." *New York*, June 2. https://www.thecut.com.

Chaudhuri, Sanjukta. 2018. *Economic Status of Minority Women in Minnesota*. St. Paul: Minnesota Department of Employment and Economic Development. https://mn.gov.

Chen, Michelle. 2018. "Minneapolis Raised the Minimum Wage, Now They Just Have to Get Employers to Pay It." *Progressive*, May 17. https://progressive.org.

Choi-Fitzpatrick, Austin. 2015. "Managing Democracy in Social Movement Organizations." *Social Movement Studies* 14 (2): 123–41.

City of Minneapolis. 2010a. *Minneapolis Fast Facts: 2010 Housing Detail*. Minneapolis: City of Minneapolis.

City of Minneapolis. 2010b. *Minneapolis Fast Facts: 2010 Labor Force and Jobs Detail*. Minneapolis: City of Minneapolis.

City of Minneapolis Residential and Real Estate Development Work Unit. 2015. *City of Minneapolis Foreclosure Response, Housing Investment Analysis: 2008–2014*. Minneapolis: City of Minneapolis. http://www.minneapolismn.gov.

Clawson, Dan, Alan Neustadtl, and Mark Weller. 1998. *Dollars and*

Votes: How Business Campaign Contributions Subvert Democracy. Philadelphia: Temple University Press.

Clegg, John, and Adaner Usmani. 2019. "The Economic Origins of Mass Incarceration." *Catalyst* 3 (3). https://catalyst-journal.com.

Clemens, Elisabeth S. 1997. *The People's Lobby: Organizational Innovation and the Rise of Interest Group Politics in the United States, 1890–1925.* Chicago: University of Chicago Press.

Cohen, Cathy J. 1997. "Punks, Bulldaggers, and Welfare Queens." *GLQ* 3:437–65.

Cohen, Cathy J. 1999. *The Boundaries of Blackness: AIDS and the Breakdown of Black Politics.* Chicago: University of Chicago Press.

Cohen, Lizabeth. 2003. *A Consumers' Republic: The Politics of Mass Consumption in Postwar America.* New York: Vintage.

Collins, Jane L., and Victoria Mayer. 2010. *Both Hands Tied: Welfare Reform and the Race to the Bottom of the Low-Wage Labor Market.* Chicago: University of Chicago Press.

Collins, J. Michael, and Carly Urban. 2018. "The Effects of a Foreclosure Moratorium on Loan Repayment Behaviors." *Regional Science and Urban Economics* 68:73–83.

Collins, Patricia Hill. 2000. *Black Feminist Thought.* New York: Routledge.

Collins, Terry. 2008. "Minneapolis: Is the Choice Worth Funds?" *Star Tribune,* April 6.

Collins, Terry. 2013. "Feb. 12, 2007: 'This Is What Drives Me.'" *Star Tribune,* June 6.

Conventions Sports and Leisure. 2009. *Economic and Jobs Impact of Metrodome Next Multipurpose Facility.* Minneapolis: Conventions Sports and Leisure. http://prod.static.vikings.clubs.nfl.com.

Corson, Ross. 2000. "Choice Ironies: Open Enrollment in Minnesota." *American Prospect,* December 5. https://prospect.org.

Cotterman, Robert F. 2002. *New Evidence on the Relationship between Race and Mortgage Default.* Washington, D.C.: U.S. Department of Housing and Urban Development.

Crenshaw, Kimberle. 1992. "Race, Gender, and Sexual Harassment." *Southern California Law Review* 65 (3): 1467–76.

Crump, Jeff. 2002. "Deconcentration by Demolition: Public Housing, Poverty, and Urban Policy." *Environment and Planning D* 20 (5): 581–96.

Crump, Jeff. 2003. "The End of Public Housing as We Know It: Public

Housing Policy, Labor Regulation, and the US City." *International Journal of Urban and Regional Research* 27 (1): 179–87.

Crump, Jeff. 2007. "Subprime Lending and Foreclosure in Hennepin and Ramsey Counties." *CURA Reporter* 37 (2): 14–18.

Crump, Jeff. 2008. "The Foreclosure Crisis in Minnesota: State Legislative Responses." *Urban Geography* 29 (8): 766–72.

Crump, Jeff, Kathe Newman, Eric S. Belksy, Phil Ashton, David H. Kaplan, Daniel J. Hammel, and Elvin Wyly. 2008. "Cities Destroyed (Again) for Cash: Forum on the US Foreclosure Crisis." *Urban Geography* 29 (8): 745–84.

Cucchiara, Maia. 2008. "Re-branding Urban Schools: Urban Revitalization, Social Status, and Marketing Public Schools to the Upper Middle Class." *Journal of Education Policy* 23 (2): 165–79.

Dahl, Robert A. 1961. *Who Governs? Democracy and Power in an American City.* New Haven: Yale University Press.

Daudt, Kurt. 2012. "Reform 2.0 Preview." Press Statement, February 13. https://www.house.leg.state.mn.us.

Davis, Angela Y. 2005. *Abolition Democracy: Beyond Empire, Prisons, and Torture.* New York: Seven Stories Press.

Davis, Don. 2012. "Gov. Dayton Signs $975 Million Vikings Stadium Bill." *Duluth News Tribune,* May 14. https://www.duluthnewstribune.com.

Davis, Mike. 1990. *City of Quartz: Excavating the Future in Los Angeles.* New York: Verso.

Day, Meagan. 2020. "Police Brutality against Protesters Only Stoked the Anti–Police Brutality Movement." *Jacobin,* June 9. https://www.jacobinmag.com.

de Certeau, Michel. 1980. "On the Oppositional Practices of Everyday Life." *Social Text* 3 (Autumn): 3–43.

Delaney, Kevin J., and Rick Eckstein. 2003. *Public Dollars, Private Stadiums: The Battle over Building Sports Stadiums.* New Brunswick: Rutgers University Press.

Delton, Jennifer A. 2002. *Making Minnesota Liberal: Civil Rights and the Transformation of the Democratic Party.* Minneapolis: University of Minnesota Press.

Desmond, Matthew. 2016. *Evicted: Poverty and Profit in the American City.* New York: Crown.

Diaz, Kevin. 1990. "Homeless Protesters Get Duplex in Deal." *Star Tribune,* May 23, 3B.

Diaz, Kevin. 1995a. "$100 Million Coming from HUD: Low-Income Units to Be Dispersed, Some Projects Rebuilt." *Star Tribune*, January 14, A1.

Diaz, Kevin. 1995b. "Mayor's Housing Proposals Stir Bitter Debate." *Star Tribune*, May 27.

Diaz, Kevin. 1996. "Trip Gave Clinton a Chance to Hear Sayles Belton's Views." *Star Tribune*, December 20, A1.

DiMartino, Catherine, and Sarah Butler Jessen. 2016. "School Brand Management: The Policies, Practices, and Perceptions of Branding and Marketing in New York City's Public High Schools." *Urban Education* 51 (5): 447–75.

Disch, Lisa. 2011. "Toward a Mobilization Conception of Democratic Representation." *American Political Science Review* 105 (1): 100–114.

Disch, Lisa. 2012. "Democratic Representation and the Constituency Paradox." *Perspectives on Politics* 10 (3): 599–616.

Draper, Kevin. 2018. "Windfall for Super Bowl Hosts? Economists Say It's Overstated." *New York Times*, January 29, D1.

Dreier, Peter. 2011. "Reagan's Real Legacy." *Nation*, February 4. https://www.thenation.com.

Dreier, Peter, and Christopher R. Martin. 2010. "How ACORN Was Framed: Political Controversy and Media Agenda Setting." *Perspectives on Politics* 8 (3): 761–92.

"Dr. Verna Price." Girls in Action. https://giaction.org.

Dunbar, Elizabeth. 2010. "Comparing the Somali Experience in Minnesota to Other Immigrant Groups." *MPRNews*, January 22. https://www.mprnews.org.

Duneier, Mitchell. 1999. *Sidewalk*. New York: Farrar, Straus, and Giroux.

Edelman, Murray. 1977. *Political Language: Words That Succeed and Policies That Fail*. New York: Academic Press.

Ehrenreich, Barbara. 2009. *Bright-Sided:* How the Relentless Promotion of Positive Thinking Has Undermined America. New York: Metropolitan.

Elbaum, Max. 2018. *Revolution in the Air: Sixties Radicals Turn to Lenin, Mao, and Che*. New York: Verso.

Eliasoph, Nina. 1998. *Avoiding Politics: How Americans Produce Apathy in Everyday Life*. Cambridge: Cambridge University Press.

Elliot Park Neighborhood, Inc. 2002. *Elliot Park Neighborhood Mas-*

ter Plan: Summary. Minneapolis: Elliot Park Neighborhood, Inc. http://www.ci.minneapolis.mn.us.

Ernst, Rose. 2010. *The Price of Progressive Politics: The Welfare Rights Movement in an Era of Colorblind Racism*. New York: New York University Press.

Estes, Nick. 2019. *Our History Is the Future*. New York: Verso.

Fagotto, Elena, and Archon Fung. 2006. "Empowered Participation in Urban Governance: The Minneapolis Neighborhood Revitalization Program." *International Journal of Urban and Regional Research* 30 (3): 638–55.

Fairbanks, Robert P. 2009. *How It Works: Recovering Citizens in Post-welfare Philadelphia*. Chicago: University of Chicago Press.

Fantasia, Rick. 1988. *Cultures of Solidarity: Consciousness, Action, and Contemporary American Workers*. Berkeley: University of California Press.

Fantasia, Rick, and Kim Voss. 2004. *Hard Work: Remaking the American Labor Movement*. Berkeley: University of California Press.

Ferguson, Michaele L. 2017. "Neoliberal Feminism as Political Ideology." *Journal of Political Ideologies* 22 (3): 221–35.

Ferree, Myra Marx. 2003. "Resonance and Radicalism: Feminist Framing in the Abortion Debates of the United States and Germany." *American Journal of Sociology* 109 (2): 303–44.

Ferreira, Fernando, and Joseph Gyourko. 2015. *A New Look at the U.S. Foreclosure Crisis*. Cambridge, Mass.: National Bureau of Economic Research.

Feshir, Riham. 2020. "Controversial Redesign Plan Goes before Minneapolis Schools This Week." *MPR News*, May 11. https://www.mprnews.org.

Fight Back staff. 2008. "Protest Demands a 'People's Bailout.'" *Fight Back News*, December 4. http://www.fightbacknews.org.

Fight Back staff. 2009. "Minnesota People's Bailout Act Introduced in Legislature." *Fight Back News*, February 12. http://www.fightbacknews.org.

Fishbein, Allen J., and Patrick Woodall. 2006. *Women Are Prime Targets for Subprime Lending*. Washington, D.C.: Consumer Federation of America. http://www.consumerfed.org.

Fisher, Mark. 2009. *Capitalist Realism: Is There No Alternative?* London: Zero Books.

Fitzpatrick, Lauren, and Art Golab. 2013. "Black Students Most Likely to Have Their School on CPS Closure List." *Chicago Sun-Times,* March 6. http://www.suntimes.com.

Flanders, Laura. 2013. "At Thatcher's Funeral, Bury TINA, Too." *Nation,* April 12. https://www.thenation.com.

Fletcher, Steve. 2020. "I'm a Minneapolis City Council Member. We Must Disband the Police—Here's What Could Come Next." *Time,* June 5. https://time.com.

Foote, Christopher L., Kristopher S. Gerardi, and Paul S. Willen. 2012. *Why Did So Many People Make So Many Ex Post Bad Decisions? The Causes of the Foreclosure Crisis.* Cambridge, Mass.: National Bureau of Economic Research.

Forrest, M. David. 2013. "Consensus and Crisis: Representing the Poor in the Post–Civil Rights Era." *New Political Science* 35 (1): 19–43.

Forrest, M. David. 2016. "For a Ruthless Criticism of U.S. Politics." *Polity* 48 (1): 5–28.

Forrest, M. David, and Dara Z. Strolovitch. 2017. "Racial Justice Advocacy, Political Representation, and the Contemporary Interest Group Universe." In *Oxford Handbook of Racial and Ethnic Politics in the United States,* edited by David L. Leal, Taeku Lee, and Mark Sawyer. Oxford: Oxford University Press. https://www.oxfordhandbooks.com.

Frase, Richard S. 2009. "What Explains Persistent Racial Disproportionality in Minnesota's Prison and Jail Populations?" *Crime and Justice* 38 (1): 201–80.

Fraser, Nancy. 2019. *The Old Is Dying and the New Cannot Be Born.* New York: Verso.

Freedom Place, Inc. 2020. "Founder—Mark Thisius." https://www.freedomplaceinc.org.

Freedom Road Socialist Organization. 2001. *Unity Statement of Freedom Road Socialist Organization.* Chicago: Freedom Road Socialist Organization. https://frso.org.

Freedom Road Socialist Organization. 2010a. *2010 Main Political Report—The U.S. Economy.* Chicago: Freedom Road Socialist Organization. https://frso.org.

Freedom Road Socialist Organization. 2010b. *Continue the Struggle against Effects of the Economic Crisis.* Chicago: Freedom Road Socialist Organization. https://frso.org.

Frymer, Paul. 1999. *Uneasy Alliances: Race and Party Competition in America.* Princeton: Princeton University Press.

Frymer, Paul, Dara Z. Strolovitch, and Dorian T. Warren. 2006. "New Orleans Is Not the Exception: Re-politicizing the Study of Racial Inequality." *DuBois Review* 3 (1): 37–57.

Gaines, Kevin K. 1996. *Uplifting the Race: Black Leadership, Politics, and Culture in the Twentieth Century.* Chapel Hill: University of North Carolina Press.

Gamson, William A., and David S. Meyer. 1996. "Framing Political Opportunity." In *Comparative Perspectives on Social Movements: Political Opportunities, Mobilizing Structures, and Cultural Framings,* edited by Doug McAdam, John D. McCarthy, and Mayer N. Zald, 275–90. Cambridge: Cambridge University Press.

Gamson, William A., and Gadi Wolfsfeld. 1993. "Movements and Media as Interacting Systems." *Annals of the American Academy of Political and Social Science* 528 (1): 114–25.

Ganz, Marshall. 2009. *Why David Sometimes Wins: Strategy, Leadership, and the California Agricultural Movement.* Oxford: Oxford University Press.

Gaventa, John. 1980. *Power and Powerlessness: Quiescence and Rebellion in an Appalachian Valley.* Champaign: University of Illinois Press.

Gilens, Martin. 2012. *Affluence and Influence: Economic Inequality and Political Power in America.* Princeton: Princeton University Press.

Gillion, Daniel Q. 2013. *The Political Power of Protest: Minority Activism and Shifts in Public Policy.* Cambridge: Cambridge University Press.

Gilman, Rhoda R. 2012. *Stand Up! The Story of Minnesota's Protest Tradition.* St. Paul: Minnesota Historical Society Press.

Gilmore, Ruth Wilson. 2007. *Golden Gulag: Prisons, Surplus, Crisis, and Opposition in Globalizing California.* Berkeley: University of California Press.

Gitlin, Todd. 1980. *The Whole World Is Watching: Mass Media in the Making and Unmaking of the New Left.* Berkeley: University of California Press.

Goetz, Edward G. 1996. "The US War on Drugs as Urban Policy." *International Journal of Urban and Regional Affairs* 20 (3): 539–49.

Goetz, Edward G. 2003. *Clearing the Way: Deconcentrating the Poor in Urban America.* Washington, D.C.: Urban Institute Press.

Goetz, Edward G. 2013. *New Deal Ruins: Race, Economic Justice, and Public Housing Policy.* Ithaca: Cornell University Press.

Goetz, Edward G. 2018. *The One-Way Street of Integration: Fair Housing and the Pursuit of Racial Justice in American Cities.* Ithaca: Cornell University Press.

Goetz, Edward G., Karen Chapple, and Barbara Lukermann. 2003. "Enabling Exclusion: The Retreat from Regional Fair Share Housing in the Implementation of the Minnesota Land Use Planning Act." *Journal of Planning Education and Research* 22 (3): 213–25.

Goetz, Edward G., Brittany Lewis, Anthony Damiano, and Molly Calhoun. 2019. *The Diversity of Gentrification: Multiple Forms of Gentrification in Minneapolis and St. Paul.* Minneapolis: Center for Urban and Regional Affairs, University of Minnesota.

Goetz, Edward G., and Mara Sidney. 1994. "Revenge of the Property Owners: Community Development and the Politics of Property." *Journal of Urban Affairs* 16 (4): 319–34.

Goetz, Edward G., and Mara Sidney. 1997. "Local Policy Subsystems and Issue Definition: An Analysis of Community Development Policy Change." *Urban Affairs Review* 32 (4): 490–512.

Goetz, Edward G., Kimberly Skobba, and Cynthia Yuen. 2010. "Housing Careers of Very Low Income Persons." *CURA Reporter* 40 (3–4): 3–11.

Goffman, Alice. 2014. *On the Run: Fugitive Life in an American City.* New York: Picador.

Goffman, Erving. 1959. *The Presentation of Self in Everyday Life.* New York: Random House.

Goffman, Erving. 1979. "Footing." *Semiotica* 25 (1–2): 1–30.

Goldstein, Tom. 2012. "Vikings Stadium Proposal Isn't for the 'People.'" *City Pages,* March 14. http://www.citypages.com.

Gorz, André. 1967. *Strategy for Labor: A Radical Proposal.* Boston: Beacon.

Gose, Joe. 2018. "Super Bowl's Minneapolis Stadium Brings a Surge in Development." *New York Times,* January 23. https://www.nytimes.com.

Grover, Michael. 2011. "On the Front Lines of the Housing Crisis: A Conversation with Julie Gugin of the Minnesota Home Ownership Center." *Federal Reserve Bank of Minneapolis,* April 1. https://www.minneapolisfed.org.

Guastella, Dustin. 2020. "To End Police Violence Fund Public Goods and Raise Wages." *Nonsite.org,* July 9. https://nonsite.org.

Gustafson, Paul. 1992. "Judge Strikes Down Law Limiting Welfare Payments for Those Coming to State." *Star Tribune,* January 10, 1A.

Hacker, Jacob S., and Paul Pierson. 2010. *Winner-Take-All Politics: How Washington Made the Rich Richer—and Turned Its Back on the Middle Class.* New York: Simon & Schuster.

Hackworth, Jason. 2002. "Local Autonomy, Bond-Rating Agencies, and Neoliberal Urbanism in the United States." *International Journal of Urban and Regional Research* 26 (4): 707–25.

Hall, Peter Dobkin. 2016. "Historical Perspectives on Nonprofit Organizations in the United States." In *The Jossey-Bass Handbook of Nonprofit Leadership and Management,* edited by David O. Renz and Robert D. Herman, 3–42. 4th ed. Hoboken, N.J.: Wiley.

Han, Hahrie. 2014. *How Organizations Develop Activists: Civic Associations and Leadership in the 21st Century.* Oxford: Oxford University Press.

Han, Hahrie. 2020. "What Happened When the Minneapolis Police Lost Legitimacy?" *New York Times,* June 10. https://www.nytimes.com.

Hancock, Ange-Marie. 2004. *The Politics of Disgust: The Public Identity of the Welfare Queen.* New York: New York University Press.

Hargarten, Jeff, Jennifer Bjorhus, MaryJo Webster, and Kelly Smith. 2018. "Fatal Police Encounters in Minnesota since 2000." *Star Tribune,* June 25.

Harrison, Roderick J., and Daniel Weinberg. 1992. *Racial and Ethnic Segregation in 1990.* Washington, D.C.: U.S. Bureau of the Census.

Hartley, Daniel. 2013. *Gentrification and Financial Health.* Federal Reserve Bank of Cleveland.

Harvey, David. 2005. *A Brief History of Neoliberalism.* New York: Oxford University Press.

Hasenfeld, Yeheskel, and Eve E. Garrow. 2012. "Nonprofit Human-Service Organizations, Social Rights, and Advocacy in a Neoliberal Welfare State." *Social Service Review* 86 (2): 295–322.

Hawkins, Beth. 2011. "'Loyal Opponents' Selected to Help Plan New North High." *MinnPost,* April 19. https://www.minnpost.com.

Hayward, Clarissa Rile. 2000. *De-Facing Power.* Cambridge: Cambridge University Press.

Hennessey, Patrick, dir. 1996. *The Homeless Home Movie.* Newberry, Fla.: Media Visions, Inc., DVD.

Hensley-Clancy, Molly. 2020. "Minneapolis Public Schools Voted to End Its Contract with the City's Police after the Death of George Floyd." *BuzzFeed,* June 2. https://www.buzzfeednews.com.

Hertel-Fernandez, Alexander. 2018. *Politics at Work: How Companies Turn Their Workers into Lobbyists.* New York: Oxford University Press.

Hertz, Susan Handley. 1981. *The Welfare Mothers Movement.* Lanham, Md.: University Press of America.

Hinck, Kaeti, Karl Pearson-Cater, and Sharon Schmickle. 2011. "You Fix the Minnesota Deficit." *MinnPost,* February 9. https://www.minnpost.com.

Hindman, Matthew Dean. 2018. *Political Advocacy and Its Interested Citizens: Neoliberalism, Postpluralism, and LGBT Organizations.* Philadelphia: University of Pennsylvania Press.

Hinrichs, Erin. 2018. "The 'Full-Service Community Schools' Model Is Getting High-Profile Political Support in Minnesota: So What Is It?" *MinnPost,* September 26. https://www.minnpost.com.

HIRE Minnesota. 2012. "How a Stadium Equity Plan Was Created: The Inside Story." *Common Ground* (Summer): 1, 10–11. http://thealliancetc.org.

Hopfensperger, Jean. 1994. "Welfare Reform Hearing Draws Crowd." *Star Tribune,* March 2, 2B.

Horazuk, Cherrene. 2020. "Labor Fights for George Floyd in Twin Cities." *Labor Notes,* June 3. https://labornotes.org.

Howard, Tanner. 2019. "Fearing Privatization: Public Housing Activists Push Back against RAD Plans." *Shelterforce,* March 21. https://shelterforce.org.

Human Impact Partners and ISAIAH. 2016. *Drowning in Debt: A Health Impact Assessment of How Payday Loan Reforms Improve the Health of Minnesota's Most Vulnerable.* Oakland, Calif.: Human Impact Partners. https://www.pewtrusts.org.

Ibrahim, Mukhtar M. 2018. "Minneapolis City Council Passes Mayor Jacob Frey's $1.55 Billion Budget." *Star Tribune,* December 6.

Immergluck, Dan. 2009. *Foreclosed: High-Risk Lending, Deregulation, and the Undermining of America's Mortgage Market.* Ithaca: Cornell University Press.

INCITE! Women of Color against Violence. 2007. *The Revolution Will Not Be Funded: Beyond the Non-profit Industrial Complex.* Cambridge: South End Press.

Institute on Metropolitan Opportunity. 2014. *Reforming Subsidized Housing Policy in the Twin Cities to Cut Costs and Reduce Segregation*. Minneapolis: Institute on Metropolitan Opportunity, University of Minnesota Law School.

Institute on Metropolitan Opportunity. 2015. *Why Are the Twin Cities So Segregated?* Minneapolis: Institute on Metropolitan Opportunity, University of Minnesota Law School.

Institute on Metropolitan Opportunity. 2017. *The Minnesota School Choice Project: Part I: Segregation and Performance*. Minneapolis: University of Minnesota Law School.

Institute on Race and Poverty. 1997. *Examining the Relationship between Housing, Education, and Persistent Segregation*. Minneapolis: Institute on Race and Poverty, University of Minnesota Law School.

Institute on Race and Poverty. 2007. *The Choice Is Ours: Expanding Educational Opportunity for all Twin Cities Children*. Minneapolis: Institute on Race and Poverty, University of Minnesota Law School.

Institute on Race and Poverty. 2009a. *Communities in Crisis: Race and Mortgage Lending in the Twin Cities*. Minneapolis: Institute on Race and Poverty, University of Minnesota Law School.

Institute on Race and Poverty. 2009b. *A Comprehensive Strategy to Integrate Twin Cities Schools and Neighborhoods*. Minneapolis: Institute on Race and Poverty, University of Minnesota Law School.

Jackman, Mary R. 1996. *The Velvet Glove: Paternalism and Conflict in Gender, Class, and Race Relations*. Berkeley: University of California Press.

Jaffe, Sarah. 2020. "A Minneapolis Worker Center Becomes a Hub of Protest." *Dissent*, June 5. https://www.dissentmagazine.org.

Johnson, Bernadeia H. 2010. Letter to Families of North Community High School, October 8. https://www.mpr.org.

Johnson, Cedric. 2007. *Revolutionaries to Race Leaders: Black Power and the Making of African American Politics*. Minneapolis: University of Minnesota.

Johnson, Cedric. 2017. "The Panthers Can't Save Us Now." *Catalyst* 1 (1). https://catalyst-journal.com.

Johnson, Cedric, ed. 2011. *The Neoliberal Deluge: Hurricane Katrina, Late Capitalism, and the Remaking of New Orleans*. Minneapolis: University of Minnesota Press.

Johnson, Creola. 2010. "Renters Evicted En Masse: Collateral Damage

Arising from the Subprime Foreclosure Crisis." *Florida Law Review* 62:975–1008.

Johnson, Dirk. 1996. "Nice City's Nasty Distinction." *New York Times,* June 30.

Jones, Elizabeth. 2018. "Racism, Fines, Fees, and the U.S. Carceral State." *Race & Class* 59 (3): 38–50.

Jones, Hannah. 2018. "Everything about the 2040 Plan You Want to Know but Are Too Afraid to Ask." *City Pages,* December 11. http://www.citypages.com.

Jones, Hannah. 2020. "University of Minnesota Cuts (Most of) Its Ties with Minneapolis Police Department." *City Pages,* May 28. http://www.citypages.com.

Kaul, Greta. 2017. "Union Membership in Minnesota Has Been Declining for Decades." *MinnPost,* March 8. https://www.minnpost.com.

Keating, Cricket. 2005. "Building Coalitional Consciousness." *NWSA Journal* 17 (2): 86–103.

Kelly, Laura Martell, and Andi Egbert. 2011. *One Minneapolis: Community Indicators Report.* Minneapolis: Minneapolis Foundation.

Kelly, Nathan J., and Peter K. Enns. 2010. "Inequality and the Dynamics of Public Opinion: The Self-Reinforcing Link between Economic Inequality and Mass Preferences." *American Journal of Political Science* 54 (4): 855–70.

Kerr, Drew. 2012. "Twenty Years of Pounding Pavement: Lyndale Walking Group Celebrates Efforts to Make Neighborhood Safer." *Southwest Journal,* April 16.

Kiel, Paul. 2012. "The Great American Foreclosure Story." *ProPublica,* April 10. https://www.propublica.org.

Kim, Claire Jean. 2000. *Bitter Fruit: The Politics of Black-Korean Conflict in New York City.* New Haven: Yale University Press.

Kimball, Joe. 2011. "Linda Higgins, Another Veteran DFL Minneapolis Lawmaker, Won't Seek Re-election." *MinnPost,* November 14. https://www.minnpost.com.

Kirkpatrick, L. Owen. 2016. "The New Urban Fiscal Crisis: Finance, Democracy, and Municipal Debt." *Politics & Society* 44 (1): 45–80.

Kirp, David L. 2010. "Cradle to College." *Nation,* June 14.

Knafo, Saki. 2012. "Occupy Protesters in Minneapolis Fight to Save Foreclosed Home, Pushing Movement's New Focus." *HuffPost,* June 2. https://www.huffpost.com.

Koch, Raymond L. 1968. "Politics and Relief in Minneapolis during the 1930s." *Minnesota History* 41 (4): 153–70.

Konechne, Deb, and Mimi Molina. 1996. "Minnesota Mustn't Cut One Welfare Dime." *Star Tribune*, December 22, A30.

Koopmans, Ruud, and Paul Statham. 1999. "Ethnic and Civic Conceptions of Nationhood and the Differential Success of the Extreme Right in Germany and Italy." In *How Social Movements Matter*, edited by Marco Giugni, Doug McAdam, and Charles Tilly, 225–51. Minneapolis: University of Minnesota Press.

Kornbluh, Felicia. 2007. *The Battle for Welfare Rights: Politics and Poverty in Modern America*. Philadelphia: University of Pennsylvania Press.

Kriz, Kenneth A. 2003. "Tax Increment Financing: Its Effect on Local Government Finances." *CURA Reporter* 33 (2): 1–7.

Kurtz, Sharon. 2002. *Workplace Justice: Organizing Multi-identity Movements*. Minneapolis: University of Minnesota Press.

Lafer, Gordon. 2017. *The One Percent Solution: How Corporations Are Remaking America One State at a Time*. Ithaca: ILR Press.

Lahm, Sarah. 2018. "Broad Support Emerges for Full-Service Community Schools in Minneapolis." *Progressive*, September 19. https://progressive.org.

Lancaster, Roger. 2020. "The Policing Crisis." *Nonsite.org*, July 9. https://nonsite.org.

Lee, Caroline W., Michael McQuarrie, and Edward T. Walker, eds. 2015. *Democratizing Inequalities: Dilemmas of the New Public Participation*. New York: New York University Press.

Lerman, Amy E., and Vesla M. Weaver. 2014. *Arresting Citizenship: The Democratic Consequences of American Crime Control*. Chicago: University of Chicago Press.

Levine, Jeremy R. 2016. "The Privatization of Political Representation: Community-Based Organizations as Nonelected Neighborhood Representatives." *American Sociological Review* 81 (6): 1251–75.

Lewis, Amanda E., and John B. Diamond. 2015. *Despite the Best Intentions: How Racial Inequality Thrives in Good Schools*. Oxford: Oxford University Press.

Lewis, Brittany. 2015. *The State of Black Women's Economics in Minnesota*. Minneapolis: Center for Urban and Regional Affairs, University of Minnesota.

Lewis, Brittany. 2019. *The Illusion of Choice: Evictions and Profit in North Minneapolis.* Minneapolis: Center for Urban and Regional Affairs, University of Minnesota.

Leyden, Peter. 1991. "A Crusade against Homelessness." *Star Tribune,* January 6, 1A.

Lichtenstein, Nelson. 2002. *State of the Union: A Century of American Labor.* Princeton: Princeton University Press.

Lichterman, Paul. 1996. *The Search for Political Community: American Activists Reinventing Commitment.* Cambridge: Cambridge University Press.

Lindblom, Charles E. 1982. "The Market as Prison." *Journal of Politics* 44 (2): 324–36.

Lipman, Pauline. 2011. *The New Political Economy of Urban Education: Neoliberalism, Race, and the Right to the City.* New York: Routledge.

Lipsky, Michael. 1980. *Street-Level Bureaucracy: Dilemmas of the Individual in Public Services.* New York: Russell Sage.

Lipsky, Michael, and Margaret Levi. 1972. "Community Organization as a Political Resource." In *People and Politics in Urban Society,* edited by Harlan Hahn, 175–99. Beverly Hills, Calif.: Sage.

Lovell, Phillip, and Julia Isaacs. 2008. "The Impact of the Mortgage Crisis on Children and Their Education." *First Focus.* http://www.brookings.edu.

Lyon-Callo, Vincent, and Susan Brin Hyatt. 2003. "The Neoliberal State and the Depoliticization of Poverty: Activist Anthropology and 'Ethnography from Below.'" *Urban Anthropology* 32 (2): 175–204.

Macklin, Christina, and Jon Pratt. 2002. *2002 Minnesota Nonprofit Economy Report.* St. Paul: Minnesota Council of Nonprofits. https://www.minnesotanonprofits.org.

Madden, Nan, and Christina Macklin. 2001. *The State of Working Minnesota 2001.* St. Paul: Minnesota Budget Project. https://www.mnbudgetproject.org.

Magan, Christopher. 2017. "15 Years Later, MN Schools Are More Segregated, and Achievement Gap Has Barely Budged." *Pioneer Press,* August 18.

Majic, Samantha. 2014. *Sex Work Politics: From Protest to Service Provision.* Philadelphia: University of Pennsylvania Press.

Mannix, Andy. 2017. "Yes, Minnesota Has a Low Prison Population, but That's Not the Whole Story." *Star Tribune,* April 2.

Mannix, Andy. 2019. "Minneapolis Police Union, Mayor Frey Still at odds over 'Warrior' Training Ban." *Star Tribune,* April 26.

Mansbridge, Jane. 1999. "Should Blacks Represent Blacks and Women Represent Women? A Contingent 'Yes.'" *Journal of Politics* 61 (3): 628–57.

Mansbridge, Jane. 2003. "Rethinking Representation." *American Political Science Review* 97 (4): 515–28.

Margolin, Emma. 2016. "How Minneapolis Became the First U.S. City to Pass Trans Protections." *NBCnews.com,* June 3. https://www.nbcnews.com.

Martin, Sloane. 2019. "Minneapolis City Council Approves 2040 Plan, 10–1." *WCCO,* October 25. https://wccoradio.radio.com.

Marwell, Nicole P. 2004. "Privatizing the Welfare State: Nonprofit Community-Based Organizations as Political Actors." *American Sociological Review* 69 (2): 265–91.

McAlevey, Jane F. 2016. *No Shortcuts: Organizing for Power in the New Gilded Age.* Oxford: Oxford University Press.

McAlevey, Jane, and Bob Ostertag. 2012. *Raising Expectations (and Raising Hell): My Decade Fighting for the Labor Movement.* New York: Verso.

McCallum, Laura. 2007. "Minneapolis Targets Six Schools for Closure." *MPRNews,* March 20.

McCammon, Holly. 2013. "Discursive Opportunity Structures." In *The Wiley-Blackwell Encyclopedia of Social and Political Movements,* edited by David A. Snow, Donatella della Porta, Bert Klandermans, and Doug McAdam. Hoboken, N.J.: Blackwell. https://onlinelibrary.wiley.com.

McCammon, Holly J., Sandra C. Arch, and Erin M. Bergner. 2014. "A Radical Demand Effect: Early US Feminists and the Married Women's Property Acts." *Social Science History* 38 (1–2): 221–50.

McCammon, Holly J., Courtney Sanders Muse, Harmony D. Newman, and Teresa M. Terrell. 2007. "Movement Framing and Discursive Opportunity Structures: The Political Successes of the U.S. Women's Jury Movements." *American Sociological Review* 72:725–49.

McDonnell, Lynda. 2004. *Seven Years of Welfare Reform—Weighing the Results.* St. Paul: Center for Advanced Studies in Child Welfare, University of Minnesota.

McElwee, Sean, Jon Green, and Colin McAuliffe. 2018. "The Left Is Winning Even When It Loses." *Nation,* August 13. https://www.thenation.com.

McKeever, Brice S. 2015. *The Nonprofit Sector in Brief 2015.* Washington, D.C.: Urban Institute. https://www.urban.org.

McKeever, Brice, and Marcus Gaddy. 2016. "The Nonprofit Workforce: By the Numbers." *Nonprofit Quarterly,* October 16. https://nonprofitquarterly.org.

McLean, Bethany, and Joe Nocera. 2010. *All the Devils Are Here: The Hidden History of the Financial Crisis.* New York: Portfolio/Penguin.

McQuarrie, Michael. 2013. "Community Organizations in the Foreclosure Crisis: The Failure of Neoliberal Civil Society." *Politics & Society* 41 (1): 73–101.

Meitrodt, Jeffrey. 2013. "Contract for Deed Can Be House of Horror for Buyers." *Star Tribune,* July 5.

Melo, Frederick. 2012. "Will New Vikings Stadium Spur More Growth than Metrodome?" *Pioneer Press,* March 3.

Mervosh, Sarah. 2021. "In Minneapolis Schools, White Families Are Asked to Help Do the Integrating." *New York Times,* November 27. https://www.nytimes.com.

Metropolitan Council. 1992. *Trouble at the Core.* St. Paul: Metropolitan Council.

Metropolitan Council. 1994. *Keeping the Twin Cities Vital.* St. Paul: Metropolitan Council.

Metropolitan Council. 2010. *2009 Metro Residents Survey.* St. Paul: Metropolitan Council.

Meyer, David S. 2004. "Protest and Political Opportunities." *Annual Review of Sociology* 30:125–45.

Meyer, David S. 2006. "Claiming Credit: Stories of Movement Influence as Outcomes." *Mobilization* 11:281–98.

Meyer, David S., and Debra C. Minkoff. 2004. "Conceptualizing Political Opportunity." *Social Forces* 82 (4): 1457–92.

Michaels, Walter Benn. 2018. "The Political Economy of Anti-racism." *Nonsite* 23. https://nonsite.org.

Mills, Charles W. 2007. "White Ignorance." In *Race and Epistemologies of Ignorance,* edited by Shannon Sullivan and Nancy Tuana, 11–38. Albany: SUNY Press.

Minkoff, Debra C. 1997. "The Sequencing of Social Movements." *American Sociological Review* 62 (5): 779–99.

Minneapolis Department of Community Planning and Economic Development. 2006. *Minneapolis Trends: 2000–2005*. Minneapolis: City of Minneapolis.

Minneapolis Department of Community Planning and Economic Development. 2007. *Minneapolis Trends: Fourth Quarter 2007.* Minneapolis: City of Minneapolis.

Minneapolis Department of Community Planning and Economic Development. 2008. *Minneapolis Trends: Fourth Quarter 2008.* Minneapolis: City of Minneapolis.

Minneapolis Department of Community Planning and Economic Development. 2009. *Minneapolis Trends: Fourth Quarter 2009.* Minneapolis: City of Minneapolis.

Minneapolis Department of Community Planning and Economic Development. 2010. *Minneapolis Trends: Third Quarter 2010.* Minneapolis: City of Minneapolis.

Minnesota Compass. 2011. *Minneapolis Neighborhood Profile: Elliot Park*. St. Paul: Wilder Foundation. http://www.mncompass.org.

Minnesota Department of Health. 2018. *Minnesota's Changing Health Insurance Landscape*. St. Paul: Minnesota Department of Health. https://www.health.state.mn.us.

Minnesota Minority Education Partnership. 2013. *Solutions Not Suspensions: Ending the Discipline Gap in Minnesota Public Schools.* St. Paul: Minnesota Minority Education Partnership, Inc. https://mneep.org.

Minnesota State House of Representatives. 1991. *Journal of the House,* May 20.

Minnesota State Senate. 1991. *Journal of the Senate,* May 20.

Mishel, Lawrence, Josh Bivens, Elise Gould, and Heidi Shierholz. 2012. *The State of Working America*. Ithaca: Cornell University Press.

Mitchell, Corey. 2011a. "Her Voice Counts for School Choice." *Star Tribune,* February 7, 9A.

Mitchell, Corey. 2011b. "North High Group Seeks Assurance." *Star Tribune,* February 22, 3B.

Mitchell, Corey. 2011c. "Enrollment Reversal Leaves Minneapolis Schools Scrambling." *Star Tribune,* October 23.

Montemayor, Stephen, and Chao Xiong. 2020. "Four Fired Minneapolis Police Officers Charged, Booked in Killing of George Floyd." *Star Tribune,* June 4.

The Movement for Black Lives. 2016. *A Vision for Black Lives.* https://m4bl.org.

Moylan, Martin. 2019. "Controversial Program Boosts Funding for Scarce Public Housing." *MPR News,* July 30. https://www.mprnews.org.

Murib, Zein. 2015. "Transgender: Examining an Emerging Political Identity Using Three Political Processes." *Politics, Groups, and Identities* 3 (3): 381–97.

Murphy, Ryan Patrick. 2010. "The Gay Land Rush: Race, Gender, and Sexuality in the Life of Post-welfare Minneapolis." In *Queer Twin Cities,* edited by Twin Cities GLBT Oral History Project, 240–68. Minneapolis: University of Minnesota Press.

Murphy, Ryan Patrick, and Alex T. Urquhart. 2010. "Sexuality in the Headlines: Intimate Upheavals as Histories of the Twin Cities." In *Queer Twin Cities,* edited by Twin Cities GLBT Oral History Project, 40–89. Minneapolis: University of Minnesota Press.

Nadasen, Premilla. 2005. *Welfare Warriors: The Welfare Rights Movement in the United States.* New York: Routledge.

Nadasen, Premilla. 2015. *Household Workers Unite: The Untold Story of African American Women Who Built a Movement.* Boston: Beacon.

National Community Reinvestment Coalition. 2007. *Are Banks on the Map? An Analysis of Bank Branch Location in Working Class and Minority Neighborhoods.* Washington, D.C.: National Community Reinvestment Coalition.

Navratil, Liz. 2019. "Affordable Units Now a Requirement for New Apartment Buildings in Minneapolis." *Star Tribune,* December 13.

Navratil, Liz. 2020. "Divided Minneapolis City Council Votes to Cut $8 Million from Police Budget." *Star Tribune,* December 10.

Nelson, Kris. 2009. "Neighborhood Responses to the Foreclosure Crisis." *CURA Reporter* 39 (1–2): 19–25.

Nelson, Tim. 2013. "Protestors: Vikings Stadium Funding Could Have Helped Poor People." *MPR News,* September 25. https://www.mprnews.org.

Newman Kathe. 2008. "The Perfect Storm: Contextualizing the Foreclosure Crisis." *Urban Geography* 29 (8): 750–54.

Nickel, Denise R. 1995. "The Progressive City? Urban Redevelopment in Minneapolis." *Urban Affairs Review* 30 (3): 355–77.

Nickrand, Jessica. 2015. "Minneapolis's White Lie." *Atlantic,* February 21. https://www.theatlantic.com.

Noll, Roger G., and Andrew Zimbalist, eds. 1997. *Sports, Jobs, and Taxes: The Economic Impact of Sports Teams and Stadiums.* Washington, D.C.: Brookings Institution.

Nord, James. 2012. "Dayton Signs Vikings Stadium Bill amid Cheers, Jeers, Familiar Faces." *MinnPost,* May 14. https://www.minnpost.com.

Norris, Mikel. 2015. "The Economic Roots of External Efficacy: Assessing the Relationship between External Political Efficacy and Income Inequality." *Canadian Journal of Political Science* 48 (4): 791–813.

Office on the Economic Status of Women. 2008. *Why Are Women among the Poorest Minnesotans?* St. Paul: Office on the Economic Status of Women, Minnesota State Legislature. https://www.oesw.leg.mn.

Oladipo, Gloria. 2021. "Minneapolis Voters Reject Bid to Replace Police with Public Safety Department." Guardian, November 2. https://www.theguardian.com.

Olson, Joel. 2004. *The Abolition of White Democracy.* Minneapolis: University of Minnesota Press.

O'Regan, Katherine, and Sharon M. Oster. 2005. "Does the Structure and Composition of the Board Matter? The Case of Nonprofit Organizations." *Journal of Law, Economics, & Organization* 21 (1): 205–27.

Orfield, Myron. 2006. "Land Use and Housing Policies to Reduce Concentrated Poverty and Racial Segregation." *Fordham Urban Law Journal* 33 (3): 101–59.

Orfield, Myron, and Nicholas Wallace. 2007. "Expanding Educational Opportunity through School and Housing Choice." *CURA Reporter* 37 (2): 19–26.

Orren, Karen, and Stephen Skowronek. 2004. *The Search for American Political Development.* Cambridge: Cambridge University Press.

Orrick, Dave. 2011. "Legislature Adjourns with No Budget Deal." *Pioneer Press,* May 23.

Osborne, David, and Ted Gaebler. 1992. *Reinventing Government: How the Entrepreneurial Spirit Is Transforming the Public Sector.* Reading, Mass.: Addison-Wesley.

Ostfield, Gili. 2020. "Ten Moves, Two Tents, and Five Months of a Housing Reckoning in Minneapolis." *New Republic,* October 30. https://newrepublic.com.

Pan, J. C. 2020. "The Wildly Unequal 'Shecession.'" *New Republic,* August 7. https://newrepublic.com.

Panning-Miller, Robert. 2010. "Rebuild (Don't Destroy) Our Public Schools." *Star Tribune,* October 31.

Pew Charitable Trusts. 2013. *Minneapolis City Fact Sheet.* Philadelphia: Pew Charitable Trusts. https://www.pewtrusts.org.

Phillips-Fein, Kim. 2009. *Invisible Hands: The Businessmen's Crusade against the New Deal.* New York: Norton.

Phillips-Fein, Kim. 2017. *Fear City: New York's Fiscal Crisis and the Rise of Austerity Politics.* New York: Metropolitan Books.

Phillips-Fein, Kim. 2019. "What's Left of Generation X." *Dissent,* Fall. https://www.dissentmagazine.org.

Phoenix, Davin. 2020. "Anger Benefits Some Americans Much More than Others." *New York Times,* June 6. https://www.nytimes.com.

Picker, Les. 2015. "The U.S. Foreclosure Crisis Was Not Just a Subprime Event." *The Digest* 8 (August). https://www.nber.org.

Pinney, George. 1991. "Most Human Resource Programs Are Kept Intact in Bill. Vote Set Today on $3.6 Billion for Welfare, Prisons, etc." *Star Tribune,* May 20, 1B.

Piven, Frances Fox. (1970) 1974. "Whom Does the Advocate Planner Serve?" In *The Politics of Turmoil: Essays on Poverty, Race, and the Urban Crisis, by Richard A. Cloward and Frances Fox Piven,* 43–53. New York: Pantheon.

Piven, Frances Fox. 1998. "Welfare Reform and the Economic and Cultural Reconstruction of Low Wage Labor Markets." *City & Society* 10 (1): 21–36.

Piven, Frances Fox. 2000. "The Link between Welfare Reform and the Labor Market." *Hybrid* 5:1–20.

Piven, Frances Fox. 2006. *Challenging Authority: How Ordinary People Change America.* Lanham, Md.: Rowman and Littlefield.

Piven, Frances Fox, and Richard A. Cloward. 1971. *Regulating the Poor: The Functions of Public Welfare.* New York: Vintage.

Piven, Frances Fox, and Richard A. Cloward. 1977. *Poor People's Movements: Why They Succeed, How They Fail.* New York: Vintage.

Polletta, Francesca. 1998. "Contending Stories: Narrative in Social Movements." *Qualitative Sociology* 21:419–46.

Polletta, Francesca, and James M. Jasper. 2001. "Collective Identity and Social Movements." *Annual Review of Sociology* 27:283–305.

Post, Tim. 2015. "MN near Bottom in On-Time Graduation for Students of Color." *MPRNews*, February 19. https://www.mprnews.org.

Quillian, Lincoln. 1999. "Migration Patterns and the Growth of High-Poverty Neighborhoods, 1970–1990." *American Journal of Sociology* 105 (1): 1–37.

Raghavendran, Beena. 2016. "North High Sees Enrollment Jump as New Year Begins." *Star Tribune*, August 30.

Reed, Adolph, Jr. 1999. *Stirrings in the Jug: Black Politics in the Post-segregationist Era*. Minneapolis: University of Minnesota Press.

Reed, Adolph, Jr., and Cornel West. 2019. "The Charter School Industry's Dishonest Attack on Bernie Sanders." *Nation*, June 19. https://www.thenation.com.

Reed, Touré F. 2020. *Toward Freedom: The Case against Race Reductionism*. New York: Verso.

Regan, Sheila. 2011. "How Much Longer for the Choice Is Yours School Integration Program in Minneapolis, Suburbs?" *Twin Cities Daily Planet*, January 4. https://www.tcdailyplanet.net.

Richman, Shaun. 2019. "The de Blasio Paradox." *American Prospect*, May 24. https://prospect.org.

Rietmulder, Michael. 2015. "8 Unscientific Reasons Minneapolis Is One of American's Most Liberal Cities." *City Pages*, September 21.

Roelofs, Joan. 2003. *Foundations and Public Policy: The Mask of Pluralism*. Albany: SUNY Press.

Rohlinger, Deana A. 2002. "Framing the Abortion Debate: Organizational Resources, Media Strategies, and Movement-Countermovement Dynamics." *Sociological Quarterly* 43 (4): 479–507.

Romero, Mary. 2011. "Are Your Papers in Order? Racial Profiling, Vigilantes, and 'America's Toughest Sheriff.'" *Harvard Latino Law Review* 14:337–57.

Roper, Eric. 2012. "Anti–Vikings Stadium Crowd Silent." *Star Tribune*, May 29.

Roper, Eric, and Randy Furst. 2012. "Cost of Last Year's North Minneapolis Tornado Estimated at $80M." *Star Tribune*, May 22.

Rosenstone, Steven J., and John Mark Hansen. 2003. *Mobilization, Participation, and Democracy in America*. New York: Longman.

Rupar, Aaron. 2012. "Mary Franson, MNGOP Rep., Compares Food Stamp Recipients to Wild Animals." *City Pages*, March 5. http://www.citypages.com.

Sainato, Michael. 2020. "'They Set Us Up': US Police Arrested over 10,000 Protesters, Many Non-violent." *Guardian*, June 8. https://www.theguardian.com.

Sakala, Leah. 2014. *Breaking Down Mass Incarceration in the 2010 Census: State-by-State Incarceration Rates by Race/Ethnicity.* Northampton, Mass.: Prison Policy Initiative. https://www.prisonpolicy.org.

Samsaraic. 2009. "Mick Kelly for the People's Coalition for a People's Bail Out interviewed—Rosemary Williams." YouTube, August 19. https://www.youtube.com.

Sandin, Erik. 2007. "MBA Antenna Gets Messages at District Meeting." *Northwestern Financial Review* 192 (20): 20.

Sangtin Writers and Richa Nagar. 2006. *Playing with Fire: Feminist Thought and Activism through Seven Lives in India.* Minneapolis: University of Minnesota Press.

Schattschneider, E. E. 1960. *The Semi-sovereign People.* New York: Holt, Reinhart, and Winston.

Scheck, Tom. 2013. "Gottwalt Resigning from the Legislature." *MPR News*, January 3. https://www.mprnews.org.

Schlozman, Kay Lehman, Sidney Verba, and Henry E. Brady. 2012. *The Unheavenly Chorus: Unequal Political Voice and the Broken Promise of American Democracy.* Princeton: Princeton University Press.

Schmickle, Sharon. 2010. "Named One of 10 'Hottest Cities' for Future Jobs, Minneapolis Also Ranks High in Economic Resilience." *MinnPost*, April 27. http://www.minnpost.com.

Schneider, Anne, and Helen Ingram. 1993. "Social Construction of Target Populations: Implications for Politics and Policy." *American Political Science Review* 87 (2): 334–47.

Schram, Sanford F. 1995. *Words of Welfare: The Poverty of Social Science and the Social Science of Poverty.* Minneapolis: University of Minnesota Press.

Schram, Sanford F. 2002. *Praxis for the Poor: Piven and Cloward and the Future of Social Science in Social Welfare.* New York: New York University Press.

Schram, Sanford F. 2015. *The Return of Ordinary Capitalism.* New York: Oxford University Press.

Schram, Sanford F., and Gary Krueger. 1994. "'Welfare Magnets' and Benefit Decline: Symbolic Problems and Substantive Consequences." *Publius* 24 (4): 61–82.

Schram, Sanford F., and Joe Soss. 2001. "Success Stories: Welfare Reform, Policy Discourse, and the Politics of Research." *ANNALS of the American Academy of Political and Social Science* 577 (1): 49–65.

Schwartz, Alex. 1995. "Rebuilding Downtown: A Case Study of Minneapolis." In *Urban Revitalization: Policies and Programs,* edited by Fritz W. Wagner, Timothy E. Joder, and Anthony J. Mumphrey Jr., 163–202. Thousand Oaks, Calif.: Sage.

Schwartz, Joseph M. 2008. *The Future of Democratic Equality.* New York: Routledge.

Schwartz-Shea, Peregrine, and Dvora Yanow. 2012. *Interpretive Research Design: Concepts and Processes.* New York: Routledge.

Scott, Ellen K., Andrew S. London, and Nancy A. Myers. 2002. "Dangerous Dependencies: The Intersection of Welfare Reform and Domestic Violence." *Gender & Society* 16 (6): 878–97.

Sentencing Project. 2004. *State Rates of Incarceration by Race.* Washington, D.C.: Sentencing Project.

Serres, Chris. 2009. "Bankers Make Case at Capitol." *Star Tribune,* February 10.

Serres, Chris. 2020. "Minnesota Welfare Payments to Increase for First Time since 1986." *Star Tribune,* February 1.

Serres, Chris. 2021. "Minnesota Gov. Tim Walz Aims to Cut Red Tape, Boost Welfare Benefits for Poor Families." *Star Tribune,* March 31.

Shah, Allie. 2009. "Minneapolis Woman, Facing Eviction-Foreclosure, Gets Last-Minute Reprieve." *Star Tribune,* July 25.

Shapiro, Eliza. 2019. "'I Love My Skin!' Black Parents Find Alternative to Integration." *New York Times,* January 8, A1.

Sidney, Mara S. 2003. *Unfair Housing: How National Policy Shapes Community Action.* Lawrence: University Press of Kansas.

Simms, Nicole. 2014. *Collateral Costs: Racial Disparities and Injustice in Minnesota's Marijuana Laws.* St. Paul: Minnesota 2020. https://www.mn2020.org.

Simons, Abby. 2009. "Minneapolis Woman Is Fighting to Stay in Home." *Star Tribune,* November 14, 3B.

Simons, Abby. 2015. "Minnesota's Working Poor Are Overdue for a Financial Boost, Task Force Says." *Star Tribune,* February 10.

Skocpol, Theda. 2003. *Diminished Democracy: From Membership to Management in American Civic Life.* Norman: University of Oklahoma Press.

Smith, Mitch. 2016. "Police and Protesters Clash in Minnesota Capital." *New York Times,* July 10. https://www.nytimes.com.

Smith, Neil. 1996. *The New Urban Frontier: Gentrification and the Revanchist City.* New York: Routledge.

Soss, Joe. 2000. *Unwanted Claims: The Politics of Participation in the U.S. Welfare System.* Ann Arbor: University of Michigan Press.

Soss, Joe, Richard C. Fording, and Sanford F. Schram. 2011. *Disciplining the Poor: Neoliberal Paternalism and the Persistent Power of Race.* Chicago: University of Chicago Press.

Soss, Joe, and Lawrence R. Jacobs. 2009. "The Place of Inequality: Non-participation in the American Polity." *Political Science Quarterly* 124 (1): 95–125.

Sparks, Holloway. 2003. "Queens, Teens, and Model Mothers: Race, Gender, and the Discourse of Welfare Reform." In *Race and the Politics of Welfare Reform,* edited by Sanford F. Schram, Joe Soss, and Richard C. Fording, 171–95. Ann Arbor: University of Michigan Press.

Spence, Lester K. 2015. *Knocking the Hustle: Against the Neoliberal Turn in Black Politics.* Brooklyn: Punctum Books.

Springer, Kimberly. 2005. *Living for the Revolution: Black Feminist Organizations, 1968–1980.* Durham: Duke University Press.

Star Tribune. 2013. "Video: Stadium Protestor: 'Our Kids Can't Eat Footballs.'" *Star Tribune,* September 25.

Stein, Judith. 1998. *Running Steel, Running America: Race, Economic Policy, and the Decline of Liberalism.* Chapel Hill: University of North Carolina Press.

Stein, Judith. 2010. *Pivotal Decade: How the United States Traded Factories for Finance in the Seventies.* New Haven: Yale University Press.

Stein, Samuel. 2019. *Capital City: Gentrification and the Real Estate State.* New York: Verso.

Streitfeld, David. 2009. "As Delinquencies Soar, One in 10 Mortgages Is a Month or More Late." *New York Times,* November 20, B6.

Strolovitch, Dara Z. 2007. *Affirmative Advocacy: Race, Class, and Gender in the Interest Group Politics.* Chicago: University of Chicago Press.

Strolovitch, Dara Z. 2013. "Of Mancessions and Hecoveries: Race, Gender, and the Political Construction of Economic Crises and Recoveries." *Perspectives on Politics* 11 (1): 167–76.

Strolovitch, Dara Z., and M. David Forrest. 2010. "Social and Economic Justice Movements and Organizations." In *Oxford Handbook of American Political Parties and Interest Groups,* edited by L. Sandy

Maisel and Jeffrey M. Berry, 468–84. Oxford: Oxford University Press.

Sugrue, Thomas. 2018. "White America's Age-Old, Misguided Obsession with Civility." *New York Times*, June 29. https://www.nytimes.com.

Swarts, Heidi J. 2008. *Organizing Urban American: Secular and Faith-Based Progessive Movements*. Minneapolis: University of Minnesota Press.

Taylor, Keeanga-Yamahtta. 2019. *Race for Profit: How Banks and the Real Estate Industry Undermined Black Homeownership*. Chapel Hill: University of North Carolina Press.

Temple, Judy A. 2015. "Whatever Happened to the Pay for Performance Bonds?" *MinnPost*, December 18. https://www.minnpost.com.

Tester, Griff. 2008. "An Intersectional Analysis of Sexual Harassment in Housing." *Gender & Society* 22 (3): 349–66.

Thompson, Derek. 2015. "The Miracle of Minneapolis." *Atlantic*, March.

Tigue, Kristoffer. 2016. "From Foreclosures to the Fight for a $15 Wage: The Rise of Neighborhoods Organizing for Change." *MinnPost*, September 2. https://www.minnpost.com.

Tilly, Charles. 2008. *Contentious Performances*. Cambridge: Cambridge University Press.

Timmermans, Stefan, and Iddo Tavory. 2012. "Theory Construction in Qualitative Research: From Grounded Theory to Abductive Analysis." *Sociological Theory* 30 (3): 167–86.

Trickey, Erick 2019. "How Minneapolis Freed Itself from the Stranglehold of Single-Family Homes." *Politico*, July 11. https://www.politico.com.

Uetricht, Micah. 2014. *Strike for America*. New York: Verso.

Uetricht, Micah, and Barry Eidlin. 2019. "US Union Revitalization and the Missing 'Militant Minority.'" *Labor Studies* 44 (1): 36–59.

United Way of Minneapolis Area. 1995. *The Face of the Twin Cities: Another Look*. Minneapolis: United Way.

Valelly, Richard M. 1989. *Radicalism in the States: The Minnesota Farmer–Labor Party and the American Political Economy*. Chicago: University of Chicago Press.

Van Wychen, Jeff. 2016. "A Closer Look at Growing Income Inequality." *Northstarpolicy.org*, August 29. http://northstarpolicy.org.

Van Wychen, Jeff. 2017. "Counties with Greatest Income Inequality Are Also the Poorest." *Northstarpolicy.org,* October 23. https://northstarpolicy.org.

Vargas, João H. Costa. 2008. "Activist Scholarship: Limits and Possibilities in Times of Black Genocide." In *Engaging Contradictions: Theory, Politics, and Methods of Activist Scholarship,* edited by Charles R. Hale, 164–82. Berkeley: University of California Press.

Wacquant, Loïc. 2009. *Punishing the Poor: The Neoliberal Government of Social Insecurity.* Durham: Duke University Press.

Wagner, Peter, and Wendy Sawyer. 2018. *States of Incarceration: The Global Context.* Northampton: Prison Policy Initiative. https://www.prisonpolicy.org.

Waldman, Annie. 2019. "How Teach for American Evolved into an Arm of the Charter School Movement." *ProPublica,* June 18. https://www.propublica.org.

Walker, Jack L. 1983. "The Origins and Maintenance of Interest Groups in America." *American Political Science Review* 77 (2): 390–406.

Wallison, Peter J. 2011. *Dissent from the Majority Report of the Financial Crisis Inquiry Commission.* Washington, D.C.: American Enterprise Institute.

Wallsten, Peter. 2011. "Activists Cry Foul over FBI Probe." *Washington Post,* June 13.

Walsh, James, and Chris Graves. 1997. "Companies' Concerns about 'Murderapolis' Fuel Anti-crime Tactics." *Star Tribune,* April 14, 1A.

Warren, Mark E. 2001. *Democracy and Association.* Princeton: Princeton University Press.

Warren, Mark R. 2001. *Dry Bones Rattling: Community Building to Revitalize American Democracy.* Princeton: Princeton University Press.

Weber, Tom. 2010. "Board Members Ask Johnson to Delay Vote on North High." *MPR News,* October 13. https://www.mprnews.org.

Webster, Jessica. 2016. *The Consequences of Doing Nothing.* Minneapolis: Mid-Minnesota Legal Aid. https://mylegalaid.org.

Weeks, Kathi. 2011. *The Problem with Work: Feminism, Marxism, Antiwork Politics, and Postwork Imaginaries.* Durham: Duke University Press.

Weinmann, Karlee, and Andy Mannix. 2009. "Are Foreclosures Helping to Improve Minneapolis' North Side?" *MinnPost,* February 3.

Weisberg, Jessica. 2009. "ICE Program under Fire." *Nation,* October 14.

Weldon, S. Laurel. 2011. *When Protest Makes Policy: How Social Movements Represent Disadvantaged Groups.* Ann Arbor: University of Michigan Press.

Wessel, Christina, Karma Sonam, and Jon Pratt. 2010. *2010 Minnesota Nonprofit Economy Report.* St. Paul: Minnesota Council of Nonprofits. https://www.minnesotanonprofits.org.

Wilder Research. 2017. *Homelessness in Minnesota: Youth on Their Own.* St. Paul: Wilder Research.

Williams, Rhonda Y. 2005. *The Politics of Public Housing: Black Women's Struggles against Urban Inequality.* New York: Oxford University Press.

Williams, Richard, Reynold Nesiba, and Eileen Diaz McConnell. 2005. "The Changing Face of Inequality in Home Mortgage Lending." *Social Problems* 52 (2): 181–208.

Winkler, Ryan. 2014. *Making Work Pay in Minnesota.* St. Paul: Minnesota House of Representatives Select Committee on Living Wage Jobs. https://www.house.leg.state.mn.us.

Wirtz, Ronald A. 2013. *Government Employment: Job Insecurity.* Federal Reserve Bank of Minneapolis. https://www.minneapolisfed.org.

Wolff, Richard D. 2005. "Ideological State Apparatuses, Consumerism, and U.S. Capitalism: Lessons for the Left." *Rethinking Marxism* 17 (2): 223–35.

Wood, Elisabeth Jean. 2006. "The Ethical Challenges of Field Research in Conflict Zones." *Qualitative Sociology* 29 (3): 373–86.

Woodly, Deva R. 2015. *The Politics of Common Sense: How Social Movements Use Public Discourse to Change Politics and Win Acceptance.* Oxford: Oxford University Press.

Wyly, Elvin K., Mona Atia, Holly Foxcroft, Daniel J. Hamme, and Kelly Phillips-Watts. 2006. "American Home: Predatory Mortgage Capital and Neighbourhood Spaces of Race and Class Exploitation in the United States." *Geografiska Annaler* 88 (1): 105–32.

Yglesias, Matthew. 2019. "The Great Awokening." *Vox,* April 1. https://www.vox.com.

Young, Iris Marion. 2000. *Inclusion and Democracy.* New York: Oxford University Press.

Zernike, Kate. 2016. "Condemnation of Charter Schools Exposes a Rift among Black Americans." *New York Times,* August 21, A10.

Zukin, Sharon. 2008. "Consuming Authenticity: From Outposts of Difference to Means of Exclusion." *Cultural Studies* 22:724–48.

INDEX

Page numbers in italics refer to figures and tables.

abolitionist demands, 12, 17, 18–19, 22, 27, 29, 34, 36, 71, 89, 91, 97, 98, 100, 101, 116, 123, 125, 133, 135, 139, 145, 146, 155, 157, 159, 181, 182, 183, 188, 213, 214, 219, 222, 230; advancing, 5, 9, 144; embracing, 20, 99; making, 70, 91, 104, 106, 137, 138, 150, 152, 178, 180, 205, 232; rhetorical underpinnings of, 147–48; supporting, 7, 8, 11, 19, 24, 25; suppressing, 16, 20, 22, 26, 30, 231

Abumayyaleh, Mahmoud, 215–16, 258n4

accountability, 188, 189, 195, 197, 200, 201, 203–4, 213

ACORN, 152

"actions," 129, 130, 131–32

activism: anti-demolition, 54–55; anti-eviction, 141; anti-foreclosure, 84, 141; antipoverty, 91; community, 83

Adams, Vincanne, 246n51

"advocacy," 125–26, 127, 128, 132, 252n55

African Americans, 4, 49, 53, 82, 89, 148, 177, 233; *Hollman* settlement and, 86; low-income, 48, 81, 101, 141; middle-class, 32, 46; policing disparities and, 87; welfare participation and, 19; working-class, 41, 42, 43, 87, 216

AFSCME. *See* American Federation of State County and Municipal Employees

AIDS Coalition to Unleash Power (ACT-UP), 161

ALEC. *See* American Legislative Exchange Council

Alinsky, Saul, 237n16

American Civil Liberties Union, 215

American Federation of State County and Municipal Employees (AFSCME), 232, 257n32; Council 5, 35; Local 3800, 14, 222; political actions of, 194, 195

American Legislative Exchange Council (ALEC), 68, 171, 176, 255n53

Annenberg Institute for School Reform, 108

Ansari, Zakiyah, 108, 109

antidiscrimination laws, 50, 58

Atkins, Joe, 150, 151, 253n22

Auletta, Ken, 47, 48

Bailout Coalition. *See* Minnesota Coalition for a People's Bailout

behavioral deficiencies, poverty discourse and, 13, 24, 48, 122, 231

"being positive," 107–9, 114, 115–16, 118, 122, 132

"big picture," giving, 170–73, 177

Black Lives Matter, 29, 34, 91, 211, 216, 221, 258n53

"blood" sacrifices, 125–26, 132, 138, 157, 169, 182, 183, 207

budget deficits, 67, 68, 129, 130

budget negotiations, 192, 194–95

Bush, George H. W., 45

capitalism, 18, 65, 81, 84, 157; Keynesian, 27; neoliberal, 16–17, 26–30, 37, 67, 219

capitalist markets, 8, 28, 64, 65, 84, 133, 157

capitalist realism, 8, 9, 89, 98, 99, 105, 137, 207, 219, 221; accommodating,

103, 116; challenging, 109, 114, 125, 138; curbing, 105, 123; described, 70; dominance of, 11, 72–73, 78, 79–80, 102–3, 150; influence of, 76–77, 90, 102–7, 108, 123, 132, 169; rise of, 73–80, 84
Carlson, Arne, 52
cash assistance, 69, 71, 76, 79, 145, 151, 152, 176, 179, 180, 256n61
Castile, Philando: death of, 216
"Celebration," 130
Centro de Trabajadores Unidos en la Lucha, 35
charter schools, 1, 59, 62, 83, 104, 242n97; competition from, 122; expansion of, 74, 75, 76, 102
Chauvin, Derek, 215, 217–18
Cherryhomes, Jackie, 56
Chicago Teachers Union, 249n27
Choice Is Yours program, 58, 61, 75, 82, 149
Choice Neighborhoods, 240n33
Cisneros, Henry, 46, 53
Citizens United, 67
civility, lack of, 193, 194, 195
Clark, Jamar: death of, 216
Clinton, Bill, 46, 47, 240n34
Cloward, Richard, 36, 244n138
collaboration, 43, 118, 119, 182, 206, 207, 256n11
collective demands: contentious identities and, 100–102; identity constructions and, *101*
color-blind rhetoric, 19, 164, 167, 177
Communities United against Police Brutality, 14
"community," 23, 96, 108, 113, 194, 199, 204; "being positive" and, 109–10, 115, 118, 123; economic disadvantages for, 118–19; North High, 93, 100, 101, 104–5, 107, 117, 120, 121, 194, 199, 200; political capacity of, 205; poor and working class, 206, 214
Community Reinvestment Act, 40
competition, 59, 84, 94, 122; market-like, 4, 13, 27, 28, 86, 102; political, 17, 36; school, 79, 82, 93, 103, 104, 105, 110, 138, 247n1
consumerism, 24, 27, 73
contentious identities, 90–91, 99, 123, 137, 144, 188, 199, 230; adversarial, 168; assembling, 100, *139*, 219; collective demands and, 100–102; fashioning, 27, 29, 30, 36, 37, 66, 70, 219, 227; intersectional, 100, 168; publicizing, 8, 146, 147, 148, 155, 181, *182*, *213*
contentious identity-building, 6, 12, 16, 20, 23, 24, 27, 29–30, 36, 72, 90, 91, 97, 133, 147, 187, 188, 192, 196, 197, 201, 211, 221, 222, 227, 232; abolition and, 219; hazards of, 7–9, 24–25, 70–72, 92; nonprofit sector and, 25
coronavirus pandemic, 10, 29, 215, 217
Costa Vargas, João, 228
crime, 44, 48, 56, 242n82
criminal justice, 17, 65, 220, 221
Cuomo, Andrew, 53
Cup Foods, 215, 216, 258n4

Dakota Access Pipeline, 29
Daudt, Kurt, 171, 176
Dayton, Mark, 67, 187, 244n2
de Blasio, Bill, 244n134
deconcentration, 48, 53, 54, 59, 63, 81, 90, 171; neoliberalism and, 44–45, 51, 58; nonprofits and, 75, 76; supporters of, 45–46, 47. *See also* poverty deconcentration
Defend Glendale and Public Housing Coalition, 222
"defund the police," 219–20, 236n20
democratic legitimacy, 187, 192, 194, 200, 203, 213, 214, 257n34, 258n43
Democratic Socialists of America, 29
Democrats, 89, 130, 211; criticism of, 128, 129
deunionization, 8, 25, 41, 65, 101, 134, 135, 144, 149, 155, 165, 166, 177, 182

development: community, 45, 50, 56, 57, 75, 167; fair-share standards and, 50–51, 52; mixed-income, 44, 45–46, 47, 54, 61, 63; public-private, 55, 62, 82; real estate, 42
Dibble, Scott, 160–61
disciplinary practices, 89, 134, 201, 230
discrimination, 4, 8, 15, 19, 46, 62, 81, 101, 119, 133, 135, 138, 145; housing, 31, 148; job, 34; laws against, 49; lending, 45; policing, 220; racial, 5, 14, 83, 100, 158, 249n21, 249n22; rental, 45
disinvestment, 100, 103, 133, 167, 220; neighborhood, 148; residential, 41
drug trade, 44, 48, 54, 85, 133, 143, 144, 145, 164, 177

Earned Income Tax Credit, 81
EBT cards, 69, 107, 135, 151, 153, 175, 178, 198, 244n5
Eckstein, Rick, 256n1
economic growth, 48, 50, 53, 56, 185
Edelman, Murray, 148
education, 56, 60, 62, 95, 119, 120, 168–69, 171, 175, 176, 177, 178, 179; access to, 4, 118, 123; free, 124; high-poverty neighborhood, 242n97; inequality in, 33; marketization of, 104; privatization of, 73, 194; welfare reform and, 172. *See also* public education
education policy, 28, 75; neoliberal, 98, 104, 107, 138, 249n27
Education Testing Service (ETS), 251n44
Eliasoph, Nina, 99
Elliot Park, 185, 256n2
Ellison, Jeremiah, 222
Ellison, Keith, 217–18
employment, 71, 87, 150, 158, 161, 173, 253n26; crisis, 161; low-wage, 85; public-sector, 14, 53, 67, 86; rate, 59–60; seasonal, 177. *See also* jobs
Ernst, Rose, 19, 145
etiquette: civic or political, 9, 11, 26, 100, 107, 109, 113, 115, 117, 124, 125, 138, 139, 147, 155, 160, 181, 182, 183, 190, 191, 204, 205, 206, 207, 213, 214, 221; concept of, 9, 26, 99; "fighting," 124–25, 157–58, 149, 169; "positive," 109–10
Every Student Succeeds Act, 235n5
evictions, 60, 233; foreclosure-related, 40, 41, 82, 142, 145, 147, 148, 152, 155, 156, 157, 158, 159, 160, 161, 162, 167–68, 171, 181; protesting, 15, 31, 168; state-level ban on, 217
exploitation, 5, 8, 15, 19, 68, 81, 83, 85, 100, 101, 103, 107, 133, 138, 145, 220; labor, 14, 27, 31, 34, 148, 170; racialized, 158; sexual, 174

FBI, 31, 237n74
Federal Housing Administration, 46
Ferguson, Michaele, 237n33
Fight Back! News, 125
Fight for 15: 29
"Fight for Justice," celebrating, 130
"fighting back," 123–39, 157, 161, 169, 175, 181, 207, 208; abolitionist demands and, 135; being positive and, 132; commitment to, 125–26, 129, 131–32; etiquette and, 124, 182
financial counseling programs, 39, 143, 155, 167
financial predation, 14, 15, 27, 220
Fiscal Disparities Program, 51, 52
Fisher, Mark, 8, 70, 73
Fletcher, Steve, 222
Floyd, George, 222, 258n4; murder of, 12, 215, 216–17, 218, 219. *See also* George Floyd uprising
food stamps, 125, 133
foreclosed homes, occupying, 196–97
foreclosures, 14, 31, 39, 40, 60, 63, 88, 141, 142, 151, 153, 156, 158, 159, 162, 164, 165–66, 167, 181, 204, 230, 231
foreclosure victims, 84, 88, 141, 142, 149, 150; poor and working, 162, 164–65, 181
Franson, Mary, 179, 180, 253n25

"fraud" prevention, 132, 133, 136, 170
Freedom Place, Inc., 126
Freedom Road Socialist Organization, 125, 157, 159, 169, 232, 251n49
Frey, Jacob, 259n19
Friends of North High Foundation, 2, 95, 103, 104, 120; "being positive" and, 110; cultural attitudes and, 119; "political" talk and, 111

gender, 177, 189, 245n42
gendered divisions, 41, 137, 149, 166
General Assistance program, 55, 135, 136, 179, 241n78
gentrification, 4, 8, 25, 31, 32, 41, 63, 75, 101, 102, 104, 144, 149, 177, 185, 216
George Floyd uprising, 211, 217, 220, 222
Girls in Action, 251n43
Glenwood public housing, 54, 247n85
Goetz, Ed, 218
Goffman, Erving, 99, 111
Gorz, André, 97
Gottwalt, Steve, 151, 152, 253n25, 253n26
grassroots mobilization, 19, 20, 26, 29, 36, 66, 85, 190, 191, 204, 206, 210, 213, 214, 219; benefits of, 188–89; building toward, 207–8; "rational prospectors" and, 189. *See also* mass engagement; mobilization; political engagement
"Great Awokening," 245n42
Great Recession, 5, 10, 11, 14, 30, 42, 53, 59, 61, 68, 72, 74, 79, 86, 87, 97, 148, 160, 164, 177, 216, 227, 232
Green Party, 164
Gruenhagen, Glenn, 179, 180, 253n25, 255n53

"habits of mind" / "habits of work," 122
Han, Hahrie, 211
Hawthorne Neighborhood Council, 142
Headwaters Foundation for Justice, 127, 157, 232, 246n52, 250n33, 252n53, 252n54
health care, 62, 77, 124, 130
health insurance, 18, 97
Heritage Park, 63
Higgins, Linda, 68, 69, 71, 72, 73, 76, 91, 92, 153, 175, 178; capitalist realism and, 70; identity politics and, 82
Hollman v. Cisneros, 54, 55, 56, 57, 61, 62, 63, 81, 82, 86, 149, 160, 247n85
Home Affordable Modification Program, 39
homelessness, 42, 87, 158
home occupations, 14, 35, 250n33; photo of, *15*
Honeywell, 56
HOPE VI, 45, 46, 48, 240n33, 240n34
House, Gerry, 251n44
House Committee on Commerce and Labor, 150
House Committee on Health and Human Services Reform, 151, 253n26; photo of, *209*
housing, 15, 56, 62, 72, 87, 93, 102, 218, 232; affordable, 40–41, 49, 50, 57, 86, 87, 124, 156, 158, 160, 167, 168; costs, 50, 177; democratic control of, 150; demolition of, 44, 241n75; low-income, 29, 47, 52, 81, 85, 174; multi-family, 217; problems, 57, 84, 150; rehabilitated, 55; subsidies for, 44, 52, 53, 148, 218; working-class, 243n124. *See also* public housing
"housing crisis," 141, 143, 144, 153, 168
housing market, 153; crash of, 40, 41–42, 58, 60, 61, 141
HUD. *See* U.S. Department of Housing and Urban Development
Human Rights Campaign, 4
human services, 42, 70, 89; spending on, 49–50, 79

identification, 69, 70, 71, 153, 199–200, 203, 204, 213
identity, 7, 10, 91, 97, 98, 117, 134, 144, 150, 189; adversarial, 101, 115, 248n20; collective movement, 236n26; intersectional, 147, 248n20; public, 6, 20, 70. *See also* contentious identities; contentious identity-building
identity politics, 71, 81, 83, 149, 220
ideology, 7, 11, 24, 70, 98, 99, 100, 137, 221, 231, 237n33. *See also* capitalist realism; consumerism
inequality, 59–66, 137, 220; economic, 110, 120, 216; educational, 110, 114, 120; growth in, 61, 63, 216; income, 60; market, 149; political, 211; racialized, 64, 110, 120, 187; regional, 52, 186
injustice, 8, 14, 68, 72, 84, 100, 101, 119, 146, 147, 149, 150, 159, 165, 170, 180, 181, 182; crosscutting, 158; economic, 103, 104, 120, 148, 150, 153, 249n22; educational, 114; market, 144, 146, 180; racialized, 104, 120; social, 151
insecurity: economic, 4; financial, 145; food, 87; health, 87; housing, 41, 57, 145; job, 156; physical, 220, 236n20; social, 41
Institute for Race and Poverty, 61
Institute for Student Achievement (ISA), 4, 121–22, 251n44
intersectional politics, 101, 136, 148, 182, 183, 248n20, 249n22, 250n42; abolitionism and, 167; importance of, 100
ISA. *See* Institute for Student Achievement

Jim Crow, 27
jobs, 153; call for, 175–83; creating, 102, 185; green, 119, 250n41; high-tech, 119; living wage, 124, 173; lower-end, 174; service, 119, 240n51; temporary, 177; training for, 18, 171; 21st century, 122; unionized, 170. *See also* employment
Johnson, Bernadeia, 1, 93, 111, 121
Johnson, Cedric, 236n20
justice: economic, 2, 152; racial, 2, 152. *See also* criminal justice; injustice; social justice

Kelly, Mick, 16
Koch brothers, 68

labor, 60; extreme, 174; gendered divisions of, 182; migrant, 42; organizations, 24; racialized divisions of, 25, 165, 182
labor markets, 41, 61, 68, 76, 86, 87, 91, 135, 151, 160, 166, 172, 173, 175, 176, 177, 178; participation in, 80–81, 170; segmentation of, 46; welfare reform and, 174
Land Use Planning Act (1976), 50
Legal Aid Society, 54, 56, 179
legitimacy, 189; achieving, 203–8, 210–11, 213–14; challenges, 191–95; mass engagement and, 195–203
lending, 45, 160, 162; predatory, 31, 40, 141–42, 145, 147, 152, 153, 170; subprime, 82, 90, 143
Lewis, Karen, 249n27
Livable Communities Act, 52
Low Income Housing Tax Credit, 241n76
Lutheran Social Services, 126
Lyndale public housing, 54, 247n85

magnification, 195–97, 203, 204
Mansbridge, Jane, 188
marginalization, 53, 54, 81, 87, 236n20, 241n72; social, 13, 59–66, 232
market actors, 77, 84, 85, 120
market-based systems, 83, 89, 114, 124, 137, 149, 168, 170, 177, 220
marketization, 2, 28, 41, 72, 79, 85,

89, 90, 104, 108, 120, 169; equating with freedom/equality, 73, 81
market participation, 28–29, 65, 81, 85, 90, 151, 191; expanding, 28, 59, 86, 149
market processes and relations, 11, 71, 75, 83, 102, 155, 165; idealizing, 80–81, 82, 149; racialized, 154, 159, 164
market rule/supremacy, 40, 73, 77, 78, 80, 91, 98, 103, 109, 110, 117, 120, 138, 150, 153, 155, 158, 159
mass engagement, 23, 190; legitimacy and, 195–203; potential for, 214. *See also* grassroots mobilization; mobilization; political engagement
McAlevey, Jane, 17, 19, 211
Metropolitan Council, 50, 51, 52, 55
Metropolitan Sports Facilities Commission, 256n1
MFIP. *See* Minnesota Family Investment Program
Midtown Exchange, 62, 63, 82, 243n124
Midtown Global Marketplace, 62
Mills, Charles, 253n14
Minneapolis Board of Education, 94; photo of, *96*
Minneapolis City Council, 51
Minneapolis College Prep, 1, 235n4
Minneapolis Federation of Teachers, 114, 199
Minneapolis Police Department, 217, 218, 258n4
Minneapolis Public Housing Authority, 54, 74
Minneapolis Public Schools (MPS), 1, 2, 32, 104, 121, 195, 233; ISA and, 4; North High and, 93, 94, 95, 247n1; poverty deconcentration and, 58–59
Minnesota Bankers Association, 150–51
Minnesota Coalition for a People's Bailout (Bailout Coalition), 5, 6, 7, 8, 9, 11, 16, 19, 30, 31, 33, 35, 36, 43, 54, 78, 79, 84, 125, 141, 155, 157, 158, 160–61, 170, 173, 176, 182, 196–97, 201, 202, 204, 210, 222, 227; abolitionist demands and, 146; accountability and, 203; action of, 32, 147, 230; anti-eviction efforts of, 152; case of, 147–48; color-blind rhetoric and, 177; constituents of, 191; contentious identity of, *182*; decline of, 32, 34; "fighting back" and, 159, 161–62, 164–68, 182–83; flier by, *163*, *166*; forum by, 149–50; leadership of, 23; legitimacy for, 203; moratorium proposals by, 150, 167; occupation by, *15*; organizational features of, *233*; outreach by, 88; political capacity and, 89; political system and, 16; PPEHRC and, 35, 164; public ignorance and, 157, 181; representational choices of, *33*; rhetoric of, 162, 165, 167, 176, 180–81; story of, 14, 15, 37; tactics of, 213; Welfare Rights Committee and, 141, 168, 169
Minnesota Family Investment Program (MFIP), 33–34, 71, 92, 124, 125, 136, 172, 175, 198; expansion of, 68; grants from, 171, 179, 180, 256n64
Minnesota Farmer–Labor Party, 51
Minnesota Immigrant Rights Action Committee, 14
Minnesota Poor People's Economic Human Rights Campaign (PPEHRC), 31, 35, 164
Minnesota Tenants Union, 141, 155, 160
Minnesota Vikings stadium, 134, 256n4; proponents of, 185–86; protesting, *186*, 187
Minnesota Welfare Rights Committee (Welfare Rights Committee), 5, 6, 7, 8, 14, 22, 30, 34, 35, 43, 55, 68, 69, 70, 71, 72, 77, 78–79, 100, 101–2, 105–7, 150, 152, 153,

185, 189, 192, 194, 198, 201, 202, 219, 221, 222, 227, 229; abolitionist demands and, 9, 139, 180; accountability and, 203; action of, 147, 230; anti-stadium campaign of, 190; Bailout Coalition and, 141, 168, 169; as base builder, 207–8, 210–11; big picture and, 170–83; capitalist realism and, 105; class/race/gender consciousness of, 177; constituents of, 191; contentious identity of, 92, 123, *139, 182, 213*, 231; coverage of, 204; deliberations of, 11, 99; democratic process and, 193; "fighting back" and, 123–39, 157, 175, 182, 207, 214; flier by, *212*; formation of, 33; leadership of, 23, 125; legitimacy for, 193, 203; mass engagement and, 190; members, *186, 209*; North High Coalition and, 105; organizational features of, *233*; outreach by, 88, 210; political capacity and, 89; protest by, 186, 195; representational efforts of, *33*, 92, 197; rhetoric of, 177, 180, 181; story of, 36, 37, 91; timeline by, *131*; trajectory of, 123–24

mobilization, 6, 9, 19, 20, 37, 207, 221; selective, 190. *See also* grassroots mobilization; mass engagement; political engagement

mortgage counseling, 31, 39, 40, 152, 156, 167

mortgages, 46, 144, 161; bad, 155, 159; fixed-rate, 167; subprime, 162, 165–66, 167. *See also* lending

MPS. *See* Minneapolis Public Schools

Nadasen, Premilla, 248n21

National Association for the Advancement of Colored People (NAACP), 53, 54, 57, 58, 107, 110, 249n28, 249n32

National Organization for Women, 4

Native Americans, 43, 49, 60, 148; poverty deconcentration and, 87

NCLB. *See* No Child Left Behind

Near North, 1, 32, 54, 55, 56, 59, 216

Neighborhood Revitalization Program (NRP), 50, 51, 52, 53, 54, 55, 74

Neighborhoods Organizing for Change (NOC), 1, 108–9, 110, 221, 246n52, 249n33

Neighborhood Stabilization Program, 39

neoliberal governance, 10, 13, 27, 28, 29, 32, 48, 53, 63, 64, 72, 158, 218, 219; rolling back, 30

neoliberalism, 8, 10, 11, 13, 15, 27, 28, 43, 59, 66, 85, 89, 110, 123, 132, 148, 161, 201, 218, 222; capitalist realism and, 73; challenging, 90, 120, 217, 219; declining legitimacy of, 29; poverty deconcentration and, 44–45, 51, 58, 72, 79, 137, 218; progressive urban regimes and, 64–65; rise of, 64–65, 90, 94; urban governance and, 45, 236n33

New Deal, 27, 42, 46, 51, 64

Nicollet Mall, 48

NOC. *See* Neighborhoods Organizing for Change

No Child Left Behind (NCLB), 1, 235n5

nonprofits, 22, 28, 39, 50, 53, 57, 74, 83, 99, 230; deconcentration and, 75, 76–77; social-justice-oriented, 49

nonprofit sector, 6, 35–36, 110, 126, 232, 238n46; contentious identity-building and, 25; social justice organizations and, 231; unequal participation and, 20–23

North High Alumni Association, 2, 103, 120

North High Community Coalition, 5, 6, 7, 8, 9, 23, 30, 35, 36, 43, 55, 57, 76, 77–78, 79, 100, 101, 117–18, 127, 132, 133, 136, 137–38, 154, 190, 195, 197, 199, 200, 210, 213, 214; abolitionism and, 139;

accountability and, 203, 204; action of, 230; "being positive" and, 107–9, 116; campaign of, 123; "community" and, 138, 201, 203; concerns of, 94; constituents of, 97–98, 191; contentious identity of, *139, 213*; decline of, 32, 33, 34; deliberations of, 11, 99; leadership of, 125; legitimacy for, 203; membership of, 103, 231; nonprofit sector and, 110; organizational features of, *233*; organizer, *205*; outreach by, 88; PEJAM and, 193, 194; political capacity and, 89; "poor and working people" and, 123; as "rational prospectors," 204–7; representational choices of, *33*; story of, 37, 93; tension in, 194; Welfare Rights Committee and, 105

North High School, 2, *2*, 3, 56, 78, 79, 93, 104, 122, 139, 194, 199, 200, 205, 233; attendance zone for, 76; closing, 1, 193; deconcentration and, 59; depiction of, 1, 83–84, 121; educational reform and, 75; future of, 95, 109, 117; market competition and, 102; performance of, 32, 113; "positive" campaign for, 115; redesign of, 3–4, 32, 33, 93–94, 96–97, 105, 109, 116, 119, 120, 121, 193, 205, 250n36, 251n47; redesign process for, 95, 105, 111, 113–15, 116–17, 120, 121–22; supporters, *3*, *96*, 250n38

Northside Neighbors for Justice, 55

NRP. *See* Neighborhood Revitalization Program

Obama, Barack, 240n33

Ocasio-Cortez, Alexandria, 29

Occupy Homes Minnesota, 84, 250n33

Occupy Minneapolis, 35

Occupy movement, 91, 211, 216

Occupy Wall Street, 6, 29, 221, 252n59

Olson public housing, 54, 247n85

open enrollment program, 74, 82, 102, 242n97

oppression, 6, 66, 100, 156, 207; abolishing, 19, 90, 97; ignorance about, 154–55; market, 8, 65, 80–84, 90, 148, 149, 150, 152–53, 154–55, 157, 161–62, 164, 168, 169, 181, 182; systemic, 10, 16, 24, 55, 70, 80, 89, 101, 124, 146

Orfield, Myron, 61

outreach campaigns, 88, 210–11, 214

Parks, Tecora: foreclosure for, 165–67

participation, 28; labor market, 80–81, 170; political, 6, 20; unequal, 20–23, 25, 230; welfare, 74, 178, 182. *See also* market participation

"partnership" (with MPS), 109, 113, 116, 117, 139, 206, 207, 213

Pawlenty, Tim, 39

PEJAM. *See* Public Education Justice Alliance of Minnesota

Phillips-Fein, Kim, 244n22

Piven, Frances Fox, 36, 188–89, 244n138, 257n26

planning meetings, observed, *228*

policing, 4, 42, 58, 64, 201, 220; community, 44, 55, 82, 216, 240n34; disparities in, 87

political capacity, 9, 11, 25, 205, 220; working-class, 73, 84–92, 191, 208, 210

political efficacy, 191, 201, 211, 221

political engagement, 31, 121, 187, 189, 195, 201, 211, 214; barriers to, 192; working-class, 88. *See also* grassroots mobilization; mass engagement; mobilization

"political" talk, 110, 111, 113, 116, 138

"poor and working people," 14, 16, 70, 105, 123, 124, 125, 128, 138, 139, 141, 143, 144, 148, 155, 156, 158, 159, 160, 168, 169, 170, 172, 179, 180, 181, 183, 187, 189, 190, 192,

198, 204, 207, 208, 211, 213, 219, 222, 255n48; as embattled class, 132–37, 161–62, 176–77, 178, 182
Poor People's Movements (Piven and Cloward), 36
poverty, 14, 24, 49, 50, 58, 60, 61, 68, 70, 123, 127, 143, 158, 171, 231, 233; Black, 25, 60; "cycle of," 47; education/training and, 179; racialized, 51; urban, 52
poverty deconcentration, 51, 53, 54, 56, 57, 58, 60, 61, 62, 63, 64, 66, 74, 148, 149, 154, 156; national push for, 45–48; neoliberalism and, 44–45, 72, 79, 137, 191, 215, 218; nonprofits and, 75. *See also* deconcentration
"poverty pimp groups," 127
Powderhorn community, 215, 258n1
PPEHRC. *See* Minnesota Poor People's Economic Human Rights Campaign
Price, Verna, 251n43
Prince, 78
privatization, 4, 32
progressives, 18, 40, 57, 84, 90, 180, 187; identity politics and, 220; neoliberal-era, 145
progressivism, 43, 44, 53, 65, 82, 86
projection, 200–203, 204, 213
"Proposal to Reconfigure Minnesota School Boundaries to Deconcentrate Poverty," 59
prostitution, 44, 54, 143, 144, 145, 164, 177
protests, 14, 15, 31, 129, 168, 177, 186, 187, 195, 216, 234; photo of, *186*
public administration, 73, 89, 102
public agencies, 28, 74, 75, 102, 230
public education, 32, 58, 97, 123, 200, 232; defending, 199; market rule and, 109; neoliberal approach to, 108
Public Education Justice Alliance of Minnesota (PEJAM), 2, 94, 95–96, 109, 114, 116, 199, 205, 206; fliers from, 111, *112*; North High Coalition and, 193, 194
public events, observed, *228*
public housing, 13, 40, 45, 47, 62, 75, 78, 85, 87, 102, 148, 160; demolition of, 44, 46, 54, 58, 65, 88; eviction from, 86; expanding, 65, 221; funding for, 241n76; neoliberals and, 48. *See also* housing
public officials, 14, 23, 43, 49, 51, 53, 57, 76, 79, 80, 81, 84, 107, 189, 204, 219, 232
public safety, 220; community-based, 236n20; transforming, 218
public schools, 3, 45, 102, 103, 120; access to, 76; African Americans and, 83; closure of, 82, 108; high-poverty, 58, 59; "orphaned," 108

queer sexual practices, policing, 50
queer youth, 43, 61

racialization, 41, 124, 137, 149, 166
racism, 68, 80, 124, 216
radical incrementalism, 9, 123, 207
rallies, 3, 30, 31, 43, 89, 113, 129, 134, 136, 139, 162, 169, 194, 195, 205, 228
"rational prospectors," organizers as, 25, 189, 190, 191, 204–7
Reagan, Ronald, 45, 52, 240n32
real estate market, 28, 81, 86, 88
recession, 13, 14, 69, 84, 147, 173. *See also* Great Recession
redistribution, 49, 51, 58, 88, 94, 98, 106, 122, 127, 149; downward, 52, 115; egalitarian, 104; social-democratic, 28; viability of, 249n24
Reed, Adolph, Jr., 247n17
Renée, Michelle, 108, 109
rental market, 81, 86, 141, 164
rent control, calls for, 65
Republican National Convention (2008), 239n74
Republican Party, 67, 151

Republicans, criticism of, 128, 129, 211
resistance, 85, 95–96, 99, 105, 160, 180; language of, 148
respectability politics, 81, 83, 149, 150
revanchism, 50, 64, 67, 68, 138, 178; urban, 41, 42, 48
rhetoric, 19, 20, 32, 37, 146, 162, 167, 176, 182, 221; anti-market, 148; anti-privatization, 65; challenges in, 180–81; class, 145, 181; color-blind, 19, 25, 31, 181; gender, 145, 181; intersectional/adversarial, 161; market-friendly, 91; misleading, 147, 175, 176; oppositional, 34, 65, 144, 146, 147–48, 150, 153, 178, 182; populist, 162, 165, 168; race, 19, 145, 181
Roelofs, Joan, 252n53
Rybak, R. T., 56, 187, 245n37

Samuels, Don, 1
Sanders, Bernie, 29, 221
Save North High Coalition, 2, 3–4, 5, 93, 227, 239n73. *See also* North High Community Coalition
Sayles Belton, Sharon, 53, 56
Schattschneider, E. E.: "chorus" of voices and, 20
school choice, 4, 13, 32, 82, 84, 105, 110, 242n100. *See also* public schools
Schram, Sanford, 9, 97, 145
Schwartz-Shea, Peregrine, 230
Seals, Leola, 57, 249n28, 249n32
Section 8 vouchers, 44, 54, 61, 82, 90, 125
segregation, 27, 46, 60, 62, 155, 167; residential, 31, 32, 41, 65, 144
self-sufficiency, 13, 172, 175
Senate Health and Human Services Committee, 67–68, 244n10
service sector, 49, 87, 119, 240n51
sexism, 80, 81, 124
sex workers, 42, 85, 143. *See also* prostitution
single mothers, 43, 46, 48, 60, 69, 71, 134, 151, 175, 207; low-income, 55, 127, 173, 177, 217; sexual exploitation of, 174; welfare reform and, 173–74
"slave labor," promotion of, 135
"slicksters," 154, 171
Smith, Neil, 42
social-democratic policies, 27, 29, 51, 57, 67, 125
social justice, 5, 10, 15, 40, 52, 53, 61, 65, 72, 97, 148, 150, 179; campaigns, 35; future prospects for, 12; upholding, 155
social justice organizations, 5, 6, 7, 11, 15–16, 27, 39, 43, 53, 64, 72, 92, 98, 99, 127, 138, 139, 213, 221, 233; abolitionist demands and, 18; citizen involvement in, 232; community-based, 30, 227; constituents of, 97, 257n14; contentious identities and, 26, 37; contributions by, 146; disadvantaged groups and, 8; examining, 227; expansion of, 232; features of, 17, 65; hazards for, 231; inclusiveness of, 20–21; legitimacy of, 193; missteps of, 16, 19, 20; mobilization of, 20, 65–66, 190; oppression and, 24, 80, 146; political system and, 4, 16, 37; potential of, 4–5, 10, 17, 36; representational work of, 4, 36, 37, 70; resources for, 25; studying, 30–37; theoretical accounts of, 22
social justice organizers, 10, 11, 23, 26, 42, 43, 44, 72, 75, 84, 89, 99, 101, 103, 125–26, 144, 147, 182, 188, 195, 204, 211, 213, 216, 227; agency of, 90–91; challenges for, 137, 180–81; disruptive movements and, 219; etiquettes of, 183, 214; grassroots mobilization and, 189, 190; intersectional identities and, 100; legitimacy issues and, 194; oppression and, 66; politics of, 22, 152; professionalization of, 25; status of, 203

social services, 39, 47, 50, 52, 65, 93, 126
social welfare, 5, 33, 68, 71, 123, 126, 134, 192
societal ignorance about oppression, 11, 145, 146, 147, 148, 154, 169, 181, 182, 207, 221, 229
Southwest High School, 59
Star Tribune, 199, 203, 204
Stein, Samuel, 65, 66, 243n124, 244n138
stereotypes, 40, 164; gendered, 47; racialized, 47, 84
Stewart, Chris, 82, 83, 193, 194, 246n52, 246n55
stigmatization, 6, 7, 13, 16, 20, 23, 26, 37, 48, 54, 55, 57, 68, 69, 70, 75, 76, 87, 89, 103, 144, 198, 220
strikes, 19, 51, 188
Strolovitch, Dara, 16
Sumner Field public housing, 54, 247n85
Sumner-Glenwood public housing, 54, 56, 62, 149, 160; demolition of, 58, 82

Take Action Minnesota, 35
TANF. *See* Temporary Assistance to Needy Families
Target Corporation, 244n2
taxes, 22, 232; income, 136; property, 45, 75; raising, 130; regressive, 65
tax increment financing (TIF), 45, 46, 48, 75
"tax the rich!," 79, 106, 124, 134, 192
Teach for America, 1
Teamsters, 1934 strike by, 51
Tea Party, 67
Temporary Assistance to Needy Families (TANF), 28, 34, 124, 217, 218
Thatcher, Margaret, 28, 73
Thisius, Mark, 126
TIF. *See* tax increment financing
Tilly, Charles, 257n34
Twin Cities Coalition for Justice for Jamar, 258n53

"underclass," 6, 20, 47, 65, 142, 143
unemployment, 14, 49, 151, 159, 162, 181, 255n48; Black–white gap in, 60; cyclical, 148; insurance, 79, 125, 173
unions, 87, 88; attacks on, 73, 177; movement-oriented, 43; weakening of, 85; workplace democracy and, 19
Up and Out of Poverty Now, 126, 241n64
Urban League, 155, 156, 160, 162, 164
U.S. Department of Health and Human Services (HHS), 136
U.S. Department of Housing and Urban Development (HUD), 44, 46, 53, 54

vacancy rates: housing, 57; office/retail, 57, 242n90; rental, 57
violence, 220; domestic, 34, 68, 80, 83, 151, 173, 174, 233; gang/drug, 55

Walz, Tim, 217
Washington, Denzel, 78
Webster, Jessica, 179, 256n61; Gottwalt and, 152; welfare reform and, 151, 172
Weeks, Kathi, 18
welfare, 48, 68, 70, 91, 171, 232; attacks on, 124, 176; cuts in, 79, 106, 124–25, 130, 134, 136, 170; expanding, 68, 178; family/child, 50; means-tested, 71; neoliberal approach to, 173; poverty and, 127; restrictions on, 82; sanctions, 85, 87; women and, 175
welfare benefits, 14, 149, 152, 170
welfare "cheats," 151, 179
welfare entitlements, 5, 9, 34, 123, 124, 136, 137, 180, 220; defending,

106; demand for, 169; strengthening, 107, 135, 182, 183
welfare policy, 44, 125, 138, 171, 176; debates on, 72; fighting, 129, 130; neoliberal, 105, 129, 134, 169, 170, 175, 178, 180
welfare programs, 19, 28, 80–81, 135, 170, 179; efficient/exclusive, 106; labor markets and, 174; national, 220; state, 244n10
welfare recipients, 18, 68, 83, 85, 88, 91, 124, 127–28, 130, 149, 153, 181, 233; background checks for, 135; Black/Hmong, 247n85; challenges for, 173; market relations and, 71; publicizing, 145
welfare reform, 13, 64, 85; education/training and, 172; neoliberal, 91, 106, 136; rejecting, 124
Welfare Reform 2.0, 170, 171, 175, 178, 179; debates over, 173; misleading rhetoric during, 176; response to, 172–73; testimony against, 174
welfare rights, 18, 19, 145, 178; expanding, 136; struggle for, 124
Welfare Rights Committee. *See* Minnesota Welfare Rights Committee
welfare state, 69, 72, 105, 132; neoliberal, 124, 126, 129, 136–37, 169
"Welfare Waste" (ABC), 68
Wells Fargo, 251n43
Wilf, Zygi, 134
Williams, Rosemary, 254–55n47
Wisconsin Uprising, 252n59
Wonder, Stevie, 78
workfare, 134–35, 136, 170
working class, 63, 128, 135, 149; political capacity of, 73, 84–92, 191, 210
"wrap-around" services, 93, 116, 122, 217, 218, 251n46

Yanow, Dvora, 230

DAVID FORREST is associate professor of politics at Oberlin College.

Manufactured by Amazon.ca
Bolton, ON

27905819R00173